Managing Sports Organizations:
Responsibility for Performance

Daniel Covell

Western New England College

Sharianne Walker

Western New England College

Julie Siciliano

Western New England College

Peter W. Hess

Western New England College

THOMSON
SOUTH-WESTERN

Australia · Canada · Mexico · Singapore · Spain · United Kingdom · United States

THOMSON

SOUTH-WESTERN

Managing Sports Organizations: Responsibility for Performance
Daniel Covell, Sharianne Walker, Julie Siciliano, Peter W. Hess

Editor-in-Chief
Jack Calhoun

Vice President, Team Director
Michael P. Roche

Executive Editor
John Szilagyi

Sr. Marketing Manager
Rob Bloom

Developmental Editor
Jennifer E. Baker

Sr. Production Editor
Elizabeth A. Shipp

Media Developmental Editor
Kristen Meere

Media Production Editor
Karen L. Schaffer

Manufacturing Coordinator
Rhonda Utley

Production House
Trejo Production

Printer
Transcontinental Printing, Inc.—
Louiseville, QC

Internal Designer
Casey Gilbertson

Photography Manager
Deanna Ettinger

Photo Researcher
Terri Miller

Cover Designer
Casey Gilbertson

Cover Photograph
© PhotoDisc

Library of Congress
Cataloging-in-Publication Data
Managing sports organizations :
responsibility for performance / Daniel
Covell . . . [et al.].
p. cm.
Includes bibliographical references and
index.
ISBN 0-324-13155-0
1. Sports administration—United
States. 2. Sports—United States—
Management. I. Covell, Daniel
GV713.M363 2002
796'.06'9—dc21   2001058172

Brief Contents

Contents

PART 3

Preface

The field of sport management is a relatively new one. It has been created in response to the ever-growing consumer demand for sports products and services, which totals more than $150 billion annually in North America alone. Increasingly, colleges and universities are creating sport management programs that emphasize management learning and organizational issues. However, many texts that are currently available do not provide a strong foundation in business management concepts within the context of sport.

A Different Approach

We feel there are three elements that distinguish our approach in this book:

The theme of management as responsible for performance runs throughout the book. Every chapter examines management principles, concepts and issues from the perspective of how to improve the performance of sports organizations.

To ensure that students understand the complexity of the sports industry, each chapter features a distinct sports segment, such as sports agency, high school and youth sports, the licensed and branded product industry, and professional league sports to name a few. Information about the structure and characteristics of the highlighted sports segment provides the background for each chapter.

We organize the material into twelve chapters for conciseness and clarity. Given the evolving range of theories and principles that define the management field and the complexity of the sports industry, we feel that our focus on integration and synthesis is essential for student learning.

In addition to these distinguishing elements, the book also includes a number of features designed to enhance learning.

Key Features

The book includes complete coverage of the full range of topics and issues currently defining the sports industry. Each industry segment, from high school athletic programs to professional sports organizations, is described from an historical perspective and in terms of current management trends. These current topics include quality and continuous improvement, teamwork, diversity, ethics and social responsibility, globalization, information technology, and change.

The book's design is characterized by simplicity. We have attempted to minimize the number of boxes and other special features in the text that at times can draw the student's eye and attention away from the key points of the chapter. Instead, we have fully integrated current examples within the chapter narrative to illustrate the concepts and challenges of sport management.

At the opening of each chapter, learners see an overview of one segment of sport industry in our "Check the Stats" feature. Information on the size and scope of the industry segment, its participants, revenue, and governance, is available at a glance.

Each chapter features an "Inside Look" at a personality or organization within the sports industry. This profile offers a real-life look at sports professionals, the challenges they face, and the management skills that enable them to meet those challenges.

A "Management Exercise" at the conclusion of each chapter provides an opportunity for students to apply the ideas they are learning in the course. The exercise involves students directly in management decisions and challenges them to solve organizational problems. The students are required to make decisions using the available data just as the manager would in comparable situations.

These key features and the distinguishing elements discussed earlier reflect our goal of integrating sports industry dynamics with management principles and concepts. Given the complexity and diversity of both sports and the management field, this goal represents a significant challenge. We hope that other instructors will view this book as an effective first step in providing students of sport management with a solid foundation for learning about sports from a management viewpoint.

Supplements

An Instructor's Manual with Test Bank, (ISBN 0-324-13156-9) has been prepared by the authors for adopters of this text. In addition, PowerPoint slides (ISBN 0-324-17099-8) are available for download from the book support website at http://covell.swcollege .com. PowerPoint slides are available for use by students as an aid to note-taking, and by instructors for enhancing their lectures.

The book support website also includes links to online resources mentioned in the text, and both students and instructors are invited to visit South-Western's online Management Resource Center at http://www.swcollege .com/management/management.html. The Management Resource Center provides access to a library of BusinessLink Videos, South-Western's exclusive online tutorials, Internet exercises, as well as links to business cases and strategic management websites.

Acknowledgments

Credit for making this book goes first to John Szilagyi, Executive Editor at South-Western. His enthusiasm for the concept and support of our efforts provided strong encouragement during the development phase. Our thanks also go to the other fine professionals at South-Western, namely Jennifer Baker, our developmental editor, and editorial assistant Molly Flynn, for important contributions relating to the text's content. We would also like to thank Libby Shipp for her thoughtful attention in editing and producing this book.

For their input on chapters, we thank Dan Weinberg, Katherine Petrecca, and Cyndi Costanzo. We also wish to acknowledge our reviewers, who read drafts of our work and provided valuable insights and suggestions for its improvement. We are grateful to:

Robin Ammon, Jr.
Slippery Rock University

Matthew Brown
Ohio University

Terry Brown
Faulkner University

Rodney L. Caughron
Northern Illinois University

LeAnne M. Conner
Denver Technical College

Nadine Forbes
Florida College of Natural Health

Charles Hammersley
Northern Arizona University

James D. LaPoint
University of Kansas

Marcia J. Mackey
Central Michigan University

Larry Marfise
University of Tampa

Larry McCarthy
Seton Hall University

Daniel McLean
Indiana University

Michael J. Mondello
Florida State University

Mark Nagel
San Jose State University

Thomas H. Sawyer
Indiana State University

David K. Stotlar
University of Northern Colorado

Peter Titlebaum
University of Dayton

William C. Vance
Central Washington University

John Vincent
University of Alabama

Joanne Washburn
Washington State University

— *Daniel D. Covell*
Sharianne Walker
Julie Siciliano
Peter W. Hess
Western New England College

Part 1

Introduction to Management of the Sports Industry

Chapter 1

Introduction to Sports and Management

Introduction

Among those not familiar with the enormous impact of sport on the American economy, the idea of a major in sport management might raise some eyebrows. "sport management? That's a real major? What do you do? Read *Sports Illustrated* in class? Watch SportsCenter on ESPN?" Actually, there should be no question about just how real a major is that prepares individuals for careers in the sports industry. Consider this: It has been estimated that the total U.S. expenditures on sports consumption, defined as sports entertainment (which includes professional sports leagues), sports products, and sports support organizations, approaches $152 billion annually. These expenditures rank sport as the eleventh largest U.S. domestic industry, ahead of chemicals, industrial machinery, and motor vehicles and equipment (Meek, 1997). If you told people you planned on majoring in chemical or industrial engineering, they might be equally clueless about the content of the major, but they wouldn't question the viability of the industry. Nor, given the kind of economic value generated by the sports industry in the United States, should there be with sport.

If they're still not convinced, you might respond to the question with a question of your own. You might ask your interrogators why are they wearing a hat or jersey from a favorite team or if they've ever written a letter to a sports hero. Or if they work out regularly or play in an organized recreational sports league. Or if the sports section of the daily paper or favored website is the first (or only) section they read. Or why fifty million Americans fish and spend $40 billion annually on angling activities and gear (Buckley, 1999). Or why a rock band called the Zambonis (named in honor of the beloved ice-resurfacing apparatus) perform songs (including "Bob Marley and the Hartford Whalers," and "Robert Moog meets Andy Moog") only about the sport of ice hockey.

Or consider these comments from former Florida A & M student Melvin Wright: "My first day I wanted to quit. My toes were hurting and I couldn't walk. I went to the dorm and called my mom to tell her I was coming home. She told me I couldn't." Wright stuck it out and became a member not of the football, baseball, basketball, or soccer teams, but of the university marching band, which is part of the proud tradition of showstopping theatrics and musicianship seen at football halftime shows at historically black colleges and universities in the United States (White, 2001, p. 150). Or why you could place any one of hundreds of bets in Las Vegas each year on the Super Bowl—not just on who wins or by how much, but on who'll score first, which team will kick more field goals, whether a team will go for it on fourth down, or, as in 2001, whether the Baltimore Ravens and New York Giants would combine to score more points than Los Angeles Laker Kobe Bryant's combined total of points and assists in his game that day versus the New York Knicks. These examples are indicators of the significant breadth of interest in sport in our society, and that interest is a major component in all societies around the world. Every culture has some kind of sports activities.

Clearly the sports industry is alive and well in the United States, both in terms of participation and in terms of growth. For example, one study found that 25 percent more Americans participated annually in bowling (ninety-one million in all, making it the nation's most popular competitive sport) than voted in the 1998 congressional elections. And total live attendance at major-league baseball, basketball, football, hockey, NCAA football and basketball games, and NASCAR races has nearly doubled since the early 1960s (Putnam, 2001).

The road to success to careers in the sports industry, however, is full of challenge. If you were to ask what their dream job might be, more than a few (most?) sport management majors would probably answer general manager of the Houston Astros, or the Seattle Seahawks, or the Toronto Maple Leafs, or the Miami Sol, or the Long Island Lizards, or whatever their favorite pro team is. With such a crowded field, does this mean these students can never get that dream job? Absolutely not. In fact, more and more of the individuals who currently hold these positions have sport management academic backgrounds. But here's the lesson from these successful sports managers: to get a job in this highly competitive job market, you must have a strong knowledge, not only of sport and the specific sports industries, but also of management and organizations in general. Knowing what Derek Jeter's lifetime average against lefties with runners in scoring position from the seventh inning on in road games is interesting (if not somewhat pathological), but in a career field where people will work for no pay as interns to get their foot in the door with an organization, it is not enough. Getting that dream job with the Maple Leafs or the Sol, with Bally's or Gold's Gym, with Nike or New Balance, or with the Ladies Professional Golf Association, requires more than being just a sports fan. Increasingly, success in a career in the sports industry requires an understanding of the best practices in organization and management as complete as the understanding of the sport itself.

This book will introduce you to both dimensions of sport management: to the various sectors of the sports industry—professional sport, collegiate sport, youth and high school sport, sports media, and so on—and to the organizational and managerial concepts, practices, and skills required for a career in sport management. To achieve this very challenging goal, each chapter contains two kinds of information:

1. Specific information about one of the major segments of the sports industry, including a segment profile and a discussion of some of the key developments and important issues confronting that segment, and

2. Consideration of one of the critical responsibilities—planning, organizing, quality, change—of managers in all organizations, and particularly of sports managers.

This dual focus in each chapter will enable you to enhance your understanding of both the various sectors or segments that make up the sports industry and the challenges and best practices of managing in sports organizations.

Defining Organizations and Management

To understand the concept of management, we need to understand first the concept of organization. An *organization* is a group of people working together to achieve a common purpose. Organizations exist to achieve goals that individuals can't achieve on their own. Besides the family, which is a special case, hunting parties were perhaps the earliest forms of organizations. They were formed to track and kill animals that were too large or too fast to be brought down by a single individual. Today, sports organizations exist to produce products or services that can't be produced by a single individual working alone. Imagine one individual trying to operate the athletic department at a school, let alone the British Open or the

Daytona 500. It couldn't happen. These and nearly all sports organizations are far too complex, with far too many related products and services and necessary tasks.

As shown in Figure 1-1, the traditional definition of management is the coordination of human, material, technological, and financial resources needed for an organization to achieve its goals. Management gathers the resources—the people, the money, the equipment—required to make work and workers more productive. Management designs the tasks and organizes the work to be done. It ensures the skills and the coordination necessary for the kind of cooperative effort that is the essence of sports organizations. Finally, it provides the sense of direction and purpose that can unify diverse people in a productive enterprise.

In this book, we use a more direct form of this larger definition of sport management: the responsibility for performance. Sports managers are always responsible for the organization's realization of its goals, even though the goals may vary depending on whether the organization runs bowling lanes, a professional league franchise, a youth ice hockey league, an international sports governing body, or a retail sporting goods store.

In summary, sports organizations exist to perform tasks that can only be executed through cooperative effort, and sports managers are responsible for the performance and success of these organizations.

Understanding Management

Over a half century ago, Henri Fayol, a French engineer, provided a job description for managers. Fayol (1949) suggested that five functions define the manager's job (see Figure 1-2). His definitions were so clear and concise that they virtually defined management for more than fifty years. According to Fayol, management must perform the five key functions of planning, organizing, commanding, coordinating, and controlling to ensure organizational success.

More recently, management researcher Henry Mintzberg (1980) provided a slightly different perspective on management. After carefully observing what executive managers actually do with their time, Mintzberg suggested that management might

Figure 1-1 Organization and Management Defined	
Organization	**Management**
Any group of people working together to achieve a common purpose or goals that could not be attained by individuals working separately.	• The coordination of human, material, technological, and financial resources needed for the organization to achieve its goals. • Responsibility for performance.

Figure 1-2 Functions of Management According to Fayol

1. Planning the work that needs to be done.

2. Organizing the work and the workplace to ensure that the work is productive.

3. Commanding or leading and directing the workers.

4. Coordinating the efforts of everyone performing the work.

5. Controlling or monitoring to ensure performance is consistent with the plan.

Figure 1-3 Mintzberg's Ten Key Managerial Roles

1. Figurehead—representing the organization at events and ceremonies.

2. Leader—exercising influence with people and events.

3. Liaison—interacting with other organizations.

4. Monitor—receiving information critical for performance.

5. Disseminator—sharing information within the organization.

6. Spokesperson—presenting information outside the organization.

7. Entrepreneur—initiating change to improve performance.

8. Disturbance handler—dealing with issues and crises inside and outside of the organization.

9. Resource allocator—determining where the organization's human and financial resources and technology will be used.

10. Negotiator—bargaining to arrive at agreements with groups and individuals both within and outside the organization.

be more effectively defined in terms of the *roles* that managers perform (see Figure 1-3). Together, Fayol's and Mintzberg's models provide an important understanding of the wide variety of functions and roles that managers are called on to perform. However, even in the relatively short period of time since Mintzberg's research, our understanding of management in general, and sport management specifically, has shifted. Perhaps the most significant change is that managers are no longer the only ones engaged in the tasks, functions, and roles of management in sports organizations.

Management as Shared Responsibility

Over the past two decades, there has been a growing recognition that organizations are too complex to be managed by managers alone. Organizations have discovered that performance is often better when management is the responsibility not only of managers, but of performance work teams as well. In Chapter 10, we examine the specifics of how the Bay Area Sports Organizing Committee (BASOC), the organization seeking to secure the 2012 Summer Olympics for California's San Francisco Bay Area, uses *employee empowerment*, the process of employees sharing the responsibility for improving performance. The input and control afforded staffers motivates them to perform at high levels, which in turn allows the organization to meet the criteria to secure the bid, which increases the potential for significant positive economic impact for the region.

The shift in management by managers to self-managing work teams can be seen throughout all segments of the sports industry. Management is increasingly a responsibility shared among work team leaders, self-managing work groups, and all of the personnel involved with the performance of a sports organization.

Remember, our understanding of sport management is true for management in every context: as true for executive managers as it is for the scouts working for the Athletics; as true for the store managers at Lids, a retail store specializing in licensed and branded headwear, as it is for the greenskeepers and grounds crew at Augusta National Golf Club in Georgia or the thousands of volunteers who work at the X Games. All of these individuals and groups are engaged in sport management; each shares in the responsibility for the performance of their organization. Increasingly, the definition of management must be expanded to include the growing dimension of shared responsibility for performance.

The New Management Environment

The responsibility for performance involves combining and coordinating human, technological, and financial resources to achieve organizational goals. Organizations by their nature are complex and therefore difficult to manage. Still, as long as society, the economy, and technology remained somewhat stable or changed only slowly, management had time to make the adjustments necessary to maintain and improve performance.

Gradual change has now been replaced by rapid change, however, and managers face new challenges brought on by a changing environment. These include intense competition and new performance standards that every management team must now achieve.

The Challenge to Compete

The task of managing organizations, described so effectively by both Fayol and Mintzberg, now complicated by the trend toward shared responsibility for performance, is obviously extremely challenging. During recent years, that task of managing has become even more challenging. The reason is competition.

First, there are more competitors as a result of the tremendous increase in global competition. While U.S. sports organizations are seeking to expand globally, as we discuss in Chapter 2, other foreign companies, especially equipment and apparel businesses like adidas and Kappa, are setting their sights on U.S. expansion. Secondly, the nature of the competition itself has become much more adversarial as global companies compete for the American sports dollar.

During the past twenty-five years, Americans have shown a seemingly limitless appetite for sports entertainment and other sports products and services. This is the result of major sports such as professional football, baseball, and basketball demonstrating the ability to generate huge revenues by responding to the American tidal wave of demand. Also, television has created an unprecedented demand for sports entertainment and for the attention and involvement of the recreational athlete. As we discuss in Chapter 11, the activities often referred to as extreme sports (skateboarding, snowboarding, in-line skating, wakeboarding, BMX biking) have grown exponentially in the last decade and been boosted by the major network presentations of extreme sports festival competitions such as ESPN's broadcasting of the X Games and NBC's broadcasting of the Gravity Games. In part because of this exposure, there are now 29 million in-line skaters in the United States (almost double the number of soccer players), almost as many skateboarders (7.2 million) as baseball players (10.8 million), and since 1999 over 600 skate parks have opened across the country, often replacing unused tennis courts and other underutilized athletic facilities (Ruibal, 2001).

With so many options now available to the sports consumer, it is no longer enough for a sports organization simply to be managed well. To compete and succeed in today's environment, the challenge for every sports organization is to be *better*. Increasingly, competition is forcing organizations to increase the quality of the products and services they offer, to increase speed and flexibility in responding to customers, and to innovate to constantly provide new products and services. Achieving these new standards is the responsibility of the sports manager.

Quality

It is common sense that given the choice between two comparably priced sports experiences or products, the customer will almost always choose the one of higher quality. Consider Greg Dallas, a former season ticket holder for the Denver Nuggets of the National Basketball Association, who gave up his two $52 seats after five years. He criticized the on-court nature of the NBA product: "It's boring, expensive, meaningless . . . the number of expensive games is 41 out of 41. The number of good games is 10 out of 41. What kind of value is that for your entertainment dollar?" (Swift, 2000, p. 76). The key to success for the NBA has clearly become quality. With so many options available in terms of where sports fans like Greg Dallas can spend their money, the leagues like the NBA simply can't afford to fall behind in terms of the quality of experience they provide. Achieving quality and continually raising the bar in terms of quality is now among the sports manager's most important responsibilities (see Chapter 7).

Speed and Flexibility

As important as quality is, it is not the total answer. Speed and flexibility have become more and more important as a way to move ahead of the competition. One executive put it this way: "Quality is your ticket into the stadium. You can't even come to the game unless you have a quality product and process in place. [But] you have to compete on other dimensions today" (Byrne, 1992).

Consider the case of Lids, described earlier in the chapter. In 2001 Lids was purchased outright by Hat World, a competitor retail and online cap sales company. Says Hat World cofounder Glenn Campbell, "Everybody either went to college, or follows a college of professional sports team. Likewise, everybody has $20. We're clearly an impulse buy, but it's one that people can afford" ("Company Information," 2001, p. 1). The newly expanded company has now grown to over 420 stores in 44 states and has won numerous awards for entrepreneurship. According to Ken Roberts, a Lids store manager, the organization keeps track of what the customer wants, "and that feedback goes directly from store managers to the district office." That way, the decisions about which products will be placed in stores as well as on the Lids's website is made with the input of customers and store managers. Lids also uses feedback from the stores in working with manufacturers in designing merchandise. This kind of speed in moving information directly from the customer and store into the company's key decision-making processes allows Lids to quickly place on its shelves exactly the kinds of products its customers want. And speed and flexibility in responding to customer desires has also allowed Lids to achieve exclusivity on the sale of certain products (K. Roberts, personal communication, July 16, 1997).

Organizations that are too large to be flexible, or too rigid in terms of policies and procedures, are unable to take advantage of opportunities that emerge and disappear so quickly in all segments of the sports industry. It is speed and flexibility in product design and distribution that allows Lids to be among the leaders in its industry segment. It is also speed and flexibility that allows Lids to maintain a leadership position in the licensed product retail market (discussed in Chapter 2).

Innovation

No matter how successful a sports organization is, someone somewhere in the world is developing a product or service that is different or better. Innovation means providing different or better products and services or finding a better way to deliver them. The need for contemporary sports organizations to innovate has become essential. Chapter 3 discusses a number of the innovations specifically in the sports media sector that have been achieved through advances in technology. But whether through technology or changes in a sport's rules, through enhanced fan participation or enhanced fan access to sports information, or even through product innovations such as the Big Bertha golf club, the pressure is on sports managers to compete by innovating.

Actually, innovation has always been a part of sport: think about the forward pass in football, the designated hitter in baseball, aluminum bats, the three-point shot. Or consider the case of Gatorade. If you ask anyone who played sports before 1970 about drinking water during practice, chances are they would say they didn't. They weren't allowed to. Many coaches believed that depriving athletes of water would toughen them up. Said Grant Teaff, former head coach at Baylor University and head of the American Football Coaches Association, "When I grew up, we were taught that if you even wanted a drink, you were less than a man" (Powers, 2001). Many coaches also believed that lifting weights was bad for athletes. Obviously, these training choices were not based on science.

In the 1960s several scientists at the University of Florida, spurred by a query from an assistant coach for the Gators' freshman football team, began to study the effects of dehydration on performance. The result was the creation of a beverage that replenishes the body with water, sodium, and sugar lost during strenuous exercise. Dubbed "Gatorade" (gator-ade, like lemon-ade), it was tested in 1965, and the next season, the gridiron Gators adopted the drink. Gatorade, now produced by the Quaker Oats Company, which was purchased by PepsiCo Inc. in 2001 for $14 billion ("PepsiCo Gets," 2001), owns 83 percent of the sports-drink market, with annual gross sales of $2.3 billion. The creators earn $6 million a year in royalties, much of which is used to fund scholarships and teaching positions (Walters, 2001).

Although the developers of Gatorade were not focused on producing a product for a market, they ended up creating an entirely new market—sports drinks—and the product that continues to dominate it. This example shows the potential value of innovation for assuring the success of all organizations. And where innovation was previously only a sometime occurrence in most sports organizations, competition has made innovation a key management responsibility in every sports organization.

Sustainable Growth

The final performance standard is of a different type than quality, speed, flexibility, and innovation. It is, in a sense, the context for the others. The concept of *sustainable growth* means that organizations neither seek to be as large as they can be nor to grow as quickly as they possibly can. Sustainable growth also means that organizations should only grow at a rate, and to a size, that can be maintained over the long term (Garfield, 1992). Certainly with so many organizations competing for the money and attention of sports fans, every sports organization must commit itself to a goal of sustainable growth.

In recent years, many sports organizations, especially apparel and footwear manufacturers, have found that bigger is not necessarily better. Growing as fast as you can in a short period may result in serious problems as time goes on. Consider the case of New Balance, a privately held footwear and apparel manufacturing company headquartered in Brighton, Massachusetts. In the wake of the up-and-down performance of companies like Reebok, and the recent demise of longtime industry stalwarts Starter and Converse, New Balance has deliberately inched its way up in sales and growth. New Balance benefited from the running boom of the 1970s, with sales growing from $200,000 annually to $80 million, and it found a niche with middle-aged and older consumers who were more concerned with performance than fashion.

Following a few failed attempts at taking on Nike and becoming a flashy and "cool" brand to attract a bigger share of the market, New Balance chairman and CEO Jim Davis said a lesson was learned. "If we try to be like everyone else, if we try to stress fashion over quality or marketing over performance, we won't be successful," he said (Denizet-Lewis, 2001, p. 129). This sustainable growth approach has allowed New Balance to retain its core market, but also because of its focus on quality, younger consumers are now discovering the brand and boosting sales. Even with this controlled focus, New Balance's domestic footwear sales reached $750 million in 2000, with another $250 million in domestic apparel and international sales. These figures surprised industry experts and company executives alike. The company learned that the right target is sustainable growth, growth at a rate and to a size that will serve the organization well regardless of the conditions. For more information on New Balance, see Chapter 2.

The New Balance story also gives us a clear example of many of the changing performance standards. The importance of these changing standards is clear: increased emphasis on quality, speed and flexibility, innovation, and sustainable growth. Ultimately, management will be judged by these standards. Successful sports organizations such as New Balance are already pursuing them.

Before considering each dimension of the further challenges for sports managers in greater detail, we first take a look at the development of management theory and thinking. We trace the roots of these ideas and theories of how to improve the performance of organizations back more than a century. And we also present the more contemporary management ideas that create the bridge between these earlier concepts and today's sports organizational climate.

The Development of Management Thought

Although earlier civilizations thought of sport as "play" in relation to the toil and labor of "work" and often linked it to fertility and religious rituals (Gorn & Goldstein, 1993), many early sporting activities were also linked to aspects of organization and management. Consider the fact that Native Americans played an early form of the game lacrosse with hundreds of players on a side, over a field several miles long. This required organization and management. In addition, the popularity of horse racing in England in the eighteenth and nineteenth centuries led to the development of a system to formally organize betting and the running of races (Mandell, 1984; Vamplew, 1989).

Although these efforts were not specifically called "management," the responsibility for organized performance has been part of human society essentially from the beginning. But it was only about two hundred years ago that the ideas which formed the basis for what we now call "management thinking" began to emerge. The following sections describe the evolution of management thinking, and more specifically, the intriguing range of answers that have been offered to what might be viewed as the key question of management: How do you improve the performance of organizations?

Some Early Ideas

Adam Smith and Task Specialization

One of the early answers to the question of performance was supplied by Adam Smith (1776/1937), author of *The Wealth of Nations*. Smith was among the first to comment on the impact of performance on the concept of the *division of labor*, or *task specialization*. Smith used a now well-known example of how a single craftsman working alone could produce no more than twenty pins in an entire day, but ten workers in a manufactory organized to perform only the specialized tasks necessary to create a pin (drawing the wire, straightening the wire, setting the head, and so on) could produce an unprecedented 12 *pounds* of pins in a day.

Without necessarily setting out to do so, Smith provided one of the early answers to the question of how to improve performance: specialize the tasks. Take every large task and break it down into smaller steps or activities, and have each worker become a specialist, an expert at one specific activity or step. This type of task specialization can be seen throughout the sports industries, from footwear, equipment and apparel manufacturing to the specialized tasks of managers in sports agency firms and intercollegiate athletic departments. Through his example of task specialization, Smith clearly established that management makes a difference. Although he never used the term *management,* it was management that organized the workers into these specialized tasks.

J. B. Say and the Concept of the Entrepreneur

A fundamentally different response to the question of how to improve performance came in the early nineteenth century from the French economic philosopher J. B. Say. Essentially, Say suggested that improved performance is the result of better ideas. In fact, Say (1803/1964) created a term to describe people with ideas for better uses of existing technology; he called these people *entrepreneurs.*

The history of sport management is replete with technological and conceptual entrepreneurs. One of the earliest and best examples was Albert G. Spalding, a standout professional baseball pitcher who in the late nineteenth century parlayed his baseball reputation and a loan of $800 to create a sporting goods manufacturing giant based on selling to the expanding American middle class. While also owner of the Chicago White Stockings of the National League, Spalding adopted technological advances to manufacture bats, baseballs, gloves, uniforms, golf clubs, bicycles, hunting goods, and football equipment.

Many other manufacturers also focused on the production of sporting goods, but Spalding also understood that he had to create and foster the markets for these products as the newly affluent middle class sought to find uses for their leisure time. Spalding produced guides on how to play and to exercise, promoted grassroots sports competitions, and gained credibility with consumers by claiming official supplier status with baseball's National League (Levine, 1985). This position of quality by association (a technique used today by every company that touts its status as the "official supplier" to any sports organization or by any company that uses a sports personality to endorse its products) allowed consumers to distinguish Spalding products from their many competitors.

Spalding also created a profitable distribution system in which the company sold directly to retailers at a set price with the guarantee that retailers would sell at a price that Spalding set. This technique created stable markets for Spalding goods and eliminated price cutting at the retail level (Levine, 1985). Spalding's company exists to this day, now headquartered in Chicopee, Massachusetts, and manufactures and sells a wide range of sporting goods products.

There are countless examples of entrepreneurial efforts throughout the history of sport management. Gary Davidson developed the American Basketball Association (ABA), World Football League (WFL), and World Hockey Association (WHA) and the concept of viable competitive professional leagues to alternative markets using innovations like the three-point shot. The Eco Golf company produces biodegradable golf tees made from corn, eliminating the need for trees, cutting down on the buildup of litter on tee boxes, and reducing damage to mower blades and cart tires caused by traditional wooden tees. And Robert Edward "Ted" Turner III, after his local Atlanta television station bought the rights to broadcast Atlanta Braves' games, bought the whole franchise for $10 million in 1975 to keep them from moving to Toronto. Turner then used the lure of Braves' games, along with *The Andy Griffith Show* reruns and old movies and the availability of satellite communications that could beam Braves' games to viewers in South Dakota, New Mexico, and all over the country, to develop TBS, America's first superstation, and later other cable offerings (Helyar, 1994). This move to use sports products as content for media companies led to the purchasing of other franchises by media companies (see Chapter 3).

Say would point out that each of these entrepreneurial efforts improved performance by finding better uses for existing technologies and better ways to develop markets and to sell to customers. He would note that each example improved performance by finding better ways for using the resources we already have.

Robert Owen and the Soho Engineering Foundry

Management experiments like those of the entrepreneurs just discussed also occurred well before our time and often took different forms. Consider the efforts

of Robert Owen, a Scottish cotton mill owner. Owen (1825) believed that improved working conditions for laborers would result in improvements in their performance. He shortened the workday from 13 to 10.5 hours, built better housing and a recreation center for his workers, provided a company store where necessities could be purchased at reasonable prices, and accessed schooling for workers' children. By all accounts, Owen's mills became highly profitable and had a significant impact on child labor laws.

Owen was able to improve performance by improving the way his workers were treated. The sports industry with the most to learn from Owen is the apparel and footwear manufacturers. Companies like Nike and Reebok have been universally criticized for paying low wages and treating workers poorly. Nike managers at a factory in Vietnam even went so far as to punish workers who wore non-Nike products by forcing them to run laps around the factory (Neuborn, 1997). In addition, Nike was found to be paying workers in El Salvador 29 cents for each $140 Duke, Georgetown, North Carolina, and Ohio State replica jersey they made (two-tenths of 1 percent of the garment's retail price) (Files, 2001). These issues are discussed in greater detail in Chapter 2, but the important point from Owen's perspective is that the way people are managed can make a significant difference in performance. To the question of how to improve performance, Robert Owen's answer was to make the workplace a community and treat people well.

These early answers to the question of management are interesting and important, but not until the twentieth century were management and organizations actually studied and analyzed in a systematic way in an effort to understand which methods worked and which didn't to improve organizational performance.

The Early Twentieth Century: Three Milestones in Management Thinking

During the first few decades of the last century, three milestone responses emerged to the question of how to improve performance: the scientific management response of Frederick Taylor, the administrative theory response of Henri Fayol, and the human relations response of Elton Mayo. These three responses, more than any others, form the basic foundations of our modern understanding of management. Each approached the central question of management from a different perspective. Each enriched our understanding of how to improve performance, and each has had a significant impact on the way all organizations are currently managed.

Scientific Management

Frederick Taylor was studying to be an engineer when he arrived at Midvale Steel Company in Pennsylvania. Not surprisingly, he applied an engineer's problem-solving acumen to thinking about the work performed at Midvale. Taylor was convinced that by carefully observing and experimenting with all the tasks performed at the mill, he would be able to identify "principles" that defined how work should be done. According to Taylor, once these principles were defined, all the workers could be trained to do the work the "one best way," rather than relying on their own various rules of thumb.

For years, Taylor studied the work performed at Midvale, carefully noting where the workers stood to do certain tasks, how far they had to reach, the kinds of tools they used—everything having to do with how they did their jobs. Based on his extensive observations, he then experimented with ways to improve the workers' performance, changing everything from how they did their jobs to the tools they used to do them. Based on these experiments, Taylor then trained the workers to perform tasks in the most efficient way. The results of Taylor's scientific approach were impressive. In one key example, the "Taylor-trained workers" loaded nearly four times as much iron per day as the other workers, and the average earnings of these men increased 50 percent (Taylor, 1947).

One of the first sports managers to adopt Taylor's scientific methods became one of baseball's most legendary and influential figures. Branch Rickey, the theatrical, pontifical, and often long-winded "Mahatma," used a Tayloresque approach to the teaching of baseball skills and the developing of players to transform several professional baseball organizations, and he was the driving force behind building the championship St. Louis Cardinal teams of the 1930s and the powerful Brooklyn Dodger squads of the late 1940s through the 1950s. Rickey, a former big-league catcher and manager with the former St. Louis Browns (now the Baltimore Orioles), spent countless hours studying the skills of the game to perfect methods in base running, hitting, defense, and pitching. In pursuit of these ends, Rickey is credited with the creation of the batting tees, sliding pits, and preseason "baseball training colleges" (Tygiel, 1993).

Along with this devotion to the study and improvement of game skills, Rickey also developed the modern farm system, in which a major-league club would use a number of affiliated "minor-league" teams for the development of future talent. In 1949 it was estimated that three out of eight major leaguers came up through the Cards' system. Rickey may be best known, however, for his entrepreneurial efforts to integrate Major-League Baseball. In an effort to reach an untapped source of talent, Rickey signed African American Jackie Robinson, a former three-sports star at UCLA and veteran of the Negro Leagues. Robinson broke the color barrier in 1947, and along with African Americans Don Newcombe and Roy Campanella, led the great Dodger teams of that era (Tygiel, 1993).

Administrative Theory

Frederick Taylor may have been the first to suggest that management is a professional set of tasks and responsibilities. Recall, however, that it was another engineer, Frenchman Henri Fayol, who first defined in a comprehensive way just what those tasks and responsibilities might be. Fayol (1949) published the details of the key elements and functions of management, listed earlier in Figure 1-2. We discuss how these elements impact a wide range of sports managers throughout the book, but stop and think for a moment about how each of these five areas impacts a job in sport. In what ways does the forecasting of events and the updating of organizational plans impact the director of product marketing for New Balance? How does the general manager for the Maple Leafs set the organization in motion and deal with unproductive personnel? How does harmony and unity of purpose impact a sports agent representing a first-round National Basketball Association (NBA) draft pick? How does a facilities manager at the Indianapolis Motor Speedway monitor worker activities and output?

Fayol's response to the question of how to improve performance might be summarized as improve the management: train managers to plan, organize, command, coordinate, and control.

The Hawthorne Studies

Like the post–World War II boom, the prosperity of the Roaring 1920s following World War I also prompted an increase in demand for automobiles, home appliances, newfangled radios and telephones, and machinery. Segments of the sports industry also benefited, as the period, often referred to as the "Golden Age of

Sport," was typified by the exploits of legendary figures such as tennis star Bill Tilden, golfer Bobby Jones, gridiron great Red Grange, baseball's Babe Ruth, and boxer William Harrison "Jack" Dempsey. Dempsey, nicknamed the "Manassa Mauler," held the heavyweight title from 1919 to 1926. With the assistance of promoter George "Tex" Rickard, Dempsey's hard-charging fighting style brought boxing to unprecedented heights of popularity. Over 80,000 saw Dempsey knock out French war hero Georges Carpentier in Toledo, Ohio, in 1921 (with gate receipts estimated at $450,000), a throng of 125,000 were at New York's Polo Grounds to see Dempsey's second-round knockout of Argentine Luis Firpo in 1923, and another 120,000 (with gate receipts totaling $2 million, of which Dempsey's cut was $717,000) saw Dempsey lose his title to Gene Tunney in Philadelphia in 1926. When he retired after losing a rematch with Tunney in 1927 (for which he earned $450,000), Dempsey was estimated to be worth $3 million. The rise of Dempsey and the boxing industry in the 1920s is often portrayed as the keynote example of the growth and establishment of spectator sport in contemporary American culture (Kahn, 1999).

Naturally the huge increase in demand for products and services of all kinds led to an increase in interest in understanding how to make organizations better at producing and offering them—in other words, how to improve organizational performance. In the early 1920s, the General Electric Company began advertising that better lighting in the workplace would result in increased output by workers. To support these claims, GE persuaded the Western Electric Company, manufacturer of telephones for the Bell Systems, to conduct illumination experiments at its huge Hawthorne Works in Cicero, Illinois, outside Chicago. Consistent with Frederick Taylor's scientific management approach, an experiment was designed to determine whether better lighting in a work area would result in increased worker productivity. Worker output was measured as lighting was increased and then decreased. The results of the experiment, shown in Figure 1-4, were totally unexpected. As the lighting was increased, productivity increased, just as GE had hoped. What was not expected was that even when the lighting was decreased, productivity continued to rise. In fact, productivity continued to rise until the lighting was as faint as moonlight; then productivity finally leveled off. These

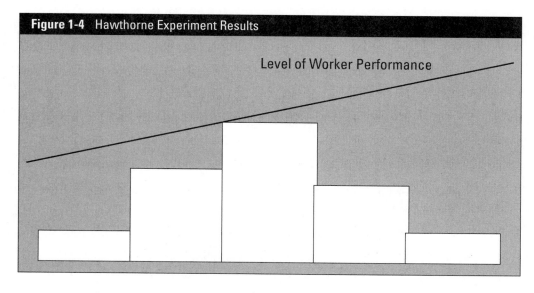

Figure 1-4 Hawthorne Experiment Results

Level of Worker Performance

were clearly not the results GE was looking for, and it promptly withdrew from the experiment. But the search was on for an explanation for these surprising results.

The Hawthorne effect. To get a clearer understanding of what had happened in the experiment at the Hawthorne Works, interviews were conducted with more than twenty thousand Western Electric workers. From the data from these interviews, Harvard University professor Elton Mayo (1953) and his research team began to piece together an explanation.

According to Mayo, the workers viewed the experiments as evidence of increased management concern for the conditions of the workplace. Mayo concluded that the workers increased their productivity in response to this increased attention from management. The experimental conditions may or may not have improved the workplace, but the workers felt that at least management was trying to do something about working conditions. The workers apparently increased their output in response to what they viewed as management's concern for their well-being. The notion that increased attention by management results in increased productivity by the worker came to be known as the *Hawthorne effect*.

Think about the sport of boxing. Although less popular today due to various organizational problems in certifying championships, ranking fighters, and perennial disputes over fixed fights and felonious activities, boxing remains a viable segment of the professional sports industry. It also remains the domain of the trainers, characters such as Angelo Dundee and Cus D'Amato, who prepare boxers for their matches. Is it possible that the research of Mayo and the impact of the Hawthorne effect could impact such a brutal and physically damaging activity as boxing? Trainer Teddy Atlas understands these seemingly unrelated spheres well. Atlas apprenticed with the venerable D'Amato, working with a young Mike Tyson in the early 1980s before he became heavyweight champ. Later, after threatening Tyson with a loaded pistol after Tyson made a sexual advance on Atlas's niece, he left Tyson and D'Amato and struck out on his own. Atlas, a former criminal himself, is known for taking a hard line with his fighters, because pushing someone to be a pro fighter, says Atlas, is against human nature. "The basis of nature is to survive. What I'm telling [a fighter] is against nature. I'm telling him how to be a brute and not just survive. A trainer's got to lead a fighter into a dark place, and not too many want to go" (Remnick, 2000, p. 153).

But as a trainer teaches a fighter to hurt and not to be hurt, he (and for now, there are no shes) must work with the fighter intimately, get to know him physically and psychologically. Between rounds in fights, trainers also nurse their wounds, give them water, and feed and boost their psyches. This practice, fight author David Remnick writes, "this babying, is unique to boxing. Bill Parcells does not water his fullback. Joe Torre does not massage the pitcher" (Remnick, 2000, p. 147).

As far as the psychological aspects, Atlas takes this role seriously as well. After the eighth round in Michael Moorer's 1994 title bout with Evander Holyfield, when Moorer had the champ on the ropes but seemed reluctant to finish him off, Atlas chided his fighter with this soliloquy:

> There comes a time in a man's life when he makes a decision to just live, survive—or he wants to win. You're making a decision just to survive. You're doing enough to keep him off ya' and hope he leaves ya' alone.

You're *lying* to yourself, and I'd be lying to you if I didn't tell you that. And if you don't change you'll be crying tomorrow! Now go out there and back him up and fight a full round [author's emphasis]. (Remnick, 2000, p. 152)

Atlas kept after Moorer throughout the fight, stating before the final round, "Michael, in your *mind* you are doing your best. But you're not doing your best. Have I ever lied to you?" When Moorer won the bout on a split decision (Moorer would later be regarded as one of the least gifted heavyweight champions ever), and as he moved to embrace his trainer, Atlas still wasn't letting up, responding, "You coulda done more, Michael" [author's emphasis] (Remnick, 2000, p. 153).

In terms of the applicability of the Hawthorne studies, then, is the realization that the impact of management is not restricted to planning and task design, as Taylor suggested, or to management principles, as Fayol suggested. Management, according to Mayo and the Hawthorne effect, and as evidenced by the cornerwork of Teddy Atlas pushing his fighters to excel, is every bit as powerful in its human impact as in its technical impact. The Hawthorne studies provided the first scientific evidence that management's attention to workers might have a major effect on their performance, and Atlas and other sports managers continue to bear this out. There was, however, an even more significant finding from the Hawthorne studies.

Mayo and the Hawthorne studies, along with the dynamics of boxing, provide a third (after Taylor and Fayol) critical response to the management question of how to improve organizational performance: improve interpersonal relations on the job. It is not enough to analyze and design each task scientifically, as Taylor suggested, or to train managers to plan, organize, command, control, and coordinate effectively, as Fayol prescribed. The Hawthorne studies pointed for the first time to the importance of interpersonal relations between management and workers, and among the workers themselves. Although later researchers criticized the way the Hawthorne studies were conducted (Rice, 1982), with questions raised about whether the experiments were sufficiently scientific to provide valid results, there is no question that with the Hawthorne studies management thinking expanded significantly to include consideration of people as a key factor in organizational performance.

More Recent Contributions

During the second half of the twentieth century, new answers to the question of how to improve organizational performance emerged. A number of the contributions to management thinking have endured, and, taken together, they provide a sense of the range and diversity of the ideas within the management mainstream. Five of the theories are (1) decision sciences, (2) systems theory, (3) contingency theory, (4) Japanese management, and (5) continuous quality improvement.

Decision Sciences

During World War II, there was a critical need to utilize scarce military resources as effectively and efficiently as possible. There were never enough personnel, aircraft, equipment, weapons, or supplies to meet the demands of all the military commanders. To aid in making the decisions about how these scarce resources should be distributed to have the greatest impact, British military technicians developed a technique called operations research (OR).

Decisions "by the numbers." OR uses mathematical equations to allow decision makers to evaluate which of all the available options represents the best use of resources. For example, World War II military planners used mathematical formulas to try out all the possible ways that various numbers and types of aircraft with various ranges between refuelings could carry various numbers and types of armaments. They also factored in the probability of each type of plane's achieving the target and the probability of each type of plane's returning safely for additional bombing runs. Thus, using all the quantitative, or numerical, information available to them, these planners were able to identify the option with the greatest likelihood of success. The U.S. military adopted OR in the course of the war; and, not surprisingly, OR was adapted to American industry following the war. It is now known as *decision sciences* (Mallach, 1994; Turban, 1990).

The impact of decision sciences is seen in all organizations. It is easy to see how such systems could be adapted to all the research and planning implemented by race teams in NASCAR, Formula One racing, and all other motor sports to achieve organizational success, but these are the more mechanized segments of the sports industries. At the most elemental level, drivers and pit crews must use similar techniques to know when pit stops must be made during the course of a race.

However, in an effort to control costs, promote driver and spectator safety, and keep competition close and fair, the management of NASCAR places certain restrictions on technological usage so that cars cannot exceed certain speeds. Although these decisions limit the actual speed of the vehicles, they actually promote organizational performance by keeping drivers, NASCAR's most valuable asset in terms of fan identity, healthy (although injuries and fatalities still occur), and assuring that the most successful teams are not those who can simply spend the most on technology to create the fastest car. This then promotes the element of driver expertise, which further develops fan identification with the drivers. Indeed, as one observer noted, when attending a NASCAR event at Darlington Raceway in South Carolina, it is simpler to purchase a T-shirt or cap emblazoned with the number and sponsor logos of Buckshot Jones, Ricky Craven, or Hut Stricklin, to steer clear of having to answer repeatedly the question, "Who's your favorite driver?" (Hagstrom, 1998, p. 8). We discuss NASCAR and other tour sports in greater detail in Chapter 11 and the licensed product industry in Chapter 2.

Other sports organizations have seen the value of decision sciences. The concessions companies that serve entertainment venues must use these methods to know which events will attract the largest crowds and what the individual tastes of each might be. It is safe to say that a World Wrestling Federation (WWF) event draws a crowd with different food demands than a performance of the Three Tenors. Health and fitness clubs keep track of the number of customers at various times of the day, what activities and equipment are involved, and for how long. The decision sciences approach can then be used to calculate what sort of activities to offer, such as power yoga, spinning, or aqua aerobics, what staffing is needed to lead them, and what time of day they are to be offered. For more details on the health and fitness industry, see Chapter 5.

Limitations of the decision sciences approach. Decision sciences have had a tremendous impact in many sports organizations, those in which the variables and factors involved can be counted and then included in quantifiable formulas. But in the area of a manager's job involving interpersonal relations, decision sciences obviously are less useful. Factors such as attitudes and norms and emotions are far more difficult to measure, and calculations involving the human factor are less reliable. In Chapter 8 we examine the efforts of NFL teams to predict the future performance of quarterback Drew Brees based largely on his physical characteristics and skills. Is this the best way to measure whether Brees will be a future star, or are there other, less tangible variables like leadership and competitiveness that more accurately predict success? The answer is not clear. Many physically gifted athletes never meet organizational expectations, and less physically imposing players succeed. Still, the decision sciences response to the question of improving performance continues to be valuable: convert the factors in the situation into numbers, and calculate the effectiveness of the various combinations of those factors until the optimum combination is found.

Systems Theory

In 1928 biologist Ludwig von Bertalanffy introduced a theory of general systems suggesting that everything in nature is interrelated. According to von Bertalanffy (1951), every entity is part of a larger system. He pointed out that in nature nothing is totally independent and self-sufficient. Every living organism is part of a system and is affected by what happens both within and outside that system. Management thinker Herbert Simon (1965) extended systems thought to organizations by viewing them as systems that make decisions and process information.

The importance of what's happening outside the organization. Traditionally, organizations were thought of as fairly closed systems. Organizations usually thought of themselves as mostly insulated or protected from whatever was happening outside their boundaries. Those in distinct organizations tended to think the events most critical to their success were those that occurred inside those boundaries.

The major contribution of a systems perspective was the recognition that organizations are in fact open systems. That is, they receive input from their environment. They transform that input into output, and the output then reenters the environment, resulting in feedback that affects subsequent input, as shown in Figure 1-5.

The systems view forces organizations to recognize that what is happening outside its boundaries does matter. As we discussed earlier in the chapter, we are a society of organizations, and when one organization falters or fails, others are almost always threatened or damaged. The example of a downturn in attendance for a professional league franchise impacting many other organizations also bears out the open systems theory, that they can indeed be affected by immediate business trends. Changes in the social, economic, political, and technological environments are also larger scale factors, as we see in Chapter 10 when we discuss the development of the Olympic movement.

Organizations also feel the impact from the other factors discussed earlier, including the changing environment and changing performance standards. Recall that bowling is the most popular sports activity in the United States. Although overall

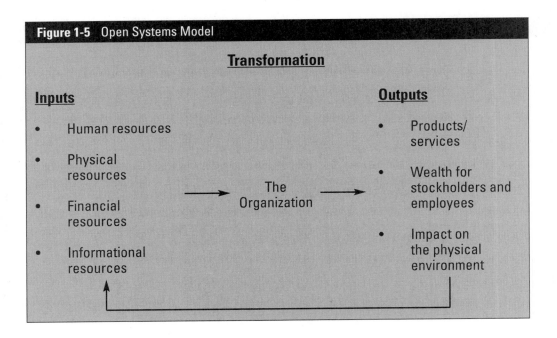

Figure 1-5 Open Systems Model

Transformation

Inputs

- Human resources
- Physical resources
- Financial resources
- Informational resources

The Organization

Outputs

- Products/services
- Wealth for stockholders and employees
- Impact on the physical environment

bowling participation is high, the number of league bowlers has dropped significantly in recent years. This is a red flag for owners of bowling lanes because league bowlers consume more beer and pizza, high profit areas for lanes. Why has league bowling declined? In *Bowling Alone*, his study of changes in American community involvement, academician Robert D. Putnam (2001) notes that this is a reflection of a general trend in American life, where people are less likely to be involved in public life, and to join civic and community groups, churches, and political parties. This also includes involvement in traditional team and sports organizations. These factors impact all sports organizations, and sports organizations can't eliminate them by their own means or own decisions. Simon's point was that, like it or not, organizations are open to the influence of their environments.

Today, successful sports organizations know they are open systems. They have learned that their environments are a key factor affecting their performance. The forms of their services and products are driven more by customer tastes and preferences than by their own. Their success in meeting customer demands is determined by many factors. Sports organizations must cultivate a workforce capable of doing the work necessary, such as certified physical trainers to teach power yoga and suppliers capable of providing affordable, high-quality materials, whether they put them in hot dogs sold at Bank One Ball Park in Phoenix, the graphite and steel in Callaway golf clubs, or the plastics to make Burton snowboards. An organization's success in selling its output is impacted strongly by what the competition offers as an alternative and by the overall state of the economy as well. Each of these environmental factors must be recognized and responded to in managing the organization.

No organization can be concerned simply with what's happening within its four walls. All organizations must be concerned equally with customer relations, community relations, employee relations, supplier relations, and government relations. Von Bertalanffy and Simon were right: all organizations—from the smallest to the largest, and regardless of the sports industry segment—are part of a system, and anything happening within this system is happening to the sports organization as well.

Contingency Theory

The search for universal or general principles of management did not end with Taylor and Fayol. The emergence of systems theory, which highlighted the many environmental variables that influenced organizations, raised the question of whether it was still possible to develop universal management principles that would apply to all organizations and all situations. Was Taylor's concept of finding "the one best way," as practiced and proselytized by Branch Rickey, still valid, given the fact that there were so many factors to be considered?

The law of the situation. Social philosopher Mary Parker Follett developed the *law of the situation* in 1928. Follett suggested that leaders would be more successful if they would adjust their style of leadership to the needs of their followers and to the requirements of the situation (Metcalf & Urwick, 1941). For Follett there was no one best way. What was best would be determined by the situation. It was up to management to recognize what the situation required and to make the necessary adjustments.

Today, this approach is called the *contingency view*, and it is reflected in nearly every dimension of management. In terms of planning, organizations now have contingency plans, options that ensure that a plan is in place for every situation likely to be encountered. In terms of organizing, the retail hat seller Lids recognizes that shipping the same products to all stores everywhere may be effective in terms of simplifying distribution, but management needs to listen to consumers and individual store managers and remain flexible to ensure that sales in stores in each market remain high. In terms of quality control, in some cases New Balance may need to inspect every product; in other cases, where manufacturing or assembly is less precise, it may make more sense to test and to inspect only a statistically selected sample of the total output. The evidence is abundant: effective organizations adjust to the situation.

Example. For a clearer understanding of the premises of the contingency view, consider the case of a college athletic department that has consistently gone over budget for several years. What can be done to balance the department's budget? First, let's consider the alternatives to contingency theory. Frederick Taylor's scientific management approach would be to examine how each coach or athletic department staff member performed his or her actual job tasks, such as recruiting or fund-raising, and make them more efficient. Henri Fayol's administrative theory answer would be to train the departmental managers so they could more effectively plan, organize, and control the activities of the department, and coordinate and direct the department's personnel. Elton Mayo's human relations theory would focus on the departmental staff members themselves, and on improving the relationships among staffers, and between staffers and department managers.

In contrast, contingency theory would say that the solution to the problem depends on the situation, and no single answer exists for how to improve the performance of the athletic department. If the problem in the athletic department is in the way the staffers or coaches are doing their jobs, and overspending their recruiting budgets or not raising sufficient revenues, the scientific management approach might be most effective. If the problem is at director level of the department, providing management training for the directors might be the best solution. If the problem is the attitudes of the staff and the coaches, human relations theory might hold the answer.

Follett's contribution was an important one, but it is often difficult to understand what is required in situations as complex and chaotic as those that organizations in the widely varied sports industries face today. And as we will learn, it can be even more difficult to implement the appropriate adjustment because the parameters and expectations of a high school athletic department are quite different from a Division I-A athletic department, which are very different again from a Division III athletic department. And these are all organizations associated with educational institutions. We will learn more about the specifics of intercollegiate athletics in Chapter 12. Still, the challenge for management is clear: to improve performance, management must learn to adjust to the situation.

Japanese Management

For most of the period following World War II, the Japanese organizational responses to the question of how to improve performance was quite different from those in America. Given the success in the automobile, consumer electronics, and steel industries, the Japanese response is one worth studying. Characteristics of this specific management style are shown in Figure 1-6 (Athos & Pascale, 1981; Ouchi, 1981). So effective was the Japanese approach to management that in the decades following a debilitating defeat in the war, it transformed a small island nation with little natural resources into an economic power and the world's most successful trading nation.

A question of culture. For many years, critics questioned the usefulness of attempting to import Japanese management to American organizations. Some theorists, researchers, and even practicing managers were convinced that Japanese management worked well in Japan because it was Japanese. They felt that the

Figure 1-6 Characteristics of the Japanese Management System

- The use of group-based problem solving or quality circles to improve organizational performance.

- Management-labor cooperation to avoid the problems associated with conflict and labor action.

- Workers' pay tied directly to the performance of the organization.

- Specific manufacturing strategies—for example, flexible production systems and JIT (just in time) inventory systems.

- Kaizen, a philosophy of continuous improvement of the products and the processes of the organization.

Japanese approach to management couldn't be as effective in America, partially because the long history of bad feelings between management and workers in the United States would not permit the kind of labor-management cooperation that is at the heart of the Japanese system. They pointed to the even longer history of American emphasis on individual rather than group achievement: the pioneer, the cowboy. In sport, it began with individuals like boxer John L. Sullivan, "the Boston Strongboy," the first nationally known sports star. It has since evolved into the notion of the superstar, with the figures of the 1920s mentioned earlier, to include many of the major figures discussed throughout the text, to the superstars and notable personalities of the first decade of the twenty-first century: Tiger Woods, Anna Kournikova, Shaquille O'Neal, Mike Tyson, Mark McGwire, and Sammy Sosa. The pundits argued that in a culture that focuses as much attention on the accomplishments of individuals as Americans do, the kind of teamwork required under the Japanese system would be all but impossible to achieve.

These were certainly legitimate and not entirely incorrect concerns, but Japanese management actually reflects the influence of American management thinkers such as Peter Drucker, W. Edward Deming, and J. M. Juran as much as it does Japanese thinking. Furthermore, many aspects of Japanese management have become commonplace in American organizations. One, in particular, is the concept of employee work teams. U.S. organizations are increasingly implementing work teams, where such teams are used not just for solving problems, as they have been in Japan, but for the design, engineering, production, and marketing of new products. As we see in Chapter 8, much of the best work done in sports agency firms is based on this model of groups working together in the areas of contract negotiation, client marketing, and financial services to best serve all clients.

The Japanese response to the question of how to improve organizational performance—to create an atmosphere of cooperation in the organization, design more effective organizational systems, and constantly seek to improve the people, the process, and the product—has come to be viewed as effective enough that elements of it are now in place in sports organizations and within the mainstream of management systems throughout the world.

However, as the U.S. economy boomed in the 1990s due to advances in information technology, and what Federal Reserve Board chairman Allen Greenspan called "irrational exuberance" in these technology-related stocks, the Japanese economy felt the pressure of this competition and encountered an extended period of recession. This has strained the effectiveness of the worker-management relations in Japan: many companies that once promised employees jobs for life have been forced to lay off and terminate workers. This has served to cast doubt on whether Japan's corporations can maintain a strong sense of worker-management partnership.

Continuous Quality Improvement

Earlier in the chapter, we emphasized increased quality as one of the new standards for sport management. Global competition, as we see in detail in Chapter 10, requires that a sports product or service be of world-class quality if the organization producing it is to succeed. Recall also the comments of Greg Dallas, the former season ticket holder for the Denver Nuggets who found a lack of quality in the

Figure 1-7 Key Elements of Deming's Fourteen-Point Program

- Require a commitment by the entire organization to improve quality.

- Advocate leadership by management to bring about changes toward improving quality.

- Eliminate the need for inspecting every product by building quality into the product from the beginning.

- Break down the barriers between departments. Solve problems through teamwork.

- Constantly seek to permanently improve the systems of production and services.

majority of the games he was asked to pay for. The message was that quality is important, but the other factors described, speed and flexibility, innovation, and sustainable growth, made quality only part of the equation toward ensuring success.

Deming's program for quality improvement. To achieve an organization that is consistently producing high-quality goods and services, Deming recommended a fourteen-point program (Deming, 1982). Figure 1-7 lists some of the key elements of his program. Not surprisingly, Deming's response to the question of how to improve the organization's performance is similar to the Japanese management response: focus on quality, continually seek to reduce the variability that is the cause of a lack of quality, and engage the entire organization in seeking to build quality into the process.

Learning Organization

An extension of the continuous improvement approach to management is the concept of the learning organization (Senge, 1990). This approach integrates the principles and practices of continuous improvement with an emphasis on continuous employee learning and development. That is, a learning organization works to facilitate the lifelong learning and personal development of all of its employees while it transforms itself to respond to changing demands and needs. Facilitating lifelong learning involves constantly upgrading employee talent, skill, and knowledge.

Boston's Fleet Center, which opened in 1995, replaced the storied Boston Garden. The new venue has been criticized by many for lacking the charm and intimacy of its hallowed predecessor. In an effort to recapture fan loyalty, the Fleet Center has sought to become a learning organization from studying the Pike Place Fish market in Seattle, a business renowned for a fun, bustling, entertaining atmosphere. The lessons learned from Pike Place help the Fleet Center focus on sales, speed, and customer service (see more detail in Chapter 11).

> **Figure 1-8** Recent Contributions to Management Thinking
>
> - **Decision sciences:** Use mathematical and statistical models to decide on the best patterns and uses of an organization's resources.
>
> - **Contingency theory:** Adjust the management approach to match the requirements of the situation.
>
> - **Systems theory:** Recognize the importance of factors and events occurring outside the organization and in the surrounding environment.
>
> - **Japanese management:** Emphasize cooperation and continuously seek to improve the people, process, and the product or service.
>
> - **Continuous quality improvement:** Focus on quality. Engage the entire organization in identifying and eliminating the sources of problems with quality.
>
> - **Learning organization:** Facilitate the lifelong learning and personal development of all employees while continuously transforming the organization to respond to changing demands and needs.

In answer to the question of how to improve performance, advocates of the learning organization approach emphasize solving problems and changing to meet demands and needs by focusing on learning. This involves learning from organizational experience and history, learning from others (benchmarking and customer input and feedback), and ensuring that the newly acquired ideas and skills are transformed into superior organizational performance.

These recent contributions to our understanding of management (shown in Figure 1-8) will certainly be followed by others. In the field of management it is clear that managers will continue to innovate and experiment with new approaches to make organizations more productive. The search will continue for more effective answers to the question of how to improve performance.

Organizations are groups of people working together to accomplish what they could not achieve separately, and management is responsible for the performance of an organization and for the organization's achieving its goals.

Sports organizations do not exist as separate units; they are interconnected. They are an integral part of a network of stakeholders, and whenever a sports organization fails to meet its performance goals, this entire network is threatened. For these reasons, management in sports organizations has never been more important. Management of sports organizations has become more challenging in the twenty-first century. The changing environment, the world that surrounds organizations, is marked by a new variety and intensity of domestic and international competition and the changing performance standards of quality, speed and flexibility, innovation, and sustainable growth.

Management is not a recent practice, and humans have been engaged in activities requiring management for millennia. Certainly many of the achievements of ancient civilizations and the developing sports industries required the type of coordination we would deem management. At the time of the Industrial Revolution, a formal train of management thinking began to emerge. From the late 1700s to the early 1900s, Adam Smith, J. B. Say, Robert Owen, and Albert Spalding all made contributions to our understanding of how to improve performance.

It was not until the twentieth century, however, that organizations were systematically studied to understand how performance might be improved. The scientific management approach of Frederick Taylor, as practiced by Branch Rickey, first recognized management as a separate and professional set of tasks within an organization. The elements of management defined by Henri Fayol provided a description and agenda for Taylor's professional manager. Elton Mayo and his research team at the Hawthorne Works, as implemented by Teddy Atlas, concluded that in improving performance, the interpersonal relations within the organization are a factor that must be recognized. From these contributions, the stream of management thinking finally gained impetus and momentum, and although these were not the only contributions of the period, they were certainly among the most important.

Since 1950 there has been a steady flow of significant contributions to our understanding of management. Decision sciences, a tool developed during World War II, converts factors of organizational concern into numbers, allowing managers to calculate the results of various options before implementation. Systems theory considers the sports organization as part of a larger system. To improve performance, sports organizations must improve their relations with every element of the system in which it operates—with customers, employees, suppliers, the government, and society at large.

Contingency theory is similar to systems theory in that it provides a way of thinking about management rather than a specific management tool. Contingency theory recognizes that there is no "one best way" to manage. To improve performance, management must understand what the situation requires and then find a way to meet the needs of the situation, whether in the area of planning, organizing, or leading. Management must adjust to what the situation requires.

Japanese management is a combination of specific management practices, some of which focus on the people in the organization, some on production and the product. In either case, in the constant effort to improve performance, the emphasis on Japanese management emphasizes cooperation and continually improving both the people and the operational process.

There has been the expanding influence of the idea that improving performance goes hand in hand with improving quality. According to Deming, real improvement in organizational performance only becomes possible when management fully commits to the very difficult transformation necessary to make quality an organization's number-one priority.

Finally, the concept of a learning organization is one that recognizes that to achieve continuous quality improvement, organizations must constantly upgrade employee talent, skill, and knowledge.

Covering Lids—Which Theories Apply?

Upon successful completion of her undergraduate sport management course work, and having worked for two summers at a nearby Lids store, Lucy Reyes accepted the position of manager at the newest Lids franchise, located at the recently remodeled Galleria at Tyler in Riverside, California. As noted, Lids is one of the country's fastest growing licensed and branded products retail chains, but sales at the store in Riverside have not been strong. The store has yet to have a profitable month.

Lucy spent her first week on the job studying the flow of customers, how her employees—most of them just a few years younger than she—handled their tasks, and the transactions with headwear suppliers. At peak periods the store was so busy that four or five customers could be waiting in line, which could mean waiting up to ten minutes to be served. At other times, when business was slow, her staff would have little or nothing to do. Customers noted the higher prices at Lids as compared to the Champs and Finish Line stores in the mall. One customer noted that prices for some Lids items such as New Era 5950 MLB replica hats were almost as expensive as those for sale at souvenir kiosks at Angels and Dodgers games.

The opening shift of employees, most of them full time, was efficient and had a checklist of duties to be performed daily. Several told Lucy that customers complained about the design and quality of the new line of Lids brand products, but no one seemed to have any positive feedback on how the designs could be improved. The second shift, however, staffed mostly with part-time workers who are full-time students at nearby Arlington, Riverside Poly, and Ramona High Schools, or at the University of California at Riverside, complained continuously about the pay level, the rudeness of customers, and each other's performance.

As Lucy begins her second week, she is ready to make changes to improve the performance at her Lids store. For each statement provided in the chart on the following page indicate the management perspective Lucy appears to be utilizing or considering.

Statement	Decision Sciences	Systems theory	Contingency	Japanese Management	Quality
1. To determine the required number of clerks for a given period, Lucy has recorded customer traffic in and out of the store for each one-hour period throughout the day.					
2. Lucy is developing a brief training program for employees on the second shift. She will personally supervise their performance for the next month. She sees no need to provide training or special supervision for the first shift because problems were minimal during that shift.					
3. Lucy has discovered that New Era has a higher markup than other of the store's suppliers, and she is considering dropping New Era products.					
4. Lucy is assigning the first shift to a work team to come up with feedback on the new Lids brand hat designs.					
5. Lucy feels the best way to eliminate excess expenses is to consider the way customers are served and to revise the processes used through the operation.					
6. Lucy has began an in-depth review of Champs and Finish Line to compare pricing policies, organization, and operations.					

References

Athos, A., & Pascale, R. (1981). *The art of Japanese management: Applications for American executives.* New York: Simon & Schuster.

Buckley, J. T. (1999, February 16). Fishing's $40 billion allure. *USA Today,* pp. 1C–2C.

Byrne, J. A. (1992, October 23). Paradigms for postmodern managers. *Business Week/Renewing America,* p. 63.

Company information. (2001, August 10). Hat World. [Online]. Available: http://www.hatworld.com/comp.html.

Deming, W. E. (1982). *Quality, productivity, and competitive position.* Cambridge, MA: MIT Center for Advanced Engineering.

Denizet-Lewis, B. (2001, April). Race against the machine. *Boston Magazine,* pp. 126–130, 168–169.

Fayol, H. (1949). *General and industrial administration.* New York: Pittman.

Files, J. (2001, May 11). 'Sweatshops' in El Salvador linked to league apparel. *New York Times,* p. C18.

Garfield, C. (1992). *Second to none.* Homewood, IL: Business One Irwin.

Gorn, E. J., & Goldstein, W. (1993). *A brief history of American sports.* New York: Hill and Wang.

Hagstrom, R. G. (1998). *The NASCAR way: The business that drives the sport.* New York: Wiley.

Helyar, J. (1994). *Lords of the realm: The real history of baseball.* New York: Ballantine.

Kahn, R. (1999). *A flame of pure fire: Jack Dempsey and the roaring '20s.* New York: Harcourt.

Levine, P. (1985). *A. G. Spalding and the rise of baseball: The promise of American sport.* New York: Oxford University Press.

Mallach, E. G. (1994). *Understanding decision support systems and expert systems.* Burr Ridge, IL: Irwin.

Mandell, R. (1984). *Sport: A cultural history.* New York: Columbia University Press.

Mayo, E. (1953). *The human problem of an industrialized civilization.* New York: Macmillan.

Meek, A. (1997, December). An estimate of the size and supporting economic activity of the sport industry in the United States. *Sport Marketing Quarterly,* pp. 15–22.

Metcalf, H. C., & Urwick, L. (eds.) (1941). *The collected papers of Mary Parker Follett.* New York: Pittman.

Mintzberg, H. A. (1980). *The nature of managerial work.* Englewood Cliffs, NJ: Prentice-Hall.

Neuborn, E. (1997, March 27). Nike to take a hit in labor report. *USA Today,* p. 1A.

Ouchi, W. (1981). *Theory Z: How American business can meet the Japanese challenge.* Reading, MA: Addison-Wesley.

Owen, R. (1825). *A new view of society.* New York: E. Bliss & F. White.

PepsiCo gets Quaker Oats nod. (2001, August 2). *Boston Globe,* p. C2.

Powers, J. (2001, August 2). Water the key to safety. *Boston Globe,* p. E3.

Putnam, R. D. (2001). *Bowling alone: The collapse and revival of American community.* New York: Touchstone.

Remnick, D. (2000, August 21 & 28). Cornerman. *The New Yorker,* pp. 144–153.

Rice, B. (1982, February). The Hawthorne defect: Persistence of a flawed theory. *Psychology Today,* pp. 70–74.

Ruibal, S. (2001, August 17). X Games roll from the edge to the burbs. *USA Today*, pp. 1A, 6A.

Say, J. B. (1964). *A treatise on political economy*. New York: Sentry Press. (Original work published 1803.)

Senge, P. M. (1990). *The fifth discipline: The art and practice of the learning organization*. New York: Doubleday.

Simon, H. A. (1965). *The shape of automation for men and management*. New York: Harper & Row.

Smith, A. (1937). *The wealth of nations*. New York: Modern Library. Original work published 1776.)

Swift, E. M. (2000, May 15). Sit on it! *Sports Illustrated*, pp. 72–85.

Taylor, F. W. (1947). *The principles of scientific management*. New York: Harper & Brothers.

Turban, E. (1990). *Decision support and expert systems: Management support systems* (2d ed.). New York: Macmillan.

Tygiel, J. (1993). *Baseball's great experiment: Jackie Robinson and his legacy* (rev. ed.). New York: Oxford University Press.

Vamplew, W. (1989). *Pay up and play the game: Professional sport in Britain, 1875–1914*. Cambridge, UK: Cambridge University Press.

von Bertalanffy, L. (1951, December). General systems theory: A new approach to the unity of science. *Human Biology*, pp. 302–361.

Walters, J. (2001, July 2). The Gatorade guys. *Sports Illustrated*, pp. 96–97.

White, H. (2001, Summer). Pay the price. *Black Voices Quarterly*, pp. 150–152.

Chapter 2

Global Licensing and Social Responsibility

Purpose: To provide apparel, footwear, and associated products for consumers.

Stakeholders: Apparel manufacturers, consumers, retailers, stockholders, organizational employees, sport organizations that enter into licensing agreements, third party licensing coordinating companies, licensed product manufacturers, government and legal trademark protection and enforcement personnel.

Size and scope:

- In 2000 sales of sports equipment, sports apparel, athletic footwear, and recreational transportation items in the United States totaled $65.5 billion, a 1.6 percent increase over 1999 ("A Sales Summary," 2001). The international wholesale value of world's market for these products was $91.8 billion (Riddle, 2001).
- Of that $65.5 billion, over half of that total ($36.3 billion) was spent on sports apparel ("A Sales Summary," 2001).
- Worldwide sales of sport-related licensed products generated $721 million in royalties on sales of $12.25 billion in 2000 (Williams, 2001). Domestic sales reached $2.2 billion (*The SGMA Report*, 2001).
- In 2000 athletic footwear sales rose 3.6 percent to $15.07 billion. Three athletic footwear categories exceeded the billion-dollar mark— running/jogging ($2.61 billion; basketball ($1.49 billion); and cross training ($1.34 billion) ("A Sales Summary," 2001).
- The $15.07 billion spent was reached by the sale of 405.4 million pairs of shoes, at an average price of $37.17. The teenage market spends the most on athletic footwear, comprising 22.7 percent of the total market ("In Depth," 2001).

Governance:

- Most individual sport leagues, tours, and players associations organize and operate their own licensing programs, as do some intercollegiate athletic departments. Other sport organizations employ third party companies to run their licensing programs for them.
- Logos (also trademarks, word marks, and service marks) are the intellectual property of sport organizations. A *trademark* is defined under the Federal Trademark Act of 1946, commonly referred to as the Lanham Act, as "any word, name, symbol, or device or combination thereof adopted and used by a manufacturer or merchant to identify his goods and distinguish them from those manufactured or sold by others" (Berry & Wong, 1993, p. 620).
- The law defines trademark infringement as the reproduction, counterfeiting, copying, or imitation in commerce of a registered mark, and it bars companies that do not pay for the right of use from manufacturing products bearing those marks. Only the owner of a mark may apply for federal registration. Sport organizations "transferred the right of use" of their names, marks, and logos to other companies so that these companies may use them in producing products for sale.
- To be claimed as property, these names and logos must be registered with the U.S. Patent and Trademark Office. Once this process is completed, these names and logos become trademarks of the organization. Sport organizations should conduct a trademark search to determine if a conflicting mark exists. A conflict may arise if an existing mark is substantially similar.

Inside Look

Glory, Glory, Man United!

Most Americans would probably choose the New York Yankees, the Dallas Cowboys, or Chicago Bulls as the world's best known team. Most non-Americans would say it is Manchester United (also known as Man U), the British soccer team founded in 1878 as the Newton Heath Lancashire and Yorkshire Railway Company Cricket and Football Club for the purpose of providing recreational opportunities for working men in the city of Manchester in Lancashire in northwest England (Bose, 2000). In the summer of 2001 thousands of people turned up in the early morning at the airport in Bangkok, Thailand, to welcome the team, and later that week, 65,000 screaming devotees jammed the city's national stadium (as another 15,000 disappointed souls unable to get in watched on a giant video screen outside) to witness the exploits of these non-native luminaries defeat the Thai national team 6–0 in an exhibition game. The scene was played out across Asia that summer, including in Singapore (where an exhibition drew 44,000) and Malaysia (with a match crowd of 100,000). In recent years the club has toured Korea, Japan, Australia, and South America, and it scheduled a U.S. tour in 2003 (Kaplan, 2001b).

So how can Manchester United, a soccer team from a fading industrial city in England, be the world's most popular team, and not the Yankees, the most successful American professional sports franchise, located in the world's best known city? First of all, soccer is the world's most popular sport, and as pointed out by Man U CEO Peter Kenyon, "Most American sports are only played on the shores of the U.S. The U.S. has got some very strong franchises, but in order for a franchise to be international, the sport has to be international" (Kaplan, 2001b, p. 31). In sports organizations seeking to expand their markets across national boundaries, or for those sports organizations that focus on international sports and international competitions, the fact that sport is a product native to all markets and cultures is a definite advantage. However, although certain sports enjoy international popularity, such as basketball and soccer (the game people outside the United States know as "football"), each culture also favors and identifies with different sports. In England and India, it might be cricket. In Indonesia, badminton. In Japan, sumo. The U.S. market is saturated with sport, but Americans tend to think of baseball as the "national pastime," and what we call football draws huge levels of spectator interest. But although baseball has strong followings in Japan, Korea, and the Caribbean, our brand of football draws little notice outside the United States.

Certainly Man U has become a global brand in part because of its degree of current on-field success in the world's most popular sport, winning the "treble" (the English Premier League championship, the English FA Cup, and the UEFA Cup [the European Club championship]) in 1999, something no English team had ever done. And United has a tradition of international success (they were the first English club to play in European competitions) and resiliency, such as when eight star members of the exceptionally gifted 1952 team were killed in a plane crash in Munich, only to have manager Sir Matt Busby rebuild the team to prominence in a few short years. After the resurrection, many staunch supporters of other football clubs adopted the Red Devils as their second-favorite side, which has eroded somewhat given the recent success of the club. Like the Yankees and Cowboys in the United States, Man U is now a team many fans love to hate (Bose, 2000).

Man U has leveraged its popularity to generate significant revenues. Sponsorships account for 6 percent of all club revenues and include a $439 million deal with Nike that runs through 2015 and a $45.1 million deal with telecommunications company Vodafone that expires in 2004. Television counts for 26 percent of revenues ($45 million in 2000), including income from the team's own network, MUTV, a cable subscription channel devoted to the club. Gate receipts totaled $55 million in 2000 (32 percent of all revenues), even though a season ticket for games at Old Trafford (capacity 67,500) costs the equivalent of $630. By comparison, the top season ticket at Yankee Stadium costs $5,022, nearly nine times that of Man U's, whose ticket prices are in the middle range of Premier League clubs. In 2001 the club turned a profit of $24 million on revenues of $182 million. The estimated value of the club is now $1.5 billion. By comparison, the Yankees, Cowboys, and Bulls, the gold-standard troika of American team sports in the 1990s, were worth only $1 billion *combined* (Bose, 2000; Dell'Apa, 2001; Kaplan, 2001a, 2001c).

Man U has reached this level of success in part because it has developed an organizational understanding that Man U is a brand, and much of that brand identity has come from attention to licensed product sales. In the early 1990s Edward Freedman came to Man U from rival Tottenham, where he had been head of merchandising. His background with soccer and retailing led him to determine that the club needed to get distribution throughout the United Kingdom for Man U products, and much of the quality of its existing products were substandard. Said Freedman of Man U's management at the time, "They did not understand what a brand was, they had never realized they *had* a brand, that Manchester United *was* a brand" [author's emphasis] (Bose, 2000, p. 188). Freedman's licensing and retailing experiences focused on improving customer satisfaction, improving the club's own retail shops (to include new huge stores in Dublin, Kuala Lumpur, Cape Town, and Singapore), creating merchandising relationships with other UK retailers, and broadening the product line to include a magazine and videos, air fresheners, and jigsaw puzzles, and agreements with banks to use the Red Devil mascot to promote youth savings accounts. Freedman used licensing and retailing to reach what he called "a large number of untapped Manchester United supporters" (Bose, 2000, p. 192).

Supporters love the Man U product for its unique combination of factors: the club's success, appreciation of athletic skill, local or national pride, style of play and player personalities, and the club's attention to brand marketing and licensing and merchandising. The off-the-field success of Man U demonstrates the potential benefits of international expansion for domestic sports organizations. But attaining success at the international level requires a change in focus for many sports organizations and makes the task of managers more challenging.

Introduction

This chapter deals with three of the issues that have gained priority as organizations move through the twenty-first century: the globalization of sport, social responsibility and ethics, and diversity. Each represents an important challenge to management. The chapter also introduces the licensed and branded products industry segment and illustrates some of the specifics of this industry segment within the context of the managerial challenges just listed.

Globalization of Sport

Like Man U, sports organizations in every segment are increasingly becoming more global in scope and trying to expand sales and market shares internationally. Consider that the U.S. population is about 275 million, much larger than that of the UK. But the population of the United States is dwarfed by that of China (1.254 billion). This means that one in every five humans lives in China. In addition, the growth in the population in the United States is virtually stagnant, whereas China's population is expected to grow by 3 percent over the next twenty years. That's quite an attractive market into which an American sports organization could tap, especially since fewer than one in twenty humans lives in the United States, and little or no increase is expected (Butler & Loth, 1999).

American companies also are attempting to capitalize on overseas sales because American markets are becoming saturated. The competition for the sports enthusiast's dollar is fierce. Americans are sport oriented and have money to spend on sport-related items, but there is intense competition for the sport and entertainment dollar, and the average American will only spend so much per year on sports services, products, and merchandise. Thus one of the best ways for most companies to achieve their increased sales targets is to broaden their product distribution. For example, companies such as Nike and Reebok expect to get better than half of their sales from markets outside of the United States.

Participation in the international marketplace can be viewed from two perspectives: (1) organizations looking to sell their products to this broader marketplace, and (2) sports leagues looking to spread the popularity of the sport overseas. Gladden and Lizandra (1998) identify five ways for sports organizations to expand internationally: broadcasting, licensing and merchandising, playing exhibitions and formal competitions, the marketing of foreign athletes, and grassroots programs. We have seen how Man U has used some of these approaches to bolster its position as the world's most popular professional sports team. In this chapter, we examine the globalization process of sports organizations through the lens of one specific step of this progression: the licensed and branded product industry.

The Licensing Process: An Overview

Licensing is "a contractual method of developing and exploiting intellectual property by transferring rights of use to third parties without the transfer of ownership" (Sherman, 1991). The "third parties" in this instance are the licensees, the companies that manufacture these products, which hold licenses to manufacture and sell products bearing the logos and marks of professional and amateur sports entities. The licensors pay a percentage royalty to the licensee on wholesale product prices as well as an up-front fee to secure the license. As shown in Figure 2-1, licensing in sport takes a variety of forms.

As we noted earlier, companies can achieve overseas sales in many ways. Licensing is not the only option. Each form of global participation has advantages and disadvantages. Effectiveness in managing the global challenge begins with understanding what these options are. New Balance (NB), the athletic footwear and apparel company introduced in Chapter 1, is pursuing a combination of these options.

As noted in Chapter 1, New Balance has grown substantially over the past few years, not by relying on flash and trends but by focusing on product attributes and, according to Katherine Petrecca, marketing manager for four NB product lines (basketball, cross training, kids' shoes, tennis), selling the product to what she calls "high-frequency users." For example, NB seeks to sell cross-training footwear to fitness and aerobics instructors, because it is this group that will be most interested in buying products with specific product performance benefits (K. Petrecca, personal communication, August 14, 2001). New Balance has also created a niche by providing footwear with extensive width sizing, and has done this, the company states, through a commitment to domestic manufacturing (the company employs over 1,600 workers at manufacturing facilities in Massachusetts and Maine) and leadership in technological innovation. In 2000 the company sold over 26 million pairs of shoes, including over 6 million pairs of cross trainers (netting nearly $200 million), over 6 million pairs of trail running shoes (netting nearly $250 million), and over 5 million pairs of running shoes (netting nearly $200 million) (*New Balance,* 2001).

Although the majority of New Balance's sales are in the United States (over 23 million pairs in 2001), the company has strong sales in Japan (3.9 million pairs), Canada (over 1 million pairs), and Australia (over 621,000 pairs), and 1 pair of NBs is sold for every 17 people in Israel (compared to 1 for every 11 Americans, the lowest ratio) (*New Balance,* 2001). These figures indicate a strong opportunity for international growth for the company. Petrecca commented that the company's sales have begun to level off in categories like running shoes, which should lead the company to look to expand sales in other product areas, such as apparel, basketball shoes, and international sales. "We still have a long way to grow," she says, "without sacrificing who we are as a company. We have all these (product) categories where we're underrepresented [in terms of sales]." The next section of the chapter focuses on the techniques used by New Balance in generating international sales.

Global Sourcing

One of the most basic forms of global involvement occurs when a business turns to a foreign company to manufacture one or more of its products. This practice is called *global sourcing,* because the company turns to whatever manufacturer or source around the world will most efficiently produce its products. Companies that engage in global sourcing take advantage of manufacturing expertise or lower wage rates in foreign countries, and then they sell their products either just in their home market or in markets around the world.

Figure 2-1   Forms of Licensing Organizations

The Approach of Professional Sports Leagues

In professional sports leagues, a for-profit branch of the organization generally referred to as a "properties division" administers licensing programs. Properties divisions approve licensees and distribute licensing revenues equally among league franchises. Properties divisions usually handle marketing and sponsorship efforts as well. League properties divisions also create mechanisms to police the marketplace for unauthorized use of marks and logos.

Other Sports Organization Licensing Programs

Many sports organizations, including the U.S. Olympic Committee (USOC) and the U.S. Tennis Association, also act as licensors to generate income and awareness. Section 110 of the Amateur Sports Act of 1978 grants the USOC the right to prohibit the unauthorized use of the word *olympic* for trade purposes (Bernstein, 1997). The USOC Licensing Program returns 82.7 percent of proceeds from sales of Olympic merchandise back to athletes through funding of training programs and athlete grants and services.

Licensing Agencies

Some colleges and universities, smaller professional leagues, tournaments, and events hire independent companies to run their licensing operations. These firms serve as "middlemen" for smaller leagues or individuals in lower-profile nonunion-ized sports that lack the resources to maintain effective licensing operations, and work for a percentage (as high as 35 percent) of gross revenues from retail sales. These organizations operate much like league properties divisions and implement much of the same protocols.

Players' Unions

Players' unions also administer licensing programs to increase revenues for their players and the union itself. These revenues can be a significant source of income for the union and its members. The same principles identified above that boost licensing as a significant revenue source for sports organizations—making the sports product more tangible, allowing the user to exhibit his or her support and involvement with the sports organization and with other fans—are also applicable to union licensing programs. However, players' union licensing efforts seek to create brand awareness less with the established recognition and interest of team colors and logos, but rather through fan identification with specific individual or groups of athletes.

Licensing in Individual Professional Sports

While players' unions handle the bulk of licensing agreements in professional team sports, athletes in individual professional sports, through their agents and advisors, usually handle licensing agreements on their own. While this makes licensing money more difficult to attain for lesser-known individuals, as with commercial endorsements, the potential exists for highly recognizable individuals to earn significant licensing revenue over which they have more control than do most athletes

Figure 2-1 Forms of Licensing Organizations *(continued)*

in professional team sports. Nowhere is this more true than for well-known drivers in NASCAR, where the top drivers earn more in licensing than from their racing salaries or winnings. Before Dale Earnhardt's death in 2001 (see Chapter 11), sales of Earnhardt's licensed products (including the most popular products, apparel, die-cast cars, and trading cards) reportedly accounted for 40 percent of NASCAR licensing sales, totaling $50 million (Hagstrom, 1998). However, following his death, the sale of Earnhardt licensed products, including a new line of memorial products, continued to boom, reaching $60 million in 2001. In addition, over 14,000 other Earn-hardt collectibles were for sale on the online auction site eBay (nearly 10,000 more than Michael Jordan items), including a $7,000 limited edition 59" tall Snap-On tool box and a $120,000 1996 Chevrolet Camaro Z-28 SS (one of three made) (Weir, 2001).

Licensing means money for extreme sports athletes as well. Skateboarding icon Tony Hawk earns $1.5 million annually for licensing agreements with companies that produce video games, action figures, equipment, and apparel, while BMX biker Dave Mirra earns $1 million (Williams, 2001).

This approach is common in the clothing and footwear industries, for example, where companies in countries such as Mexico, China, and Malaysia have much lower production costs because workers are paid at much lower wage rates than American workers. The foreign producer or source manufactures the product to a particular company's specifications and then attaches the company's label or logo to the product.

Nike, Reebok, Benetton, and Banana Republic are examples of companies that do a great deal of global sourcing. The Gap is the only major U.S. apparel retailer that manufactures all of the products it sells (Riddle, 2001). However, as we noted in Chapter 1, these practices have gotten manufacturers such as Nike into trouble due to the poor working conditions and low wages paid to workers in Vietnam, China, and Indonesia. New Balance uses global sourcing, but unlike Nike and other competitors who do no shoe and apparel manufacturing in the United States, New Balance assembles 20 percent of its footwear in U.S. factories (by comparison, 60 percent of the world's footwear is manufactured in China [Riddle, 2001]). At one plant in Lawrence, Massachusetts, 220 workers operate high-tech machines and make $14 an hour, versus the $65 a month Nike pays workers in Indonesia. New Balance employs only about 2,400 workers worldwide; Nike employs some 500,000 factory workers globally ("Boston by the Numbers," 2001).

According to Petrecca, New Balance would like to manufacture more products domestically because "Some customers see this as a positive product attribute and like to support those companies that manufacture products domestically, but the cost of doing so would make our products too expensive." However, a survey conducted by the Sporting Goods Manufacturers Association (SGMA), an industry trade group representing the interests of 1,600 organizations involved in this industry segment, lists "price" as the most important factor for sports apparel buyers, followed "fit and comfort" and "quality." "Made in USA" ranked fifth (*The SGMA*, 2001).

www.SGMA.com

Companies must rely on global sourcing for increasing both international and domestic sales, because companies like Nike, which make all their shoes in Asia, then look to sell the shoes made there to local consumers as the local economies continue to boom and incomes continue to rise. This gives Nike and others a potentially significant advantage in reaching these future consumers. In support of these efforts, Nike has embarked on endorsement deals with emerging Chinese athletes, including female tennis phenoms Peng Shuai and Li Na, and men's hoop star Wang Zhi-Zhi. The Chinese hope the support from Nike will help bolster the country's performance in the upcoming 2008 Beijing Summer Games (see Chapter 10) (Kaplan, 2001d).

Exporting

Another common form of participation in global markets is *exporting:* the practice of selling goods or services produced in one country directly to customers in foreign markets. Most major corporations use exporting as part of their overall mix of global strategies, but for small businesses, exporting frequently is the only global strategy, because it represents the most direct form of involvement in global markets. Exporting allows a small business to participate in global markets by finding a means or channel through which it can distribute its product in the foreign market.

The advantage of exporting over other kinds of global involvement is greater control over the quality of the product as well as receiving the full share of profits. The complicated aspect of exporting is that it often requires the assistance of local agents or local representatives with expertise in how best to gain entry and acceptance in their country's markets. As we discussed above, New Balance currently exports much of its manufactured products around the world, with 27.8 percent of all sales outside the United States (*New Balance*, 2001).

Local Assembly and Packaging

Sometimes trade restrictions in a foreign country prohibit the direct import of some large products, such as automobiles or large pieces of machinery or equipment. To enter markets with these kinds of restrictions, a company ships major components of the finished product to a company-owned facility in the foreign country for final assembly. This is the approach taken by Honda, Toyota, and other foreign car manufacturers doing business in the United States. Major components, such as the engine and transmission, are manufactured in Japan or Europe and shipped to the American facility for assembly of the finished automobile. Although this approach can be more expensive than exporting a final product to a foreign market, trade restrictions in that market may leave no other alternative for gaining access to that market. New Balance uses this approach through global sourcing for much of its international sales, but does utilize local domestic assembly at plants for 20 percent of its products sold in the United States. As we note later, the company sees this as a positive approach to corporate responsibility, which in turn influences certain buyers to purchase New Balance products because the company supports domestic jobs and does not exploit foreign workers to the degree that other companies do.

Joint Venture/Strategic Alliance

One of the more complex levels of participation in global markets involves a company from one country pooling its resources with those of one or more foreign companies. Sometimes the joint venture is necessary as a result of laws in foreign countries prohibiting a company from another country from owning more than 49 percent of a business in the host country. Other times, these agreements provide faster entry into a marketplace.

In other cases, called *strategic alliances,* the purpose of the partnership is to take advantage of particular expertise or other resources in the foreign companies. Both joint ventures and strategic alliances represent highly complex approaches to participating in the global marketplace. Achieving effective overall management of a shared-ownership venture with companies from different countries is challenging, but works well when both parties have a strong need for the venture or strategic alliance. New Balance currently has joint venture agreements in Japan and Taiwan.

Direct Foreign Investment

The most fully developed form of participation in the global marketplace is when a corporation produces and markets goods or services in a foreign country through a wholly owned company or subsidiary in that country. A wholly owned local company is an existing company that has been purchased by the corporation to allow it to take advantage of the market position, management, workforce, or other resources already in place in that company.

Forming a wholly owned subsidiary in a foreign market (versus buying an existing company) has the advantage of allowing the corporation to do business entirely its own way. The disadvantage of this approach is that it requires the corporation to develop its own market position and its own workforce, its own facilities and suppliers, all in a foreign market. New Balance has subsidiaries in countries around the world, including France, Germany, Sweden, and the United Kingdom.

As shown in Figure 2-2, the various levels or forms of participation in the global marketplace can be thought of as stages or degrees of involvement, from the simpler levels of exporting and licensing to the more complicated stages of strategic alliances and wholly owned foreign business units. Sports managers must recognize the advantages and disadvantages of each and pursue the option that presents the greatest opportunity for successful involvement in the global marketplace.

Figure 2-2 Stages of Global Involvement	
• Licensing	• Local assembly and packaging
• Global sourcing	• Joint venture/strategic alliance
• Exporting	• Direct foreign investment

Social Responsibility and Ethics

We can view the study of social responsibility and ethics from two perspectives. At the larger level is the obligation of organizations to be good corporate citizens, to provide society not only with goods and services, but also to contribute to the social well-being of the communities where they operate. At the more individual level is the ethical conduct of workers and managers in performing their daily tasks and planning for long-term growth. We review both perspectives.

Socially Responsible Organizations

Through the 1950s, the relationship between business and the American public was always a good one. Consumers were eager to purchase products that had not been available during the Great Depression of the 1930s or during World War II, and businesses expanded rapidly to satisfy that demand. Business was viewed as the source of the jobs and the products that were at the heart of the American dream. A saying popular at the time was "What's good for General Motors is good for America." Large corporations made financial contributions for community projects, and most companies were strong supporters of the United Way and similar social service funds.

Beginning in the 1960s, however, the public began to view business differently. To meet the exploding consumer demand in the years following World War II, organizations increased production at such rapid rates that the results unfortunately included pollution of the air and water, environmental decay from the dumping of industrial waste, and ineffective and sometimes unsafe products and services. Frustration with the Vietnam War added to the public's discontent. Many people blamed big businesses with defense contracts, such as McDonnell Douglas and Du Pont, for profiting from the prolongation of the war. An even stronger sense of resentment was directed toward Dow Chemical Company, maker of napalm, a chemical used by U.S. forces with tragic consequences for the landscape of Vietnam and its people. Additionally, there was the growing sense that business organizations were not offering equal employment opportunity to the minority members of society. "Suddenly consumerism, stockholderism, racial equalitarianism, antimilitarism, environmentalism, and feminism became forces to be reckoned with by corporate management" (Jacoby, 1973).

The result of all of these factors was a significant increase in the public's demand that organizations of all types act in a more socially responsible way. Some areas of social responsibility, including protection of the environment, equal employment opportunity, and safe working conditions, are now regulated by law and monitored by federal agencies. In the areas not covered by laws and regulations, however, the question of how much social responsibility business organizations should take on has generated a wide range of responses.

Two Views of Social Responsibility

The most common approaches to social responsibility reflect either of two very different philosophies. As summarized in Figure 2-3, these two views vary in their

Figure 2-3 Two Views of Social Responsibility of Organizations

Arguments for Classical Economic Approach

- Management's responsibility is to earn profits for owners (stockholders).

- Potential conflict of interest occurs when managers must meet profit goals and simultaneously enhance social welfare.

- Businesses lack expertise to manage social problems.

Arguments for Activist Approach

- Business is a member of society and has responsibilities stakeholders, such as employees, customers, suppliers, distributors, creditors, government, unions, special interest groups, and the general public.

- Business has technical, financial, and managerial resources to help solve social problems.

- Government intervention is less likely when business takes the initiative in addressing social problems.

conception of the level and type of involvement management should undertake in terms of activities to benefit society.

The Classical Economic Approach

The classical economic approach to social responsibility suggests that a business organization should limit its involvement to activities that improve its own economic performance. This approach maintains that the first and foremost responsibility of management is to earn profits for owners (stockholders). According to esteemed economist Milton Friedman (1970), a strong proponent of this view, there is a potential conflict of interest when society holds managers responsible to owners for meeting profit goals and at the same time holds them responsible to society to enhance social welfare. From this perspective, every dollar spent on social problems or donated to a charity is one less dollar distributed to the owners in the form of dividends and one less dollar available for the kind of investment that creates jobs.

The classical economic approach further argues that requiring management to pursue socially responsible activities could be unethical, because the managers are spending money that belongs to other people: "Insofar as the actions of [an employee of the owners of the business] . . . reduce returns to stockholders, he is spending their money. Insofar as his actions raise the price to customers, he is spending the customers' money" (Friedman, 1971).

A final argument against managerial involvement in social responsibility programs is that businesses lack the expertise to determine which programs have the greatest needs. For example, should an organization donate to the local YMCA to support athletic and recreational activities, or should it, like the founding of Manchester United and many contemporary organizations in the United States, found its own organization to provide such opportunities? Which would serve the needs of the community better?

In summary, the classical economic approach to social responsibility insists that business organizations have the social responsibility only to do no harm to customers, employees, or the environment. In this view, managers do not have the right to invest stockholders' profits in activities focusing on social problems. Management's only responsibility is to follow the legal and ethical rules of society while making the business organization as profitable as possible.

The Activist Approach

The activist model of social responsibility argues that business does in fact have a responsibility to deal with social problems, because business is both part of the cause of the problems and part of society (Davis, 1975; Sturdivant & Vernon-Wortzel, 1990). And social responsibility activists argue that organizations do have the technical, financial, and managerial resources to help solve society's difficult problems.

Growing evidence indicates that to some extent businesses agree with this view. For example, large and small companies all over the United States have entered partnerships with local schools; they provide training for teachers and administrators in key skill areas and donate surplus computers, furniture, and other equipment that the school might not otherwise be able to afford.

Another part of the activist argument is that business has a responsibility not just to owners and shareholders, but also to everyone who has a stake in the company's operations. These include employees, customers, suppliers, distributors, creditors, government, unions, special interest groups, and the general public. In the activist view, business—as a corporate citizen of a large community—has an obligation to respond to the needs of all these stakeholders while also pursuing a profit. In other words, business has an obligation to be responsible to all of the elements of the communities from which it profits. This argument gains strength considerably the more closely the success of the business is presented as linked to the health of the community that supplies it with workers and customers.

Lastly, the activist argument holds that when business itself takes the initiative in addressing social problems, costly government intervention is less likely. In recent years, for example, both the cable TV industry and video game producers have taken the initiative to create commissions to monitor the level of violence in their products. Their actions came in response to consumer concerns as well as concern on the part of management that the government would impose potentially more costly standards if these industries did not take the initiative and act on their own.

A Difficult Choice

In the classical economic approach, business is viewed exclusively as an economic entity whose nearly exclusive purpose is profit. The activist approach, in

contrast, views business as a member of society, with broader social responsibilities. When an action is required by law or when investment in a socially responsible activity is profitable, there is no conflict between the two views, and both approaches would support the activity.

It is when the socially responsible activity is neither required by law nor profitable that the two approaches differ. The classical approach would argue against business becoming involved; the activist view would support involvement if the costs were not prohibitively high. The degree to which a business advances societal versus economic objectives depends to a great extent on factors such as the organization's size, the nature of competition in the industry, the type of problems involved, and the costs of pursuing an activity versus the consequences of not doing so. Many sports organizations and individual athletes donate to local charitable organizations (and in the case of the September 11, 2001 terrorist attacks, donated millions to the American Red Cross and to funds set up to benefit those families who lost loved ones) or set up their own tax-exempt public charitable organizations. These organizations funnel more than $100 million annually to charitable programs (led in 2001 by the Andre Agassi Charitable Foundation, which raised $5.4 million for programs for neglected and abused children and a Las Vegas Boys & Girls club), but unfortunately many are inefficiently run and spend far too much on administrative costs.

PGA Tour pro Tom Lehman's charity golf event for children's cancer research in Minnesota spent 85 cents for every dollar raised, when the industry standard for such expenses should be 40 cents (Dodd, 2001c). Several such organizations, including the Sammy Sosa Foundation, have run into trouble because associates of the athletes are put in charge of the firms but have no training or experience in managing them. Said one Internal Revenue Service auditor responsible for reviewing the operations of such organizations, "All of these athletes start these things, but they never finish them because they don't understand what it entails. . . . They're hiring brothers, mothers and fathers" (Dodd, 2001a, p. 2A)—a practice followed by Barry Bonds, Drew Bledsoe, and Tiger Woods. Other charitable organizations, such as those initiated by NBA players Dikembe Motumbo and Terrell Brandon, and New York Yankees outfielder Bernie Williams, have virtually no funds or activities (Dodd, 2001b). This example underscores the difficulties for some organizations, even those organized to perform social activism, to execute these duties fully and responsibly. We examine further the difficulties associated in this choice as it relates to the licensed and branded products industry in the managerial exercise at the end of the chapter.

Ethical Conduct of Individuals

Ethical organizations encourage and enable people at all levels to exercise ethical judgment. We expect our organizations to conduct themselves in a way that is honest and fair in terms of how they treat their customers, employees, and society in general. To influence employee judgment and behavior properly, ethical practices must shape the organization's decision-making processes and be a part of the organization's culture. In sports organizations, the complexity of competing interests in sport makes moral and ethical dilemmas difficult to resolve.

For the most part, athletic competition is a test of skill, strategy, and physical prowess. However, the industries and structures that have grown around sport have complicated the roles played by all sports organization personnel, from athletes, coaches, and managers, to league officials, manufacturers, and retail and wholesale sales personnel. For example, the licensed and branded footwear and apparel manufacturers have had a significant impact in the world of high school and intercollegiate athletics. Both Nike and adidas, for example, have jumped headlong into sponsorship and equipment provision agreements with summer all-star basketball camps, and high school and Amateur Athletic Union (AAU) basketball traveling all-star teams in hopes of finding the next Michael Jordan. These companies engage in these activities to establish connections early with high-profile young players so that these prospects will later be more likely to attend colleges and universities with whom these companies have sponsorship agreements. Ultimately, the hope is that if these young athletes continue to perform at high levels, they might eventually be seen wearing Nikes or adidas shoes in the NBA.

As part of the no-holds-barred efforts to snap up potential future stars like Dermarr Johnson, Lamar Odom, and Tracy McGrady, however, these companies have established connections with prep school coaches and other individuals of questionable reputations (Wetzel & Yaeger, 2000).

From a business standpoint, this early action on the part of Nike and adidas is understandable. Locking up the next Jordan could mean millions, maybe billions, in future sales. Unfortunately, this results in the future of these young athletes being placed in the hands of schools and individuals who are more interested in furthering their own interests than those of the athletes. This potential for conflict makes decision making more difficult and more critical for sports managers who seek to run successful organizations and also act in a manner that protects the best interests of young men and women.

One way to simplify the decision-making process and to encourage morality in sport is to make the requirements and standards of behavior of a job or institution clear. Codes of conduct or codes of ethics provide that clarification and outline the guidelines for employee behavior.

Implementing such codes is not always simple and straightforward for organizations in the licensed and branded apparel and footwear industry, for example. Although licensors have quality control over the images on licensed products, they do not control all operations of the licensees. Licensees are independent businesses, and as such conduct their businesses as they see fit. Nike, as the industry leader, has received significant negative publicity for its business practices in assembly facilities in Vietnam. Nike has borne the brunt of public criticisms for such actions and certainly cannot be excused entirely for the business practices of its overseas partners, but the fact remains that nearly every clothing and footwear manufacturer that assembles product outside the United States (and free from U.S. labor laws) is guilty of some degree of improper labor exploitation, ranging from using child labor to paying (by U.S. standards) paltry wages.

Because of these poor standards and practices, it is not uncommon for licensors to be seen as responsible for them as well. Colleges and universities are especially susceptible to this sort of scrutiny, given the heightened sensitivities of educational communities and institutional educational missions, which are further enhanced by the religious affiliations at some schools. When the University of Wisconsin made public its licensing agreement with Reebok, certain personnel at the university questioned Reebok's business practices and labor relations with Southeast Asian manufacturers, claiming that Reebok shoe assemblers in Indonesia received only $2.45 per day. A petition circulated by professors stated, "If the University of Wisconsin advertises a firm like Reebok, it accepts the conditions under which Reebok profits." The university's agreement with Reebok also contained a clause stating that university employees would not disparage Reebok, but after considerable campus outcry, the clause was omitted from the contract (Naughton, 1997, p. A65).

In response to this sort of criticism, many schools have published a code of conduct for all licensees. Notre Dame, affiliated with the Congregatio a Sancta Cruce (CSC) order of the Catholic church and particularly susceptible to such criticisms given its combined status as a religious institution and a perennial football power, has composed a code that states the school is "committed to conducting its business affairs in a socially responsible manner consistent with its religious and educational mission." Consequently, Notre Dame stipulates that all licensees must meet the university's stated standards for legal and environmental compliance, ethical principles, and employment practices ("Code of Conduct," 1997). Codes of conduct such as that of Notre Dame establishes norms that reinforce individual ethical behaviors. When firmly and consistently supported by top management, these ethical guidelines provide an important decision-making tool for employees throughout the organization.

The social responsibility and ethical behavior demands of American society represent complex challenges for all organizations. For sports managers, the challenges can vary depending on the nature of the sports organization, but as organizations that provide highly discretionary products and services, they rely heavily on the goodwill and positive associations held by consumers, and as such must carry out business practices that meet their ethical expectations.

The Diversity Challenge

A third emerging challenge for sports managers is the diversity challenge. The number of ethnic groups in the workplace has increased dramatically in recent decades, with the influx of immigrants from Asia, Europe, and other parts of the world. The workforce is becoming older as members of the huge baby boom generation move through their fifties and into their sixties. In addition, the Americans with Disabilities Act passed in 1990 seeks to remove many of the barriers that formerly prevented individuals with physical disabilities from joining the workforce. The net effect of all of these changes is that the American workforce is now and will continue to become increasingly diverse in terms of gender, race, age, and physical abilities.

The coordination of human resources has never been easy, and this growing diversity in the workplace represents a challenge as well as a special opportunity for management. The greater the differences that people bring with them to the workplace, the greater the management effort needed to blend these differences and to unify efforts in a single direction. Yet, as difficult as this challenge may be, many organizations feel this growing diversity also presents a special opportunity. The more the workforce inside the organization mirrors the diversity of the customers outside, the more likely it is that the organization will satisfy the needs of those diverse customers.

Many sports organizations, especially professional sports leagues like the National Football League (NFL) and National Basketball Association (NBA), and Division I intercollegiate athletics programs, which have a high percentages of nonwhites and women as players, have been criticized for a lack of commitment to organizational diversity by maintaining managerial staffs that do not reflect the team rosters' racial or gender composition. In terms of New Balance's commitment to diversity, Petrecca says the company has pushed hard to become a more diverse organization. In her view, not only does a diverse workforce enable the company to access a range of perspectives and input from a wide variety of employees, which in turn allows the company to produce better footwear and apparel, but also the company has made it clear that it is the right thing to do. Thus, in the case of New Balance, they believe that doing right is also doing good—for society and for the corporate bottom line.

Despite its best intentions, however, New Balance has become diverse in terms of gender, but in a stratified way. For example, the marketing and promotions staff is nearly all female, but the research and development personnel—the science and technical staff—are predominantly male. This delineation by task exemplifies the tendency in many schools for males rather than females to be encouraged to excel in computer, math, and science courses. Such a separation may lead to disconnects in how the company communicates across departments and within departments as well, if only a single male works in marketing and promotions or a solo female in research and development. The continuation of this trend could hinder New Balance from achieving organizational success.

Guidelines for Managing Diversity

Given the lack of diversity in the sports industry (Ashe, 1992; Blum, 1993; Hums, 1996; Lapchick, 1996; Shropshire, 1996), steps must be taken to increase access to the industry. What follows are several guidelines for managing diversity (Rice, 1994).

Get the CEO's Commitment

Addressing diversity issues is difficult to do well and is therefore easy to place on a back burner. When the head of the organization makes diversity a priority, everyone pays closer attention.

Set Specific Diversity Goals

Set specific targets, such as 30 percent representation of females and minorities at all levels of the organization, especially management, by the year 2005. Measure managers' performance in terms of their contribution to these goals, and base compensation on their level of success.

Adopt a Plan for Addressing the Concerns of White Males

White males still constitute roughly half of the overall workforce and hold 60 percent of all management positions. Individuals from this group may feel threatened when preference is given to women and minorities in the workplace, and they may view this practice as "reverse discrimination." Organizations need to acknowledge and directly address their concerns. It needs to be made clear to every member of the organization why it is in everyone's best interest to participate in the development of a diverse workforce.

Provide Training in Valuing Diversity—Carefully

It is important, but difficult, to provide training that allows others to experience what it is like to be a minority in our culture without also seeming to point a finger of blame at nonminority participants. People often feel threatened and uncomfortable when they are required to role-play difficult diversity situations. This is not the most effective emotional state for learning. One promising approach to diversity training is to present movies such as *Thelma and Louise, Malcolm X*, or *Philadelphia* and involve participants in discussions of what they experience and feel, and how this can be applied to improve their own organization's performance in the area of diversity.

Other guidelines for creating an organization where diversity is valued include celebrating differences among workers through special events, videos, and newsletters, as well as developing strategies to identify sources of diverse workers for the organization. Even with the most effective guidelines, however, creating a diverse force of skilled and talented workers and teaching them to work together in an atmosphere of genuine teamwork remains a major challenge.

Although Manchester United has become the world's best known and most valuable team sports property, it and the sport of soccer still face challenges in some of these areas. There is virtually no female or ethnic minority representation in the club's management, and indeed, as is the case throughout English football, women cannot have access to most of the club's business meeting rooms and facilities. In addition, some supporters exhibit virulent strains of racism, an ugly offshoot of the hooliganism that still plagues the sport, in the way they treat opposing nonwhite players. Nick Hornby, a lifelong Arsenal fan and author of *Fever Pitch*—an excellent book on the subject of being a fan—tells of games where visiting white Liverpool fans threw bananas and made monkey noises when Arsenal's John Barnes took the field. And at Arsenal, says Hornby, "you can even now hear idiots who jeer the black players. One night I turned around to confront an Arsenal fan making monkey noises at Manchester United's Paul Ince, and I found that I was abusing a blind man. A blind racist!" (Hornby, 1992, p. 189).

It would seem to be hard for even the most internationally focused sports organizations to eradicate racial and diversity problems. Some, such as the South Africa Rugby Football Union, have set quotas on the numbers of black players on teams. The guidelines also stipulate that at least two black players are required to be on the field at all times in matches (Burris, 2001). While seemingly extreme, these measures were instituted to promote opportunities for South African blacks in light of the country's decades of racial apartheid. However, in the ever-more-global sports industries, those sports organizations that embrace the key issues discussed in this chapter will ultimately be the most successful in meeting the demands that come with global expansion.

Epilogue

When asked what one thing New Balance should do in the next twelve months to improve the company, Katherine Petrecca said,

> We need to build relationships from the marketing and promotions side directly with the retail buyers. That way the money that I'm spending, they feel that I'm spending it on them. So if I'm doing "Girls on the Run" [New Balance's promotion to build grassroots running programs with young women], in 50 cities tied in with 50 New Balance–only stores, that's going to increase the sales of kids shoes. So it's not only targeting the consumer, but it's also closing the loop between promotions, the consumer, and the retailer. So all these efforts are focused toward creating more sales.
>
> For example, the Girls on the Run program in Holland, Michigan, had 500 girls enrolled this year. The program had money to buy shoes, but they could only do it at a discount. So I set it so [local retailer] Gazelle Sports gets a discount off the wholesale price and a certain amount of a certain style of shoe, then they turn around and fit all the girls in the program, and sell them to them at 30 percent off the retail price. So there's a direct correlation between my sponsorship that led to New Balance sales for my retailer. And next year, they're going to have a thousand girls, and they're going to sell a thousand pairs of shoes. (Petrecca, personal communication, August 14, 2001)

Petrecca's point is that for New Balance and its associated retailers, as with all companies and organizations that do business in the licensed and branded footwear and apparel industry, all of their activities ultimately revolve around the sale of product. SGMA president John Riddle agrees, indicating an industry trend toward fewer, larger retailers commanding more of the total annual sales. Riddle (2001) comments that slower economic growth and excess inventory in these stores have made "timing the key" in meeting the demands of these fewer, more powerful retailers, and that manufacturer-retailer partnerships are a crucial component.

The directness of mission can have complications for the issues of social responsibility and ethics, diversity, and their relationship to the globalization efforts of sports organizations. If sports organizations look toward short-term financial success only, it could come at the expense of long-term organizational success in these other areas.

Three issues have gained priority as sports organizations move into the twenty-first century: social responsibility and ethics, diversity, and globalization. Each represents an important challenge to management.

Social responsibility is the concept that organizations, especially business organizations, have a responsibility for more than just economic performance; they have a responsibility to contribute to the social well-being of the communities where they operate. The classical economic view rejects this concept, saying that business organizations exist exclusively to generate profits for owners and stockholders. The activist perspective holds that all organizations have the obligation to involve themselves in solving problems in the communities from which they profit.

On an individual basis, sports managers need to be aware of the importance of ethics in the sport workplace. Incorporating codes of conduct or codes of ethics is one way to make the requirements and standards of behavior of a job or institution clear.

Also demanding attention from management is the lack of diversity in the sports industry. Guidelines for managing diversity include getting the commitment of the chief executive officer (CEO), setting specific diversity goals, adopting a plan for addressing the concerns of white males, and providing training in valuing diversity. The goal is to create a diverse workforce of skilled and talented workers and teach them to work together in an atmosphere of genuine teamwork. Finally, there is competitive pressure for organizations to become involved in global markets.

With intense competition in U.S. markets, sports organizations must learn to succeed in markets around the world. There are a variety of options or degrees of global involvement, but regardless of the approach, success in global markets requires that management learn the culture, customize the product or service, recognize the risks involved in global environments, and be patient and persistent.

Summary

¡Viva Neuva Balance!

Although New Balance's stated mission is to be recognized as the world's leading manufacturer of high-performance footwear and apparel, and even though the company has grown from a $100 million company to a $1 billion company over the last decade, New Balance has approached the concept of growth very cautiously. However, facing an international economic slowdown with sluggish economies in the United States, Japan, and Europe, and increasingly unstable political and security issues following the September 11, 2001, terrorist attacks, New Balance is now facing challenges in expanding its sales in some of the potential growth product lines, like basketball, tennis, and cross training.

New Balance touts the fact that it is the only U.S. footwear manufacturer that assembles shoes domestically at facilities in Lawrence, Massachusetts, and Norway, Norridgewock, and Skowhegan in Maine, and many customers make purchasing decisions with this in mind. However, New Balance still makes 80 percent of its footwear products outside the United States, and as it faces cooling economies and increased sales expectations, the company may have to consider going the route of its major competitors and sending all manufacturing to foreign countries. As we have also learned, such a move could also help bolster New Balance's sales in those countries to which it seeks to move production, like Nike hopes to do in China. This has led CEO Jim Davis and the company's management to look south of the border, down Mexico way, as a potentially beneficial site to shift its U.S. manufacturing operations.

As noted earlier, a number of American businesses have moved to Mexico to take advantage of low labor wage rates. The passage of the North American Free Trade Act (NAFTA) has also provided for ease in transport of goods across the border, allowing for huge cost savings when compared to shipments from Asia or Central America. The weaker environmental laws and lack of strong union organizing in Mexico also hold the potential for cost savings in product manufacturing. In addition, to date New Balance sales in Mexico, Central America, and the Caribbean—which has a combined population approximately equal to that of the United States—have come nowhere near to matching U.S. sales levels. For example, Mexicans bought only 433,000 pairs of New Balance shoes in 2001. That's only 100,000 more than purchased by an Israeli population of six million, but Mexico's population is over 100 million. Moving manufacturing to these countries would serve to bolster potential revenues from these growing economies with populations certain to grow.

Although the potential for sales growth in Mexico, Central America, and the Caribbean is good with such a move, there are associated risks as well, but if New Balance is to meet its goal of selling 11 million pairs of shoes worldwide, it must act to increase sales, because many other U.S. footwear manufacturers are also eyeing Mexico for these same reasons. CEO Jim Davis, president and chief operating officer (COO) Jim Tompkins, vice president (VP) of manufacturing John Wilson, VP of international sales Edward Haddad, VP of human resources Carol O'Donnell, and Katherine Petrecca now have to consider how this proposed move could impact New Balance in the key areas of social responsibility and ethics, diversity, and globalization of sports organizations. Given your expert knowledge of these areas, you have been asked to advise this group as they debate the move. The group is assembled in a conference room on the ninth floor of the company's headquarters, with a view overlooking the Massachusetts Turnpike below. Jim Davis looks to you and says, "What do you have for us?"

1. First, explain to those in the meeting how the concept of social responsibility applies to New Balance's consideration to move operations to Mexico. Using this concept, explain what New Balance owes and to whom.

2. Several of the managers in the meeting are devotees of Milton Friedman and are advocating for the company to move more in the direction of the classical economic view; others are promoting the activist perspective. Explain each of these views to the others in the meeting, and assess which approach is more or less in line with New Balance's current approach and how a change in approaches might impact the company and future sales.

3. John Wilson, VP of manufacturing, says if New Balance moves all domestic assembly to Mexico, it will face much of the scrutiny applied currently to major competitors Nike, Reebok, and adidas in the areas of worker pay, treatment, and working conditions. Wilson then asks you to explain the role of codes of conduct and codes of ethics, and how these can help New Balance avoid the problems encountered by these other companies.

4. Carol O'Donnell, VP of human resources, is concerned about how the company will address diversity issues given this proposed move. She asks you what guidelines the company should implement to manage the new diversity demands associated with this proposed move.

A sales summary of sneakers, shirts, socks, softballs, and more. (2001). Sporting Goods Manufacturers Association [online]. Available: http://www.sgma.com/press/200198879042-4066.html.

Ashe, A. (1992, August). What does the future hold for blacks in sport? *Ebony*, pp. 132–133.

Basic facts about registering a trademark. (1994). Washington, DC: U.S. Government Printing Office.

Bernstein, A. (1997, February 10). Eye on licensing. *Sporting Goods Business*, p. 22.

Berry, R. C., & Wong, G. M. (1993). *Law and business of the sport industries: Common issues in amateur and professional sports, Vol. 2,* (2d ed.). Westport, CT: Praeger.

Blum, D. E. (1993, April 21). Forum examines discrimination against black women in sport. *Chronicle of Higher Education*, pp. A39–A40.

Bose, M. (2000). *Manchester Unlimited.* New York: Texere.

Boston by the numbers. (2001, April). *Boston Magazine*, p. 30.

Burris, J. (2001, October 24). Mixed results. *Boston Globe*, pp. F1, F6.

Butler, D., & Loth, R. (1999, October 3). Now we are 6 billion. *Boston Globe*, p. E1.

Code of conduct for University of Notre Dame licensees. (1997). Notre Dame, IN: University of Notre Dame.

Davis, K. (1975, June). Five propositions for social responsibility. *Business Horizons*, pp. 19–24.

Dell'Apa, F. (2001, February 13). Promotion unites Manchester, Yankees. *Boston Globe*, p. F2.

Dodd, M. (2001a, July 20). Athletes' charities small, but most hit their mark. *USA Today*, pp. 1A–2A.

Dodd, M. (2001b, July 20). Charitable help all over the field. *USA Today*, pp. 1C–2C.

Dodd, M. (2001c, July 20). Do events raise funds or fun? *USA Today*, p. 3C.

Friedman, M. (1970, September 13). The social responsibility of business is to increase profits. *New York Times Magazine*, pp. 13–14.

Gladden, J. M., & Lizandra, M. (1998). International sport. In L. P. Masteralexis, C. A. Barr, & M. A. Hums (eds.), *Principles and practice of sport management* (pp. 208–242). Gaithersburg, MD: Aspen.

Hagstrom, R. H. (1998). *The NASCAR way: The business that drives the sport.* New York: Wiley.

Hornby, N. (1992). *Fever pitch.* London, UK: Indigo.

Hums, M. A. (1996). "Increasing employment opportunities for people with disabilities through sports and adapted physical activity." *Proceedings from the Second European Conference on Adapted Physical Activity and Sports: Health, Well Being and Employment.* Leuven, Belgium: ACCO.

In depth report on U.S. athletic footwear statistics now available. (2001, August 8). Sporting Goods Manufacturers Association [online]. Available: http://www.sgma.com/press990112393-25831.html.

Jacoby, N. H. (1973). *Corporate power and social responsibility.* New York: Macmillan.

Kaplan, D. (2001a, February 12–18). Yanks-Man U team leaves U.S. soccer on bench. *Street & Smith's SportsBusiness Journal*, p. 4.

Kaplan, D. (2001b, August 6–12). Manchester's red tide. *Street & Smith's SportsBusiness Journal*, pp. 1, 30–31.

Kaplan, D. (2001c, August 6–12). Club's financial rise dates to market debut. *Street & Smith's SportsBusiness Journal,* p. 30.

Kaplan, D. (2001d, October 1–7). Medal-hungry China loosens grip on athletes. *Street & Smith's SportsBusiness Journal,* pp. 1, 39.

Lapchick, R. (1996). *Racial report card.* Boston: Northeastern University Center for the Study of Sport in Society.

Naughton, J. (1997, September 6). Exclusive deal with Reebok brings U. of Wisconsin millions of dollars and unexpected criticism. *Chronicle of Higher Education,* p. A65.

New Balance Athletic Shoe Company, Inc. fact sheet. (2001). Brighton, MA: New Balance Athletic Shoe Company, Inc.

O'Toole, T. (2001, October 3). Copyright case over 'Buzz' costly to Georgia Tech. *USA Today,* p. 1C.

Rice, F. (1994, August 8). How to make diversity pay. *Fortune,* pp. 79–86.

Riddle, J. (2001, October). *State of the U.S. sporting goods industry.* Presentation at the International Sport Business and Entertainment Conference, Columbia, SC.

Sherman, A. J. (1991). *Franchising and licensing: Two ways to build your business.* New York: AMACOM.

Shropshire, K. L. (1996). *In black and white: Race and sports in America.* New York: New York University Press.

Sturdivant, F. D., & Vernon-Wortzel, H. (1990). *Business and society: A managerial approach* (4th ed.). Homewood, IL: Irwin.

The SGMA report: Sports apparel monitor (2001). North Palm Beach, FL: Sporting Goods Manufacturers Association.

Williams, P. (2001, August 20–26). Niche licensing grows to multimillion-dollar market. *Street & Smith's Sports Business Journal,* p. 23.

Weir, T. (2001, June 22–24). Earnhardt's image alive and collectible. *USA Today,* pp. 1C–2C.

Wetzel, D., & Yaeger, D. (2000). *Sole influence: Basketball, corporate greed, and the corruption of America's youth.* New York: Warner.

Chapter 3

IT Management and Sports Media

Purpose: To provide sport information to the general public in a variety of formats including game broadcasts, stories, and feature articles.

Stakeholders: Fans, athletes, coaches, administrators, leagues, commissioners' offices, media personnel (writers, reporters, broadcasters), alumni, sport governing bodies, licensees, corporate partners, and local, state, and federal government.

Size and scope:
- The sports media consists of thousands of outlets including magazines, newspaper sports sections, sports talk radio, and sports networks (national and regional).
- The sports broadcast media includes not only the on-the-air talent (play by play, color analyst, on-field reporter, etc.), but also includes the behind-the-scenes staff that encompasses a wide array of broadcast specialists including camera crew, producers, sound technicians, editors, statisticians, and video technicians.

Governance:
- Individual sports media outlets and members operate under policies and guidelines established by its ownership; however, individual leagues and sport organizations establish rules pertaining to the media (e.g., when media members may enter the locker room).
- Members of the sports media often belong to affiliate professional organizations such as the National Collegiate Baseball Writers of America (NCBWA) or the College Sports Information Directors of America (CoSIDA).

Inside Look

Foxifying Sports Coverage

In 1993 Fox Network CEO Rupert Murdoch hired David Hill, president of Britain's Sky Television, to launch Fox Sports, a new division of the fledgling Fox Network. In an effort to make significant gains on staunch traditional broadcast network competitors ABC, NBC, and CBS, Murdoch had a vision that he would make Fox a major network by entering into the bidding for that perennial ratings powerhouse, the National Football League (NFL). Hill successfully executed Murdoch's plan with a multibillion-dollar bid on an NFL package that would change the shape of sports broadcasting for decades to come.

When Murdoch and Hill introduced Fox Sports and its presentation of the National Football Conference (NFC) of the NFL, industry traditionalists suggested the sports network was doomed to fail and the NFL had made a terrible mistake by aligning itself with a network that had built its reputation by flying in the face of broadcast convention. Fox had positioned itself as a youth-oriented, pop culture savvy network that built its young audience through nontraditional programming such as the edgy sitcom *Married with Children* and the animated counterculture series *The Simpsons*. Fox Network positioned itself as trendy, hip, flashy, and irreverent. Its image seemed in direct opposition to the NFL and the NFC, which had enjoyed a long broadcast partnership with CBS, a network that had traditionally attracted an older audience and had historically cultivated an image of being more serious, more conservative, and more family oriented in its broadcast strategy.

Hill believed the NFL on Fox had to be different from existing coverage of the sport in order to win over fans and advertisers. He was convinced that Fox must promote an entertainment package that would draw viewers into the game, create excitement about the product, and deliver NFL broadcasts in a way never seen before by sports fans. For Hill, technology was the key to the NFL's success on Fox (Mullen, 1998). Hill utilized advancements in IT to greatly enhance game production values. He introduced several technology-based broadcast innovations that not only changed how games are produced and distributed, but he also raised fan expectations of sports broadcasting. Hill brought fans inside the game by putting microphones on NFL game officials that would allow the audience to hear the sounds of actual play on the field.

He also introduced interesting and visually appealing and exciting graphics, such as exploding footballs, football players who appeared as robot-type animated characters, flashy statistical graphics, and colorful action clip lead-ins and fades. Hill also introduced the Fox Box, a graphic that has now become a standard for the industry. The Fox Box is an on-screen electronic scoreboard with game clock that allows fans to follow other game scores and receive updates while watching sports action in real time. Hill's "foxifying" of traditional sports coverage was designed to excite and engage fans and to produce sports in a way that was both fun and interesting for viewers. Hill believes the success of Fox Sports rests in its ability to bring a new attitude to sports broadcasts and to utilize new technology in a way that provides a higher quality fan-friendly sports broadcast product (Mullen, 1998).

Hill and Fox's influence have extended to other professional sports as well. It was Hill's idea to visually enhance

http://
www.foxsports.com

hockey pucks with a bright light that would be seen on NHL broadcasts so fans might be able to more easily follow the action. He also encouraged pregame coverage and halftime shows that had an irreverent tone. Sports celebrities, ex-athletes, and broadcasters focused on presenting information to the viewer in a way that was designed to both entertain and educate. Somehow, the Fox approach characterized an attitude that sports are supposed to be games; the viewer is supposed to enjoy the spectacle of the experience; and the traditional stuffiness and seriousness of sports broadcasts needs to be abandoned for high-tech innovation. Technological advances such as "catcher cams" in baseball and ESPN's "First and Ten Yellow Line" are now standard fare for the sports home viewer. This new technology imposes a yellow line on the field that shows home viewers how far the offensive team needs to go in order to achieve a first down. New computer mapping technology produces a yellow graphic that actually appears to be under the feet of the players (King, 2000). Sportvision, Inc., the company that developed this technology, is now exploring its application to automobile racing. The result would allow viewers to see cars illuminated in different colors. The colors would shift as the car's velocity changed so viewers could see a more graphic representation of comparative speed.

The application of new information technologies intended to provide better and more complete information to the viewer, thereby enhancing the sports experience, has not been without its detractors. Fox received a great deal of publicity and created a boost in NHL ratings with the introduction of the illuminated puck, but critics argued that such technologies are little more than gimmicks and electronic wizardry that take away from the sport itself. Although Fox gained much positive publicity for its innovation, it also received criticism from sports purists and letters from disappointed viewers who found the glowing puck to be both distracting and invasive. Technology in Fox broadcasts became the topic of great public debate, and for many fans, the glowing puck became the story, and the game itself seemed to be little more than secondary news.

Sports organization managers and members of the sports media will continue to develop new ways to utilize technology to enhance the sports experience for consumers. But as they proceed, they must consider the important issue raised by critics of these new sports media information technologies. Does media technology necessarily enhance our games or does it somehow detract from the purity of sport? Does this approach to sports broadcasting diminish the integrity of the games? Have sports managers become obsessed with technology to the point that they are providing useless information to viewers only because they want to showcase emerging technologies? Does advanced audio technology such as personal microphones worn by officials, players, and coaches impede game personnel comfort and behavior? Should sports managers fully utilize media technology like instant replay video and on-the-field monitors to assist officials in decision making? At what point does media technology enhance the game and at what point does it become invasive? For sports executives like David Hill, the utilization of emerging media information technology has only just begun, and its development will continue irrevocably to shape how we produce and view sport for generations to come.

Introduction

Advances in information technology (IT) over the past ten years represent perhaps the most dynamic set of opportunities and challenges in all of sport management. In this chapter, we take a look at both. First, we survey the enhancements both in organizational performance and in the range and scope of products and services offered. Then we consider the challenges that must be met by sports managers if the full potential of IT is to be realized.

We also explore sports media, which has significantly embraced IT innovations. The sports media is defined by its ability to produce and distribute sports information in a variety of forms ranging from live game broadcasts, to statistical analysis, to sports reporting, to sports skills instruction, to athlete personality profiles. IT has significantly shaped the growth of sports media in the last decade. The sports media has become an increasingly powerful entity that both shapes our games and also our participation and perceptions of sport.

The Sports Media

The sports media segment is made up of thousands of related organizations. These range from broadcast (television and radio) media outlets such as national broadcast network sports divisions (e.g., CBS Sports, HBO Sports, and ABC Sports) to national sports broadcast networks (e.g., ESPN or The Golf Channel) to regional sports networks (e.g., Madison Square Garden Network). The sports media also includes the print media, which encompasses national sports publications such as *Sports Illustrated*, *ESPN Magazine*, and *The Sporting News* as well as sports divisions at virtually every newspaper, radio, and television station throughout the country. The segment also involves a full spectrum of sports talk radio personalities, sportswriters, authors, reporters, producers, broadcasters, color and play-by-play announcers, commentators, and journalists. It also includes allied technicians such as camera people, editors, and sound specialists. A burgeoning electronic media segment includes sports websites that provide sport information, services, and products.

The sports media has traditionally had a complex relationship with sports organizations. The media's traditional role is to report objectively on game outcomes and the operation of sports organizations. However, in some instances, specifically at the professional level, the media engage in commercial partnerships with sports organizations through the purchasing of broadcasting rights. For the sports organization, the sports media is critically important to the operation of the sports business. Not only does the media serve as an important conduit for information sharing with organizational stakeholders, but it may also serve as a product distribution channel for constituents who consume the sports product through the media. As a result, organizational relationships with the media may be complex. Whereas the sports manager is interested in representing the organization and its personnel in the best possible light, the media is interested in selling newspapers or magazines and generating listener or viewer ratings. Relationships among sports managers, athletes, coaches, players, and members of the media can become contentious as sports media members seek to uncover material for compelling stories while sports organization personnel seek to control the flow of information and present the organization in a positive light. The responsibility for

managing these complex relationships often rests with the sports organization's public relations director, marketing or communications specialist, or sports information director.

The relationship among the media and the sports organization is often complicated because the media outlet, in purchasing broadcast rights, depends on the existence of a good working relationship with the sports organization management. Sports broadcasts have delivered important target markets and viewer audiences to advertisers. Sports media executives are aware that sports have traditionally provided important programming for networks, and bidding wars over broadcast rights have developed as a result of the perceived value of the product to the network. Therefore, although the sports news division is interested in reporting objectively on the operation of the sports organization, sports media executives are cognizant that the sports organization provides a valuable product to the media entity.

In the past several years, the line between the sports media and the sports organization has become increasingly blurred. ESPN, for example, is owned by Disney, which also owns ABC Sports, the NHL's Mighty Ducks, and MLB's Anaheim Angels (Ostrowski, 1998). Media giant Time Warner Inc., which is the parent company of TNT (television network), owns MLB's Atlanta Braves and the NBA's Atlanta Hawks, and major publishing powerhouse Tribune Company owns MLB's Chicago Cubs (Ostrowski, 1998). Such cross-ownership allows for synergistic partnerships between commonly owned companies. Opportunities for the parent company to capture broadcast and advertising revenues are created. Shared control also allows for the development of complex marketing deals that leverage the media and sports properties. Some critics suggest that media and sports organization shared ownership creates inherent conflicts of interest and allows for market exploitation through inflation of advertising rates and single-interest control of game broadcasts, which results in less than objective coverage of the sports organization.

Advancements in media IT, specifically the development of cable television, digital signals, high-definition television (HDTV), wireless technology, and the Internet, have all resulted in an increasingly fragmented sports media segment. There are more sports media products and services than ever before. We need only scan the cable or satellite television lineup, visit the local newsstand, or surf the Internet to become fully aware of the breadth and depth of sports information and sports media coverage available. Not only is there a wealth of sport, recreation, and fitness programming on television and radio, but that coverage extends to the web, where sports fans may follow team websites, participate in fantasy leagues, engage in online discussions with sports celebrities, get real-time sports information as well as listen to online game broadcasts. Wireless technology allows fans to use their cell phones or handheld personal sports information terminals to receive updated scores and game information. There are also thousands of sports publications for every interest and every audience. Examples of the vast array of sports publications include *Sports Illustrated for Kids, Men's Health, Outdoor Life, WWF magazine,* and so on. An example of a sports media organization that has successfully capitalized on advancements in IT is ESPN. The development of cable television can be linked directly to the creation of ESPN in 1979. The network's sports news show, *Sports Center,* the first uniquely positioned sports news–only broadcast, has become an icon of the American sports industry. The

network's success has resulted in spinoff ventures: ESPN2, the ESPN website, and *ESPN* magazine. ABC purchased 85 percent of the network for $202 million in 1994, and ESPN, currently owned by ABC parent company Walt Disney Company, is now worth an estimated $5 billion (Ostrowski, 1998).

IT has dramatically shaped not only how the sports media produces and broadcasts games and how sports information is presented, but how sports media organizations are managed as well. Sports media organizations are certainly not alone in their integration of IT in their operation. In fact, most sports organizations have embraced IT advancements and are learning to develop and adopt technology that will help them provide better products and service to consumers and become more efficient. Sports managers recognize that IT is a useful tool that presents both unique challenges and opportunities for enhancement to the sports organization.

Improved Performance Through IT

Information technology (IT) refers to all of the resources—the processes, practices, and systems—an organization uses to gather, retain, and process the information it uses to pursue its mission. Most of us are familiar with the range of information technologies now in use in everyday life, everything from PCs and the Internet, to cell phones, e-mail, voice mail, and fax machines. All of these technologies, as well as an ever-expanding variety of information systems (software), have for more than a decade been challenging managers to discover how IT can best be used to enhance performance and achievement of the organization's goals. To understand this challenge, let's first become familiar with some of the IT systems that are not part of our everyday lives as individuals.

Information Systems

Several levels of information systems are actually available to organizations (see Figure 3-1). The most basic is called a *transaction-processing system (TPS)*, which

Figure 3-1 Levels of Information Systems

Level I TPS—Transaction-processing system
Designed to perform most basic and recurring transactions

Level II MIS—Management information system
Provides managers with information about organizational operations and performance

Level III DSS—Decision support system
Supports managerial decision making, identify needs, monitor effects of environmental change

consists of a computer system designed to perform the most basic and recurring transactions of an organization. In a sports organization, a TPS would be used to handle ticket purchases, for example, as well as payments to vendors, facility scheduling, tee time reservations, and payroll checks to employees. In general, a TPS is most useful for transactions that occur regularly and frequently, and in their basic format involve little or no change from transaction to transaction.

The next level of information system is called a *management information system (MIS)*. An MIS is used to provide managers with information about the operation and performance of the organization. A sports media organization's MIS might be used to monitor the amount of repair or downtime required for the various kinds of production equipment (cameras, video machines, etc.) it uses, for example, or the percentage of advertising time sold for various upcoming programs or events. This type of information allows managers to stay current on how various elements of the organization are performing, and to recognize when problems occur.

A more sophisticated form of MIS is called a *decision support system (DSS)*. A DSS allows managers not only to monitor current performance in such areas as costs, or sales, or revenues, but also to analyze trends over time in any of these areas, or the effects of changes in any of these areas on other areas of performance. DSS also enables managers to monitor and factor in variables from the environment such as competitors' pricing or advertising expenditures, inflation, conditions in the national or regional economy, or any other external factor that might affect the organization's performance. Finally, using DSS, managers can evaluate the impact of various options or alternatives before actually implementing them. For example, a sports network can evaluate the impact of various levels of increases in the rate it charges advertisers on its broadcasts, taking into account such factors as inflation, the prices its competitors charge, industry trends in advertising rates, the condition of the national economy, and so on.

In short, as a result of IT advances in TPS, MIS, and DSS, organizations now have the ability to dramatically streamline their day-to-day operations, to monitor virtually every performance area of the organization, and to enhance significantly the quality of analysis, problem solving, and decision making as the organization pursues its mission.

Organizationwide Feedback on Performance

One important change resulting from the use of IT in organizations is the availability of continuous feedback on performance, not just to managers, but also to individuals and teams at every level of the organization. It is no longer enough for the manager alone to know how things are going; for organizations to continuously improve, everyone must have access to information on performance. Through IT, this kind of organizationwide feedback on performance becomes possible.

Two examples of the integrated application of computer technologies utilized by sports organizations are the Computerized Maintenance Management System (CMMS) and the Enterprise Asset Management (EAM) System (Hernandez, 2001). These systems, used by sports organizations ranging from professional sports facilities to college athletic departments to municipal park and recreation departments, consist of a series of relational database modules that communicate with one another. These modules may include equipment record management, work order management, preventive maintenance schedules, and inventory control modules. They may also include purchasing modules, personnel modules, report writing, and scheduling modules. Because the individual modules are interconnected, a manager can generate a history of an individual piece of equipment or vehicle and determine the actual cost of the equipment overtime as well as analyze maintenance practices, materials, and labor costs. The manager, for example, may also generate a report that details maintenance cost per vehicle, tire life, project staffing efficiency, and so on. This technology provides the manager with continuous feedback on performance, and it also allows the manager to improve maintenance, staffing, and inventory control efficiency. For sports managers, savings generated through streamlined management of these functions represents new dollars that can be used for capital improvements, training of personnel, or the creation of additional programs (Hernandez, 2001).

Sports organizations are not unlike businesses in every industry that are now seeing improvements in performance that are the result, at least in part, of the much wider range of feedback made possible by IT. According to Harvard Business School professor Gary W. Loveman, "gains [in performance] come not because the technology is whiz-bang, but because [IT] supports breakthrough ideas in business processes" ("The Technology Payoff," 1993, p. 57). In other words, the kind of organizationwide feedback made possible through IT allows not just managers but also individual and team performers to see what kind of progress they are making toward performance goals and to identify performance problems more quickly.

Enhanced Communication Through IT

Children everywhere ten years old or even younger are familiar with most of the recent IT-based advances in communication, particularly with wireless (cellular) telephones, e-mail, and voice mail. What is less widely understood are the dramatic improvements that these technologies, as well as faxes and teleconferencing, have made possible in terms of organization performance.

To appreciate the scope of the improvements in these areas, let's consider what communication in organizations looked like prior to these advances. Even at the management level, if an individual or group identified a problem, or came up with an improvement idea, most often a memo had to be prepared, typed by a secretary, and sent through the company's mail system to the appropriate parties. These parties would then respond through the same process of typed, mailed memo, most often independently, with little or no knowledge of the reaction of the others who had received the initial memo. This process might continue back and forth for as long as it took to make a decision on the issue. Before voice mail and e-mail, telephone messages could only be left for individuals with secretaries or assistants, necessitating messages that were brief and less than complete.

In an effort to short-circuit this extremely time-consuming process of memo and return memo, a meeting might be called bringing together all of the parties required for discussion and decision. Of course the more parties required for this process, the more difficult it was to schedule a meeting, especially if some of the individuals involved were from outside of the area. The meeting form of communication does result in less time wasted in sending memos back and forth and does provide an opportunity for interaction between participants. The logistics of scheduling meetings can often be cumbersome, however, and frequently long periods of time pass before a mutually agreeable time can be found when all of the parties can come together at the same location.

With IT, all of this has changed. Problems and ideas can now be identified and shared nearly instantaneously through e-mail, reducing the back-and-forth process of information exchange and feedback from weeks to days or even hours. Meetings involving parties separated by thousands of miles can be arranged much more easily using the teleconferencing and videoconferencing made possible through IT. Voice mail now makes a third channel of communication available to virtually anyone in the organization with a telephone. In short, advances in IT have both accelerated and expanded communication processes throughout organizations, greatly enhancing their ability to respond rapidly and effectively to both problems and opportunities.

IT has also significantly affected the organization's ability to communicate with stakeholders. Web-based technologies such as e-mail and organizational websites have allowed sports organizations to provide instantaneous information including game broadcasts, game stories, game results, press releases, and statistics to both the media and other stakeholders including fans, sponsors, and parents of student athletes. Sports facilities, recreation departments, youth leagues, and professional sports teams as well as other sports organizations are able to provide important information such as schedule changes, announcements about upcoming events or promotions, and directions to sports facilities online. Some organizations encourage stakeholders to register for regular e-newsletters or bulletins that provide important information, special offers, or event announcements. This approach to communication can result in significant savings in publication design, printing, and mailing costs.

Many college athletic departments have been particularly successful in utilizing the web to communicate with key stakeholders including alumni, parents, donors, and prospective students who are located throughout the country. Parents, who may be located thousands of miles from the school, are now able to follow their student athlete's team performance. Prospective students can research the school's athletic teams, coaches, and student athlete services from the privacy of their own homes, and alumni around the world can easily follow their alma mater's sports teams.

Internet technology is also used to collect important feedback from stakeholders. Organizations may provide opportunities for online chats with sports stars or coaches, and may encourage fans to contact the organization for additional information or to provide comments on products, services, or policies the organization is considering. For many sports organizations, web technology creates a link to a broad-based constituency by facilitating information exchange.

Web technology plays a role in facilitating other exchanges with stakeholders as well. Sports organization websites may offer online purchase of goods such as tickets or merchandise as well as membership or registration services. The Giants and Seattle Mariners have created virtual marketplaces where season ticket holders can resell tickets, and the Giants claim this service prevented more than forty thousand no-shows in one season alone (Williams, 2001a). E-companies such as Global eTicket Exchange, LiquidSeats Inc., and E-TicketBoard Inc. have created online auction communities where fans can sell and trade tickets without having to go through a scalper.

Constituents may use a sports organization's website to register for aerobics classes, youth soccer, summer camp, or tennis lessons. Some sports facilities offer online tee time and court reservation service, and others may create a player or competitor database, offer to find appropriate opponents, and set up matches between users. Some sports teams allow fans to swap or trade unused tickets online or to see the actual sight lines of any seat in the house through virtual facility tours.

Product and Service Innovations Through IT

Yet another area of tremendous opportunity for organizations is the development of new products or services, or of new delivery mechanisms through the use of IT. Not too long ago, a major sports industry publication reported the following innovations, all based on advances in information technology.

Trakus Inc., a small technology firm in Somerville, Massachusetts, is building a system that places electronic sensors on football and hockey players. While the athletes are practicing or even actually competing, Trakus would generate information on everything from pulse, body temperature, and speed to measures of exertion and intensity of hits or collisions. Trainers and conditioners would use these data to track athletes' stamina, endurance, strength, and other performance variables, and the media and fans would have a whole new source of information to evaluate and compare the performance of athletes.

The New York Jets and other NFL teams have begun using a "virtual playbook." The traditional printed football playbook contains all of a team's plays and formations, which players are expected to memorize as the road map for their performance. The virtual playbook is presented on a CD and contains all of the information included in a traditional playbook, but also uses animation to "put the plays in action," as well as video clips to allow players to see the play in actual game conditions. And after studying the virtual playbook, the players can then test themselves (or be tested)—complete with game clock and crowd noise—on such tasks as formation recognition and offensive and defensive adjustments.

Professional teams in all three major sports (football, baseball, and basketball) have begun to experiment with "smart" seats in their stadiums and arenas. These seats have small screens mounted on their armrests, allowing fans to call up replays from various angles, see scores and plays from other games, track statistics, review player profiles, order concessions and team merchandise, and compete with other fans for cash and prizes.

Perhaps no IT-based change, however, has been more far-reaching for organizations than the changes that have come as a result of the development of the Internet and the World Wide Web. And perhaps nowhere has the impact of the Internet been greater than in the sports media industry.

The Web and the Sports Media

In every industry, organizations have been changed forever by the Internet. Transactions of every kind, from banking and stock market transactions, to catalog viewing and the purchase of everything from clothes to cars to music, are now commonplace on the Internet. To remain competitive, virtually every organization must at least make available to its customers the ability to do business with the organization over the Internet. As we discussed earlier, the Internet not only allows the opportunity for information exchange, but for commercial exchange or business transactions as well.

Sports media organizations are certainly not exempt from this pressure. To satisfy their customers, these organizations must inform and entertain. The earliest Internet innovations for sports media organizations were websites (Internet locations) that fans could visit as an alternative means of accessing the information provided in a broadcast or article. Then sports media websites were enhanced to provide information that wasn't available simply by watching or listening to a broadcast or reading an article. Websites not only gave information and results, but detailed statistical information, historical records, profiles, feature stories, upcoming game previews and so on. In Figure 3-2, the top ten sports websites are presented along with numbers of visitors to that site for a one month period, suggesting the growing popularity of sports websites.

Figure 3-2 Top Sports Websites in the United States*

Site	Unique Visitors
http://www.espn.com	6,276,000
http://www.mlb.com	4,482,000
http://www.sportsline.com	4,462,000
NFL Internet Group	2,630,000
http://www.cnnsi.com	2,491,000
http://www.nascar.com	2,425,000
http://www.sportingnews.com	1,551,000
http://www.fansonly.com	1,442,000
http://www.nba.com	1,242,000
http://www.sandbox.com	1,161,000

*Figures provided for July 2001.
 Source: Sportbusiness International.

The combination of the Internet with the development of high-speed cable access is resulting in an ever-evolving range of innovations in terms of what sports media organizations can offer their customers. The comments from Ross Levinson, senior vice president at News Digital Media, paint a vivid picture of what becomes possible through the marriage of traditional sports media and IT: "You'll have chats and messaging (with players, coaches, other fans), you can predict plays, track your fantasy team in real time, order a pizza or the jersey of your favorite player. . . . Or you can have an ongoing interactive game with yourself or others, or call up the stats on any player, or archive a play you just watched" (Liberman, 2000). One of the great promises of new media technology is its ability to be customized to the user. One sports media company, ACTV, Inc. in Dallas, Texas, has developed technology that allows fans to select their favorite camera angle for game viewing (Williams, 2001b); some sports websites allow fans to receive individual reports on a favorite player's performance including up-to-date statistics and actual game-highlight video clips. Other advances include TiVo, an automated broadcast delivery system that allows viewers to record and view any programming at anytime and to stop or pause real-time action and then restart viewing without interrupting the broadcast.

In short, through the use of IT, sports media organizations can now offer their customers more than just information or the opportunity to watch an event or program. Through IT, sports media organizations can now provide their customers with the opportunity to become active participants in a multifaceted sports-based experience.

The Management Challenges of IT

The demonstrated benefits of recent advances in IT, both in terms of enhanced organizational performance and expanded and improved products and services for customers, are impressive. But significant challenges must be met if organizations are to achieve the full dimension of these benefits. Among the most significant of these challenges are the need for quality information, the risk of information overload, and how to manage telecommuters and virtual teams, ensuring continuous training to keep up with the continuing advances in IT, the challenge of maintaining security in terms of the organization's information systems, and the cost of IT development, training, and application.

The Need to Convert Data into Information

In all of the ways already described, advances in IT have significantly enhanced organizations' ability to use information. For IT to yield its full benefits, however, the information being processed must be *quality* information. Actually, a fairly common distinction is drawn between information and data. *Data* consist of numbers or facts that represent some aspect or aspects of a situation. Nielsen ratings of a televised sports event, the prices competitors charge advertisers, and the number of hits on a sports organization's website are all examples of data, facts or figures that in and of themselves have no meaning.

Information, in contrast, consists of data that have meaning. A program's Nielsen rating, for example, when related to the ratings for other similar programs, or to the target rating established for that program, becomes information. By relating the data to other factors, the data become information. In many ways, converting data to information is one of the critical tasks of the manager. IT can help ensure the availability of a continuous flow of essential data such as prices or ratings or website hits, but it is the manager's job to apply knowledge and expertise based on education and experience and convert raw data into information useful for problem solving, decision making, and innovation. This means that one of the key challenges for organizations in optimizing the impact of IT is to ensure that throughout the organization the knowledge and skills exist that are needed to convert data into useful information.

This is one of the reasons why higher levels of education are becoming required for more and more jobs in the workplace. Higher levels of education translate into an increased ability to interpret, analyze, and understand data, in other words, to convert data into useful information. A major or degree in sport management has little value in itself; it is the knowledge of the sports industry gained through the major or degree program that is of value, because it is this knowledge that enables the sports manager to analyze and interpret data from the field, to convert that data into information that enhances decision making and problem solving.

Ensuring Information Is on "TRAC"

A second management-challenge related to IT is ensuring that the information developed and used in organizations is quality information. Quality, in this case, generally means that information is timely, relevant, accurate, and complete, or as shown in Figure 3-3, on "TRAC."

Timely

Even the best information, if it is not available at the time needed for decision making or problem solving, is of little use to the manager. This is true in all organizations, but it is even truer in media organizations whose mission is to provide the most up-to-date information available. For example, game results and statistics must be con-

Figure 3-3 The "TRAC" Model of Quality Information	
Timely	Providing the most up-to-date information available
Relevant	Giving information that relates to and enhances understanding of key issues
Accurate	Ensuring that the information is a reliable and valid representation of what is happening
Complete	Providing information that is sufficiently comprehensive to represent all of the important aspects of the situation

tinuously updated and reported in order for them to retain their value to users. But even in the operation of these organizations, timely information is essential. For example, sports media advertising executives must have timely information about advertising sales, available inventory, and audience ratings.

Relevant

For information to be truly useful, it must relate to and enhance understanding of the issues and questions of direct concern to the organizations. On the one hand, this means not cluttering the organization's information systems with information that simply does not relate to the organization's needs, that is not used in the organization's decision making. On the other hand is the challenge of ensuring that each decision maker in the organization has access to the kind of information needed for the particular decisions in which he or she is involved. For example, a national sports magazine manager would be particularly interested in collecting and maintaining a database of subscribers. The manager must determine what type of information would be important to collect and record about subscribers. Does the manager want to know the age, gender, and income of the subscriber? Would it also be valuable to know what other magazines the subscriber reads, what products he or she uses, and what professional team the subscriber considers a favorite? Clearly, all of this information is considered in the magazine's marketing efforts and is therefore relevant to the organization.

Accurate

Of course for information to be of value to an organization, it must be accurate, a reliable and valid representation of what is really happening. In many ways, this is the most difficult challenge relating to information, especially in situations where the data are unclear. In these situations, the information used is often the result of individual or group judgments about a situation, which are naturally subject to bias and interpretation. For example, members of the sports media are often faced with the challenge of reporting on games and events in the sports industry when few facts are known or may be unavailable. Consider the case of the "behind clubhouse doors" spat between the team's star player and manager. Although very little may be known about the actual content of the argument, members of the media may ask other players what they know, may speculate about the cause with other members of the press, or may rely on secondhand reports of the incident. In this case, the resultant story in the evening's sports section may be little more than personal opinion, half-truths, and innuendo; yet the reader has come to view the reporter as a legitimate news source and interprets the reporter's opinion as fact. The media must shoulder the responsibility of verifying the accuracy of information it presents as fact while assuring that opinions or subjective reporting is represented as such.

For the sports organization utilizing data to make managerial decisions, it is the manager's responsibility, as much as possible, to develop better data on the situation, either in the form of more reliable facts and figures, or by seeking the opinions of a wider group of people, preferably including experts with extensive experience with the situation under consideration. For example, the sports media executive must have data that accurately shows costs of production, as well as trends in advertising revenues in order to develop an appropriate bid on broadcasting rights. Without good information, he or she is likely to over- or underbid, thereby either losing the property or paying too much—in either case, potentially losing millions of dollars for the network.

Complete

Finally, information must be sufficiently comprehensive to represent all of the important aspects of a situation. Incomplete information results in decision making that fails to take into account one or more important factors. This in turn jeopardizes the likelihood of the success or effectiveness of the decision or solution. For example, consider the case of the broadcast executive preparing to bid on a sports broadcast rights package. If he or she considered costs of production and advertising revenue forecasts, but did not consider information about competitors such as what were they likely to bid, how much they had bid in the past, and how much were advertising rates for a similar event in the past, he or she would be basing the bid on only part of the picture. The executive would also want to consider the state of the economy and industry trends as well. Sports managers must be aware that basing decisions on incomplete information often results in poor decisions.

Information that is on "TRAC" provides a solid foundation for an organization's decision-making and problem-solving processes. Shortcomings in any of these four areas results in decisions built on inadequate foundations, and the results are not likely to be positive.

The Risk of Information Overload

One of the downsides of the recent advances in IT is the attendant risk of organizations being overwhelmed with information. On average, humans are somewhat limited in their ability to process anything more than a fairly moderate amount of information at any one time. The amount of information pouring in from cell phones, e-mail, the Internet, and other sources has increasingly begun to threaten to exceed our capacity to organize and make sense of it all. Research suggests, for example, that corporate workers in America who use e-mail receive an average of thirty messages a day, and they spend approximately two hours each day responding to and completing tasks related to the messages (Hymowitz, 1999). The existence of so much information means risking either drowning as we immerse ourselves in this unending flow of information or failing to recognize the most important information because it is buried in so much other information. Thus the organization is challenged to develop practices and procedures that ensure, as much as possible, that everyone in the organization receives only the information they need to perform their jobs well.

The Challenge of Telecommuting and Virtual Teams

One promising area of change as a result of advances in IT is in the way work is done, or more accurately *where* work is done. *Telecommuting* is the use of IT to allow workers to perform their jobs at sites other than where the organization is located, usually at home. Telecommuters use PCs, the Internet, fax machines, and

other technology to complete their work without the pressures and time loss of actual commuting. The organization gains access to a wider range of workers, with reduced needs in terms of office and parking space and furniture.

Virtual teams consist of individuals who perform as a team without necessarily working at the same location. Virtual teams use the same technology as telecommuters as well as teleconferencing, videoconferencing, and electronic meetings. Virtual teams enable organizations to involve individuals working anywhere in the world in problem solving and decision making. This ensures that teams are composed of members with the best available skills and knowledge for whatever issues the team is addressing.

Several challenges arise in managing both telecommuters and virtual teams. The first is obvious: How do you provide the kind of supervision, direction, and support that happens easily on a face-to-face basis to individuals who may be physically present only occasionally, or even rarely? The second is less obvious: How do you compensate for the lack of social interaction among virtual team members and commuters, which appears to be an important source of motivation in the workplace? The kind of cohesiveness among group or team members that is an important factor in members' productivity appears to be more difficult to achieve for telecommuters and virtual team members.

In fact, organizations have begun to experiment with ways to reduce these problems. Most approaches involve building in at least some face-to-face meetings involving all members of any virtual team, especially at the beginning of the team process. Similarly for telecommuters, many arrangements now require that, at least occasionally, regular time be spent in the office, and just as important, at lunch, interacting directly with coworkers and managers.

As continuing advances in IT make both telecommuting and virtual teams more common, managers will need to continue developing approaches for ensuring high levels of performance—and a strong sense of involvement—for employees who are working elsewhere, on their own.

The Continuous Training Challenge

Obviously, IT is only as good as the skills of the people who use it. This has always been the case between people and technology, but now there is a difference. In every age prior to the present, technology changed slowly. In fact, until the past decade or so, the technical skills one learned at the beginning of a career most often were sufficient for an entire career. Whether in the factory or the office, a change in technology rarely required significant additional training. With the advent of computer technology, this pattern has changed dramatically. Since the early 1990s, advances in IT have been continuous, requiring organizations to develop continuous training capabilities just to keep pace.

Traditionally, employee training has been viewed as "lost time," time when the employee is not working. Increasingly, this view is changing to recognize that training is an absolutely necessary investment to ensure that managers and employees have the skills needed to make maximum use of the capabilities of IT. Even with this changed mind-set, however, arranging for continuous training in IT is difficult. As competition forces the requirement of greater efficiency on every organization, it becomes more and more challenging to find the time for training. But organizations are using innovative approaches to ensure that training occurs. One such approach uses IT to respond to this challenge. In this approach, training is available online, allowing employees to access training materials whenever they can, without ever leaving their desks. There may be disadvantages to this approach as well, including the problems associated with employees being required to find the time for training on their own. But whatever questions specific approaches to training might raise, if the full advantages of IT are to be realized, continuous training must become a reality.

The Question of Security

The potential for improved performance through IT is significant, but even when used effectively it is not without risks. An additional area of challenge for managers is to effectively manage the access to information made possible by IT and required in the workplace.

IT: The Need for Access and the Threat of Leaks

Increasingly, employees are sharing the responsibility with management for speeding up and improving the organization's performance. This shared responsibility increases their need for access to information on such factors as inventory levels, delivery schedules, costs, and levels of staff, as well as the performance of various units within the organization. Obviously, this greater access to information throughout the organization results in an increased possibility that important information might leak outside the organization to competitors, the media, and elsewhere. Organizations must learn to manage this reality and the risk it represents.

Yet on closer examination, it appears that the fear of leaks may be greater than the actual threat. Companies like General Motors and Herman-Miller have been sharing what some companies consider secret information with front-line employees for a number of years, with no evidence of any damaging leaks. Tom Peters also makes the point that because information is everywhere anyway, competitors can get the kind of information they are seeking without the help of leaks. Finally, the potential performance advantages of sharing information with employees far outweigh the value of keeping this information secure (Peters, 1987).

The Possibility of Sabotage

Perhaps more serious than the potential for damaging leaks is another risk arising from the presence of IT in the workplace: the risk of employee sabotage of the company's information system. A single angry employee armed only with a computer virus is now capable of doing irreparable harm to a company's databases and information systems. There is also the possibility of the one-person strike, where a single anonymous, dissatisfied employee could interrupt the information system to call attention to a particular issue or to attempt to gain concessions from management. No laws, programs, nor security arrangements can totally protect against this. The best defense is social pressure from one's peers or an employee's feeling of being treated with dignity and justice (Toffler, 1990).

To guard against viruses, employees can be trained to not use software and disks from unknown sources. In addition, security software has been developed to protect against viruses. However, as with leaks of crucial information, organizations must now learn to manage their employees in ways that minimize the likelihood they will want to do damage to the information and the IT to which they have now gained access. Fortunately, surprisingly little evidence to date exists of this kind of sabotage. In essence, it will have to be the employees' sense of fair treatment that management will have to satisfy, if the threat of information leaks and IT sabotage is to be minimized effectively.

Sports Gambling

Sports managers have long been concerned with the effect of sports gambling on the industry. After professional baseball's Chicago Black Sox scandal of 1919 when several players were accused of fixing the World Series, there were increasing concerns about maintaining the integrity of our games so fans would continue to support sports teams and organizations. The development of IT, however, has played a role in facilitating sports gambling. Fans may utilize the web to place bets with foreign gambling operations (where gambling is legal in the host country) and offshore gambling establishments where sports gambling may be conducted beyond the purview of the U.S. government. Additionally, sports websites provide detailed information that supports gamblers in their attempts to analyze every facet of a game before placing a bet. Sports gambling websites facilitate gambling by bringing the gambling opportunity directly into the home of the gambler where he or she may place a bet in private. This system also encourages the gambler to use a credit card and to place bets frequently. For the sports manager and law enforcement agencies, control of online gambling has become increasingly difficult, and it is likely that because of its convenience and anonymity, sports gambling websites will continue to proliferate.

Cost Considerations

One of the greatest challenges faced by managers seeking to develop and integrate IT into the operation of the sports organization is its associated cost. Sports technology and related dotcoms boomed in the 1990s. The onset of the new millennium saw a massive shakeout of the industry, and many technology-based companies and websites failed. Research and development of new technologies is very expensive. Sports organizations must consider not only the upfront cost of securing the technology, but also training and maintenance costs must be considered as an ongoing expense. Sports managers must recognize the extensive technology start-up costs such as building infrastructure, purchasing hardware and software, and staff training. For example, many sports stadiums and teams have been slow to adopt "smart seat" technology for various reasons including the cost of installation, concerns that promised revenue streams will not be realized, and fears that the technology will quickly become obsolete.

Interestingly enough, in the fall of 2001, Fox shelved the "First and Ten Yellow Line" technology in its NFL broadcasts discussed earlier because of cost considerations. Without sponsorship of this technology, Fox executives claimed that the related costs of $50,000 per game had become prohibitive to its use (Lefton, 2001). Sports managers are carefully assessing both the costs and benefits of new technologies and looking closely at the bottom line. Sports managers must determine whether the new technology results in realizable gains in sales, revenues, or other quantifiable benefits. It is not surprising then that Gregg Hamburger, director of advanced media and emerging technologies at the Marketing Arm, a Dallas-based sports consultancy, suggests the best investment in information technology is one designed to enhance revenue streams: "It's in ticket sales. It's in the merchandise. It's in monetizing all the research that's at your fingertips, whether it's the season-ticket database or whether it's cutting costs in production areas" (Bounds, 2001, p. 30). One example of information technology that has been successfully utilized by the sports media to generate new revenues is virtual advertising in game broadcasts. Whereas the fan in the stadium sees a blank space on the court or on the backstop wall behind the batter, broadcasting technology allows the network to superimpose advertising signage in these areas that is only seen by the home viewer. The advertising can be sold on a per quarter or by inning basis, providing the broadcaster with a new inventory of advertising opportunities that may be sold to sponsors.

For most sports organizations, it is no longer a question of *if* the sports organization should consider integrating advancements in IT, but *how* the organization can successfully implement, realize, and sustain the competitive advantage that can be brought about through IT.

Epilogue

While Fox television continues to utilize technology to enhance sports broadcasts and attract viewers, there are signs that league officials are wary of the changes. When Fox announced that it would be dropping its "First and Ten Yellow Line" technology because it was too expensive to maintain at $50,000 per game over the course of the season, critics and NFL insiders suggested that Fox had a bigger agenda. It has been argued that Fox was merely putting pressure on the league to allow sponsorship of game enhancements, which had been banned by the NFL as part of its last broadcast agreement (Lefton, 2001). The NFL had eliminated sponsorship of game enhancements such as the "Budweiser Starting Lineup" because of fear of overcommercialization of the game. Such ploys were thought to alienate the viewer and were seen as an unwelcome distraction by the league. By pulling the "First and Ten Yellow Line" technology and claiming that it was too expensive, Fox knew it was likely to anger viewers. Public outcry over the loss of the technology might put pressure on the league to allow sponsorship of enhancements. At the core of the debate is the intrusion of advertising into sports programming and the games themselves. Technology has made it possible for these new saleable enhancements as well as creating an entirely new stream of virtual advertising revenues. While the tendency has been to embrace technology and to laud the value it brings to sports broadcasting, sports organizations such as the NFL are likely to continue to recognize and debate the potentially negative consequences brought about by the lucrative marriage of sport and technology.

Summary

The sports media segment plays an integral role in connecting stakeholders to sports organizations. The sports media not only reports game outcomes, but serves as a marketing distribution channel by which sport is delivered directly to consumers throughout the world. The sports media continues to reinvent itself through technologies that allow sports consumers to gain more immediate access to sports information and organizations.

The sports media has successfully utilized developing information technology (IT). IT refers to all of the resources—the processes, practices, and systems—an organization uses to gather, retain, and process the information it uses to pursue its mission. IT provides organizations with the ability to develop new products and services while improving management's ability to make effective and efficient decisions. Managers utilize several levels of information systems including Transaction Processing Systems (TPS), Management Information Systems (MIS), and Decision Support Systems (DSS). These systems help organizations dramatically streamline their day-to-day operations, monitor virtually every performance area of the organization, and enhance significantly the quality of analysis, problem solving, and decision making as the organization pursues its mission. Computer-based technologies, especially the Internet and World Wide Web, have greatly expanded the role of the sports media and provided sports consumers with greater and broader access to sports information and sports organizations.

Sports organizations have recognized the associated challenges of IT including content quality, information overload, telecommuting and virtual teams, training, security, sports gambling, and cost considerations. Advances in information technology will continue to shape the management of sports organizations. As the sports media plays a leadership role in the sports industry in developing and integrating new technologies, it will continue to become an increasingly powerful entity that shapes not only our games but also our participation and perceptions of sport.

Pro Sports Collectibles, Memorabilia and More!

Paul Hunter has recently purchased Pro Sports Collectibles, Memorabilia and More!, a local sports memorabilia and sports collectibles store that had been family owned for forty years. Hunter, a longtime sports memorabilia collector, who was well known and respected in sports memorabilia circles, was excited about beginning his own business. He thought he had done his homework before purchasing the store. He had created a business plan, secured the capital to support his investment, and had developed deals with several suppliers who would provide him with quality memorabilia and sports items.

One hour after Paul signed the papers, he walked into his new store and arranged to take Cy Thompson, the store's only full-time employee, to dinner that evening. What he learned during that dinner made him truly realize for the first time what he had undertaken. Paul carefully took notes as Cy began to talk about the operation of Pro Sports Collectibles, Memorabilia and More! The following list is what he wrote.

- Only one full-time employee. Eight part-time college student workers. Schedule made up by owner and posted on the bulletin board on Saturdays. Sometimes part-time workers change hours. By the end of the week, the schedule is a mess with eraser marks, penciled-in names. Sometimes no one shows to take a shift and the full-time employee or owner is stuck working the shift. Employees complain that hours are not distributed evenly and paychecks, handwritten by the owner, are sometimes sent days late.

- Inventory arrives by truck on Wednesday. Sometimes it is not unloaded until Saturday.

- Inventory system is maintained by hand on index cards.

- Shoplifting is a serious problem.

- Phone calls from out-of-state collectors take a great deal of time. Must search back room or index cards to see if item is available.

- Most transactions take place with customers who live within 60 miles. No online transactions.

- Only cash and checks accepted for transactions.

When Paul got home that evening, he reviewed his notes and realized that he needed a plan to integrate technology into the management of Pro Sports Collectibles, Memorabilia and More!

1. Develop a technology plan for Pro Sports Collectibles, Memorabilia and More! Identify the challenges outlined in Paul's list and how they might be addressed by the use of technology.

2. Pro Sports Collectibles, Memorabilia and More! has failed to utilize Internet technology. Work with a team of students to identify what content would be important to include in a new store website.

3. Design a web page for Pro Sports Collectibles, Memorabilia and More! or any other sports organization of your choice.

Management Exercise

References

Bounds, J. (2001, April 16–22). It's a brave new world of enhanced TV, Internet. *Street & Smith's SportsBusiness Journal*, p. 30.

Hernandez, V. (2001, June). Computerized maintenance management systems. *Parks & Recreation*, pp. 65–69.

Hymowitz, C. (1999, September 26). Flooded with e-mail? Try screening, sorting, or maybe just phoning. *Wall Street Journal*, p. B1.

King, B. (2000, July 24–30). Sportvisions's idea guru puts Star Wars technology into play. *Street & Smith's SportsBusiness Journal*, p. 26.

Lefton, T. (2001, November 26–December 2). Did Fox really draw the line over $50,000 a week? *Street & Smith's SportsBusiness Journal*, p. 9

Liberman, N. (2000, October 23–29). Technology is future's wild card. *Street & Smith's SportsBusiness Journal*, pp. 29, 38.

Mullen, L. (1998, December 21–27). Off-the-wall ways put Fox on the map. *Street & Smith's SportsBusiness Journal*, p. 23.

———. Top sports websites in the United States. *Sportbusiness International*, p. 33.

Ostrowski, J. (1998, December 21–28). In any currency, ESPN a cash machine. *Street & Smith's SportsBusiness Journal*, p. 25.

Peters, T. (1987). *Thriving on chaos.* New York: Harper & Row.

The technology payoff. (1993, June 14). *Business Week*, p. 57.

Toffler, A. (1990). *Powershift.* New York: Bantam.

Williams, P. (2001a, April 16–22). End of the line for ticket lines. *Street & Smith's SportsBusiness Journal*, p. 27.

Williams, P. (2001b, April 16–22). Sports TV sprints toward future. *Street & Smith's SportsBusiness Journal*, p. 25.

Critical Management Tasks

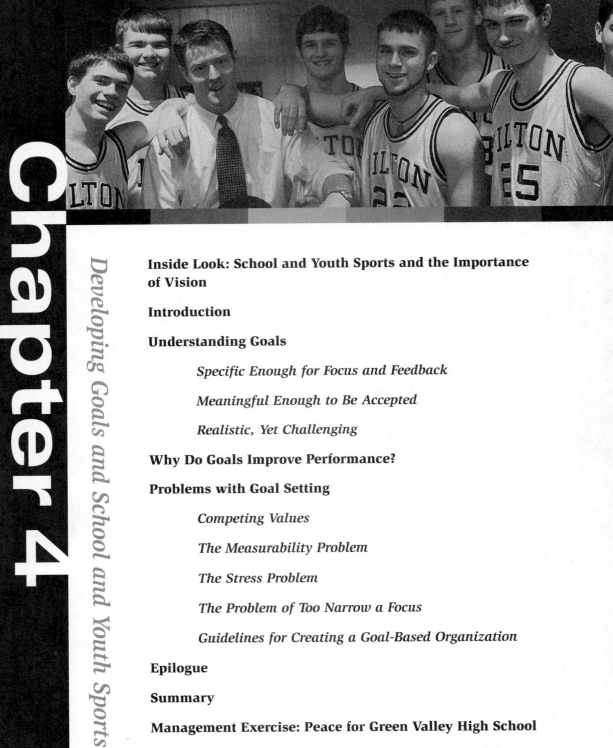

Chapter 4

Developing Goals and School and Youth Sports

Purpose:

To provide athletic participation opportunities for boys and girls up to and including high school.

Stakeholders:

Participant athletes, parents, coaches, related support personnel (trainers, officials), equipment suppliers, league administrators, school administrators, state association administrators, elected officials (local school boards, state and federal legislators), local, state, and federal taxpayers.

Size and scope:

- Nearly 4 million young men and over 2.5 million young women participated in high school athletics during the 1999–2000 school year. Over a million play football, the sport with the most participants ("Highlights," 2001).
- More than 70 million parents, 3.5 million coaches, and between 30 and 35 million children ages 3 to 14 are involved in youth sports in the United States each year (Zheutlin, 2001). However, 44 percent of children ages 6 to 17 participated in only one organized team sport ("Highlights," 2001).
- Over 650,000 boys and girls ages 4½ to 18 participated on approximately 50,000 teams run by the American Youth Soccer Organization (Kinsey, personal communication, March 29, 2000), and over 210,000 participated on teams aligned with the Amateur Athletic Union (AAU), an increase of approximately 200 percent since 1990 ("Highlights," 2001).
- Membership in USA Hockey, the national governing body for ice and in-line hockey in the United States, includes approximately 550,000 ice and in-line players, coaches, officials, and volunteers ("This Is USA Hockey," 2000).

Governance:

- The National Federation of State High School Associations (NF) serves as the coordinator for high school sports, as well as activities such as student council, debate, and drama. The NF encompasses all fifty individual state high school athletics and activity associations, as well as similar governing bodies operating in the District of Columbia, Bermuda, Guam, St. Croix, St. Thomas, St. John, and ten Canadian provinces.
- In addition to compiling national records in sports and national sport participation rates, the NF coordinates official certification, issues playing rules for sixteen boys' and sixteen girls' sports, prints eight million publications annually (including officials' manuals, casebooks, magazines, supplemental books and teaching aids), holds national conferences and competitions, and acts as an advocate and lobbying agent for school-based youth sports (*What Is the National Federation?* 1997).
- The legislative body of the NF, the National Council, is comprised of one representative from each member state, provincial, or territorial association. The council meets to conduct business twice each year.
- The NF model is typically replicated at the state level by state associations. State associations, also nonprofits, have a direct role in organizing state championships and competitions in athletics and activities, and they are the final authority in determining athlete eligibility.

Inside Look

School and Youth Sports and the Importance of Vision

In 2000 five small private high schools in Miami-Dade County in Florida were accused of recruiting foreign players to bolster their boys' basketball teams in violation of Florida High School Activities Association (FHSAA) rules. All of these schools were highly successful, including Berkshire Academy, where all fourteen of the team's players were international transfers from countries such as Cameroon, Uruguay, and Yugoslavia. The Berkshire boys' team compiled a gaudy 32–2 record and was the top-ranked Class 1A team in the state; the girls' team, with four international players, was 28–2.

The FHSAA, the state's governing body for high school sports, reacted quickly to the complaint lodged by a competitor school, banning the Berkshire boys' and girls' teams from the state's postseason tournament for using "undue influence in athletic recruiting" (Fonteboa, 2000, p. 1D). Another school, Miami Christian, was forced to forfeit twenty-three regular season games for using three male players who had exhausted their high school eligibility in the Dominican Republic. Miami Christian was also under investigation for illegally recruiting six other Dominican players. Milos Nikolic, one of the four Yugoslavian players on the Berkshire boys' team, said, "I just wanted a chance to get away from the war areas. . . . I came here to finish my education, improve my English, and hopefully go on to college" (Fonteboa, 2000, p. 8D). Many supporters echo Nikolic's comments, citing that these athletic programs provide opportunities for athletically gifted students who might not otherwise attain a college degree to gain access to a college education via athletic scholarships.

These incidents bring into question just what precisely are the proper goals of high school and youth sports programs, and therefore complicate the process of providing the clear sense of purpose for school and youth league managers. Although the Berkshire basketball program was successful on the court, the methods deemed to attain this success were deemed inappropriate. But why? Aren't wins and losses the true measure of success for a sports organization? Or is it something else? In the case of these Florida schools, it is clear that one competing value, the desire to produce wins over losses, superseded the values of providing educationally sound experiences that school and youth league programs are often presumed to provide.

Chances are, you yourself have participated in either or both youth and school sports. Many of you had good experiences, and some of you probably didn't. What makes an experience at this level either positive or negative? Did it come down to conflicts over winning and losing? Did the adults—your coaches, your parents, or others—seem to be more interested in winning than you were? Maybe. Research by Michigan State University's Institute for the Study of Youth Sports found that kids in youth sports play to have fun, be with their friends, and learn. "It isn't until kids are in their early adolescence that they develop an adult sense of winning and losing," says the institute's Mike Clark. Bob Bigelow, a former NBA player who has studied youth sports extensively, puts it this way: "The fundamental chasm in youth sports is the difference between adult needs and priorities and the kids' needs and priorities. The question is: whose needs are going to prevail?" (Zheutlin, 2001, p. 18).

Management expert Peter Drucker (1973) has suggested that "it is the first responsibility of the manager . . . to give others vision and the ability to perform." Drucker defined vision as the clear, shared sense of direction that allows organizations to achieve a common purpose. He insisted that vision is the first contribution of management because a shared sense of direction makes possible the cooperation and commitment necessary for organizations to succeed. Only with a common vision can individuals and groups perform with a clear sense of the destination they are working toward and a clear sense of the direction of the organization. But in the context of youth and school sports, the question, as Bigelow points out, is what direction is most important?

More recently, management thinkers James C. Collins and Jerry I. Porras (1998) described a well-conceived vision as having two parts: core ideology and envisioned future. Core ideology is defined as the enduring characteristics of an organization and includes core values and core purposes. Core values are those values an organization would keep even if it were penalized for retaining them, and core purpose as what defines an organization's reason for being. The envisioned future includes BHAGs, or "big, hairy, audacious goals," bold long-range goals that influence the direction of an organization for ten to thirty years, and a vivid description of what it will mean to achieve these BHAGs.

In the early part of the twentieth century, football coaching legend John Heisman (for whom college football's famous trophy is named) attempted, as did many others, to define what might be considered the core ideology of youth sports organizations. Heisman declared that football taught willpower, self control, clear thinking, sportsmanship, and the formation of good habits in young men. Asked Heisman, "The doctor regulates his liver, the dentist looks after his teeth, the (teacher) undertakes to give him the all-essential dose of geometry, the gymnasium instructor makes sure that his muscles become firm and reliable—are these not enough? . . . Is there a school of any kind where a boy's Will or Temper or Disposition can be trained?" (Heisman, 2000, p. 2).

The training of will, temper, and disposition in young boys might be considered BHAGs and certainly would be viewed as a worthy and challenging envisioned future. In fact, the development of youth and school sports in America during the twentieth century provides an excellent example of the power of vision and what is possible when people share a committed sense of direction. But the challenge over this period was how to determine this direction, and in whose interests.

During the early 1900s, educators aligned with the Progressive Movement, including John Dewey, G. Stanley Hall, and William James, first articulated the vision of athletics as a tool to prepare young people for the rigors of modern life in American society. Several years later, in the period during and immediately following World War I (1914–1918), the nation began to recognize the health benefits of athletics for male youths and adults alike. In particular, school sports for males were promoted as a source of physical training for the armed forces without directly encouraging militarism and a means to encourage the cooperation and discipline valued by an increasingly ethnically diverse and industrialized society. During the period, when only one in three children entered high school and only one in nine completed it, educators began to recognize interscholastic athletic programs as an important way to keep students in school and to boost graduation rates. These became part of the envisioned future for those organizations promoting youth sports.

With this recognition, the vision of youth sports as a potentially valuable learning experience took root and began to grow. By 1931 thirty-six states had passed laws pertaining to physical education in high schools, and forty-seven states had athletic associations that monitored and controlled boys' high school athletics and conducted state championships in baseball, basketball, football, and track and field (O'Hanlon, 1982).

Not surprisingly, this period was also marked by dramatic growth for youth sports outside the high school arena. As a result of the Great Depression and the difficult conditions for youth at that time, a number of private and parochial sports organizations emerged to promote youth participation in sports. These included American Legion Junior Baseball (1925), Pop Warner youth football (1929), the Catholic Youth Organization (basketball, boxing, and softball) in 1930, the Amateur Softball Association (1933), and Little League Baseball (1939). Today, nearly 4 million young men and nearly 2.5 million young women participate in high school athletics, and as many as 70 million children are involved in youth sports programs. These numbers are clear testimony to the success of the articulation of the vision of youth sports and school athletics as valuable learning experiences.

As with the pioneers of youth and school sports, the first responsibility of sports managers in every segment of the sports industries is to provide a clear sense of vision, to provide the direction that will ensure effective organizational performance, and to enable every member of the organization to contribute meaningfully to the organization's success. According to Peter Drucker, the most effective way to achieve a shared understanding of the organization's vision is through well-defined goals. The challenge in school and youth sports continues to be how to define program goals. This means it is management's first responsibility to develop a system of goals that provides a sense of direction so clear that it guides the organization on its course.

Introduction

Within the context of the school-based and youth sports industry segments, this chapter describes goal setting and how clearly stated goals can provide people and sports organizations with the focus, direction, and understanding needed for optimum performance. We define the task of developing effective goals in terms of several key criteria, review the numerous benefits from developing goals in this manner, and examine the challenges and difficulties that are part of the goal-setting process.

The chapter also illustrates some of the specifics of the school-based and youth sports industry segment, how goal setting impacts this segment, and, once goals have been defined, how managers in this segment work to achieve them.

Understanding Goals

Consider the following two statements that might be made by a new community sports group or high school:

1.   To provide high-quality athletic opportunities for youth.

2.   To provide a sports program for each season of the year at both the interscholastic and intramural levels within three years.

The first statement is not a goal; the second is. What is the difference?

A goal is a commitment to a specific outcome within a specific time frame. The first statement describes a general direction of having high-quality athletic opportunity for youth, but it is not as specific as it might be in terms of exactly what the desired outcome is and when it is to be achieved. The second statement is much more specific in terms of both desired outcome and time frame. It commits to organizing a different sports activity on a year-round basis at different levels of competition (interscholastic and intramural) within three years. This type of specificity is a fundamental requirement for developing goals.

Specific Enough for Focus and Feedback

Being specific contributes to improved performance in two ways. First, goals that specify a targeted outcome provide a clear focus for everyone in the organization. For example, a program that provides opportunities at different levels of competition must include intramural sports as well as interscholastic sports (if we are talking about a high school athletic program). The more general statement of providing "high-quality athletic programs" can be interpreted in many different ways, with some people perhaps focusing on intramurals as a way to ensure maximum participation and others focusing on making the interscholastic teams as competitive as possible. The more specific statement makes it clear that the focus includes both intramural and interscholastic sports.

The more specific the goals, the more likely that everyone in the organization will have the same understanding, rather than his or her own individual interpretation, of the target. And when the destination is clear to everyone, it ensures both better decisions about how to get there and better cooperation along the way.

Second, goals that are specific make it possible to track progress toward the goal. This information about progress toward a goal is called *feedback*. When there has been steady or significant progress toward the goal, feedback can be a source of positive reinforcement, increasing motivation to continue toward the goal. For example, with the general goal statement of "quality athletic opportunities for youth in the community," it would be difficult to know how much progress the addition of any particular program actually represents. With the more specific goal we have been discussing, it is possible to understand exactly what kind of progress the addition of a specific program, such as coed intramural football, represents. Coed intramural field hockey covers the fall season of the commitment to a program for each season of the year, and the overall goal is both reinforcing and makes clear what the focus should be now that this piece of the goal is in place.

Conversely, where progress has been less positive, feedback can serve as a warning, indicating that either greater effort or a different approach is needed if the goal is going to be achieved. In our example, if it took nearly two years to add the coed intramural football program, the specified overall time frame of three years makes it clear that greater effort or a different approach is likely to be needed if the several other pieces of the goal are to be achieved within the goal's time frame. Figure 4-1 shows a formula for expressing goals in the most specific terms possible.

Commitment to an outcome specific enough to provide focus and feedback, however, is not the only requirement for a goal to be effective. For goals to increase performance, they must also be meaningful enough to be accepted by those involved, as well as both realistic and challenging.

Meaningful Enough to Be Accepted

Earlier, we noted that significant progress toward the vision of athletics as a part of the curriculum throughout public schools gained momentum when educators

---

Figure 4-1 Goal-Setting Formula for a School Athletic Department

A goal-setting formula can assist managers and employees in developing goals that satisfy the specific and time-framed criteria. The first component is an action statement that includes a specific outcome that should be expressed in numbers, whenever possible (as the first three goals demonstrate). When the outcome can't be expressed using numbers, then satisfactory completion of an activity is the next best way to ensure the desired outcome is specific (as in the fourth goal statement).

	Specific Outcome	Time Frame
Goal 1.	To decrease the number of athletic injuries by 20 percent	by the end of the school year.
Goal 2.	To recruit ten girls for the school soccer team	by 2002.
Goal 3.	To reduce the number of positive results in random drug tests of athletes by 50 percent	by 2003.
Goal 4.	To add a new sports program for the fall season	by the end of the school year.

realized that interscholastic sports programs are an effective way to keep students in school and to increase graduation rates. With this realization, the goal of establishing athletic programs in the schools became meaningful to educators. Because they viewed this goal as consistent with their own goal of educating students, they became motivated to accept this goal and to join the effort to achieve it.

When the people involved view a goal as a means for satisfying their own needs and for achieving their own goals, we say the goal is meaningful for them. When the goal is meaningful enough to be accepted, performance improves. More recently, educators recognized the importance of making goals meaningful by linking performance in the classroom to eligibility to play high school sports. The "no pass/no play" policies that have become common in recent years are an effort to make the goal of acceptable classroom performance more meaningful to student athletes. With "no pass/no play," educators attempt to make the goal of passing grades in all courses more meaningful by making this goal a requirement for participation in interscholastic sports, a goal they know is already meaningful to student athletes.

For goals to improve performance, then, they must not only reflect the goals of the organization, they must also meet the needs of the individuals and groups involved in attaining the goals. In the first example, the goal of athletic programs in the schools became meaningful to educators when these programs became recognized as an important means of support for their own goals of educating all students. In the second example, educators hope that the goal of participating in interscholastic sports will be meaningful enough to motivate students to put in the effort required to pass all of their courses.

Realistic, Yet Challenging

The policy of "no pass/no play" reflects the efforts of educators to define a goal for student athletes that is realistic. The goal of at least passing all academic courses represents for some students a definite increase in performance, but to a level that is realistic in terms of attainment. Some critics of this policy suggest that merely passing all courses is hardly an appropriate goal for any educational institution and that students are capable of higher performance that just passing courses.

Reflecting this latter view, some communities have raised the minimum standard for participation in interscholastic sports. These communities have adopted what might be called a "less than C/no play" policy for student athletes. This is consistent with the concept of stretch goals, which are purposely set at levels that are attainable, but only with a level of effort significantly greater than what has been typical. Supporters of "less than C/no play" argue that this approach attempts to use students' intense desire to play sports to fuel greater effort toward academic goals. And, in fact, classic research in this area of management shows that difficult goals result in greater improvements in performance than goals that are perceived as easy to attain (Stedry & Kay, 1964). People work harder to achieve challenging goals and are inspired to rise to a challenge, as long as that challenge is meaningful and *realistic*.

The last point is the potential problem with the "less than C/no play" rule. There has been concern that some students will view the goal of C or better in every course as unattainable, unrealistic. This is important. Goals that are viewed as *too* challenging can actually result in diminished effort and lower performance because the group or individual may simply withdraw effort and not perform even to previous levels.

Figure 4-2 shows the relationship between the perceived difficulty of a goal and the level of effort likely to be invested in that goal. Performance increases as goal difficulty increases. The higher the goal, the higher the performance, up to a point. Beyond a certain point that varies depending on the task to be performed and the people performing it, as goal difficulty continues to increase, performance actually declines. The key is to define goals in such a way that they are challenging, but not too challenging.

Some school systems, recognizing the potential negative effect of goals that are too challenging, have modified the "less than C/no play" approach. These systems are concerned that the goal of a grade of C or better in every course may be viewed as unrealistic and unattainable by some students, based on their own past experience with courses and grades. The concern is that these students may actually work less hard at their studies, thinking they'll never achieve the goal, so why even try. In an effort to avoid this kind of thinking, some school systems have implemented a "less than C *average*/no play" rule, for example. This encourages improved performance in school, but allows students to remain eligible for sports (and other extracurricular activities) by offsetting any grades lower than C with grades higher than C in other courses.

The key for managers everywhere is to define goals that are both challenging enough to improve performance and realistic enough for the group or individual

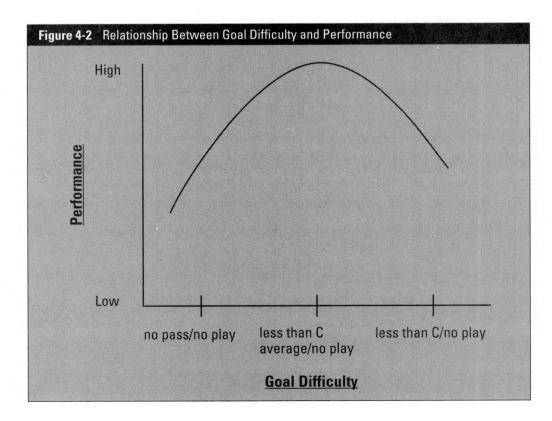

Figure 4-2 Relationship Between Goal Difficulty and Performance

to feel the goal is attainable. The "less than C average/no play" approach is an excellent example of setting a goal that is both challenging and realistic.

In summary, just having goals is not necessarily sufficient to improve performance. For goals to be effective, they must be specific enough for focus and feedback, meaningful enough to be accepted, realistic, and challenging, and time framed. Figure 4-3 adapts an acronym suggested by Hersey and Blanchard (1981) as a way to remember the essential characteristics of effective goals (1981). For goals to improve performance, they must be SMART.

Why Do Goals Improve Performance?

A reasonable question at this point is why SMART goals do lead to consistently higher levels of motivation and performance. There are several reasons, as shown in Figure 4-4.

The passage of Title IX of the Education Amendments of 1972 resulted in many school administrators defining goals that have had exactly the impact on performance described in Figure 4-4. Briefly, the legislation in Title IX requires that female students must be afforded the same opportunities as males in terms of access to participation in athletic programs. To ensure Title IX compliance, a high school athletic director, for example, might set a target of 38 percent female and 62 percent male participation in school sports programs, because these percentages are based on the school's enrollment. In addition, the athletic director identified three years as the time frame to achieve this goal.

First of all, it is worth noting that this goal is a SMART goal.

- It is *specific*. The Office of Civil Rights advised schools can show compliance with Title IX when opportunities are provided to both sexes proportionate to enrollment. The number of slots on inter-scholastic and intramural sports teams must be in the proportion each season for males and females.

- The goal is *meaningful* enough to be *accepted*. Failure to achieve the goal leaves the school open to legal charges of discrimination and potentially jeopardizes any federal funding the school receives.

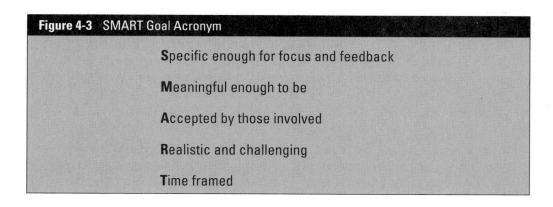

Figure 4-3 SMART Goal Acronym

Specific enough for focus and feedback

Meaningful enough to be

Accepted by those involved

Realistic and challenging

Time framed

Figure 4-4 Why SMART Goals Improve Performance

SMART goals improve motivation and performance in the following ways:

1. Increased attention toward goal-related activities.

2. A higher level of effort demanded by the more difficult goal.

3. The development of action plans to achieve the goal.

4. Increased persistence in the face of obstacles or difficulties.

- The goal is *realistic* and challenging. It does not necessarily require any additional funding for athletics. The existing budget can just be redistributed to ensure equal opportunity to participate for both women and men. Realistically, however, there is a real challenge in somehow continuing to offer the kinds of athletic opportunities historically available to young men and now making the same level of opportunity available to young women.

- The *time frame* is specific in this example. The athletic director has set a three-year period to reach the targeted percentage of participation.

The goals set as a result of Title IX resulted in dramatic improvements in providing young women with the opportunity to participate in sports. And achieving Title IX goals has required school systems to develop action plans and to overcome budgetary, alumni, parental, and other obstacles to find ways to provide young women with greater opportunities to participate in school sports without seriously reducing the opportunities historically enjoyed by young men.

Again, remember that just having a goal may not be enough to motivate and improve performance. Only when goals are SMART are they likely to cause the level of increased attention and effort necessary for improved performance.

Problems with Goal Setting

Four major hurdles must be cleared to fully achieve the potential for improving performance that goals can bring. The first is the problem of competing values. The second involves the challenge of setting goals for outcomes that are difficult to measure. The third is the longer term problem of setting challenging goals without also creating unwanted stress. Finally, the last is the problem of avoiding too narrow a focus in defining goals. Each of the problems potentially can hinder the development of an effective goal-based management system.

Competing Values

There are potential conflicts in managing school and youth sports effectively. Robert Quinn commented that organizational effectiveness is difficult to understand because it is inherently paradoxical. To be effective, an organization must possess

© COMSTOCK IMAGES

attributes that he calls competing values, such as control and flexibility, and internal and external focus (Quinn & Rohrbaugh, 1983). In school and youth sports, these competing values are operating programs that emphasize educational values while simultaneously being successful in terms of wins and losses. It is this paradox that can complicate the goal-setting process.

Consider the Florida high school recruiting violations discussed earlier. Situations like this remind us that sports managers must craft a vision that reflects a shared sense of direction to achieve the cooperation and commitment necessary for his or her athletic program to be successful. These examples of competing values and conflicting goals in high school and youth sports provide a clear message: achieving organizational performance requires the development of a comprehensive network of effective and appropriate goals.

The Measurability Problem

We discussed the importance of goals being specific enough for focus and feedback and emphasized the importance of defining goals in such a way that it becomes possible to measure progress toward the goal. However, for some types of performance, it can be extremely difficult to define goals that are specific enough to be measurable. Every youth or school sports organization wants to offer "quality programs," for example, or to have "effective coaches." Yet at the level of youth and high school sports programs, what is meant by the terms *quality programs* and *effective coaches* can be fairly complicated to explain. In fact, different people might define these two ideas very differently. Despite the difficulty of providing specific, quantifiable goals to define what "quality" and "effective" mean, that is exactly what sports managers must attempt to do. Otherwise, coaches and others throughout the organization will interpret what they are supposed to do based on their own understanding of what these ideas mean. This can result in inconsistency and sometimes conflict across the organization.

www.soccer.org

Recall the point made earlier. Even when it is not feasible to include numbers as part of the goal statement, satisfactory achievement of an activity is an option that helps to ensure goals are measurable. The American Youth Soccer Association (AYSO) provides an example. AYSO defines "quality programs" in youth soccer as programs in which there is open registration rather than tryouts, teams are competitively balanced, everyone plays at least half of the game, coaches emphasize positive instruction, and the emphasis is on sportsmanship and mutual respect rather than winning at all cost. Although only the one aspect of every participant playing at least half of the game is quantifiable, the definition of quality programs is clearly spelled out. Taken together, each of the targeted activities provides a much clearer sense of direction for the members of this organization than the phrase "quality program" ("The Five," 2000).

The Stress Problem

Earlier we emphasized the importance of defining goals so they are realistic but sufficiently challenging to raise motivation and performance. We also cautioned that unrealistic, overly challenging goals can actually discourage those involved, possibly resulting in a decrease in motivation and performance. Another problem with goals that are too challenging, however, is the problem of stress. Some goals are so challenging that they place a high level of pressure on groups and individuals to perform. Over time, these kinds of very demanding goals can result in fatigue and burnout rather than improved performance. They can also cause individuals or groups under pressure to make compromises or cut corners to reach these goals. Sports managers working with youth have a special responsibility not to encourage goals that cause performance-sapping stress.

An example of the burnout problem is the pattern sometimes seen in young athletes who are pushed by themselves, their parents, and their coaches to achieve extremely demanding goals in terms of athletic competition. What we see are young people who practice and compete year round in order to achieve top regional or national rankings in a sport such as tennis or to be selected to an elite regional team such as the Olympic Development Team in soccer. It is not unusual to hear stories of some of these young athletes, especially as they engage in this type of intense pursuit of very difficult goals year after year, eventually taking time off or quitting the sport altogether.

An example of cutting corners or compromising standards can be seen among high school athletic directors (ADs) in meeting what Robert Quinn identified as the competing values. For ADs, these competing values are operating programs that emphasize educational values that are simultaneously successful in terms of wins and losses. Consider the plight of the AD who manages "James R.," a twenty-five-year-old head high school basketball coach and teacher at a Catholic high school in Pennsylvania. In James's first year, his team finished 15–6, but didn't qualify for postseason play. So he responded, "fifteen and six, which to me is average . . . and I was like, we're a Catholic school—we can go and get whoever we want . . . there's no reason we should ever be bad." James then embarked on recruiting efforts, attracting players from Finland and Philadelphia, whose tuitions were paid for by wealthy alumni. This move angered some parents, whose sons were now riding the bench. James responded, "'Well, things happen.' But I should have told her, 'Tell your kid to make a jump shot and I wouldn't have to bring in these kids from Finland.'" In James's defense, he claims, "Everybody knows [about his recruiting exceptional outside players] . . . the people in the office—they were joking, saying like, 'when are the ringers starting?' So everyone knows . . . it's what you've got to do to win. The priests come to the games. They all . . . like winning." According to James, his supervisor, the school AD, has warned him not to get caught recruiting. "Actually I don't know what the [recruiting] rules are," says James. "I have no idea. . . . You can't be overt. You're recruiting, but you can't say that you're doing it . . . and I've never gotten caught" (Bowe, Bowe, and Streeter, 2000, pp. 318, 320–321). So you have an AD who knows his coach is cheating, and his actions in response are to tell him not to get caught. It is not hard to imagine the stress that this manager experiences in trying to meet the expectation of building winning programs.

Given the potential of stretch goals to cause stress, it is the responsibility of the sports manager to ensure that program and organizational goals encourage improved performance and motivation and not stress and burnout. With coaches like James and the expectations of priests and administrators who tacitly condone cheating to produce winning teams, one wonders how long that Pennsylvania Catholic school AD will be on the job.

The Problem of Too Narrow a Focus

An effective goal statement provides direction and focus. But when this focus is too limited, it could cause unwanted results. A goal with too narrow a focus has led to a problem for high schools in terms of staffing certain coaching positions. In an effort to retain personnel, many schools have allowed full-time teachers who are also coaches to step down from coaching but keep their full-time teaching positions. This decision was meant to keep qualified personnel, but as a result schools are then forced to look outside the school to fill what are now only part-time coaching positions. Although these individuals may have some basic qualifications, they often lack the knowledge of basic principles of child development, adolescent growth and development, and information concerning proper training and conditioning (Seefeldt, 1996).

The goal of increasing participation opportunities, coupled with frequent budgetary limitations, has exacerbated the pressures to hire qualified coaches. As a result, more and more schools, and virtually all youth leagues, are forced to rely on insufficiently trained personnel. Bob Scharbert, regional manager of the Miami Metro-Dade Park and Recreation Department, underscores concerns over the training of volunteer coaches: "Would you think of enrolling your children in a school if you knew their teachers had not one bit of training in education? This is what you're doing with your young athletes" ("Kids' Programs," 1997, p. 25A).

To deal with these unwanted results, more and more schools and youth leagues are looking toward independent organizations to provide coaching certification to assure competency in basic coaching and educational skills. As of 2001 thirty-six states required some form of mandatory coaching certification program for high school coaches, twenty-one of which required certification only for those coaches who were not also full-time faculty members ("Summary Chart," 2001). One such organization, the American Sport Education Program (ASEP), offers courses intended to help coaches, administrators, and parents develop expertise in training, conditioning, and motivation. ASEP training and coaching education programs are recommended by many state associations. The NF also offers similar certification programs for administrators.

We have emphasized that goals must be specific enough to provide focus, but the challenge for sports managers is to develop goal statements that do not limit the focus to the point where unwanted outcomes result. The potential problems with defining sports organizational goals are summarized in Figure 4-5.

These problems of measurability, employee stress, and too narrow a focus are significant challenges for managers working to set goals with the greatest performance-enhancing potential. As significant as these challenges may seem, however, they have not diminished the commitment of sports organizations to the development of effective goal-based systems of management.

Guidelines for Creating a Goal-Based Organization

The potential of goals to improve performance is clear, as are the challenges that must be met in setting organizational goals. Effective goals, however, are only part of the solution. To maximize the overall impact of goals on organizational

Figure 4-5 Potential Problems with Goal Statements

- **Competing values:** Operating programs that emphasize competing organizational values can complicate the goal setting process.

- **Measurability:** In some areas performance results are difficult to quantify or measure.

- **Stress:** Goals that are too demanding can result in stress and performance problems over the long term.

- **Too narrow a focus:** Some goals are so concentrated in their focus that they could have unwanted results.

performance and to create a truly goal-based sports organization requires following the four guidelines.

Create a Network of Goals

The concept of a network of goals suggests that specific end results should be identified for every department, team, and individual in a sports organization, and the desired results should contribute to meeting the organization's larger goals. In other words, the individual, department, team, and overall organization goals should build on one another, with the attainment of each goal moving the sports organization closer to achieving its purpose. Figure 4-6 provides an example of such a network, with specific goals for each individual at different levels of a sports organization.

Another way to state this approach is that goals must be consistent and coordinated throughout the sports organization, both top to bottom (vertically) and across every department and level (horizontal). Figure 4-6 illustrates vertical consistency. The school administrator's goal is in line with that of the coaches' goal, which is in line with that of the guidance counselors' goal, and so on. The consistency achieved through a network of goals is an important criterion for a sports organization's success.

The first requirement of a network of goals, then, is that the network be comprehensive, that there be specific goals for every unit and every position in the organization, and that all the goals in the network point in the same direction.

Prioritize Among Specific Goals

A network or total system of goals would be easier to carry out if only one goal were identified for the entire sports organization and if individuals and departments each pursued only that goal. In today's complex and dynamic environment, however, most sports organizations must pursue multiple goals. A high school program might have the goal of high participation numbers for all students, encouraging high academic achievement for all participants while also seeking to keep related costs low. To deal with multiple goals, organizations must learn to prioritize them—they must determine which goal is first in terms of importance, which is second, and so on. Multiple goals make the job of managing sports

Figure 4-6 A Portion of a Network of Goals

School Administrators

Goal = Have 80 percent of students involved in athletics

Coaches

Goal = Athletes have a minimum C grade point average to keep them eligible (or BHAG of B average)

Guidance Counselors

Goal = X percent of athletes awarded scholarships for college

organizations much more complicated. But they are often unavoidable, even in small nonprofit sports organizations, and sports managers need to prioritize them if the organization is to be successful.

Benchmarking: Set Goals from the Outside In

Benchmarking is the process of researching other sports organizations' goals and setting goals that match those of the best managed organizations. With benchmarking, the search is on for role models. For many sports organizations, benchmarking is a simple process, because a competitive sports product will always be measured against other organizations. For every contest, there is a basic measurement tool—the scoreboard. The fact that the scoreboard gives a precise measurement on an organization's effectiveness is clear. However, although the teams that win usually score the most points (or, in sports like cross country, the fewest), the score does not provide examples of how to achieve that measure of success. Other measurements are needed. For example, a basketball coach might research what winning college coaches have as goals. These might be to hold your opponent to less than 40 percent shooting percentage from the field or to shoot 70 percent from the free throw line.

The recent increase of players jumping directly to professional teams and bypassing college has set a new and somewhat problematic benchmarking challenge for high school athletic programs. This has long been an accepted practice in baseball (see Chapter 8 for a discussion of the career path of pitcher Matt Kinney) and ice hockey, with the vast majority of players serving long apprenticeships in the minor leagues. However, the emergence of basketball talents such as Kevin Garnett, Kobe Bryant, and Tracy McGrady, who moved directly from high school to NBA stardom, now may cause high school programs to be evaluated not on how successfully students are prepared to pursue educational goals or to help prepare students for collegiate academic and athletic success, but rather on how well the program can produce players so good that they can become the next Kobe, KG, or T-Mac. This is a benchmarking standard that very few schools will be able to meet, and it can bring significant problems for those programs that seek to meet it.

Such was the case at Dominguez High School in Compton, California, a school in a district that has insufficient funds to buy textbooks for all its students, few functioning libraries, and poorly maintained school buildings. The Compton district is in such disorder that the state appointed administrators to run the schools in lieu of local authorities. But students still want to transfer to Dominguez because the boys' basketball team wins and, thanks to generous funding from Nike for gear and travel expenses, can give them the exposure they seek to advance their basketball careers. These are players looking for a coach to help them make it to the NBA. The Dons, led most recently by 7-foot 1-inch Tyson Chandler, who attracted NBA scouts to games and was selected in the first round of the 2001 NBA draft, as well as those looking to give Chandler money and cars, were coached by Russell Otis, who directed the Dons to the top sport in the 2000 *USA Today* high school hoop poll. Otis was fired in 2001 amid allegations of sexual abuse of a former player, even though many in the local community dismissed the allegations and strongly supported him because of the Dons' success. Compton mayor Omar Bradley opined that the allegations were concocted to get Otis fired by those who wanted to get closer to Chandler to share in his future NBA riches (Wolff & Dohrmann, 2001). Using the goals of national prominence and attracting future NBA stars for benchmarking has unquestionably created more problems for a school that has too many to begin with. However, Dominguez could serve as a negative benchmarking example for other high school and youth sports programs.

Build in Flexibility

Some critics charge that commitment to specific goals results in sports organizations that are too rigid to respond to changes in their particular environments. A focus on specific goals, according to this view, restricts the ability of organizations to be flexible enough to take advantage of unexpected opportunities or unanticipated changes in their environment.

It is difficult to argue against the importance of flexibility. Speed and flexibility, as you recall from Chapter 1, are among the key emerging performance standards. But it is also difficult to argue against the effectiveness of goals in improving organizational performance. The solution to this dilemma is not to eliminate specific goals, but to ensure that the goal system includes the ability to review and revise goals in response to significant changes as they occur.

This kind of flexibility is an important element in assuring that high school and youth sports programs are focused on maintaining educational goals. At Richmond (California) High School, players on the boys' basketball team signed a contract that required them to attend classes, to sit at the front of the classroom, to study at least ten hours a week, and to maintain a 2.0 grade point average (GPA). After a third of the players started skipping classes and getting poor reports from their teachers, the coach, AD, and principal decided to lock the whole team out of practice. "We win basketball games as a team; we lose basketball games as a team," said head coach Ken Carter. "Basketball is just a small part of their lives. I think they got the message. My whole goal was to replace bad habits with good habits" (Kaneshiro, 1999, p. 14C). As a result, the team missed a league game and an alumni exhibition, but after teachers turned in favorable reports, the lockout was lifted.

Flexibility is an essential performance standard for sports organizations competing in the changing environment. The key to flexibility is not to eliminate goals, but to develop a system in which goals are continually reviewed to ensure they make sense in terms of the changing environment. Many programs might seek to punish individuals, but not force them to miss games, or selectively punish individual players. The managers at Richmond High believed that approach would not be effective.

They had to be flexible and bold to make an impact and to help the students meet their goal of academic improvement, and they were willing to lose games to do it.

The practice of creating goal networks, prioritizing among multiple goals, setting goals from the outside in, and building flexibility into the system are all essential elements of an effective goal-based management system. If well implemented, such a system makes possible the kind of performance improvements seen at Richmond High and other goal-based sports organizations.

Epilogue

The need to compete and excel in every segment of the sports industries mandates that organizational vision consist of a clearly defined, fully developed network of goals. Much progress has been made in our understanding and implementation of goal-based systems, but significant challenges remain. It is in finding effective responses to these remaining challenges that sports managers will fulfill what Peter Drucker defines as management's "first responsibility": to give others vision and the ability to perform.

In the case of Danny Almonte, his father, Felipe de Jesus Almonte, and Rolando Paulino, another adult who founded the South Bronx league in which Almonte played, conspired to pass off the fourteen-year old Almonte as two years younger. The boy, who was 5 feet 10 inches tall and threw near 80 mph, pitched a perfect game in 2001 Little League World Series play and led his team to a third place finish. Almonte and the team then enjoyed a parade in New York City and were feted by Mayor Rudolph Guiliani, and the pitcher fielded congratulatory calls from major leaguers Randy Johnson and Ken Griffey, Jr. This incident followed a similar occurrence a decade earlier, when a team from the Philippines was stripped of its title for using ineligible players.

School officials in the Dominican Republic reported that Almonte attended school in Moca in the D.R. until June 15, 2001, which would have prevented him from playing the required six Little League games to qualify for championship eligibility. In response to the incident, Little League officials banned Almonte's father and Paulino from further involvement with Little League, but did not revoke the charter of the league or sanction the other eligible players, allowing them and other South Bronx youths to continue to play. Little League President Stephen Keener also said that Almonte had never attended school since emigrating to the United States in 1999. In addition, D.R. public-records officials brought criminal charges against Almonte's father, threatening to arrest him as soon as he set foot back in the D.R. If convicted, Almonte's father could face up to five years in jail (Cala, 2001; Fritz, 2001).

Although it is clear that all school and youth sports, including Little League and the competitions run by the Florida State High School Athletic Association, and the vast majority of these sports activities are run by responsible adults, the desire to win complicates the sense of vision for high school and youth sports organizations. In the case of the high schools in Florida and the South Bronx league managers, the clearly defined, fully developed network of goals did not exist, were disregarded, or were significantly misdirected. Future managers in these groups will face the task of setting past ills right, providing a corrected vision, and enabling those in the organization to meet these newly established goals.

The first responsibility of management is to give others vision and the ability to perform. Vision can be established by a total network of goals. Goals must satisfy several criteria to ensure that they provide individuals with the kind of focus, direction, and understanding they need to perform well. The acronym "SMART" identifies the key criteria for effective goals. Each should be specific enough for focus, meaningful enough to be accepted, realistic yet challenging, and time framed.

Goals that are "SMART" provide for consistency throughout the organization and a blueprint for effectiveness. They ensure that individuals focus on achieving the organization's goals rather than their own. Effective goals provide a basis for cooperation and teamwork, help coordinate the efforts of different departments, and provide decision makers with the criteria for generating and evaluating options.

In areas where output or performance are not easily measured, defining specific goals is more difficult. In addition, goals that are too challenging can cause stress or burnout for participants.

The most effective goals are part of a larger system or network. First, goals are most effective when they are defined for every task and area of the organization and when they work to move the organization toward its overall purpose. Second, goals must be prioritized. Organizations must have complex, sometimes competing goals and care must be taken to establish priorities, identifying which goals are most important. Third, benchmarking, or setting goals from the outside in, compares the goals of other sports organizations and mirrors what they do to improve performance. Finally, building flexibility into the goals system is essential. Goals must be reviewed and revised to ensure that they are right for the sports organization and its changing environment.

Summary

Peace for Green Valley High School

Don Damone is worried. Lately, it keeps him up at night. Even after a full day of games and classes and the contact with the hyperactive life at school, he sees those images in his head and can't sleep, because he knows it could happen at his school.

Damone is the athletic director at Green Valley High School (GVHS), the home of the Dragons, student population of 1,300 and growing, grades 9–12, located in an affluent suburban area. Wins and losses are not the problem, as GVHS teams are quite strong, winning several recent Class 5A state championships in football, wrestling, field hockey, and softball. Money isn't the problem either, as the recent U.S. economic boom and the general local affluence has left Dragon teams well equipped and facilities well maintained. Staffing isn't an issue either. The salaries paid to coaches by the GVHS district are among the best in the state.

But still Damone is worried. He has seen schools like his, with students who have plenty of parental support and plenty of financial and educational resources, schools that on the surface seem so perfect, devastated by terror, violence, and death. It's those images that keep him up, those images from Columbine and others, students fleeing school buildings, students lying wounded or dead, because fellow students turned on them, gunning them down in the very place they are supposed to be growing, learning, and becoming adults. Everyone in America, stunned by these same images, asked the same question: Why? Why did this happen? Aren't the urban schools the violent places? How could that happen there? Could that happen in my town?

While America wondered and debates raged among the experts, Damone can't sleep because he knows if it could happen at Columbine, it could happen at GVHS. Schools have cliques. Always have, he thinks. The stereotypes persist. The jocks, the druggies, the metalheads, the rich kids with the SUVs, the computer geeks, the band and drama types, and those kids who just sort of occupy the fringes, skirting the walls in the hallways in the hubbub between classes. The "jocks" are the group he knows the best. They are looked on with reverence by some, with disdain by others, and with loathing by a few. Some of this respect is deserved, as some are great kids and very positive role models. But there are others who are jerks—kids who like to fight, who take drugs, who pick on those kids who are weaker or not as "cool" just because they can. Again, nothing new there either.

But times are different. He remembers the stories his father told him about when he and his friends brought guns to school—but these were hunting rifles so they could go deer hunting after classes. They would bring them to the principal's office for safekeeping. But that was in the 1940s, in the sticks, during the war and just after the Depression. Everybody hunted back then; they had to to live. God, he thinks, do that today and just imagine the furor. It actually makes him laugh to think about it. It is like a Norman Rockwell drawing on the cover of the *Saturday Evening Post*. Too quaint. And unreal.

Today there are tensions that didn't exist then, couldn't have. Terrorist attacks, violence in video games, on TV, in movies, and in the dark corners of the Internet. All of a sudden, thinks Damone, it seems that a reasonable response to a petty transgression is to kill someone. Because of this, Damone doesn't find it so aberrant that a kid who was picked on, or felt marginalized, or was just not "cool," would decide to lash out and settle the score with the business end of a semiautomatic handgun purchased by an adult friend at a gun show.

So Damone wants to stop it from happening at GVHS. No Columbine here, he mutters. Damone can't control the Al-Qaeda, video games, TV, movies, or the Internet, but he can do something. He wants to break through the clique mentality. He wants to educate his athletes about their power and the roles in the school. He wants to stop them from picking on other kids, and he wants to protect them and everyone else and stop that one teenager from snapping and pulling the trigger. This isn't about video cameras and metal detectors, he thinks. This is about education.

1. Write a goal statement that helps Damone prevent school violence from occurring. Review the statement to see if it is SMART.

2. Assess your goal statement against the four common problems associated with goal setting.

3. Using each of the guidelines for creating effective goals, list the three activities that might be undertaken to ensure that your goal will be achieved.

Bowe, J., Bowe, M., & Streeter, S. (2000). *Gig: Americans talk about their jobs at the turn of the millennium.* New York: Crown.

Cala, A. (2001, September 5). Almonte's father is charged. *Boston Globe,* p. C3.

Collins, J. C., & Porras, J. I. (1998). Building your company's vision. In *Harvard Business Review on Change.* (pp. 21–54). Boston: Harvard Business School Press.

Drucker, P. (1973). *Management: Tasks, responsibilities, practices.* New York: Harper & Row.

Fonteboa, P. A. (2000, February 23). Foreign exchange. *Miami Herald,* pp. 1D, 8D–9D.

Fritz, M. (2001, September 1). Say it ain't so: Little Leaguer was overage. *Boston Globe,* pp. A1, G7.

Heisman, J. (2000). *Principles of football* (rev. ed.). Athens, GA: Hill Street Press.

Hersey, P., & Blanchard, K. (1981). *Management of organizational behavior.* Englewood Cliffs, NJ: Prentice-Hall.

Kaneshiro, S. (1999, January 14). California coach hopes players have learned their lesson. *USA Today,* p. 14C.

Kids' programs look for volunteers who are both competent and caring. (1997, January 12). *Miami Herald,* p. 25A.

O'Hanlon, T. P. (1982, Spring). School sports as social training: The case of athletics and the crisis of World War I. *Journal of Sport History, 9*(1), pp. 15–25.

Quinn, R. E., & Rohrbaugh, J. (1983). A spatial model of effectiveness criteria: Towards a competing values approach to organizational analysis. *Management Science, 29*(3), pp. 363–377.

Seefeldt, V. (1996). The future of youth sports in America. In F. L. Smoll & R. E. Smith (eds.), *Children in sport: A biopsychosocial perspective* (pp. 423–435). Indianapolis: Brown & Benchmark.

Stedry, A. C. & Kay, E. (1964). *The effects of goal difficulty on performance.* New York: General Electric: Behavioral Research Service.

Summary chart of state coaches education requirements for 2001. (2001). *Blueprint for success: 2001 national interscholastic coaching requirements report.* Champaign, IL: Human Kinetics.

The five philosophies. (2000). American Youth Soccer Organization [online]. Available: http://www.soccer.org/abc/a_5philo.htm.

This is USA Hockey: Administrative organization. (2000). USA Hockey [online]. Available: http://www.usahockey.com/news/thisis.htm.

U.S. trends in team sports. (2001). North Palm Beach, FL: Sporting Goods Manufacturers Association.

What Is the National Federation? (1997). Kansas City, MO: National Federation of State High School Associations.

Wolff, A., & Dohrmann, G. (2001, February 26). School for scandal. *Sports Illustrated,* pp. 72–84.

Zheultin, P. (2001, July 8). Out of bounds. *Boston Globe Magazine,* pp. 10–11,18–22.

References

PHOTO: © COMSTOCK IMAGES

Chapter 5

Decision Making in Sports Organizations

Purpose:

To promote health and physical fitness; to promote lifelong wellness and to heighten awareness of the benefits of exercise and healthful living.

Stakeholders:

Clubs, professional organizations, member clients, personal trainers, club employees, equipment suppliers, media, licensees, corporate partners, retailers, home fitness enthusiasts, medical community, federal, state, and local government.

Size and scope:

- Over 20,000 health clubs in the United States including commercial and nonprofit clubs. Clubs are also based in hospitals, military bases, resorts, living communities, educational institutions, and businesses.
- 30.6 million adult health club members in the United States.
- Estimated $11 billion in health club revenues generated every year with an additional estimated $8 billion spent on fitness-related products and services.
- Estimated $3.4 billion spent on health and fitness equipment annually.
- Thousands of fitness product manufacturers and fitness service providers.

Governance:

- Federal, state, and local regulation.
- Professional organizations and trade groups including International Health, Racquet and Sportsclub Association (IHRSA), American College of Sports Medicine (ACSM), National Strength and Conditioning Association (NSCA), International Association of Fitness Professionals (IDEA), Aerobics and Fitness Association of America (AFAA), and the National Athletic Trainers' Association (NATA).

Inside Look

Bally Undergoes a Makeover

Lee Hillman, incoming president and CEO of Bally Total Fitness, did a careful assessment of the fitness club chain he was about to take over in late 1996. He recognized that Bally was considered the premier name in the discount health club category, yet services were limited and corporate revenues were falling (Iknoian, 1999). Hillman looked at Bally's clubs and recognized that many of the clubs seemed out of date and needed renovation. Others seemed to use their space inefficiently. For example, some clubs had swimming pools that were expensive to maintain and operate but were used by only a small percentage of members. Hillman was also aware that the fitness club industry, which had experienced tremendous growth in the 1970s and early 1980s, had seemed to slow in the 1990s. The health and fitness club business was clearly changing, and Hillman was concerned that unless Bally underwent a makeover, the chain would continue to decline.

Although Americans were more aware of health and fitness issues than ever in the 1990s and health club membership numbers were booming, Bally Total Fitness was in a precarious position. The competition for health and fitness club memberships had intensified. New clubs were entering the market. Corporations had begun to build their own fitness centers for employees, and nonprofit groups like the YMCA were building bigger and better workout facilities and offering more health and fitness programs. Even local recreation departments, schools, and colleges had begun to build workout facilities to meet the fitness needs of their constituents. Consumers seemed eager to join the newest club that offered classes and services featuring the latest fitness trends such as kick boxing, climbing, or spinning. Health and fitness club members had grown more sophisticated in their needs and desires. They expected technologically sophisticated equipment and were attracted by those clubs that offered a wide variety of amenities such as personal trainers, steam and sauna rooms, child-care areas, well appointed locker rooms, and massage therapists. Consumers not only demanded a higher quality workout environment but also expected excellent customer service from their clubs. Interest in health and fitness products and services grew as members sought not only to improve their condition, but to monitor their progress as well. Clubs began to offer body fat percentage testing, blood pressure and heart rate monitoring, and a broad spectrum of health and fitness products ranging from herbal health supplements to the newest workout gear and equipment.

Hillman knew that Bally had made its mark in the industry by positioning itself as a leader in the discount category. They had offered basic programs and services at a good price. Bally had succeeded by adopting a high-volume, low-margin approach to membership. By keeping their membership fee low, they generated a high volume of single club pay-in-advance memberships and had been able to generate $639.2 million in operating revenues in 1996 (Iknoian, 1999). Yet Hillman believed Bally was underperforming. Revenues were falling and costs were escalating. Members were defecting, and Hillman believed Bally's previously successful discount approach no longer offered a strategic advantage in the changing health and fitness club marketplace.

Customers seemed to want more than what Bally had to offer. For Hillman, Bally was clearly losing ground. To him, Bally's "total fitness" promise no longer rang true, and he recognized he would need to make and implement many decisions in order to move the company back to the forefront of the industry.

Introduction

This chapter introduces the health and fitness sports industry segment, which includes not only health and fitness clubs but also several related health and fitness services and spin-off products. Health and fitness clubs and programs can be found in a variety of settings ranging from commercial chain clubs and corporate fitness clubs to nonprofit wellness programs. Within this setting we examine the managerial challenge of decision making and problem solving. Sports managers make hundreds of decisions every day, and their actions not only shape the sports organization, but ultimately influence the organization's ability to fulfill its mission and meet its goals.

The Health and Fitness Industry

Bally Total Fitness is just one example of the types of businesses that make up the very complex health and fitness segment of the sports industry. The International Health, Racquet and Sportsclub Association (IHRSA), the premier trade association of health and fitness clubs, reports that in 1999, 54.8 million Americans, or 22 percent of the total U.S. population, exercised at a health or fitness club, and approximately 30 million of these people were health or fitness club members. IHRSA states that as of January 2001, there were 16,983 clubs in the United States and industry revenues reached over $10.6 billion in 1999.

Three Segments

IHRSA divides health and fitness clubs into three distinct segments: commercial clubs, not-for-profit clubs, and miscellaneous for-profit health/fitness enterprises (see Figure 5-1). Commercial clubs make up the clear majority of all health and fitness clubs. Currently over thirteen thousand such clubs are in the United States (http://www.ihrsa.org), and they consist of investor or member-owned businesses that may either be individually owned entities or part of a larger fitness club chain. Commercially owned clubs operate as for-profit businesses. They pay taxes and may not collect charitable donations. Not-for-profit clubs make up the second largest segment and consist of clubs that are owned and operated by nonprofit organizations such as churches, educational groups, municipal entities, and the military. These clubs do not pay taxes and may conduct fund-raising programs.

Figure 5-1 Types of Health and Fitness Clubs

Segment	Examples of Segment Members	Percentage of All Health Club Memberships
Commercial	Gold's, Bally Total Fitness, Fitness USA Individual entrepreneur-owned club American Club Systems	50 percent of members
Not for Profit	YMCA, Jewish Community Center University or college health club Military fitness center City community center Hospital-based club	37 percent of members
Miscellaneous for Profit	Corporate fitness center Hotel health club Resorts, spas, country clubs	13 percent of members

Source: IHRSA/American Sports Data Health Club Trend Report
(http://www.ihrsa.org).

In the opinion of many people in the health and fitness club industry, the nonprofit status enjoyed by these clubs results in an unfair competitive advantage (*Health & Fitness Business News*, 2000). For example, the local Young Men's Christian Association (YMCA), a nonprofit organization, is planning to construct a new fitness and strength and conditioning room. The YMCA is able to raise money through fund-raising programs to pay for the construction of the new area. They are able to keep their existing membership price because fund-raising provides an independent revenue source for construction. The local commercial fitness club decides to renovate its fitness center to compete with the new facility at the YMCA. The same project is more expensive for the commercial club (they have no tax-free status and must pay taxes on new equipment and materials purchased). The commercial club must bear the cost of the construction or pass the cost on to members in the form of higher membership fees. Additionally, the commercial club will pay property taxes based on the valuation of their property and building, whereas the YMCA, as a nonprofit organization, is exempt from property taxes. Fitness club owners argue that the nonprofit status of their competitors makes it increasingly difficult for the commercial club to compete.

The third group of health and fitness clubs, miscellaneous for-profit health/fitness enterprises, is made up of clubs run as an amenity or secondary part of a business. They include, for example, hotel and motel fitness centers, resort-based clubs, apartment complex fitness centers, retirement community health clubs, and corporate fitness centers.

Characteristics of Health and Fitness Clubs

Traditionally, health and fitness clubs have been thought of as places where members and guests gather to engage in exercise activities that promote the general health and well-being of the individual. Club-based exercise programs and activities may be formal and structured (e.g., an aerobics class or supervised weight training program) or they may be informal and unstructured (e.g., open swim time or walking on the treadmill). Health and fitness clubs have greatly expanded their programs and services in the last decade to include nontraditional activities such as wall-climbing and self-defense classes. They may also include recreational-type activities including sports programs, skills instruction, or tournament and league competition. Many clubs have evolved as fitness or wellness complexes that not only feature traditional facilities such as locker rooms, courts, and aerobics rooms, but also provide retail space, spa components, food service areas, saunas, therapy centers, meeting rooms, and child-care centers. These hybrid top-of-the-line facilities are becoming more prevalent and construction costs for such complexes can easily reach $25 million (Babish, 2001).

Some clubs choose to be highly specialized and emphasize one particular sport or type of activity. Examples of this approach include an aerobics, yoga, or karate studio or a tennis, squash, or sailing club. Despite the health and fitness component of the type of activities offered through these clubs, it may be argued that certain types of clubs should be considered part of the recreation industry as well. Because many people engage in fitness-type activities during their leisure time, crossover between the two sports industry segments is appropriate and necessary. In fact, recreation professionals suggest that the recreation segment of the sports industry (see Chapter 9) necessarily encompass several programs and activities that promote health and well-being.

Perhaps the most well-known specialized health and fitness club in the industry is Gold's Gym. Gold's originally built its reputation by catering exclusively to the serious bodybuilder. The original Gold's Gym in Venice, California, came to be known as the "mecca of bodybuilding" where club members were intensely committed to building bigger and better bodies and to competing in bodybuilding contests (Hoffman, 1998). The member base of Gold's, however, has broadened in the last two decades to include more mainstream athletes such as professional, college, amateur, and recreational athletes who have joined the club to improve their general conditioning, appearance, and performance in sports (Hoffman, 1998).

Some health and fitness clubs emphasize the concept of wellness and focus on the development and general well-being of the entire person. These types of clubs are often community based, and their membership consists of individuals who are members of a particular organization or group. For example, a university or college fitness or wellness center devises programs and services targeted to enhance the health and well-being of the campus community that includes not only students and faculty, but staff, alumni, and administration as well. A hospital-based, senior center-based, or retirement community health and fitness club would necessarily provide programming that would focus on rehabilitation, health care, or prevention of sickness or injury. Such a program may also seek to teach new skills, develop community spirit, and actively engage participants in social settings for the purpose of building relationships, keeping the individual actively involved in life and from becoming depressed or socially isolated.

The corporate fitness center or municipal employee wellness club provides activities designed to appeal to employees and encourage employee participation. Employers see these clubs and services as an investment in their organizations because they recognize that healthy employees are more productive, less likely to be absent from work, and less likely to make sickness- or injury-related insurance claims. The corporate health and fitness center also encourages employee social interaction, a sense of community, employee loyalty, and team building. These clubs can also sponsor health improvement initiatives such as weight control, stress reduction, or smoking cessation programs, thereby improving the general health of the work force.

Spin-Off Organizations, Products, and Services

Although health and fitness clubs are the primary component of the health and fitness industry, several other spin-off organizations by extension must be considered within the scope of this segment. Professional service providers such as personal trainers and instructors or fitness gurus (ranging from Tae Bo's Billy Blanks to diet phenomenon Richard Simmons and actor/fitness celebrities Suzanne Somers and Chuck Norris) may be included in this segment. Health and fitness media aids such as videotapes, television shows, magazines, and books as well as products and supplements such as those distributed by companies like GNC, Joe Weider, or Twin Labs should be included in this ancillary services and products category.

Another large component of the ancillary services and products category is health and fitness equipment manufacturers and distributors. Companies such as Nautilus, Nordic Track, and Cybex develop, manufacture, and sell equipment to clubs. They also sell directly to home users. These consumers represent what is known as the home fitness market. Infomercials on television promote the benefits of the latest home fitness equipment including the newest ab-flexing, thigh-shaping, or tummy-busting gizmo. Home fitness enthusiasts also purchase equipment and products through their local sporting goods store or discount chain where they select from a vast array of equipment and products including ankle weights, pedometers, energy supplements, and cellulite creams. All of the companies that create and market these products are part of the health and fitness industry as well (see Figure 5-2).

In the opinion of some health and fitness professionals, the growth of the industry to include these various spin-off or ancillary products is problematic. Critics of some types of spin-off products such as supplements and home equipment or services question whether these products are little more than shams or schemes to make money. Ionized wristbands, herbal mud wraps, and rolling contraptions with elastic resisting bands may or may not help the user to lose weight, eliminate a paunch around the middle, or create life-affirming energy flow in the extremities. Often the advertising for these products is designed to capitalize on consumers' naïveté and desire for a quick fix to their fitness or wellness problems. Consumers must carefully evaluate the claims made by various fitness product manufacturers and marketers.

Certainly the sale and distribution of health/sports supplements has been very controversial and has generated heated debate in the health and fitness community. Supplements have been designed to offer the individual a physical advantage in athletic performance or create an attractive, healthy well-toned body. These supplements traditionally have not been subject to federal review and approval. Often products come to market without extensive testing or approval, and the medical community has

Figure 5-2 The Health and Fitness Industry

Health and Fitness Clubs

Commercial/Not for Profit/Miscellaneous for Profit

Spin-Offs or Ancillary Services and Products

Personal trainers and instructors

Fitness gurus

Media products (videotapes, magazines, books, television/radio shows)

Health and fitness equipment (Nautilus, Cybex)

Supplements (herbs, Creatine, vitamins)

Products (food scales, pedometer, no-fat energy bars, magnetic bracelets, weight-lifting belts)

Apparel, shoes

---

been very skeptical of the benefits of these products. Some doctors and fitness experts have claimed these products are effective and safe; others have suggested that the use of these products is detrimental to the individual's health. Without extensive research and review of these products, consumers may be taking their lives into their own hands. For example, one herbal supplement, Ephedra, which has been included in many weight loss supplements, has been allegedly linked to several deaths, yet is still commercially available. The lesson for consumers is clear. Products that claim to help the user lose 20 pounds in ten days, develop six-pack abs overnight, or slow the aging process should be viewed with skepticism. Health and fitness industry professionals have come to realize the popularity of these types of products and the power of consumers' desires to gain every advantage available to them in their quest for fitness, and they will undoubtedly continue to wrangle with the ethical issues of developing and distributing products that may not only be ineffectual, but detrimental to the health and well-being of the consumer.

Because of their shared interest in health and well-being, the health and fitness industry segment is often considered to be connected to the sports medicine segment. Sports medicine professionals including doctors, therapists, certified athletic trainers, psychologists, and surgeons play a critical role in the diagnosis and treatment of sports-related injury. The sports medicine segment is a medical specialization and is therefore most closely allied with the medical community, yet because of their common concern, the human body and human performance, the two segments (sports medicine and health and fitness) are linked. This chapter focuses primarily on the health and fitness industry segment. Additional information about the allied sports medicine segment can be found through the American College of Sports Medicine (http://www.acsm.org).

Chapter 5: Decision Making in Sports Organizations

Future Trends

Although the health and fitness industry has expanded to include each of these various spin-off components, American Sports Data (ASD) suggests that the fitness phenomenon in the United States actually peaked in 1990 (Carr, 2000). ASD president Harvey Lauer points to a trend of declining exercise participation rates in the last decade as evidence that there may be some erosion in Americans' commitment to fitness (Carr, 2000). Club memberships have risen slightly during the same period, but an astounding number of Americans have engaged in fad dieting and become increasingly sedentary, possibly due to the pervasiveness of cable television, technology, and home computers (O'Sullivan, 2000). For Lauer, the issue is not Americans' understanding of the importance of exercise, fitness, and good health, it is finding ways to translate that understanding into permanent lifestyle change (Carr, 2000).

Despite the fact that club membership has seemed to plateau, the industry has remained vital and dynamic. New hybrid fitness and wellness centers continue to attract users, and the many spin-off enterprises already discussed have fueled growth and expansion of the industry. The development of these spin-off or ancillary products and services has contributed to the expansion of the definition of a health and fitness club beyond just "a place to work out." The club has now become the health and fitness product retailer, the social center, and the health and fitness educator. Club staff members have become beauty consultants, child-care providers, social directors, fitness counselors, and personal shoppers. Health and fitness club managers have recognized that this approach has been successful in meeting customer demands for more convenience and flexibility, better technology, safer equipment, and more products and services designed to help them become more physically fit. This approach has also allowed them to reach new markets and develop new sources of revenue to ensure the stability of their businesses.

It is likely that health and fitness club managers will continue to follow this path. Certainly they will continue to promote healthy lifestyles, but they will also remain committed to developing new products and services that will extend the role and definition of the health and fitness industry so they may better position themselves to achieve their own organizational goals.

Decision Making in Sports Organizations

For health and fitness industry managers like Bally's Lee Hillman (introduced at the beginning of this chapter), this basic question of how to position the organization to succeed is at the core of every business decision. Once the organization has defined the goals that determine its direction, the manager must make decisions that move the organization closer to its goals. We've defined management as responsibility for an organization's achievement of its goals. Success in exercising this responsibility is determined to a large degree by the effectiveness of the manager's decisions. Just as Frederick Taylor tried to understand how a task could be organized to make it as productive as possible, we consider here how decisions can be made to make them as effective as possible.

Hillman made three key decisions as he began his efforts to return Bally to the forefront of the health and fitness club industry. He decided to revamp the Bally physical plant, he decided to expand Bally's product offerings, and he decided to venture into e-commerce. Each decision played an important part in Hillman's plan to revitalize Bally. Only three years after Hillman took control of Bally, the club demonstrated remarkable success. Revenues were up by about $100 million, and in an independent survey taken in 1999, nine out of ten people said they think of Bally first when they think of fitness (Iknoian, 1999). Membership increased. Strategic partnerships were created and sales figures rose. The number of clubs rose to 350 and the chain moved into several new states. Bally currently considers itself to be the largest and only nationwide commercial operator of fitness centers in the United States and reports that the club now has over four million members in twenty-seven states and Canada.

An examination of these three important decisions demonstrates how each decision played an important role in Bally's eventual success. Each decision also provides specific evidence of just how important the decision-making process is to the sports organization and its achievement of its stated goals.

- In 1996 Bally offered only traditional fitness and exercise programs based at clubs. Products and services were distributed on site only, and members needed to be physically present on site in order to utilize their membership. Hillman visited several clubs and found that many facilities were aging rapidly and were out of date. Physical plants were obsolete and overhead costs were growing. Some facilities were aesthetically unappealing. Hillman was concerned that the facilities were not attractive enough to attract new members or keep existing members coming back. He knew something needed to be done with Bally's physical plants, and he reviewed his options. He could close all the clubs and rebuild. He could make small cosmetic changes. He could target reconstruction efforts on those clubs that were the most profitable. He could renovate the clubs on a predetermined schedule. He could do nothing. His first decision was that something had to be done to create a uniformly attractive and efficient physical plant for the Bally chain. He began by creating a master plan for addressing the physical plants of all Bally's clubs. His plan would involve closing some clubs. He would expand and upgrade others. He devised plans for newer and more efficient clubs and set out to construct additional clubs based on the new design in several new markets. As he reviewed each club and made a decision about how to proceed, he kept in mind his initial plan: to create efficient and attractive physical plants to support the operation of Bally's clubs. His first decision to address physical plant issues proved to be a resounding success. Membership increased and retention rates improved. With the new design and more space, clubs were now able to operate more efficiently while controlling overhead costs.

- Bally offered only standard on-site exercise and fitness programs when Hillman arrived in 1996. Hillman decided that Bally's promise of "total fitness" was inaccurate. He decided that one of the best ways to halt Bally's declining revenue problem was by expanding Bally's programs and services. He decided to create off-site opportunities for potential consumers by creating a new line of nutritional supplements in 1997. He also made these products available through a new Bally website. In the first year, $9.3 million in sales were realized from the supplements. By 1999 the line included forty-four items and sales continued to grow. Hillman recognized that he would need additional revenue streams beyond membership fees and recognized the booming interest in supplements. By making these products available at sites other than Bally Clubs, Hillman could reach the market of non-Bally members.

- Hillman was concerned with the decline in Bally's membership roles. He needed to find new ways to contact potential members and to encourage them to buy products and to come to the club. He was certain that once they had entered the facility, his staff could sell them a membership. Hillman decided to capitalize on the traffic generated by visits to the Bally website. He added new features to the site and instituted a program whereby anyone who visited the website could print out a free guest pass. In 1998 over 25,000 guest passes were printed and $3.5 million in membership sales were realized.

After reviewing each of these decisions and seeing them within the context of a larger vision for Bally's success, it is easy to see it is the decision making process that drives the operation of the sports organization. Decisions are what move the organization either closer to or further away from goal attainment. In effect, the sports manager is constantly engaged in the decision-making process, and his or her ability to make the right decisions determines the success of the organization.

The Decision-Making Process

Decision making is the process of selecting and implementing alternatives consistent with a goal. It is a series of activities that begins with defining the purpose or goal of the decision and then involves developing and evaluating alternatives, selecting and implementing the optimal alternative, and monitoring the results to ensure that the decision goals are achieved. This entire process, from setting the decision goal to making sure the goal has been achieved, is called decision making. There are a variety of ways to describe the activities in the decision-making process. They can be reduced in number to three or four, or increased to eight or more. Virtually every decision model, however, includes in one form or another the phases or steps shown in Figure 5-3. Each of these phases of the decision process is worth considering in greater detail.

Figure 5-3 Steps in the Decision-Making Process

- Define the goals of the decision.

- Gather relevant information.

- Generate the broadest possible range of alternatives.

- Evaluate the alternatives for strengths and weaknesses.

- Select the optimal alternative.

- Implement the decision and monitor it for effectiveness.

Step 1: Define the Decision Goals

The purpose of any management decision is to move the organization closer to the attainment of its goals. When we speak of the "goal of a decision," we mean the need to establish, in very specific terms, just what the decision is intended to accomplish. As we discussed in Chapter 4, goals that are specific provide a target to aim for and make feedback possible. In that sense, decision making is like any other activity. Performance is enhanced when the decision process itself is in pursuit of specific goals. When a goal is defined, decision making has the critical focus necessary to ensure that the decision will actually move the organization closer to attaining the goal(s). Also, specific goals enable feedback to be provided in progress reports.

In addition to focus and feedback, there are benefits in defining specific goals that are unique to the decision process. Specific decision goals, for example, provide criteria for focusing the information search, for determining which alternatives might be most relevant, and for evaluating the relative strengths and weaknesses of each alternative. When a university fitness center set the goal of improving safety for students using free weights, it eliminated the alternative of leaving the fitness centers open 24 hours a day. It would be impossible to provide 24-hour supervision of the area and the lifters, a condition required to facilitate safe lifting. Specific decision goals also provide the standards for evaluating the effectiveness of the decision itself once the selected alternative is actually implemented. Only with specific decision goals can the organization evaluate whether the decision is actually moving it closer to those goals.

Step 2: Gather Information

Once the decision goals are clear, the next step is to gather as much information as possible relevant to them. Clearly defined decision goals help focus the information search. At the community senior center, the fitness club director was asked to provide aerobic exercise programming. She needed to decide what types of classes to offer that would be most beneficial to her clients. She recognized that she would need to provide aerobic activities that would be safe for seniors and appropriate for their abilities. She began to search her health and fitness programming resource guides in an attempt to generate programming ideas for consideration. In the first guide, she discovered aerobic exercise alternatives including step aerobics, kick boxing, and cross-country skiing. Were these types of programs viable alternatives?

This is a very important point. What she needed to do was focus on information relevant to health and fitness programming for seniors, an important advantage to goal-based decisions. In an age when the amount of information available to management is expanding rapidly, clearly defined decision goals allow managers to set boundaries on their information search to target the most relevant information. Efficiency in gathering information is essential, but it is important to gather as much information as possible before moving too quickly through the rest of the decision process. Quality decisions require quality information. Before our senior center fitness club director can make an appropriate decision, she must not only have good information about appropriate programming for seniors, but she must also have a sense of the physical abilities and interests of her clients as well as information about available facilities, resources, and equipment. For example, she might decide to begin a water aerobics class for her senior clients that would be offered at 9:30 P.M. in the community pool. Certainly this type of aerobic activity would be an appropriate component of a senior fitness or wellness program, yet the program would be doomed to fail if her seniors were afraid of the water, did not like to swim, or were unable to secure transportation to the community pool at that hour. If she had obtained good information about the lifestyles of her senior clients, she may have realized that a 7:30 A.M. program would attract more seniors than a program held at night. The lesson of this example is clear. Having the right information on which to base a decision is absolutely critical to the effectiveness of the decision.

Barriers and One Solution

A variety of barriers can prevent management from having the information needed to make effective decisions. Managers often feel they lack the time to fully research important information. Some managers consciously try to avoid becoming overwhelmed by information especially during the crunch time of decision making. Consider the example of a health or fitness club manager being asked to purchase new fitness equipment. There are several brands and types of equipment, and any manager could spend hundreds of hours researching different models and new technology. Additionally, the manager may be busy with the daily operation of the club and feel he or she just doesn't have the time to read and learn about all the new equipment on the market or meet with every sales representative who wants to demonstrate a new exercise apparatus. The manager might also feel ill prepared to digest or interpret the available information about the equipment. As a result, the manager might tend not to ask others for information or recommendations for fear of appearing uninformed or not qualified to make a good decision.

To understand the enormity of the challenge of equipping a health and fitness club, we need only go to a health or fitness equipment retail outlet and examine the wide variety of options available to the home fitness enthusiasts. Literally hundreds of types of stationary bikes, treadmills, and stair climbers are available. The salesperson will be only too happy to give complete demonstrations of the equipment while pointing out the variety of features available on each model. Sales staff will share countless brochures, complicated diagrams, fitness equipment reviews, and catalogs with consumers. All of this information is designed to help home fitness enthusiasts make a good decision about what to buy. Sometimes what results is information overload. Consumers can't remember everything that was said about what piece of equipment. They don't understand the differences between an upright and recumbent bike, nor are they certain of the different features available on the electronic heart rate monitor control panel. Consumers view the promotional video, study the brochure, and talk to the salesperson again, but they are still not sure if they have accurate information or what that information means. Because our consumers are eager to start their home fitness program this weekend and they don't have any more time to put into their search, they buy the first exercise bike they see at the next sporting goods store they walk into. In this scenario, it might be argued that information gathering contributed little more than frustration to the decision-making process.

One approach to overcoming these information barriers is called "management by walking (or wandering) around," or MBWA. Management theorists Tom Peters and Nancy Austin suggest that managers in effective companies get the information they need simply by walking around, by getting out of their offices and talking with people—employees, suppliers, other managers, and customers (Peters & Austin, 1985). MBWA enables managers to avoid both appearing uninformed and having to frantically search out essential information when an unexpected decision suddenly needs to be made. Through MBWA, managers maintain a constant flow of information, and they keep that information continuously updated.

In the case of our fitness club manager who is faced with the daunting task of purchasing new equipment, she might engage in MBWA by talking with clients and asking them what features they would like in new equipment. She might also talk with other club managers at professional meetings, where she might also meet informally with suppliers and discuss new industry innovations. Many managers admit that for all of the reasons presented—but time and pride chief among them—MBWA isn't easy at first. But they've also found that MBWA is a powerful tool for making sure they are hearing what they need to hear, so their decisions reflect the broadest possible range of information.

Decision Step 3: Generate Alternatives

In the third phase of decision making, the challenge is to not move too quickly to a consideration only of the obvious alternatives. In this era of accelerating change and global competition, the obvious alternatives, the traditional solutions to organizational problems, have become increasingly ineffective. Innovative alternatives need to be generated, and as this need intensifies, creativity becomes an ever more critical ingredient in the decision-making process.

The Importance of Creativity

For the purpose of this discussion, we describe creativity as the ability to discover relations between things that were formerly considered unrelated (Sternberg, 1985). The main barrier to creativity, according to researchers, is our lack of flexibility in the way we view things. We tend to place the elements of our experience in fixed categories. The longer we operate using these categories, and the longer they work for us, the more difficult it is for us to see beyond them. If we place two elements in unrelated categories, over time it becomes more and more difficult for us to relate them.

Take, for instance, the child-care problem that faced so many health and fitness clubs so many years ago. Mothers with young children often suggested that because of their role as primary caregiver, they were unable to utilize their memberships fully. They were unable to leave their small children at home and go to the club to work out. It was often difficult to find a babysitter, especially during school hours or weekday evenings when they hoped to use the club. As a result, many mothers with young children would use the facility sporadically and might even allow their membership to lapse. Originally, health and fitness club managers saw this as a barrier to membership of mothers and other child caregivers. Eventually, managers came to realize they could capitalize on the situation not only by offering on-site quality child care, but also by offering programs that catered to young children (e.g., toddler swimming lessons or gymnastics and mother and baby fitness classes).

Over the years, a number of techniques have emerged to help loosen up categories and patterned thinking, to enhance creative capacity. The most familiar of these techniques is *brainstorming*, a group technique for generating the broadest possible range of alternatives. The rules for brainstorming are summarized in Figure 5-4.

These rules reflect two basic realizations about the creative process. The first is that creativity is very often a synergistic process. One person's ideas can spark ideas in someone else's mind. The rules emphasizing quantity, strangeness, and piggybacking ideas are intended to encourage the synergistic potential of the group. These rules also reflect the fact that judgment or critics tend to restrict the flow of ideas. It takes courage to suggest an unusual idea, especially in a group setting. The knowledge that our ideas might be judged or criticized is usually enough to convince us not to risk sharing them. The no-judgments-allowed rule helps create a climate that enhances the willingness of group members to risk sharing their ideas, again increasing their potential for developing innovative alternatives.

Step 4: Evaluate Alternatives

When the broadest possible range of realistic alternatives has been identified, the focus of the decision process shifts to evaluating those alternatives, to identifying the strengths and weaknesses of each option. Perhaps no dimension of the decision process has been as well developed as the evaluation phase.

Quantitative Approaches for Evaluating Alternatives

One set of methods used to evaluate decision alternatives has been found to be extremely useful in situations where all of the variables relative to the decision goals and alternatives can be expressed in numbers. These are called *quantitative approaches* because they use mathematical and statistical techniques to analyze the decision alternatives.

Linear programming. In Chapter 2 we discussed *linear programming*, a decision sciences technique that allows the decision maker to use mathematical formulas to analyze and evaluate the full range of decision options before committing to one option. In the health and fitness industry, a club manager might use linear programming to decide how many staff members will be needed on a particular day, given the number of clients expected, the areas of the club to be utilized, and the types of activities that will be held on a particular day.

Break-even analysis. Another common quantitative evaluation technique, called *break-even analysis*, is used to determine how many units of a product (or service) must be sold at what price for the producer or service provider to at least break even, given the cost of producing or providing that item or service. The break-even point occurs when revenues from the sale of a product or service exactly equal the cost of producing and selling it. For example, a club manager can decide exactly how many personal training sessions he must sell before he begins to make money. The break-even point (BEP) for a product or service can be calculated whenever three things are known: fixed costs for operation, variable costs per unit, and the selling cost per unit (see Figure 5-5). Break-even analysis allows the decision maker to understand clearly the financial impact of various alternatives before deciding which one to pursue.

Decision tree analysis. Another technique for evaluating decision options is called the *decision tree*. In some decisions, certain important information can't be known ahead of time. For example, the senior center fitness director is trying to select a date for the club's annual season-opening member guest golf tournament. It is impossible to know for certain what the weather will be on any given day, so probability estimates about the likelihood of cold weather or rain can be made based on current forecasts and weather data from previous years. Decision tree analysis uses probability estimates to help compare various alternatives.

Consider the case of the club manager trying to choose between the construction of a climbing wall and the purchase of a dek hockey rink. The dek hockey rink would be less expensive to buy and could be used by more people at a time, but would it generate as much revenue as a climbing wall? But why construct the more expensive climbing wall if there is limited interest in rock climbing among the membership? The manager would also like to make the new facility available to nonmembers and expects to charge nonmembers a higher user fee than members. The manager would gather information from other clubs and talk to members in an attempt to estimate what percentage of the time each facility will be used and by whom. It is only by estimating patterns of use that the manager will be able to evaluate each facility and attempt to determine which would be more profitable to the club. Of course, this kind of analysis is only as accurate as the probability estimates, which depend on the quality of research undertaken and the amount of experience the manager has had with the business being estimated. A manager who has had a great deal of experience with dek hockey rinks or climbing walls is in a much better position to make appropriate probability estimates of use than a manager unfamiliar with either facility. Nevertheless, quantifying expectations enables the manager to evaluate alternatives in a way that is extremely objective and would not otherwise be possible.

Qualitative Techniques for Evaluating Alternatives

Not all decisions involve factors that can be easily quantified or measured. For example, suppose a decision has to be made about which employee should be promoted to fitness program director. Imagine there are two excellent internal candidates for this job and management needs to assess the strengths and weaknesses of both. When quantitative techniques seem inappropriate, the manager can turn to the T-chart, one of the most widely used qualitative decision-making tools.

T-Chart. One tool used to compare alternatives in this kind of situation is the T-chart, which gets its name from the T-shaped format used to list and compare alternatives. A T-chart for the decision described here is shown in Figure 5-6.

Figure 5-5 Determining Cost Per Session for Personal Trainer Using Break-Even Analysis

Fixed Costs (fixed costs for operation—items like rent, the cost of equipment, utilities, legal—costs that will be there whether one training session is produced/sold or two hundred sessions are produced/sold)

Rent for new training room area	$ 6,000
Utilities	$ 1,000
Equipment and room renovation cost	$ 2,500
Legal/Insurance	$ 500
Total fixed cost	$10,000

Variable Costs (variable costs per unit/session, such as labor and material costs that will vary depending on how many units/sessions are produced)

Trainer's salary	$20 per session
Supplies	$ 2 per session
Total cost per session	$22 per session

Selling Price Per Unit/Session

$50 per unit/session

Break-Even Analysis

$$\frac{\text{Total fixed cost}}{\text{Selling price} - \text{Variable cost per unit}} = \text{BEP (units/sessions)}$$

$$\frac{\$10,000}{\$50 - \$22} = 357 \text{ (units/sessions)}^*$$

*In order for the club owner to break even (where revenues equal costs) on personal training services, he or she would have to sell 357 sessions per year. To make a profit, he or she would have to sell more than 357 sessions a year.

The characteristics compared in T-charts aren't like the costs or the number of items in quantitative-type decisions. They are more qualitative or subjective in nature. They might include communication and organizational skills, for example, which are not easily expressed in numbers. The value of the T-chart is that it puts on paper the qualitative considerations that otherwise would have to be juggled in the decision maker's brain. The T-chart registers all the factors the manager is attempting to consider in a decision and freezes action so each factor can be considered carefully. In the example in Figure 5-6, the T-chart allows the decision maker to compare the two job candidates on each factor relevant to the decision. As with the earlier phases of the decision process, the emphasis in the assessment phase is on not moving too quickly to select an alternative. Like the other phases,

Figure 5-6 T-Chart for Use In Hiring a Fitness Program Director

Evaluation Criteria	Candidate A	Candidate B
Time with company	Five years	Ten years
Education	Bachelor's degree	Master's degree
Interpersonal skills	Excellent	Good
Management skills	Weak organizer Excellent motivator	Strong planner Detail oriented
Knowledge of fitness	Extensive	Extensive
Certifications/ Professional organizations	CPR, IHRSA	CPR, ACSM NASPE, IHRSA
Other	Creative programmer	

the evaluation phase is an attempt to impose a discipline on the decision maker to ensure that appropriate evaluation criteria are brought into focus and each alternative is considered carefully.

Step 5: Select the Optimal Alternative

The fifth phase of the decision process is to select the alternative that comes closest to satisfying the decision goal. Nobel laureate Herbert Simon was among the first to recognize that there is no such thing as a perfect decision. Simon uses the term *bounded rationality* to describe the fact that no matter how systematic the manager has been, in most cases, it is impossible to have all of the relevant information, to generate every possible alternative, or to comprehend fully the advantages and disadvantages of each option. Furthermore, because most decisions are attempting to achieve a variety of goals, a single alternative will rarely satisfy all of them. These limitations of the decision process "bound" or reduce the rationality of the decision. Recognizing these realities about decision making, Simon coined the term *satisfice* to describe the way alternatives really are selected (Simon, 1957). According to Simon, about the best we can do in making a decision is to select the best available alternative, recognizing our lack of time, the lack of complete information, and the variety of goals most decisions are attempting to satisfy. Satisficing, says Simon, is the way most selections of alternatives are actually made.

Health and fitness instructors have found that their clients often satisfice when it comes to making decisions about their own health and fitness programs. For example, a typical client has a variety of responsibilities including work, family, and social obligations. For example, consider the variety of personal and professional

obligations facing Bill on Friday. His calendar is filled with a late afternoon meeting at work, family events, and social obligations that all occur simultaneously, each involving separate goals (e.g., late afternoon meeting with sales team to prepare a new strategy for a sales pitch to a client; attend daughter's first softball game; mow the lawn; attend son's youth baseball game; eat a healthy dinner; attend evening wedding and reception of work associate; complete a scheduled 5:30 P.M. workout with personal trainer at fitness club). Because it would be virtually impossible for Bill to achieve all of the desired outcomes, he will have to satisfice by selecting an alternative that is not ideal but is the best one available. His decision might be to cancel the workout, forgo the wedding, and put off the yard work in favor of attending the late afternoon meeting and then grabbing a fast-food meal on the way to the youth baseball/softball complex to watch the children's games.

Bill's personal trainer recognizes that for many of his clients, sticking to a health and fitness regime is often compromised as part of the process of satisficing. Certainly the optimal healthful alternative for Bill would be to work out with his personal trainer and eat a healthy home-cooked meal as prescribed in his diet plan. Most health and fitness professionals recognize that clients often satisfice when it comes to personal fitness choices. For that reason, health and fitness professionals have developed a variety of strategies to help counter the negative effects of satisficing when it comes to personal fitness. In an effort to address clients' lack of time, personal trainers might offer early morning or late evening sessions in an attempt to minimize work conflicts. To address the lack of information problem, a club might provide a brochure or newsletter that features articles about best fast-food choices for healthy eating. As a result of these types of efforts, Bill might have scheduled a 6:30 A.M. appointment with his personal trainer and would have purchased a salad and a plain grilled chicken sandwich rather than a double-sized cheeseburger and fries at the fast-food chain. Although Bill still has to satisfice (ideally, he would have chosen his 5:30 P.M. usual workout and his healthful home-cooked meal), his personal trainer and club can help him to make better if not ideal fitness decisions when planning his Friday.

The challenge for Bill and for managers is not to compromise too easily, but to ensure that the alternative selected is truly the best available, given the bounded rationality of the decision-making situation. As Simon suggests, satisficing is not only how most decisions are made, but is necessary given the reality of time and information constraints.

Step 6: Implement the Decision and Monitor It for Effectiveness

All too often, especially with difficult decisions, we tend to consider the decision process complete once we have selected the optimal alternative. There is often a definite sense of relief once the decision has been made. However, all the effort invested in the decision process will have been wasted unless the alternative selected is put into action effectively. A decision is just a choice until it is acted on.

Lee Hillman decided to expand Bally by creating new lines of fitness products, but the chain's effective implementation of the decision is what led to a dramatic increase in profits. Quality products had to be developed. Manufacturers were secured. Packaging and marketing materials were created and new channels of distribution both at Bally's clubs and online were put into place. If Bally had not implemented a comprehensive strategy to develop and bring these products to market, Hillman's decision would have failed.

Effective implementation, however, does not complete the action phase of the decision-making process. Once the choice has been implemented, the decision must be monitored to ensure that the alternative put into action is in fact moving the organization closer to its goals. As we said at the beginning of the chapter, moving the organization closer to its goals is the ultimate purpose of every decision, and this cannot be assumed to be happening just because the decision has been implemented. An organization that attempts to improve performance by implementing a particular management approach, for example, needs to evaluate how well that approach is actually meeting the goals of that decision. Only when the monitoring phase confirms that the decision goals have been achieved is the decision-making process finally complete.

The Decision Maker

As important as the decision process is, another key variable determines the effectiveness of decisions: the decision maker. The decision maker is not a neutral factor. Decisions reflect the person making them as much as the process by which they are made. A number of dimensions of the decision maker are worth considering.

Intuition and the Impact of Experience on Decisions

As part of his research on decision making, Simon studied chess masters to try to understand how they are able to consistently make high-quality decisions when there are so many variables and so little time. What Simon discovered is that chess masters do not use a purely logical or rational decision process of the type that has been presented. It would be virtually impossible for them to evaluate systematically the consequences of each of the available alternatives at every point in a chess match, especially in the very brief period of time allowed between moves. Based on his observations, Simon concluded it must be "intuition" that allows chess masters to select such effective alternatives in so little time (Simon, 1979). For Simon, however, intuition is not merely a "hunch" or a "gut instinct"; it is ability based on extensive experience. Intuition based on years of experience allows the chess master or the veteran manager to select and implement the most appropriate course of action without exhaustively evaluating each alternative (Agor, 1986). In management, as in sports, the experienced player tends to make the better decisions.

Personality, Values, and Power

Like any behavior, a person's decision making reflects his or her personality, values, and power. Personality may be interpreted as the individual's consistent pattern of behavior. An *aggressive personality*, for example, is revealed in a consistent pattern of risk taking and confrontation. Similarly, the *perfectionist personality* emerges from a pattern of constantly pursuing the one best way, the only right answer. The *impulsive personality*, in contrast, shows a pattern of leaping to conclusions and preferring action to analysis (Etzioni, 1989).

We can reasonably expect that when confronted with all of the same goals and information, and even sharing all of the same experiences, each different personality might actually decide very differently. The aggressive personality might be expected to make decisions in ways that some might find argumentative or confrontational. The perfectionist might postpone taking action, preferring to seek the ideal alternative. The impulsive personality might hurry through the decision process, just to have it over. For this reason, managers must recognize the powerful influence of personality in decision making and minimize any negative effects a decision maker's personality might have on the effectiveness of the decision process.

Beyond personality, decisions tend also to reflect the values of the decision maker, those things that are personally most important to him or her in the decision context. Paul Grymkoski, president and international director of Gold's Gym Franchising, Inc., and Rich Minzer, associate director of franchising and gym operations at the Gold's Gym headquarters in Venice, California, are two such managers whose personal values impact their decisions. Both Grymkoski and Minzer value the immensely personal nature of individual fitness. They value the creation of fitness programs and services that are client centered and maintain only the highest standards for service quality, product excellence with an underlying commitment to assuring safety for all members. Because of these values, both men only work with vendors whose primary concern is helping every club create the best possible workout environment for members (Hoffman, 1998). Because of their distrust of fitness equipment companies that set and emphasize sales quotas for their representatives and encourage sales over all else, Minzer and Grymkoski have consciously made the decision to deal only with companies that share their commitment to personal attention to clients and the provision of quality fitness programs and services.

Another example of how the values and beliefs of the decision maker influence the decision-making process may be found in the debate over the sales of health and fitness supplements. Some clubs and personal trainers have refused to sell or promote the use of Creatine and androstenedione (the supplements that came to national attention in 1999 when professional baseball player and home run hitter Mark McGwire publicly acknowledged his use of the supplements) because of possible long-term negative effects of use, but other clubs and individuals have chosen to continue to distribute these controversial substances. The decision to halt the sales of these substances that have been banned by some professional sports leagues and governing bodies is made by some personal trainers and health club managers when the act of selling the products runs counter to their own personal values and belief systems. For others, the decision to stop selling these products will only be made when irrefutable evidence is presented that the use of these substances causes real and serious long-term damage to the human body. The same issues have arisen in the area of tanning. Some club managers feel comfortable providing tanning services for clients. In fact, 9.7 percent of clubs in an IHRSA survey reported that tanning bed rental was one of their top five revenue-producing programs (http://www.ihrsa.org). Other club managers have decided not to offer tanning services based on their concerns about a possible connection between tanning bed use and skin cancer. For each individual decision maker, personal values and beliefs strongly color and influence both the goals and outcomes of the decision process.

Finally, there is the issue of power. Some alternatives, including sometimes the best alternatives, are beyond the power of the decision maker to implement. Managers, especially team leaders and middle managers, often do not have the power to implement these changes. Unfortunately, experience has shown us that the managers with the best understanding of the situation and often the ability to devise the best course of action do not always have sufficient power to ensure the best alternative is selected and implemented. Like experience, personality, and values, the power of the decision maker strongly influences the effectiveness of the decision-making process. Consider the college student who has worked at the YMCA reception desk on nights and weekends for several years. Based on her front-line experience and knowledge of members' concerns, she would like to institute a program where members needing squash partners register at the reception desk every week. She would pair registered singles, set up matches, and then call each registrant to confirm arrangements. She believes this service would greatly benefit members and would give her something productive to do on Monday evenings when things are slow at the registration desk. She presents her idea to the manager, who then tells her he does not want her to do anything more than greet members, scan identification cards, and answer the phone during her shifts. Although her idea may have great merit, she has no power to make a decision to implement the plan.

Groups and Decision Making

Organizations are built on the need for people to engage in cooperative efforts to get things done. Frequently, the effectiveness of decisions hinges not on the decision maker's ability to take direct action, but on how successfully he or she involves other people in making and implementing the decision. Typically, this includes both those whose input would improve the decision and those whose commitment is needed for the decision to be effectively implemented.

The Advantages and Disadvantages of Involving Others

Although group involvement can improve the decision-making process, there are both advantages and disadvantages to group-based decisions. A summary of these is shown in Figure 5-7.

Unquestionably the involvement of others, no matter how great the potential benefits, complicates the decision-making process. Anyone who has ever been involved in a group project or committee has experienced firsthand the difficulty of actually making a group decision. The price of not involving others in decisions can also be high, however, particularly in terms of lack of valuable input, understanding, and commitment to the decision from them.

Figure 5-7 Advantages and Disadvantages of Group Decision Making

Advantages of Involving Others in Decisions

- A better understanding of the reasons for the decision

- A greater commitment to making the decisions work

- Greater creative potential

- More careful evaluation of alternatives

Disadvantages of Involving Others in Decisions

- Increased time spent in discussion at each stage of the process

- Difficulty in reaching a consensus

- Creation of winners and losers as suggestions are reviewed and adopted

- Compromise rather than selection of the optimal alternative

---

Levels of Involvement in the Decision Process

Management theorist and consultant Victor Vroom and his associates have described five levels of involving others in decision making (Vroom & Yetton, 1973). These levels are shown in Figure 5-8.

In Vroom's model (Vroom, 1973), a decision about what to include in a report summarizing a work group's activities for the year would require very little participation, if any. Participation is probably not essential for identifying the group's accomplishments, and there is little need of the group's commitment to the report. A decision on how to redesign the group's work area, however, would almost certainly benefit from a higher level of group participation. Both the group's input and its commitment would be essential to the success of the new design.

Vroom's point is that the same level of participation is not necessary in every decision. But the more important the group's acceptance of the decision is, or the more the decision might benefit from group input and ideas, the higher the level should be of individual and group participation, at least to the extent that time permits.

Interestingly, the amount of group-based decision making has increased significantly in recent years as teamwork has become one of the key elements of the changing workplace. One of the defining characteristics of this trend has been the steadily increasing responsibility of teams for making many of their own decisions. Organizations now recognize that for them to compete in the changing

Figure 5-8 Levels of Group Involvement in Decision Making

1. The manager alone makes the decision, using the information immediately available.

2. The manager alone makes the decision, involving others only for the information they are able to provide.

3. The manager shares the problems with specific group members and receives input from them, but makes the decision alone.

4. The manager shares the problem with the group as a group and receives input from the group, but makes the decision alone.

5. The manager works with the group throughout the decision process to achieve a consensus shared both by the manager and the members of the group.

environment, decisions must reflect the commitment, the expertise, and the creativity that can only come with highly participative decision making. For this reason, the challenge for managers is to improve not only their own skills as decision makers, but the decision-making skills of their teams as well.

Groupthink: A Potential Problem with Group Decisions

Although group-based decision making unquestionably offers the potential for more effective decisions, it also has potential drawbacks, even beyond those we mentioned earlier. One of the most serious is *groupthink*. Psychologist Irving Janis coined the term *groupthink* to describe the tendency of close-knit groups to lose their ability to function effectively in the decision-making process (Janis, 1982). In reviewing group decisions around famous events in recent history, Janis found that the more cohesive or unified a group was, the less willing the members were to present their own opinions, especially when they differed from the opinions of other group members. Instead of benefiting from the differing points of view of various group members, the decision process in groups suffering from groupthink unconsciously focused on not changing the status quo.

Recall the example of the seniors' fitness club introduced earlier in this chapter. Imagine that the manager decided to involve several staff members and club members in the decision-making process to create a new aerobics program for seniors. The unspoken desire to avoid creating conflict within the group might encourage group members to offer only traditional alternatives for aerobic programming. Alternatives offered might include bowling or walking clubs, but might not include more creative alternatives such as bicycling or jazz dancing. Individual members of the decision-making team may have creative suggestions or serious doubts about any one alternative, but when groupthink takes over, individuals never forcefully state their ideas or objections to the group. Instead, they just go along with the momentum, apparently for fear of being viewed as disloyal to the decision team. Although the failure of a senior fitness club member to express her interest in jazz dancing doesn't seem to be earth shattering, the consequences of groupthink are always serious. Groupthink decisions are lacking both in terms of challenging the status quo and in critically evaluating the alternatives presented. For example, if the group seems satisfied with one member's interpretation of what a particular issue or problem is and how it should be addressed, not only are alternative points of view not raised, but suggested alternatives tend not to be evaluated very critically or carefully.

Janis describes a number of symptoms of groupthink, including self-censorship by members and the appearance of total agreement, even when consensus does not exist. Perhaps more importantly, he suggests strategies for avoiding groupthink. Some of these strategies are summarized in Figure 5-9.

With the trend toward more group and team-based decisions, the tendency toward groupthink becomes an increasingly serious problem. By implementing Janis's strategies, groups can take much greater advantage of their potential for making higher quality decisions.

Ethics and Decision Making

Ethical behavior continues to be a key challenge to management in an ever-changing sports world. *Ethical behavior* may be best defined as behavior that recognizes the difference between right and wrong, behavior that conforms to society's standards and expectations. Two easily justifiable moral standards might be honesty and fairness. We expect sports organizations to conduct themselves in a way that the average person might consider honest in terms of telling the truth, and fair in terms of how equitably they treat their customers or clients, employees, and society in general. In no area of organizational performance is ethical behavior more important than in decision making.

In sports organizations, ethics must matter. At the most basic level, our free market society is based on honesty and fair play. In the sports industry, our games and the operation of our organizations rely on the integrity of individuals who

Figure 5-9 Strategies for Avoiding Groupthink

- Assign the role of critical evaluator to every member of the group.

- Make sure the group leader avoids stating preferences or positions early in the process.

- Encourage input from individuals and experts outside the group.

- Assign one member to play devil's advocate at each group meeting.

- Hold a "second chance" meeting to review the decision once a consensus has been reached.

participate in and manage the sports enterprise. In that sense, unfair and dishonest behavior threatens the very existence of not only the sports industry, but society as well. Every unethical act by organizations threatens the trust that is the foundation of a free society. At the industry level, there is a very real concern that a growing lack of trust in sports organizations may result in demands for additional legislation and regulation to control their operation. The fear is that such restrictions would not only make operations more difficult, but would further limit the ability of the sports organization to compete globally against businesses from other societies that operate without such regulations. Finally, unethical behavior of sports organizations, when discovered, invariably results in a loss of confidence in the organization by customers, investors, and employees. For example, during the health and fitness club boom in the 1970s, many health and fitness club managers induced members to sign long-term contracts. These long-term membership contracts were expensive, yet seemed to offer members a much better deal than monthly renewal fees. Unfortunately, some of these clubs went out of business and literally shut down and moved in the middle of the night. Members were left with long-term memberships to nonexistent clubs with no way to secure a refund. This pattern of ethical abuse of consumers put a black mark on the health and fitness club industry and left many consumers with doubts about the credibility and integrity of the fitness club business.

What this example suggests is that sports managers need to pay attention to the ethical dimensions of decision making. They must work to establish ethical organizational cultures that embrace ethics training, adherence to professional ethical codes and standards, internal ethics committees or teams, and outside review by professional organizations. The key to ethical decisions in organizations is the commitment to ethical behavior by top management. In order to avoid the making of unethical decisions, top management not only must support a system for dealing with ethical questions once they are raised, but they must actively encourage people to raise and discuss ethical concerns whenever they exist. Without that kind of managerial support, even the best internal ethics committees and organization systems and procedures are likely to be ineffective.

In other words, ethical decision making in an organization may have much more to do with the climate and standards that management creates than with the decision-making process itself. This means that if organizations are to achieve the goal of ethical decision making, they must commit themselves to creating an environment in which questions about ethics are a required part of the evaluation phase of every decision. Top managers must serve as ethical role models and must create an environment in which ethics is a key priority in every decision process. Management must insist that the question "Is this decision fair and honest?" be answered for all of the organization's decisions.

The health and fitness segment of the sports industry includes not only health and fitness clubs, but encompasses other spin-off or ancillary organizations including personal training businesses, fitness equipment companies, and nutritional supplement manufacturers. Health and fitness clubs can be considered to fit into one of three categories including commercial clubs, not-for-profit clubs, and miscellaneous for-profit health/fitness enterprises including hotel health clubs and corporate fitness programs.

Making effective decisions is a critical task of all sports managers. Only decisions that actually move the organization closer to its goals can be considered effective. Decision making must be viewed as a series of activities. These activities begin with an understanding of the decision goals followed by information gathering, generating and evaluating alternatives, selecting and implementing the optimal alternative, and concluding with the monitoring of the effectiveness of the decision. The decision process concludes only when the decision has actually achieved its goals. Management's responsibility is to ensure a decision process equal to this challenge. MBWA (management by walking around), creativity, and satisficing are all essential elements of effective decision making.

Besides recognizing the importance of an effective decision-making process, managers also need to recognize the importance of process itself and the influence of the decision maker on that process. The decision maker's intuition, if based on extensive experience, represents a significant asset in the decision process. The personality, values, and power of the decision maker are likely to shape the decision process and the decision itself.

There has been an increasing emphasis on involving others in the decision process. There are advantages and disadvantages to shared decision making and various degrees of group involvement. But clearly, the greater the value of group input to the decision, or the more important the group's commitment to the decision, the greater the need for group involvement in the decision-making process.

However, with group decisions there is also the risk of groupthink, a decision process that reflects the group members' desire not to change the status quo that overrides the desire to achieve the actual decision goals. The challenge for management is to maximize the advantages of involving others in decisions while managing that process to minimize the potential disadvantages. Finally, the decisions reached in the decision-making process must be ethical. Meeting this requirement begins with developing a code of ethics. Managers must also establish a body to review questions of ethics in an organization and offer management training that includes instruction in ethical decision making. Ultimately, ethical decisions require a belief that pervades the organization from top to bottom: the decision process and all decisions must be both fair and honest and must move the organization closer to the realization of its goals.

Teams at Young Rehabilitation Hospital

You are a member of the management team at Young Rehabilitation Hospital. The hospital is named after its founder and CEO, Dr. Sydney Young, and specializes in the rehabilitation of patients with spinal cord injuries. Because of its excellent reputation, the hospital receives patients from all over the United States. In the last five years, the hospital has begun to work with an increasing number of patients who have sports-related spinal cord and neck injuries. They include hockey players, soccer players, lacrosse players, baseball players, football players, race car drivers, and equestrians.

During the past year, the hospital has been experimenting with the creation of a sports-related spinal cord and neck injury unit that would be managed utilizing a team-based approach. The professional staff had suggested that sports patients share unique emotional and physical needs. A sports-related spinal and neck injury unit could further enhance the hospital's reputation, attract top sports medicine specialists, and develop new research funding. It had been agreed that the creation of such a unit could result in immediate and long-term benefits for patients and their families. The experiment created a team of twenty employees (three doctors, two social workers, two sports psychologists, two physical therapists, six nurses, and five nurses' aides). This team cares for only one ward of ten patients. The rest of the staff works on patients throughout the hospital, as they traditionally did.

The team has been in operation for a full year, and as a member of the hospital's management team you are part of the group that will evaluate the success of the treatment team's approach. The evaluation group will be meeting to prepare its recommendation later in the week, and you have begun to prepare for that meeting by reviewing your e-mail messages.

Date:	April 4, 2002
From:	syoung@youngrehab.com
Subject:	Treatment Team Experiment

As you know, I am requesting a recommendation from your group based on our experience with the sports-related injury treatment team. I am asking that your group review the information about patients and staff members who have participated in the team experiment, and suggest whether we should expand the team concept, discontinue the experimental team, or pursue some other course of action.

Please identify at least three alternatives, assess the strengths and weaknesses of each, and provide me with your recommendation of which alternative we should pursue and why. I ask you to keep in mind that our reason for trying the treatment team approach was to improve the process of rehabilitation for the patients, enhance the reputation of the hospital in the area of sports-related spinal cord and neck injury treatment, and improve the performance and job satisfaction of the staff.

I look forward to receiving your report by the end of this month.

Sydney Young, M.D.

Date: April 4, 2002

From: aduclos@youngrehab.com

Subject: Data from survey of treatment team members

The following is a summary of the results of our survey of staff members who have been serving on the treatment team. As you can see, their reaction to the experiment is mixed.

1. Team members reported greater satisfaction with their team-mates.

2. There was concern about a lack of a true supervisor to provide overall direction for the team.

3. There is significantly lower satisfaction among team members because of fewer opportunities for promotions.

4. Overtime hours were 48 percent lower for team members.

5. Frequent conflicts were reported about who had primary responsibility for patient care.

6. Significant satisfaction was reported with having the opportunity to focus on a limited number of patients for their entire treatment process.

7. Absenteeism was 42 percent lower for team members.

8. Ten of twenty team members have requested a return to their departments.

9. Sports-related spinal cord and neck injury referrals have increased by 42 percent.

10. Three new research grants have been secured by doctors and one has been secured by the sports psychologists.

Angela Duclos

Director of Staff Services

Date: April 5, 2002

From: vsanchez@youngrehab.com

Dr. Young asked that I share with you the information we have gathered about patients who participated in the team treatment experiment. I would be happy to provide clarification of any of these points.

1. Patients recovered significantly faster with team-based treatment.

2. Patients put forth more effort during exercise periods.

3. Patients appeared less accepting of staff who were not team members.

4. Patients were discharged 10 percent earlier than the average ninety days.

5. Closer relationships were established between patients and team members.

6. Patient treatment costs were 12 percent higher for the team approach.

Victor Sanchez

Coordinator of Patient Services

1. Define the goal(s) of the decision Dr. Young must make.

2. Identify three options as alternatives.

3. Create T-charts to assist you in assessing the strengths and weaknesses of each of these options.

4. Based on your analysis, indicate which option you would recommend to Dr. Young and why.

References

Agor, W. (1986, January–February). How top executives use their intuition to make decisions. *Business Horizons*, pp. 49–53.

Babish, G. (2001, May). Downsize this. *Athletic Business*, pp. 55–59.

Carr, B. (2000, September). ASD: Fitness slows despite increased awareness. *Health & Fitness Business*, p. 7.

Etzioni, A. (1989, July/August). Humble decision making. *Harvard Business Review*, pp. 122–126.

Health & Fitness Business News. (2000, February). YMCAs take another hit in tax wars with private clubs, p. 23.

Hoffman, M. (1998, July). Buyer profile: In Gold's we trust. *Health & Fitness Business*, p. 16.

Iknoian, T. (1999, September/October). Bally keeps its total fitness promise. *Health & Fitness Business*, pp. 41–43.

Janis, I. (1982). *Groupthink.* Boston: Houghton Mifflin.

O'Sullivan, E. (2000, October). Play for life. *Parks & Recreation*, pp. 99–106.

Peters, T., & Austin, N. (1985). *A passion for for excellence.* New York: Random House, p. 6.

Simon, H. A. (1957). *Administrative behavior.* New York: Free Press.

Simon, H. A. (1979). Information processing models of cognition. *Annual Review of Psychology, 30*, p. 363.

Sternberg, R. J. (1985). Implicit theories of intelligence, creativity and wisdom. *Journal of Personality and Social Psychology, 49*, pp. 607–627.

Vroom, V. (1973). A new look at managerial decision making. *Organizational Dynamics, 1*, p. 66–80.

Vroom, V., & Yetton, P. (1973). *Leadership and decision making.* Pittsburgh: University of Pittsburgh Press.

Part 3

Planning for Performance

Chapter 6

Strategic Planning in Sports

Purpose:	To provide packaged events to spectators at a venue or via the mass media (Mullin, Hardy, & Sutton, 2000).
Stakeholders:	Players, agents, player unions, coaches, individual franchise management personnel, individual franchise employees, franchise owners, league management personnel, league employees, broadcast networks, franchise and league sponsors, franchise and league advertisers, sports broadcast, print, and online media, fans.

Size and scope:

- Over 72 million fans attended Major League Baseball (MLB) games in 2001, with eight clubs (Cardinals, Dodgers, Giants, Indians, Mariners, Orioles, Rockies, Yankees) each drawing over 3 million fans (Pro Sports Tracker, 2001).
- Attendance for the 181 affiliated minor league baseball franchises totaled over 37 million in 2000, an increase of 4 million since 1994 (Williams, 2001).
- In 1998 the NFL league average for revenues was $81.6 million, MLB teams averaged $79.1 million, NBA teams averaged $64.6 million, and NHL teams averaged $51.4 million. Together, these leagues combined accounted for $7.9 billion in revenues (Ozanian, 1998).

Governance:

- The league system has centralized considerable management power at the league level rather than with individual franchises. Rules followed by franchise owners were created to support this centralization, including playing a regular schedule solely against other league clubs. This led to a league championship, setting uniform admissions process, and promising not to poach players from other league teams (Leifer, 1995; Seymour, 1960). The power to uphold these rules would eventually evolve to the commissioner.
- The current commissioner system emerged from a model initiated by professional baseball in response to the 1919 "Black Sox" scandal. Eight players for the Chicago White Sox were accused of throwing games in that year's World Series against the Cincinnati Reds. MLB owners, in an effort to deal with the fallout, hired former federal judge Kenesaw Mountain Landis as its commissioner, dismantling the former three-person governance model. Landis responded to the Black Sox scandal by banning all eight players from organized baseball for life (Pietrusza, 1998).
- Although current commissioners do not wield the absolute power held by Landis, they do possess discretionary powers in the following areas:
  1. approval of player contracts
  2. resolution of disputes between players and clubs
  3. resolution of disputes between clubs
  4. resolution of disputes between player or club and league
  5. disciplinary matters involving players, clubs, front office personnel, and owners
  6. Rule-making authority. (Yasser, McCurdy; & Gopelrud, 1997).

Thrashing Toward Expansion

In 1999, on a June afternoon in Boston's FleetCenter, the National Hockey League's expansion team, Atlanta Thrashers, participated in a draft of current NHL players to put together a roster for its inaugural season. Media and sports mogul Ted Turner's Turner Sports, Inc., which also owned the NBA Atlanta Hawks and MLB's Atlanta Braves, paid $80 million for the rights to the NHL's twenty-eighth franchise. These three properties, as well as parts of many other professional franchises such as the Colorado Avalanche and the New York Knicks, are now owned by media conglomerate AOL/Time Warner (Gruen, 2001). Two other ownership groups also forked over that tariff for the rights for franchises in Columbus, Ohio, and St. Paul, Minnesota, that were slated to begin play in 2000, bringing the league's franchise total to thirty. In 1998 the Nashville (Tennessee) Predators joined the league, also having paid the $80 million entrance fee (Krupa, 1999).

It wasn't that long ago when the NHL consisted of only a half dozen teams—often referred to as the "Original Six"—Boston, Chicago, Detroit, Montreal, the New York Rangers, and Toronto. In 1967 the league doubled in size, with new franchises in Bloomington (Minnesota), Oakland, Los Angeles, Philadelphia, Pittsburgh, and St. Louis, at a cost to join of $2 million each. By 1992 the league had doubled in size again, when the owners of the Tampa Bay Lightning and Ottawa Senators paid $50 million each to enter the league (Krupa, 1999). Some of these expansion efforts were in response to the creation in 1972 of a rival league, the World Hockey Association (WHA).

But Atlanta? Columbus? Nashville? Hardly hockey hotbeds. Most NHL players hail from places like Moose Jaw, Saskatchewan, the Upper Peninsula of Michigan, or the Czech Republic, not from the region whose residents pledged allegiance to the likes of NASCAR icons Richard Petty and Dale Earnhardt.

NHL commissioner Gary B. Bettman explained that the National Hockey League is always searching for opportunities for growth. According to Bettman, "The expansion will make the league stronger, a more vibrant factor in the entertainment sports marketplace"(Krupa, 1999, p. C12).

In fact, the factors that influenced the NHL's expansion were mainly the opportunities to develop revenues from television and advertising. The National Football League, as discussed in Chapter 3, recently signed television deals worth $17.6 billion. The current NHL deal with ABC and ESPN is worth a comparatively paltry $600 million. In part attributable to media revenues, the NFL average franchise value is twice as much as the NHL average (Ozanian, 1998). These new markets afford the NHL's television partners more attractive markets of viewers and more promising tickets, concessions, and licensing revenues for local owners. If the NHL intended to grow and to avoid being totally eclipsed by other sport/ entertainment competitors, it clearly had to expand into new, somewhat surprising markets, such as Columbus and Nashville. The ultimate success of the NHL's expansion efforts will be revealed in future revenues from local tickets sales, facility revenues, and local and national media contracts, and the early financial returns have been promising.

In today's environment, with its constant and rapid changes, most sport organizations have learned what the NHL learned: They can no longer react to circumstances around them. They must be proactive and take the initiative to develop strategies that minimize threats and maximize opportunities. Can you imagine the NHL with only six franchises today? Would they be making the most of their opportunities to generate revenues nationally and globally? Through planning, sport organizations are able to keep pace with changes in the environment, rather than simply react to them. Strategic planning is the responsibility for understanding the mission of the organization, for anticipating and recognizing changes in the world outside the organization, and for developing strategies for positioning the organization to compete in the changing environment.

Introduction

This chapter introduces the strategic management process within the framework of the professional league sports industry segment and focuses on its initial stages. In these stages, professional league sports organizations define their missions and strategic goals, analyze the environment and their own strengths and weaknesses, and then develop strategies to achieve their stated missions and goals. The information that specifically defines and impacts the professional league sports segment is also presented in detail.

Strategic Planning

Between 1965 and 1972, about the time when the NHL was undergoing its first growth period, the concept and process of strategic planning came into wide use (Schendel & Hofer, 1979). Global competition first began to escalate as the Japanese and European economies completed their recoveries from the ravages of World War II. Also, computers were just then beginning to change the way business was done, and changes in transportation and communications were impacting organizations as well. As we outlined in Chapter 3, communications, especially in the area of broadcasting and media, would (and continue) to impact professional sports organizations significantly. Perhaps the biggest change in professional league sports would be the advent of free agency for players, which, over time, led to gigantic increases in player salaries. We discuss this environmental change in detail later.

As the rate and magnitude of these changes in the environment increased, organizations began to pay more attention to how they affected market conditions and other key factors. They began to develop goals and plans reflecting these changes. This process of monitoring and analyzing key changes in the environment and developing strategies to increase the organization's effectiveness in response to those changes came to be known as strategic planning.

Initially, the emphasis in strategic planning was on a top-down approach: top-level managers and professional corporate planners analyzed the environment, developed very specific goals and highly detailed plans, and then passed them down to front-line managers. Because a lack of communication often existed between those who developed the plans and those who were supposed to put them into action, these top-down strategic plans were almost never effectively implemented.

Companies also learned of the potential problems when so-called experts such as top managers and professional planners rely solely on their own judgment and opinions to analyze the environment or forecast the future. Here are some classic and humorous examples of the type of thinking that results when even highly qualified individuals rely on their own analysis:

> "Do you think I want every kid in this city walking around with a Yankee cap?"
>> —George Weiss, general manager, New York Yankees, in the 1960s (Helyar, 1994, p. 70). Professional leagues in North America now sell billions of dollars in licensed products each year.

> "What? Preempt *The Doris Day Show*?" [a popular variety show in the 1970s]
>> —An executive at NBC when presented with the concept of "Monday Night Football," the prime-time broadcasting of NFL football, in 1970 (Murphy, 1999b, p. 56). Over the course of the twentieth century, the NFL became the preeminent professional sports league in North America, in large part due to innovative broadcasting scheduling and techniques.

In an effort to avoid such tunnel vision, as well as the communications problems just mentioned, the top-down approach to planning began to change in the 1980s. To ensure both broader input into the planning process and more effective implementation once the plans were developed, organizations began to involve managers from all parts of the organization. This strategy reflects a trend identified by management thinkers Hamid Bouchikhi and John R. Kimberly (2000) in their efforts to encourage managers to create a customized workplace: a shift from the nineteenth century model of power concentrated at the top, through the twentieth century model of a limited and functional sharing and empowerment, to a twenty-first century model where power is diffused and shared. In terms of planning, this process of encouraging all managers, employees, and work teams to think strategically and to focus on the organization's environment is called *strategic management*.

The Strategic Management Approach to Planning

The major components of the strategic management approach to planning are summarized in Figure 6-1. Because the sports environment is continuously shifting and changing, strategic management must be an ongoing, continuous examination of how well sports organizations are aligned with that environment. In the professional sports league system, the lead person responsible for strategic management is the commissioner.

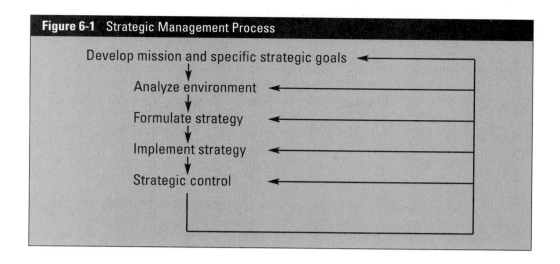

Figure 6-1 Strategic Management Process

Develop mission and specific strategic goals

Analyze environment

Formulate strategy

Implement strategy

Strategic control

More recently, commissioners have gained responsibilities in other areas, especially in marketing and revenue generation. In the 1960s NFL Commissioner Alvin "Pete" Rozelle lobbied the U.S. Congress for an exemption to the Sherman Anti-Trust Act that allowed the league to sell its TV rights collectively (Murphy, 1999b). This boosted each team's TV take from $330,000 annually in 1962 to $75 million a year in 2001. Rozelle promoted this concept, defined by Helyar (1994) as "league-think," to NFL owners, emphasizing that the pooling and sharing of revenues would make for a better overall product because all teams could share equally in the league's success. As a result of all teams in the NFL sharing equally in the league's revenues, the fans of the Green Bay Packers, for example, know they have a realistic chance to reach the Super Bowl in any given year. Yet those same fans who cheer for the Milwaukee Brewers are virtually certain that, because of the lack of revenue sharing in MLB and the huge disparity in local revenues between franchises, even though the Brewers began playing in state-of-the-art Miller Park in 2001, their team will struggle just to reach .500.

Among contemporary pro league top managers, NBA Commissioner David J. Stern is generally acknowledged to have assumed these new responsibilities most effectively. He had the good fortune to preside over a league that had the world's best known and most marketable athletic commodity (Michael Jordan) and had built momentum through the presence of standout players (Larry Bird and Earvin "Magic" Johnson). In addition, Stern has been able to expand the league's international presence through efforts such as the 1992 Barcelona Olympics "Dream Team" (see Chapter 10). He has built consensus among owners and has dealt effectively with labor disputes (Masteralexis, 1998). Lastly, Stern has wielded a swift and potent disciplinary club, as evidenced with the attempts by the management of the Minnesota Timberwolves and the agent representing star player Joe Smith to circumvent the league's salary cap in 2000. Stern voided Smith's contract, which barred the team from resigning him, and he suspended the Timberwolves' managers who were responsible (Pickeral, 2000). Despite these successes, current troubles such as skyrocketing ticket prices, dwindling attendance, sagging TV ratings, dysfunctional on-court play, and fan perceptions of indifferent player efforts will be new challenges for Stern and league managers.

Although responsibility for strategic management is increasingly shared through organizations, in professional sports the league commissioner provides the focal point for ensuring a strategic management approach. We turn now to a fuller consideration of that approach. This chapter focuses primarily on the first three phases of the strategic management process: from defining the organization's mission and strategic goals to developing the strategies for achieving those goals.

A clear, compelling sense of direction is the starting point of the strategic management process; it is management's responsibility to give the organization this sense of its own enduring purpose (Carlson-Thomas, 1992). The most common way that organizations attempt to communicate this sense of purpose or direction is through a mission statement.

Step 1: Establishing the Organization's Direction

As we noted in Chapter 4, the first responsibility of management is to provide vision. Consider the case of the Arena Football League (AFL). In 1981 James Foster attended an indoor soccer game and began doodling on a manila envelope. Six years later, the AFL was founded. Figure 6-2 outlines some of the distinctive AFL rules.

The rules promote scoring: AFL teams score a combined 95.9 points per game. Says AFL commissioner David Baker, "some NBA teams don't score as many points as an Arena team does" (Murphy, 1999a, p. 56). Its popularity is still growing. The league drew just under 140,000 for 12 games in 1987 and attracted nearly 1.2 million for 119 games in 2000. Said Detroit Fury coach Mouse Davis, "There's two things [a fan sees at AFL games]. There's lots of scoring, and guys get the crap knocked out of them right in front of you" (Weiner, 2001a, p. 2C).

Figure 6-2 Arena Football League Rules of Play

- **The field:** The game is played indoors, on a surface 50 yards long by 28.3 yards wide, surrounded by 4-foot-high padded walls. The end zones are 8 yards wide. The goal-side rebound nets are 30 feet wide and 32 feet high. A forward pass that rebounds off the net is live and in play until it touches the playing surface.

- **Players:** 20-man active roster, 8 players on the field. Players play offense and defense, with the exception of the kicker, quarterback, offensive specialist, and two defensive specialists.

- **Substitutions:** All nonspecialists may substitute only once during each quarter.

- **Kicking:** Drop kicks are allowed. Four points for a field goal by drop kick; two points for a conversion by a drop kick after a touchdown. Punting is illegal. On fourth down, a team must go for a first down, touchdown, or field goal. The receiving team may field any kickoff or missed field goal that rebounds off the net.

The AFL has been so successful that franchises which would have sold for $500,000 a few years ago now could go for $7 to $15 million (Sandomir, 2001). The league began a new twelve-team developmental venture, arenafootball2, in 2000 in southeastern and midwestern U.S. markets such as Bossier City, Louisiana, and Lincoln, Nebraska. The league expanded to 28 teams in 2001, with plans to expand to 40 in 2002 (Weiner, 2001b). Said Commissioner Baker, "our vision is to have a fan friendly, year-round, worldwide football league for a new generation" (Murphy, 1999a, p. 57). The NFL has also recognized this success and purchased an option to buy up to 49.99 percent of the AFL. "Our goal is to support football at all levels," said NFL Commissioner Paul Tagliabue. "This deal helps us in the growth of the game" (Murphy, 1999a, p. 57). One NFL owner, the Detroit Lions' William Clay Ford, Jr., owns the Detroit Fury, and two others, Dallas Cowboys' owner Jerry Jones and Washington Redskins' owner Daniel Snyder, will own franchises soon (at the discounted franchise price of $4.5 million). Says NFL executive vice president Robert Goodell, the league's high scoring and two-way player skills is "a tool to introduce football to a different demographic," especially young fans (Sandomir, 2001, p. C18). Perhaps the AFL's most well-known on-field contribution to the NFL is Kurt Warner, the St. Louis Rams' quarterback named the league's most valuable player (MVP) in 1999. Warner apprenticed as the quarterback for the AFL's Iowa Barnstormers.

In terms of strategic management, visions such as these provide an organization's general and enduring sense of direction through its *mission*.

The Mission Statement

The mission statement is a summary of what business the organization is in or seeks to be in, and it often includes a statement of its philosophy and values. The mission statement reveals an organization's long-term vision—what it wants to be and whom it wants to serve. An effective mission statement provides a sense of direction for every individual and group in an organization.

Before we discuss the characteristics of an effective mission statement, let's consider why we have professional sports teams and leagues at all. What business are they in? As we noted earlier, professional sports teams and leagues exist to provide packaged events to spectators at a venue or via the mass media. The first organization to undertake this mission was the Cincinnati Red Stockings, the first fully and openly professional American sports team. The Red Stockings were organized in 1869 by Cincinnati investors, led by Aaron Champion, who felt they could make professional baseball a profitable business by charging admission to games (initially 10 cents). The club hired Harry Wright, an experienced, inventive, and hardworking baseball man, to manage the team and to recruit the best talent from across the country. The payroll for the ten Red Stockings was $9,300, with Harry's brother, George, the team's pitcher, making the most at $1,400. These salaries, seemingly minuscule by today's standards, were substantial for the day, when the average skilled worker made approximately $525 to $700 annually (Guschov, 1998).

Although many criticized this new model as crassly mercenary with players whose only interests would be their salaries, the Red Stockings were successful on the field, winning their first sixty-nine games against a mix of amateur, collegiate, and semipro teams. The professional model meant that Wright's charges could train and work to perfect their craft full time. After losing the first-ever extra inning game to the Brooklyn Atlantics in 1870, interest in the team waned at home, and gate receipts dwindled. The club owners decided to dismantle the professional model before the 1871 season. That year, however, the National Association of Professional Base Ball Players was formed, leading to the eventual formation of the National League in 1876 (Guschov, 1998). The Red Stockings were the first example of organizing a professional sports team for profit, and serves as the organizational template for today's professional sports teams and leagues.

Definition of the Business

It may appear that every professional sports team's mission is to organize for profit, but simply defining a team's mission this way does not provide direction or keep the team focused on its stakeholders. Rather, a mission statement should clearly answer the questions, "What business are we in?" and "What business should we be in?" These questions must be answered in terms of customer needs and not in terms of the products or services the company currently offers (Abell, 1980; Collins, 1997; Collins & Porras, 1996). This emphasis on customer needs helps sports teams avoid being left behind by changes in technology or consumer preferences and keeps them focused on ways to satisfy the mission. For example, consider the mission statement of MLB's Colorado Rockies, shown in Figure 6-3.

The statement clearly identifies the fans' needs. First and foremost, it is baseball entertainment. By being very clear about the mission, it provides a foundation for strategies and plans for new activities. For example, if management is looking for ways to increase attendance, its focus is on enhancing the baseball entertainment experience of fans, what are commonly referred to product extensions, first established by Bill Veeck, one of sports' marketing pioneers. While owner of several major- and minor-league franchises, Veeck strived to make baseball fun and entertaining for all fans. Veeck's efforts included promotional giveaways such as bat day, fireworks after home runs, improved rest room and concessions facilities, and stunts such as using a midget to pinch-hit, and "Grandstand Manager Night," when fans in the stands, not the team's manager, decided whether the players on the field would bunt, or steal, or what pitches would be thrown (Sugar, 1978). Thanks to the approaches of Veeck and others who built on this concept, such as former Oakland Athletics' owner Charlie Finley (who in the 1970s clad his team in ultrabright green and yellow uniforms, white shoes, and encouraged them to sport flowing hair and moustaches to create an image of "the Swingin' A's"), the Rockies understand that everyone associated with the team should work toward the same purpose—baseball entertainment—and the focus is clear.

Philosophy and values. Beyond the business it is in or seeks to be in, a mission statement should also define the organization's philosophy—its basic beliefs, values, and priorities. The Colorado Rockies' mission statement makes these points

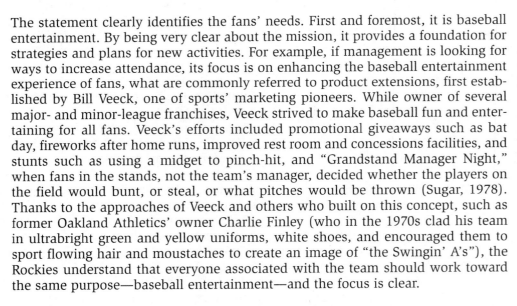

Figure 6-3 Colorado Rockies' Mission Statement

To provide the highest level of baseball entertainment in an excellent stadium environment at prices affordable for families, and to support the development of youth baseball throughout the Rocky Mountain region.

very clearly. The team is committed to providing a quality stadium environment at prices affordable for families, and it values the development of youth baseball. These are the team's top priorities.

Another example of effective statements about an organization's philosophy and values can be found in the Arena Football League's (AFL) Fans' Bill of Rights (see Figure 6-4).

Throughout this statement, the AFL reinforces that it is dedicated to serving its customers and providing them with a "first-class entertainment experience . . . at an affordable price," and they are entitled "to interact with and have access to players and coaches for autographs and conversation in recognition for their support at every game ("The Arena," 1999). Part of the mission statement is printed on the back of every league employee's business card. This approach is intended to make AFL fans feel that their enjoyment and satisfaction are the league's highest priorities. And the AFL players are also more like their fans than their NFL counterparts. Kurt Warner worked the graveyard shift stocking shelves at a Hy-Vee supermarket while playing for the Iowa Barnstormers, and most other players also work full time in jobs such as construction (like 2000 ArenaBowl MVP Rick Hamilton of the Orlando Predators) and high school education (like lineman Rod Williams of the Tampa Bay Storm) (Weiner, 2001b).

The mission statement, then, defines for employees, customers, and all other stakeholders the organization's highest and most enduring goals in terms of the needs of the customers it is seeking to satisfy and the organization's philosophy and values

---

Figure 6-4 Excerpts from the AFL's Fans' Bill of Rights

- We believe that every Fan is entitled to a wholesome environment for guests and family members, free of violence, profane gestures and language, or rude and invasive behavior that could in any way interfere with a first-class entertainment experience.

- We believe that every Fan deserves our best effort on a consistent basis, on every play on the field, every action in the stands, every call to our office, and every involvement in the community.

- We believe that every Fan is entitled to a total entertainment experience at an affordable cost for all members of the family from the time they arrive at the arena to the time they depart.

- We believe that every Fan is entitled to interact with and have access to players and coaches for autographs and conversation in recognition of their support at every game.

- We believe that Fans expect the Arena Football League to be comprised of gentlemen and ladies who are examples and role models for youth, free of physical violence, drugs, alcohol, and gambling abuse.

Source: "The Arena," 1999.

in pursuing these goals. Once its mission and philosophy are clear, an organization is ready to turn its attention to the environment in which it must pursue these goals.

Step 2: Analyzing the Situation: Comparing the Organization to Its Environment

In terms of planning, even organizations with clear missions often tend to get so caught up in the day-to-day problems that they fail to recognize and respond to what's happening around them. Remember, the estimated total U.S. expenditures on sports consumption approach $152 billion annually (Meek, 1997). These numbers would seem to indicate outstanding growth potential for pro sports leagues and would support expansion moves like the NHL's. Other environmental factors have impacted these leagues, however, and have made such expansion efforts problematic.

Recall NHL commissioner Bettman's observations about the love of hockey in the NHL's decision to return to Minnesota. If love of hockey was a key determinant, then why were none of the expansion teams headed for Canada, where hockey is far more a part of the national culture than in the United States? Part of the rationale was that two Canadian cities—Quebec City (to Denver in 1995) and Winnipeg (to Phoenix in 1996)—recently lost their teams. In addition, the six current Canadian franchises are facing severe financial difficulties due to highly unfavorable exchange rates between U.S. and Canadian dollars (because Canadian clubs collect revenue mostly in Canadian dollars, but pay salaries in U.S. dollars [Cohen, 2000]), and a tax system that is highly unfavorable for franchises when compared to the U.S. system. Because of this, in 2001 brewer Molson Inc. sold approximately 80 percent of the storied Montreal Canadiens and 100 percent of their home venue, the Molson Centre, for the comparatively low price of $183 million (US), but only after the city of Montreal cut the team's annual tax bill of $7.3 million (CD) by nearly a third. Although Molson retained around 20 percent ownership in the Canadiens and the deal stipulated the team could not be moved from Montreal (Dupont, 2001b), the Calgary, Vancouver, and Ottawa franchises may be forced to move to the United States (Allen, 1999a), further calling into question the wisdom of expansion. Vancouver Canucks' general manager Brian Burke criticized the Canadian government's response to the plight of the NHL franchises, stating, "I don't get it. How many cars of this train have to go off the cliff before they figure out the rest of the cars are in trouble?" (Dupont, 2001a, p. C7).

The fact that several U.S. franchises are also on shaky ground casts further doubt on the NHL's recent expansion. In the midst of a surprising 1999 Stanley Cup playoff run, the Pittsburgh Penguins filed for bankruptcy due to conflicts over their facility lease, local media revenues, and a dwindling season ticket base. The franchise was saved in large part because of the efforts of then-retired star Mario Lemieux, who stepped in to broker a deal to take over the team and saved it from dissolution (Allen, 1999b). Lemieux took over the team in lieu of the $32.5 million in deferred salary owed to him by the Penguins. "Still-Super" Mario returned to the ice from a three-year retirement in late 2000, in part because the franchise's fortunes were sagging again and his return served to boost ticket sales (McDonough, 2000). The figures bear this out, as the Pens sold 65,000 extra tickets in the ten days after Lemieux announced his return, generating $2.9 million (Bernstein, 2000). Road opponents were also benefiting at the gate, and TV ratings on ESPN for games involving Lemieux increased 50 percent (Allen, 2001). The

Carolina Hurricanes, New York Islanders, and the Phoenix Coyotes have also experienced similar problems. Critics of expansion also claim that expansion dilutes the pool for available talent, even though the league has developed strong connections with countries outside North America in search of players, with nearly 30 percent of league players now coming from Europe (sixty-three from the Czech Republic alone) (Ellick, 2001).

The North American landscape is littered with the detritus of leagues that were founded and failed, or franchises that were added unwisely. Major-league baseball teams could once be found in Troy, New York, and Worcester, Massachusetts. The NFL had franchises in Decatur and Rock Island, Illinois, and Duluth, Minnesota. The NBA formerly called Buffalo, Vancouver, and Fort Wayne, Indiana, home. And all leagues have been and will continue to be challenged by rival leagues. The NFL has merged with the All-American Football Conference (from whence came the San Francisco 49ers and the original Cleveland Browns [now the Baltimore Ravens]), and the American Football League (which merged in total with the NFL in 1970). The newly expanded NFL outlasted competitors the World Football League in the 1970s (with teams like the Shreveport [Louisiana] Steamer and the Honolulu Hawaiians), the United States Football League in the 1980s (with the late Pittsburgh Maulers and the Memphis Showboats), and created partnerships with the Arena Football League in the 1990s. And even the Arena League, with its recent success, had franchises fail in Cincinnati, Charlotte, and Cleveland, to name a few. The latest challenge to the NFL came from the XFL, a joint venture between NBC and the World Wrestling Federation (WWFE), which began play in February 2001 with franchises in Birmingham (Alabama), Chicago, East Rutherford (New Jersey), Las Vegas, Los Angeles, Memphis, Orlando, and San Francisco, but quickly folded after one season due to low TV ratings and attendance, poor on-field play, and substantial financial losses experienced by both partners ($40 million for NBC, $35 million for the WWFE) (Hiestand, 2001b).

All these leagues and franchises were seemingly poised to cash in on the ever-increasing consumer demand for sports entertainment. And although some new leagues and franchises were successful, the increased competition for talent drove up salaries, the largest single expenditure for professional league teams. The newer leagues were generally less able to afford these increases over time, and, when unable to generate significant revenues from ticket sales, stadium revenues, and, most critically, television, either failed or merged fully or in part with the established league. This would then reduce competition for talent, and salaries would, for a time, decrease. This would also reduce competition for television viewers and raise ratings for the surviving league.

These kinds of experiences convince sports organizations of the critical importance of monitoring the trends in their environment. In the strategic management view, before deciding on a game plan, or a strategy to achieve that mission, an organization must analyze the situation: not only in its own strengths and weaknesses, but also those of competitors. Recognizing what is actually happening in the environment and evaluating the organization in terms of those trends is what a *situation analysis* is all about. Situation analysis examines the complex set of interactions between factors both inside and outside the organization. It begins with a review of conditions in the environment to see if they pose opportunities or threats and then uses this review as a basis for assessing the organization itself for potential strengths and weaknesses.

Figure 6-5 shows the relationship between the organization and its environment. The outer circle represents the *general environment*, which includes broad trends and conditions in society. These are factors outside the organization that tend to affect society and organizations in general. The middle circle represents the *task* or *specific environment*, which consists of individuals, groups, and organizations that directly affect a particular organization but are not part of it. The inner circle is the organization itself, the dimensions of the organization that impact performance. All three elements require management's constant attention.

The Two Environments

The first step in analyzing the organization's situation is to assess the environment for opportunities and threats. As we stated earlier, two categories of environments must be monitored: the general environment, which is shared by every organization in a society, and the task or specific environment, which is unique to a particular organization.

General environment. As Figure 6-5 shows, the general environment can be divided into five dimensions or subcategories of change: social, economic, political/ legal, technological, and global.

Social change includes changes in social patterns, demographics, values, and institutions. The increased interest and involvement in physical activity and sports spectatorship by women has been reflected in the development of new leagues such as the Women's United Soccer Association (WUSA) and the NBA's Women's National Basketball Association (WNBA). In addition, established "male" leagues have recognized the levels of interest of women and have developed efforts to

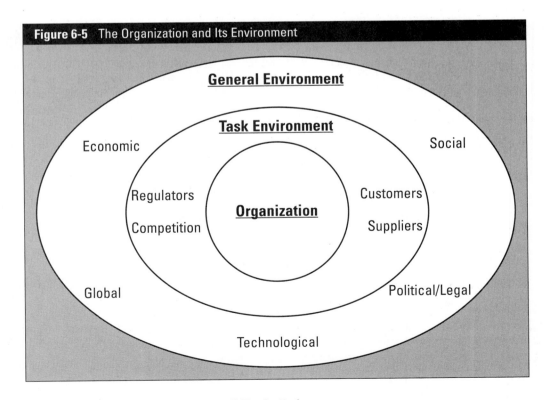

Figure 6-5 The Organization and Its Environment

cultivate these interests. A recent survey indicated that women comprise 44 percent of the NFL's fan base, buy 70 percent of the $3 billion's worth of the league's licensed products, that 40 million women watch NFL games weekly, and nearly half a million attend games weekly. Sara Levinson, president of NFL Properties, the for-profit marketing arm of the league, said of women customers, "They control the TV dial on Sunday afternoons and decide what sport their kids will get involved with. We have to make these gatekeepers comfortable." One effort to cultivate these female gatekeepers is a course called "NFL 101 for Women," in which participants can screen game films, try on equipment, talk with NFL referees, and meet players. Said one excited San Diego attendee, "They were so muscular and sexy-looking when their uniforms were off" (Meyers, 1997, p. 2A). Sex appeal is apparently part of the attraction as well.

Economic change refers to the overall status of the economy, which varies over time. Times of economic prosperity, when demand for services and goods is high, as was the case for the United States throughout most of the 1990s, represent periods of tremendous opportunity for sports organizations. In reaction to this relative affluence, the average ticket price for the "Big Four" (MLB, NBA, NFL, NHL) has increased 80 percent—four times faster than the Consumer Price Index. The price of Seat 1 in Row 7, Aisle F at Dodger Stadium in Los Angeles cost $3.50 when the stadium opened in 1962, and remained there until 1976. Since then, however, the price has been increased fourteen times, to $31 for the 2000 season, representing a total increase of 785.7 percent. But a ticket is only part of the cost of attendance. Should you and three friends choose to attend a New York Knicks' game at Madison Square Garden and park your car nearby, sit in midpriced seats, drink four sodas, two beers, eat four hot dogs, and take home two programs and two souvenir caps, you had better bring along at least a "Benjamin" each. The total cost: $455.26 (Swift, 2000).

Although some fans and consumers are shocked at these prices, and others refuse to pay them and seek out other leisure activities (leading to the 1990s boom in the development and expansion of minor-league professional sports leagues), University of Chicago economist Allen R. Sanderson argues that relative expense should be determined on two factors: closely related leisure alternatives and personal income. Sanderson notes that one can attend an MLB game in Chicago for $15, which compares favorably to the cost of tickets for the Chicago Symphony, the Great America amusement park, a Dixie Chicks concert at the United Center, or the Museum of Science and Industry (which includes watching an IMAX film of Michael Jordan). Sanderson also avers that the economic expansion of the 1990s has meant that for most families these events have become more affordable, and that players' salaries have increased in large part not to free agency, but because spectators and consumers are willing to pay the prices set by teams, although team owners often find it easy to blame greedy players for price increases (Sanderson, 2000).

Political and legal change includes the impact of governmental laws and the legal system, as well as the relationship between government and business. Although we would cite many examples of such changes impacting professional leagues, the most significant is probably the gradual dismantling of the reserve clause. Professional baseball's National League initiated the reserve clause in 1879 to reduce player salaries, the most significant expenditure for professional teams. Before this, players would often leave teams in midseason for better offers from other teams. It was the functional equivalent of Alex Rodriguez choosing to leave the Texas Rangers in mid-July if the New York Mets offered him just one penny more, even though he was set to make $22 million that year from the Rangers.

At first, teams reserved five players who were not permitted to sign with other teams. Other teams effectively bound those players to that club by agreeing not to sign them away. This also meant that teams could then trade and sell players under contract as well. Eventually a clause, Paragraph 10A, was inserted in the Uniform Players Contract stipulating that clubs had the right to renew a signed contract for a period of one year on the same terms (Helyar, 1994).

Players and rival leagues made a few attempts at destroying this system. The formation of the Brotherhood of Professional Baseball Players, led by John Montgomery Ward, a player for the then-New York Giants, led to the formation of the Players League (PL) in 1890. The Players League, formed on a profit-sharing model in conjunction with owner-investors, lured away many of the game's best players, but through the efforts of Albert Spalding and other National League owners and facing first-year financial peril, the Players League owners sold their franchise interests to the NL owners, killing the PL and reinstating the reserve system (Lowenfish, 1980).

Another competitor league, the Federal League (FL), challenged the reserve system of the then established American and National Leagues in 1914–1915, but the FL met the same fate as the Players League when owners were bought out or coopted, except for the owners of the Baltimore franchise. In response, they sued the established leagues, claiming the reserve system was an antitrust violation that kept them from acquiring the talent necessary to compete equally. In 1922 the U.S. Supreme Court ruled against the Baltimore franchise, stating, somewhat curiously, that professional baseball did not qualify as interstate commerce, so the reserve clause could stand (White, 1996).

The clause withstood several challenges over the next fifty years, including another unsuccessful Supreme Court decision initiated by former St. Louis Cardinals' outfielder Curt Flood, who challenged the right of the Cardinals to trade him to the Philadelphia Phillies in exchange for slugging first baseman Dick Allen. The Court used the 1922 decision as precedent in ruling against Flood, and it recommended that any change in professional baseball's antitrust exemption be addressed by the U.S. Congress (Lowenfish, 1980).

The reserve clause effectively ended not from a court decision but from a salary arbitration hearing. In the 1960s and 1970s, the emergence of a more powerful and united MLB Players' Association, under the leadership of Marvin Miller, negotiated an agreement with MLB owners that many disputes between players and clubs be adjudicated not by the commissioner, an employee of the owners, but by an independent arbitrator whose decision both sides were bound to follow.

The hearing that broke the stranglehold of the reserve clause occurred just before Christmas 1974. Because of a protracted salary dispute with Los Angeles Dodgers' management, star pitcher Andy Messersmith played the entire year without signing a contract. The arbitrator, Peter Seitz, ruled that although Messersmith had been renewed automatically by the Dodgers as permitted under Paragraph 10A of the Uniform Player Contract, the fact that he had not signed a contract in 1974 meant the one-year renewal clause had expired. Therefore, Seitz decreed that Messersmith was no longer contractually bound to the Dodgers and was free to sign with whatever team he chose. The current system of salary arbitration after three years of major-league service and free agency after six years was then negotiated and agreed to by the union and ownership (Helyar, 1994).

Other such significant legal changes can come from other leagues' cases. In 1982 the union for the now-defunct North American Soccer League won a suit that permitted union access to all player salary data. The NFL's players union used this case so their players could compare salaries. Before that, Tommy Kramer, the starting quarterback for the Minnesota Vikings who threw for 3,912 yards in 1981, made $100,000; Guy Benjamin, the backup for the San Francisco 49ers who threw for 171 yards, made $130,000. Dick Berthelsen, the NFL's general counsel who won the case, underscored the ruling's significance: "What it did was make sure that false information was no longer being passed around. Players felt they would get in trouble if they talked about salaries" (Forbes, 2001, p. 14C).

Technological change refers to the advances that create new products and new ways of producing goods and providing services. As noted in Chapter 3, information technology has transformed every sports organization's environment with revolutions in manufacturing, communication, information processing, and shopping. Virtually every professional league team and league has its own Internet website, where fans can access statistical information, experience live game video or audio, chat with other fans, and, most importantly for teams, purchase tickets or licensed products.

The San Francisco Giants, with its proximity to California's Silicon Valley, the epicenter of the technology boom of the 1990s, have used technology to take the time-honored, if often illegal, practice of ticket scalping online. The Giants, who moved into state-of-the-art Pacific Bell Park in 2000, created a service through the team's website that allowed season ticket holders to sell unneeded tickets to other fans at a cost that could be well above the face value of the ticket. The club charges a 10 percent fee to buyer and seller for each transaction, and the tickets are verified by a UPC bar code printed onto each ticket. The system allows for potentially greater season ticket holder satisfaction, now that they can easily sell tickets for one of the eighty-one regular season home games they may not be able to attend. The service also draws fans to the team's website. Many other teams at the major- and minor-league level have initiated such ticket exchange service for season ticket holders, but the Giants are the first to enter into "e-scalping" (Jenkins, 2000).

Global change has been perhaps the most volatile recent environmental factor. International politics and economic conditions have been dramatically altered by the sudden shift of whole geographic regions to more capitalist economic systems from communist or totalitarian models, where governments planned and controlled production and distribution of goods and services, and set prices. The satellite countries and states now independent from the Soviet Union have become sources of talent for the recently expanded leagues like the NHL (with stars such as Dominek Hasek, Pavel Bure, and Jaromir Jagr) and the NBA (with standouts such as Dirk Nowitski, Toni Kukoc, and Peja Stojakovic). Currently, approximately half of the NHL's players are from outside North America. The home countries for these players have now become potential markets for these leagues. For example, when the Penguins (with Jagr) and Buffalo Sabres (with Hasek) played in 2001, the NHL's Czech website hits tripled, and walking down the streets of Prague one is likely to see many Jagr and Hasek jerseys. When Jagr moved to the Washington Capitals and Hasek to the Detroit Red Wings in 2001, local merchants in Prague stocked up on merchandise from the new clubs (Ellick, 2001). All professional leagues have made strides to broaden their consumer base internationally, through efforts like the "North American v. World" format in the NHL All-Star Game, where two teams

of fan-selected stars are formed based on these geographic distinctions, to the participation of pro league players in international competitions like the Olympics.

Globalization has also brought changes to the American pro league landscape through the advent of professional soccer. Major League Soccer (MLS), founded in 1995 after the United States hosted the 1994 World Cup, is the latest soccer league to try its luck in a country that embraces soccer for its children (with millions of youth participants) but has yet to make it a significant part of its consumer experience. Ironically, technology and globalization have, to a degree, hurt the nascent MLS, because it is often easier to find a tape-delayed broadcast of an English Premier League match on TV featuring Manchester United, or to watch matches from Mexico and Central and South American in Spanish on a Univision affiliate, than to view a live English-language network MLS broadcast.

Changes in the social, political, economic, technological, and global environments, then, can have a dramatic effect on any organization. It is the responsibility of management to monitor continuously these key dimensions of the general environment to recognize as early as possible the changes that might impact the organization. This responsibility extends also to the task environment.

Task environment. The *task*, or *immediate, environment* includes the factors in the environment that directly impact a specific organization. Thus in Figure 6-5 the elements of the task environment are located closer to the organization. Like the general environment, the task environment consists of several dimensions. Among the most important are customers, competition, suppliers, and regulators.

Customers are the individuals, groups, and other organizations that purchase the products and services an organization provides. Changes in customers' needs and priorities can have a significant effect on a professional league organization. Recall the argument of economist Allen Sanderson that the economic expansion of the 1990s has meant that for most families attending pro league events has become more affordable. As a result, he argues that this affluence has meant sports consumers now seek higher levels of goods and services—microbrews instead of Old Style or Bud, theatre-style seats with chair-back video screens linked to the team's website for stats and video replays instead of bleacher seats, $250 fully embroidered authentic replica jerseys instead of an adjustable cap. This in part has fueled the efforts of many major-league franchises to develop facilities that offer consumers more amenities and allow teams to charge consumers more in return (Sanderson, 2000). The luxury suites and club seats, which offer augmented services and comforts, net the new Cleveland Browns' franchise nearly $25 million in annual revenues (Ozanian, 1998).

Competitors are other organizations that vie for an organization's customers. In the contemporary pro league task environment, we have noted that some fans are appalled at the cost of attending events, but they express other concerns as well. Remember Greg Dallas from Chapter 1, the former season ticket holder for the NBA's Denver Nuggets who gave up his two $52 seats after five years? Apparently, his sentiments are not unique to him, as one poll found that only 1 percent of Colorado sports fans indicated that the Nuggets were their favorite team ("Go Figure," 2001). Even so, although the NBA is unlikely to be threatened by any other professional basketball league, the real competition for the Denver Nuggets is what else Greg Dallas and his family could do on a typical February day instead of attending a Nuggets' game. They could go out to eat, to a movie, to a Colorado Avalanche game, ski at any one of the region's numerous mountain resorts, attend a University of Denver men's hockey game, travel to Boulder to attend a University of Colorado men's or women's basketball game, attend a local high school game, or sit at home and watch any one of dozens of pro or college hockey or basketball games available on cable, pay, or free TV.

In addition, as we noted earlier, the price and value issue has led to the expansion of minor professional leagues throughout the United States. As the NHL has expanded south and west, so have minor leagues such as the East Coast Hockey League (with franchises in cities such as Columbia, South Carolina, and Estero, Florida) and the Western Professional Hockey League (with franchises in locales like Odessa, Texas, and Albuquerque, New Mexico). Some minor leagues and lower priced professional leagues have expanded into so-called major-league markets. The Philadelphia Phantoms, the American Hockey League affiliate of the NHL Philadelphia Flyers, play in the building next to the Flyers' home, during the same season. The Phantoms survive as a lower cost alternative to their NHL neighbors, and they routinely draw well.

Suppliers also can exert a strong outside influence on organizations. They may raise their prices, or the quality of their goods may become a problem. As we noted previously, the labor supply may be limited in its skill or number, thus requiring organizations to train new hires or seek new source of talent. As we discussed in Chapter 2, apparel and footwear manufacturers such as Nike, adidas, and Puma enter into agreements with pro leagues to supply uniforms, footwear, and sideline and practice clothing in exchange for the right to sell products bearing the NFL and NFL team logos and trademarks. The NFL then earns a royalty (4 to 6 percent) on the wholesale price of products sold. However, many individual players have their own personal endorsement agreements with these companies. For example, in 2001, New York Giants defensive back Jason Sehorn, who endorses Nike products, was fined $10,000 for wearing a hat without a Reebok or adidas logo, the two companies that have agreements to produce sideline apparel for the NFL, even though Sehorn was injured and not in uniform, and wasn't even wearing a Nike hat. Because of Sehorn's Nike deal, he couldn't wear another logo hat, so he and other Nike endorsers must go hatless on the sidelines (Weisman, 2001). Confused? So was Sehorn. These agreements then must be clearly defined so the rights and responsibilities of teams, leagues, and suppliers are specifically delineated, or it will be costly.

Increasingly, pro sports leagues are viewing suppliers as potential sources of competitive advantage. Pro leagues understand that licensing partnerships with high-profile companies such as Nike and adidas mean that these companies will work to promote their league affiliations in their efforts to promote their own product sales.

Regulators are the final component of the organization's task environment. These outside agencies have the ability to control or influence the internal workings of an organization. For example, twelve U.S. cities collect nonresident local and state taxes from visiting players (the city of Columbus, Ohio, home of the NHL expansion Blue Jackets, collects a 2 percent tax from visiting players, coaches, and *trainers*). Players who live in states that collect income taxes get tax credits, so they aren't taxed on the same income twice (Lombardo, 2001). Philadelphia has a provision in its tax code that requires all professional athletes who play in the city, either for a local franchise or for a visiting team, to pay a certain percentage of their income to the city. For Philadelphia residents, the rate is 4.5635 percent, for nonresidents, 3.9672 percent. The amount of compensation subject to taxation is determined by multiplying the amount of compensation received by the factor resulting from dividing the total number of "duty days" within Philadelphia by the total number of "duty days." "Duty days" are defined as all days spent in training camp, in practice, and actual game days (McTamney, personal communication, February 26, 2001). For example, if the Florida Marlins play nine games against the Phillies at Veterans Stadium during the course of a season, the Marlins are required to withhold from each member of the Marlins 3.9672 percent of his income earned in those nine games. So if the Marlins begin practice in Florida on February 20 and end the season on October 1, that, excluding days off, would amount to approximately 210 "duty days." As a result, 4.29 percent of each Marlins' income would be subject to this tax. Local taxes also have implications when players switch teams. When pitcher Kevin Brown left the Florida Marlins to sign a seven-year $105 million deal with the Los Angeles Dodgers, he moved from a state with no income tax to California, which cost him $9.7 million (Lombardo, 2001).

Other taxes also impact leagues. When the Los Angeles Lakers played three games in Philadelphia against the 76ers in the 2001 NBA finals, the city realized $34,991 from the Lakers from the city's nonresident payroll tax (center Shaquille O'Neal paid $11,424 himself), $239,000 from the 5 percent amusement tax on tickets, and $25,000 from a 15 percent parking tax, for a total of close to $300,000 ("Lakers Expect," 2001).

Private interest groups also attempt to influence an organization's policies and procedures. When pro teams want to expand or build facilities, they often face scrutiny and outright opposition from local private interest groups who are against the team's efforts to take land or use local tax revenues to finance construction. As a result of efforts of such groups, several municipalities have recently voted against the use of such funds to finance pro team facilities, including Minneapolis, Charlotte, and San Francisco. Because of this fourth such voter rejection, the San Francisco Giants were forced to secure private financing for the construction of Pac Bell Park, making the new stadium the first sports team facility built with exclusively private funds since 1962 (Kaplan, 2000a).

At the minor-league level, citizens' groups in Springfield, Massachusetts, successfully fought to overturn Mayor Michael Albano's efforts to take by eminent domain a parcel of land for a proposed minor-league baseball stadium. Citizens' groups brought a suit against the seizure because the site supported a collection of shops, including a supermarket, on which local low-income residents without transportation relied. Other citizens' groups later mobilized to research and suggest other more acceptable sites.

Management's purpose in studying the general and task environments is to identify trends that represent opportunities or threats to the organization's ability to achieve its goals. This process of monitoring and evaluating puts the organization in a proactive rather than reactive position and reduces the likelihood of being caught off guard by shifts in the environment. This phase of the strategic management process can be thought of as a kind of early warning system that allows management to take the initiative either to maximize the opportunity or to minimize the corresponding threat resulting from the environmental change.

The Organization's Competencies*

There is more to a sports organization than its mission, philosophy, and goals. An organization consists of human, technological, and financial competencies as well. Once it is clear what changes are taking place in the environment, the next step is to analyze these competencies. A checklist of key areas of organizational competency might include the following.

Management. An analysis of organizational successes and failures indicates that one crucial ingredient in virtually every case is management expertise. Does the organization possess the management skill and experience necessary to address a potential threat or to pursue a potential opportunity? Perhaps the worst professional franchise in North America is the NBA's Los Angeles Clippers, owned by successful real estate developer Donald Sterling. Under Sterling's eighteen years of ownership, the Clippers have had exactly one winning season. A former player blames Sterling directly: "To have a decent team you need to keep a core of players together and let them grow. Sterling doesn't do that. He's not a builder, he's a meddler . . . money is the root of all evil, and Sterling likes to hold on to his" (p. 64).

Sterling has also refused to add players when the team's roster was reduced by injuries. As a result, midway through the 2000–2001 season, the Clippers were again next to last in the league in attendance, playing to an average of 64.1 percent of capacity in the new state-of-the-art Staples Center. In contrast, their arena neighbor, the 2000 NBA champion Lakers, draw on average seven thousand more fans each game while charging more for tickets.

Corporate culture and values. Is the value system of the organization consistent with the demands of the environment? For example, there is a problem if the organization values conservative decision making and the environment requires risk taking. There is also a problem if the environment requires a focus on customer demands and the organization does not value customer input. If the environment demands speed and innovation, are these also valued inside the organization? Are there cultural and values issues that the Lakers have that the Clippers do not? Is there any reason the Clippers can't be as successful as the Lakers? A Los Angeles sportswriter summed up owner Sterling's values when he remarked, "Sterling's agenda is as much social as professional. He loves the status that owning even a bad team confers." Player agent David Falk is more direct: "At some level, Sterling must be content being the losingest NBA owner ever" (pp. 64, 67).

Human resources. Do the organization's employees have the skills necessary to respond effectively to changes in the environment? As technology becomes more complex, does the organization have the people able to operate complex systems? As the environment requires competition on a global basis, does the organization have the people with the language skills and cultural understanding necessary to compete?

Unless otherwise noted, information in this section is from Lidz, 2000.

A former Clippers' general manager concedes the team's woes stem from the fact that "there have been a lot of bad decisions by people who have worked for him, including me," but Sterling once appointed a close friend and former model (with no basketball experience) to the position of assistant general manager. One might not have to think long about why. Says Sterling, "I'm only as good as my advisers" (pp. 64, 68).

Operational systems. Does the organization possess, or can it develop, the systems necessary for the business to succeed? The Clippers have had significant problems in their efforts to secure and retain talent. In 1987 the team drafted Reggie Williams over Scottie Pippen and Reggie Miller; in 1989, they opted for Danny Ferry over Glenn Rice; and in 1990, the team passed on Jayson Williams and Toni Kukoc in favor of Bo Kimble. Poor trades have also been routine, as evidenced by the trade of twenty-seven-year-old Danny Manning for an aging Dominique Wilkins in 1993. The Clippers have also failed to lure any significant free agents or retained any of value, which may happen when one of their few strong picks, 1999 pick Lamar Odom, is eligible for free agency.

Marketing. Does the organization have the ability to evaluate customer needs and to effectively price, promote, and advertise its products and services? Sterling once slashed the Clippers' advertising budget from $200,000 to less than $9,000. Enough said.

Financial resources. Does the organization have access to the financial resources necessary to respond effectively to the environment? Can it afford the management, human resources, technology, research, and marketing that will allow it to compete? Even though the Clippers share the Los Angeles market with the far more successful Lakers, the region can easily support two NBA franchises. The NBA shares revenues and controls salary expenses among teams. Sterling has shown the ability to be successful in other business ventures, but a clear and realistic understanding by the organization of its own competencies is essential to analyzing the situation. Only with an understanding of its competencies can the Clippers or any other pro sports franchise or league begin the process of determining its strategic strengths and weaknesses.

SWOT Analysis

The process of considering an organization's competencies in terms of changes in the environment is called a *SWOT analysis* (Andrews, 1971; Hofer & Schendel, 1978). SWOT stands for the *s*trengths and *w*eaknesses of the organization and the *o*pportunities and *t*hreats in the environment.

Any SWOT analysis of a professional sports league must consider what Much and Gotto (1997) define as the key elements in determining franchise value: the degree of revenue sharing within the league and the stability of the league's labor agreements. A third factor, which is related to labor relations, is how well the league controls its most significant expenditure, player salaries.

Pro league revenues and expenses. Professional leagues rely on two revenue sources most heavily: ticket sales and media revenues. Although often overshadowed by emerging revenue sources such as naming rights, sponsorships, and facility revenues such as personal seat licenses and luxury box rentals, revenues from ticket sales remain the most prominent revenue source for pro league teams. Media revenues, including television rights' fees paid to teams and leagues, are the next most important income source for most leagues and franchises. The exception is the NFL, which, as outlined in Chapter 3, generates a far greater percentage and overall amount of media revenues than other leagues. However, facility revenues are becoming a more important factor in determining franchise values because much of these revenues are not part of revenue-sharing agreements or used to determine salary cap figures, and they are one of the main driving forces in motivating pro league teams to seek new venues in which to play (Ozanian, 1998). The greatest expense for pro league franchises is player costs, which includes most prominently player salaries. Figure 6-6 shows a percentage breakdown of revenues for the Big Four pro leagues.

Although the overall average for media revenues totals 39 percent, this is mainly because 51 percent of NFL team revenues come from national and local media sources, whereas other pro league franchises derive only 15 percent of revenues from these sources. As noted in Chapter 3, the big differences here are the money from national TV deals. In 2001 NFL franchises earned $75 million each from network deals; NBA teams got $30.3 million and MLB teams, $22 million.

Revenue sharing. As we discussed earlier in this chapter, through the concept of league-think, where national television revenues were shared equally among all teams, former NFL commissioner Pete Rozelle established the NFL as the most effective and profitable pro sports league. Leagues also share revenues from licensing royalties (usually equally among all franchises) and a percentage of ticket sales. For example, the NFL shifted its ticket revenue–sharing plan in 2001 from a 60/40 spilt of each individual game, where the home team gave 40 percent of ticket and other game-day revenues to the visitors, to a plan where 40 percent of all ticket revenues throughout the league would be distributed to each team equally. This plan was agreed to by the owners to pave the way for league realignment, which would have otherwise been opposed by franchises such as the Arizona Cardinals, who balked at the idea of moving from the NFC East and losing the big paydays from annual visits to Dallas, New York, and Washington (Elliott, 2001). Because of this

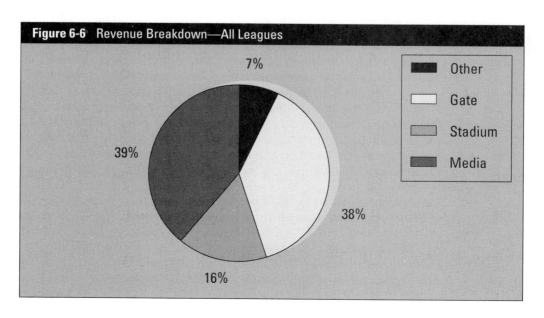

Figure 6-6 Revenue Breakdown—All Leagues

- Other
- Gate
- Stadium
- Media

7%
39%
38%
16%

plan, and the fact that Commissioner Paul Tagliabue had the power to make it happen based on the provisions that recent expansion teams could not oppose the moves, league realignment based on geographic proximity was approved in May 2001 for the 2002 season, with a four-division structure in each conference.

The key revenue-sharing difference among pro leagues is not how they share national media revenues, because leagues share that equally, but rather the nature of local TV media revenues. This is seen most acutely in MLB, where the national media revenues are overshadowed by the impact of local media revenues. The most telling comparison that highlights this disparity is between the New York Yankees and the Montreal Expos. In 2001 the Yankees earned $53 million in their local TV deal with the MSG Network. The Expos had no local TV deals and generated nothing (Rofe, 2000). As a result, the Yankees were able to fund a payroll of close to $120 million and won their twenty-fifth World Series, whereas the Expos' payroll hovered at $20 million as the club again finished below .500, twenty-eight games out of first place. In comparison, the Washington Redskins generated total revenues of $148.7 million in 1999, the most in the NFL; the Cincinnati Bengals earned the least, bringing in $90.9 million. Although this is a difference of nearly $60 million, the Bengals still made over $8 million (eighteenth in the league), and the Redskins made $32.3 million (second in the league) ("NFL Team," 2001).

Labor relations and salary control. The ability of a professional league to maintain consistency in its labor agreements with players' unions and control the major expense of player salaries directly impacts the value of a pro league franchise and its level of profitability. The league that has had the most problematic relationship with its players' union is MLB, underscored by its player strike and subsequent cancellation of the World Series in 1994. Previously, MLB experienced eight stoppages in play from 1972 to 1994 due to player strikes or owner lockouts (Helyar, 1994). The strength of the players' union has earned it the right to salary arbitration, which has contributed to the increase of the average MLB payroll from under $20 million in 1988 to $63 million in 2001 (Blum, 2001; Bodley, 1999). The NFL has had the most control in dealing with its players' association, following the breaking of the player strike in 1987 through the use of replacement players. Said one agent who represents NFL players, "It's incredible how much power the owners have, and how little the players get" (Cafardo, 2001, p. F5). In 2001 the league and the players' union agreed to extend their current collective bargaining agreement (see Chapter 8) through 2007. The deal, which continues to preserve NFL labor peace, increases minimum salaries for rookies and certain veterans in an effort to end the recent trend of cutting certain veteran players due to salary cap concerns (Willing, 2001).

Salaries are controlled in the NFL and NBA by salary caps, which put strict controls over how much individual teams can spend on player salaries and in some cases, places limitations on the salaries of individual players. The NHL and MLB have no set caps, but the latter does charge a luxury tax on those teams whose payrolls exceed a certain level. The tax is then distributed to the poorest teams in the league.

Salary caps are set based on a percentage of team revenues. In the NBA, the league and players' union agreed that the salary cap would be tied to all "basketball-related income" (BRI), such as ticket sales, media revenues, and licensing (but excludes a portion of facility revenues such as stadium-naming rights and luxury box rentals). In 2000–2001, the estimated total NBA BRI was $2.1 billion, which meant the individual team cap was set at $34 million.

The cap also sets maximum individual salaries for star players and sets minimums and maximums for other players based on years of experience. For example, a player with seven years of experience or less can make either 25 percent of the team's cap total, 105 percent of his previous salary, or $9 million. These limitations are in place to distribute money evenly to more players, rather than allowing a star player to make far more than his teammates.

However, the NBA's cap is considered soft, because there are certain exceptions. Teams can spend whatever they want to sign their own free agents. This clause is in place so teams may maintain fan interest by retaining those star players who have established their careers with a certain club. The NFL, because of its stronger bargaining power with its players' union, has the "hardest" cap in pro league sports, meaning it has the fewest exceptions, and allows teams to control costs most effectively.

The strengths and weakness of pro franchises are revealed in their relative values, as shown in Figure 6-7. Due to the levels of revenue sharing, labor relations, and salary control, three of the top eight most valuable franchises are in the NFL, and eight of the top ten most profitable franchises are either NBA or NFL teams.

Through a SWOT analysis involving these factors of revenue sharing, labor relations, and salary control, a pro sports organization can determine whether its level of competencies represents strategic strengths or weaknesses given the current environment. Once a SWOT analysis has identified strengths and weaknesses in terms of opportunities and threats in the environment, an organization can begin to consider strategic alternatives for achieving its goals.

Figure 6-7 The Top 10 Most Profitable Professional League Franchises	
1. **Dallas Cowboys (NFL):**	**$41.3 million**
2. Colorado Rockies (MLB):	$38.3 million
3. **Portland Trailblazers (NBA):**	**$34.2 million**
4. **Washington Redskins (NFL):**	**$31.7 million**
5. **Miami Dolphins (NFL):**	**$31.6 million**
6. **Detroit Pistons (NBA):**	**$30.0 million**
7. **Los Angeles Lakers (NBA):**	**$24.8 million**
8. New York Yankees (MLB):	$21.4 million
9. **Utah Jazz (NBA):**	**$20.7 million**
10. **Houston Rockets (NBA):**	**$20.3 million**
Source: Ozanian, 1998.	

Step 3: Developing Strategy

The term *strategy* comes from the Greek term "to lead an army." In that sense, a strategy is a kind of battle plan. In strategic management terms, strategy is the course of action an organization selects to minimize threats and maximize opportunities that emerge in the environment.

As shown in Figure 6-8, the strategies an organization selects must reflect its mission, the opportunities and threats in the environment, and its own strengths and weaknesses. The process of developing strategy, shown as the shaded area in Figure 6-8, helps the organization find its best fit among the three sets of forces.

Developing Strategic Alternatives

Strategic alternatives are the options that management can select as the possible courses of action for obtaining its goals. *Corporate-level strategy* deals with the alternatives a company or organization explores as it conducts business across several industries or markets. For example, most professional leagues have a non-profit division that organizes the activities of the league and a for-profit division (usually referred to as a properties division) that handles licensing, sponsorships, and media negotiations. These individual properties divisions are then further divided. For example, the NBA's licensing division is subdivided into a sales segment (serving as a liaison with retailers), a marketing segment (developing retail promotions), an apparel licensing segment (for licensing agreements with apparel manufacturers), and a nonapparel licensing segment (for licensing

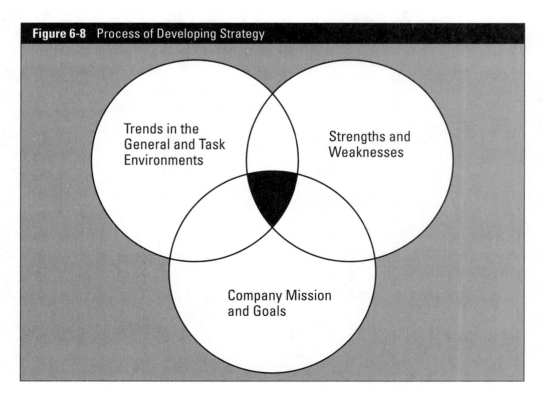

Figure 6-8 Process of Developing Strategy

Trends in the General and Task Environments

Strengths and Weaknesses

Company Mission and Goals

agreements with nonapparel manufacturers) (Covell, 2000). Organizations with interests in more than one industry or more than one market require corporate strategies that lead its various divisions in a unified direction.

Business-level strategy deals with alternatives for a company operating in a single industry. Individual league franchises are more likely to fit this description and are more likely to require a strategy for the success of that single franchise.

Functional-level strategy involves plans for each of the organization's functional areas. Key areas typically include research and development, operations, finance, marketing, and human resources. Strategies at the functional level are designed to implement the higher level strategies at the corporate or business level. Figure 6-9 summarizes the characteristics of the three levels of strategic alternatives. The following is a more detailed discussion of each of these three levels.

Corporate-Level Strategy

At the corporate level, strategy deals with an organization's decision about either expanding or retreating in general or from industry to industry. These decisions are not made in a vacuum. The strategic alternative a corporation chooses depends on the environmental conditions of today and the forecasted trends of tomorrow.

Merger and acquisition. These strategies involve an organization's merging with or purchasing an organization in another industry to offset threats in its own environment and/or take advantage of opportunities in the environment of another industry. In the professional league environment, more and more franchises have been acquired by media companies. Disney (which owns ABC and the ESPN networks) owns the MLB Anaheim Angels and the Anaheim Mighty Ducks, Fox owns the Los Angeles Dodgers, and AOL/Time Warner owns the Braves, Hawks, and Thrashers. These acquisitions allow for these media companies to provide game and other various related content for their various broadcast outlets, rather than paying some other ownership group for the right to broadcast games, and they allow them to control expenses as well.

These acquisitions are also an example of the trend away from individual ownership of professional league franchises to a corporate ownership structure. Fewer and fewer franchises are owned by individuals or families. The increased financial

Figure 6-9 Different Levels of Strategic Alternatives	
Corporate Level	Strategies pertaining to companies that conduct business across several industries and several markets.
Business Level	Strategies for companies operating in a single industry.
Functional Level	Strategies for the organization's functional areas or departments.

risk that has emerged due to the ever-increasing cost of purchasing franchises (including the $1 billion expansion fee paid in 1998 by the ownership group of the NFL's thirty-second franchise, the Houston Texans) and the ever-increasing costs associated with salaries and facility construction have rendered individual ownership virtually obsolete.

Retrenchment. When an organization is not competing effectively, *retrenchment*, or turn-around strategies, are often needed. One retrenchment option involves divesting, selling off divisions in industries an organization no longer wants to do business in. The other involves downsizing, which typically involves a significant reduction in the size of an organization and the number of employees working for it. Many new and emerging leagues often go through a retrenchment period when financially shaky or poorly managed franchises are dropped or merged with other stronger franchises. The purpose of such a strategy is to enable a league to become more effective as it competes in its environment.

Business-Level Strategy

The second level of strategy deals with an organization or corporate business unit operating in a single industry. The purpose of defining a business-level strategy is to give the organization an advantage over its competition in the same industry. At the business level are three approaches for achieving a competitive advantage: differentiation, cost leader, and focus (Porter, 1985).

Differentiation. When an organization attempts to gain a competitive advantage through a differentiation strategy, it strives to be unique in its industry or market segment by designing product characteristics to satisfy customer needs in ways that competitors find difficult to match. This uniqueness may come from physical characteristics of the product, such as quality or reliability, or it may lie in the product's appeal to customers' psychological needs. Consider the WUSA, the premier women's professional soccer league owned by cable TV distributors including Time Warner, Cox, and Comcast, which began play in 2001. Each investor committed $8 million and company resources and cable network promotion airtime (Lee, 2001). Men's soccer remains the world's most popular sport, but it has gained only limited popularity in the United States (see later). However, the U.S. women's national team is a perennial power, winning the 1996 Olympic gold medal along with the 1999 World Cup before a packed house in the Rose Bowl in Pasadena, California, on Brandi Chastain's sports-bra baring overtime penalty kick goal.

www.wusa.com

To build on this success and fan interest, the WUSA began play in April, with playoffs in mid-August, with franchises located in Atlanta, Boston, Chapel Hill, North Carolina (to capitalize on the local market interest in the University of North Carolina's dominant women's soccer team), Philadelphia, San Diego, San Jose, Washington, D.C., and Uniondale, New York, and many of the national team stars (who are also part owners in the league) will be distributed throughout the WUSA, along with some of the world's best non-U.S. players such as Chinese goalkeeper Gao Hong, Norwegian midfielder Dagny Mellgren, and Brazilian forward Pretinha (Weeks, 2001).

Grassroots marketing will be a key strategy for the WUSA. The league will target female fans as its main support base and promote the league as a pioneering opportunity for women in professional sport, because according to Lauren Gregg, vice president of the league, girls "can grow up knowing that boys and girls are going to be great athletes and they can be successful in whatever they do" (Brennan, 2001, p. 3C). Says Joe Cummings, general manager of the Boston Breakers, "We have to get into the communities, talk to people, and form relationships" (Lee, 2001, p. 43).

Cost leader. The alternative to differentiation is the cost leader strategy. A cost leader strategy is pursued by companies that strive to produce goods or services at the lowest cost in the industry, thereby enabling them to offer the lowest prices. The WUSA controls player costs through its single-entity structure (where all franchise ownership and team decisions are made by the league) so that teams will not bid against each other for player services as with most other leagues. The league's minimum salary is $25,000, the maximum is $85,000, and the average is $40,000. The league's average ticket price is $11 (Hiestand, 2001a), $8 less than the average ticket price for MLB. Based on these figures, the league's plan is to break even in 2006 based on an initial $64 million investment, and it seeks to attract an average game attendance of 7,000 and between $15 and $20 million in corporate sponsorships (Lee, 2001).

Focus. In the focus strategy, an organization targets a particular customer or geographic market or follows a focus strategy that specializes it in some way. As noted, the WUSA will target female fans and TV viewers. Twenty-two games will be broadcast nationally on TNT and CNN/SI, and the league hopes to earn ratings between 0.5 and 1.0. However, this focus does not guarantee success, because according to ESPN research vice president Artie Bulgrin, a viewer's interest in a particular sport is "absolutely" more important than the gender of its participants. Bulgrin notes that women comprise only 33 percent of ESPN's women's college basketball, so targeting women primarily may be shortsighted. However, according to WUSA vice president Gregg, at the league's inaugural game, a fan won a car during a halftime promotion. When player Judy Foudy presented her with the car, the fan said, "I don't care about the car. Can I have a picture of you?" Gregg stated, "The fact that she was face to face with this heroine for her, that's what we're about" (Hiestand, 2001, p. 3C). Female leagues like the WUSA must also target potential sponsors to associate with them for additional revenues. According to Bart McGuire of the Women's Tennis Association (WTA), "We need to persuade businesses to recognize that women's sports in general are a really good investment vehicle. We're still a cheap date. A good company could obtain a significant sponsorship position (in any women's league) for less than half what they pay for one 30-second spot on the Super Bowl" (Brennan, 2001, p. 3C).

Functional-Level Strategy

Functional-level strategies deal with plans that must be developed in each of the organization's key areas of functioning to support and implement corporate-level and business-level strategies. For example, a typical NFL franchise has separate function areas such as general counsel, finance, marketing, football operations, and coaching. The general counsel handles all legal and contract matters for the team, human resources issues and policies, and litigation coordination. *Finance* area handles all team financial and tax matters, concessions operations, ticket sales, facilities, and coordinates with the league on all financial matters. The *marketing* area is responsible for all team marketing efforts including sponsorship, public relations, special events, and coordinating with the league on marketing issues. *Football operations* coordinates player contract negotiations, salary cap administration, and serves as a liaison between coaches and scouts. The *coaching* segment, overseen by the head coach, is responsible for all team-related operations and player personnel decisions (*Executive organization*, 1999).

Steps 4 and 5: Implementing Strategy and Strategic Control

As important as it is, the development of strategy is not enough to ensure that an organization will achieve its mission and goals. For strategies to be effective, they must be translated into action. This brings us to the final two stages of the strategic management approach to planning: implementing strategy and strategic control. We discuss each of these two areas briefly here. Implementing strategy, or operational planning, and strategic control are the focus of Chapter 7.

Implementing Strategy

The implementation of strategy is actually the first stage of what is called the operational planning phase of strategic management. *Operational planning* is the process of determining how the corporate- or business-level strategy will be put into action.

The implementation of strategy is key for YankeeNets. The organization was formed in 1999 by major partners George Steinbrenner of the Yankees and the NBA's New Jersey Nets' owners Lewis Katz and Raymond Chambers. In 2000 the organization purchased through a subsidiary the NHL's New Jersey Devils for $175 million. The firm also signed a deal to sell joint sponsorships with the NFL's New York Giants. YankeeNets' business-level strategy is focus. It was formed, in the words of Randy Vataha, president of Game Plan LLC, a sports business advisory firm (and himself a former NFL wide receiver), "to become a multifaceted sports and entertainment company. The sports assets are just there to build off of" (Kaplan, 2000b, p. 24). The firm oversees business operations for the three teams, including ticket and stadium operations, advertising and sponsorships, and television rights. Steinbrenner, who purchased 57 percent of the Yankees with partners for $10 million in 1973, made $160 million when the firm was formed, and he now owns 28 percent of YankeeNets (Gruen, 2001).

Recall that in implementing a focus strategy, an organization targets a particular customer or geographic market or follows a focus strategy that specializes it in some way. The focus, therefore, for YankeeNets is to build a regional sports firm that can now provide an opportunity for the development of bundled sponsorships and media rights for all three properties, thereby increasing the value of each. In addition, the Devils and Nets, often perceived as second-tier franchises in the competitive New York sports market, benefit from the affiliation with the Yankees' brand. The Yankees gain sales and marketing expertise from these firms that have always had to work harder and be more innovative in selling tickets and sponsorships.

Long-terms plans also called for YankeeNets to form their own broadcast subsidiary, which is a twist on the trend where media companies acquire pro teams for broadcasting purposes (Kaplan, 2000b). A firm such as YankeeNets could then acquire the means to produce their own broadcasts and retain all the generated revenue. For this strategy to work, it must then be translated into programs, policies, and procedures that constitute "strategy in action."

Strategic Control

The last step in the strategic management process involves continuous monitoring of the organization's progress toward its long-range goals and mission. It involves evaluating the effectiveness of the organization's strategy on an ongoing basis. Is the strategy working, or should it be revised? Is it still consistent with current environmental conditions? Are there problems with implementation? Where are the problems likely to occur?

One of the key motivations for creating YankeeNets had been to form its own regional sports network, but in 2001 TV broadcaster, MSG Network, owned by Cablevisions Systems Corporation, negotiated a one-year extension of its current $50 million a year deal. The presence of that much money on the table, plus MSG's threatened lawsuit over the contract, put the idea on hold. Then YankeeNets negotiated a deal with MSG to buy out its cable rights and created YankeeNets Entertainment Sports (YES), valued at $800 million by Goldman Sachs & Co., which promptly bought 40 percent of the venture in partnership with a former AT&T Broadband CEO (Kaplan & Bernstein, 2001).

YankeeNets also has plans to build a new facility for the Nets and the Devils in Newark, New Jersey, with the possibility of building a new home there for the Yankees as well. The firm has already been able to raise $214 million through the sale of high-risk junk bonds, but in November 2001, the project, expected to cost $355 million, was put on hold by the New Jersey state legislature (Kapla, 2000b; Kaplan & Bernstein, 2001). In light of some of the opposition to public financing of private sports facilities, this will make the task for YankeeNets more difficult. Also, the firm can expect a significant level of opposition from municipal and state political and community leaders, not to mention fans and the sports media, if it should try to move the storied "Bronx Bombers" ouf of the "House That Ruth Built" to downtown Newark and "A House That Junk Bonds Built." After the New Jersey legislature put the project on hold, Leonard Coleman, the former president of the National League now leading the stadium project for YankeeNets, issued a veiled threat that the Devils and Nets would leave New Jersey and "find someplace else to do business," but because the teams need to stay in the New York area to remain part of YES and no other cities have indicated interest in attracting the team, YankeeNets has little leverage (Kaplan & Bernstein, 2001). Based on the monitoring of the effectiveness of its strategy, YankeeNets changed its immediate approach to the regional sports network and may have to alter its facility construction plans.

Financial controls, in the form of budgets, often provide warning signals that potential problem areas might exist. *Budgets* are statements of expected results in financial terms. Discrepancies between budget targets and actual results may be an indication of unanticipated occurrences. Monitoring performance, in this case financial performance, allows an organization to measure the success of its strategies.

Nonfinancial controls are used for the same purpose and include areas such as productivity and quality controls and feedback from customers. Most organizations use a combination of financial and nonfinancial controls to provide early-warning systems.

The strategy scorecard is based on the concept of a balanced scorecard, which is a means for reviewing and controlling performance (Kaplan & Norton, 1992). Like the balanced scorecard, the strategy scorecard involves setting targeted "scores" for four different areas of an organization: financial, customers, operations, and human resources. However, the strategy scorecard goes one step further by defining measures linked specifically to the organization's mission and long-term strategies.

For example, consider the Colorado Rockies' mission to provide the highest level of baseball entertainment in an excellent stadium environment at prices affordable for families, and to support the development of youth baseball throughout the Rocky Mountain region. What measures can be set forth to determine whether this mission and strategies to achieve it are being implemented successfully? Figure 6-10 shows the types of measures that might be developed in each of the four different areas and their relationship to the mission. When the measures are linked to the organization's mission, the strategy scorecard provides the basis for successful strategic measurement and management. In essence, it links the energies, abilities, and specific knowledge of people throughout the sports organization to specific measures, and everyone knows the score.

Epilogue

The NHL has now established its markets and is beginning a new era in which player salaries, although not yet approaching those of baseball and basketball,

Figure 6-10 Colorado Rockies' Strategy Scorecard

		Mission
1. Financial	Revenue target (a,c) Expense ratios (c) Profit targets (c) X percent of revenue allocated for youth baseball training camp (d)	a. Highest level of baseball entertainment
2. Customers	Level of customer satisfaction based on survey data (a) Number of fans' visits per season (a) Number of families attending each game (c)	b. Excellent stadium environment
3. Operations	Stadium sound levels (b) Number of broken seats (b) Amount of unsold food discarded after each game (b)	c. Prices affordable to families
4. Human resources	Employee turnover rates (a, b) Salary levels (a, b) Employee surveys to determine satisfaction (a, b)	d. Support of youth baseball

nonetheless are rising at an accelerated rate. Third- and fourth-line players are now commanding salaries previously held only by the game's elite. It would seem that the NHL would seek not to emulate this pattern of escalation experienced in baseball, but the lack of an NFL-like hard cap has seen payrolls grow exponentially. As we discuss in Chapter 8, during the 1990s, the average salary in the NHL grew 517 percent to $1.4 million ("Sports Salaries," 2001).

Following the 2001 season, the Washington Capitals signed recently acquired former Pittsburgh Penguins star forward Jaromir Jagr to a two-year $20.7 million contract, making him the highest paid NHL player by annual salary. Caps owner Ted Leonsis justified the expenditure even though the Caps lost $20 million in 2001 because "you have to spend money to make money . . . we got somebody who made the needle move on all the metrics—ticket sales, TV contract, merchandise." Several weeks later, the New York Islanders signed formerly recalcitrant Ottawa Senators forward Alexi Yashin to the richest contract in NHL history (ten years, nearly $90 million). While Philadelphia Flyers general manager Bobby Clarke admitted that "in every sport it seems like the team with the highest payroll are the top teams" (La Canfora, 2001, p. D6), Canucks GM Brian Burke, who as noted earlier must deal with the limitations of the Canadian exchange rate and lack of government support, referred to this and other signings as "crazy money . . . I know we can't support the salaries. I know that some of the teams who have spent that money are doing it without financial capability to pay the money. I'm running my business like a business. I'm going head to head with people who are crazy, as far as I'm concerned" (Griffiths, 2001, p. 42; La Canfora, 2001; "Yahsin Scores," 2001).

Former Minnesota Twins part owner Clark C. Griffiths disagrees with Leonsis's assertion, because the Capitals, unlike AOL, the company through which Leonsis made his fortune, cannot expand beyond its home market and generate additional revenues other than what they can acquire in tickets, sponsorships, and local broadcast revenue. Whereas NHL teams rely most heavily on gate receipts for revenue, the Caps don't have enough stadium capacity at the MCI Center to make the income to cover Jagr's salary, so they'll have to raise prices. In fact, Griffiths (2001) argues that a high-priced player like Jagr will contribute little to making the Caps, a playoff team in 2001, better and able to generate more revenue. In fact, in 2001 the expansion Minnesota Wild had a payroll of $15.3 million and earned 68 points; the New York Rangers spent $55.5 million and amassed 72 points. The cost of those four additional points—either two wins, four ties, or a win and two ties—is $40.2 million, at a cost of $20.1 million a win or $10.05 million a tie.

Although the NHL reacted to environmental changes over the past few decades with a generally successful approach to franchise expansion and relocation, many of the leagues' franchises now face financial peril because of burgeoning salaries. We have learned that through planning, sports organizations are able to keep pace with changes in the environment, rather than simply react to them. Strategic planning is the responsibility for understanding the mission of the organization, for anticipating and recognizing changes in the world outside the organization, and for developing strategies for positioning the organization to compete in the changing environment. Whether the NHL will adapt this approach to control upwardly spiraling salaries remains to be seen, but as Commissioner Bettman stated, "If the system is not working correctly, it will have to be addressed" (La Canfora, 2001, p. D6), either by strike or lockout. Stay tuned.

Summary

One of the most powerful tools that management has for ensuring an organization's long-term success is planning. The process begins with a review of the organization's mission, which identifies the organization's business and goals. A detailed situational analysis follows, beginning with an assessment of trends in both the general and the task environment of the organization. The organization's competencies are then evaluated and assessed in terms of opportunities and threats in the environment. Referred to as a SWOT analysis, this process of assessing the organization's competencies in light of environmental conditions helps management identify potential areas where the organization may be weak or strong or where the environment is threatening or promising.

Based on the SWOT analysis, strategies at the corporate, business, and functional levels are formulated to maximize opportunities and minimize threats to the organization as it seeks to achieve its mission and goals. Corporate-level strategies consist of strategic choices made when organizations compete in several industries. At this level, organizations may pursue strategies of merger and acquisitions as a way of growing or may reduce the size of the organization by retrenching or downsizing.

Business-level strategy deals with strategic alternatives for a company operating in a single industry. The approaches available at the business level include differentiation, cost leader, and focus strategies. All three provide an organization the opportunity to achieve a strategic advantage over competitors in the same industry.

Functional-level strategies define the plans of action that are necessary in each of the organization's functional areas to carry out the corporate- and/or business-level strategies. This level of planning—operational planning—is part of the implementation stage of the strategic management process.

Finally, strategic control involves constantly monitoring the organization's progress toward its long-term goals and mission. Financial and nonfinancial controls provide information to the organization about whether its strategies are working, whether they are consistent with the environment, and where problems are likely to occur.

The strategic management process puts the organization in an offensive, proactive position. Identifying shifts and trends in the environment enables management to respond more effectively to new technologies, new competition, social changes, and changes in the political and legal environment. When sports managers deal with challenges today by revising their mission, goals, and strategies, they are in a better position to avoid crises tomorrow and to take full advantage of tomorrow's opportunities.

The Big Four Plus One?

Throughout this chapter we have referred most often with our examples to the "Big Four" professional sports leagues. But there are many other leagues across the country as well. Major League Soccer (MLS) is one of those "other" leagues.

Although soccer (the sport referred to as "football" outside North America) is the world's most popular sport, and many American boys and girls participate on school and youth league teams (three million on youth teams and more than half a million in high school ["Soccer," 2001]), professional league soccer has never broken into the ranks of the "Big Four."

MLS, which began play in 1996 with franchises in Foxboro (Massachusetts), East Rutherford (New Jersey), Washington (D.C.), Tampa, Columbus (Ohio), Kansas City, Dallas, Denver, San Jose, and Los Angeles, is the most recent professional soccer league incarnation, following the failure of the North American Soccer League in 1984. The league ownership and operating structure is unlike most other pro leagues. The league is structured as a single limited liability company (referred to as a "single entity") with individual investors not owning franchises themselves, but rather owning a financial stake in the entire league. The league states that this allows the investors to operate autonomously, but with the incentive to see that all teams are successful ("About MLS," 2001). The league owns the member clubs, negotiates national media, sponsorship, and licensing deals, and signs players and allocates them to teams. Teams hire staff, negotiate local media deals and run local promotions, and keep 50 percent of ticket, parking, and concessions revenues, all local sponsorship revenues, any local broadcast revenues up to $1.1 million annually, and 30 percent of any local broadcast revenues above the $1.1 million level (Gruen, 2001). This might seem like a logical extension of Rozelle's league-think, but what the single-entity structure really does is serve to counteract any antitrust claims by players hoping to increase salaries through contract bidding between franchises.

The league has hoped to capitalize on the buzz created after the United States played host to the 1994 World Cup, soccer's international championship. MLS expanded to Chicago and Miami/Fort Lauderdale in 1998 and has attracted by its count more than eleven million fans in its first four years—an average of more than fifteen thousand a game—at an average ticket price of $14. The league has attempted to create on-the-field play that "encourages attacking and entertaining soccer" and to promote the development of native-born players ("About MLS," 2001) in part as a reaction to common criticisms by nonsoccer fans that games are boring 1–0 (or "nil") affairs played by a bunch of foreigners they've never heard of. Says one expert, "Any sport needs nationalism and stars. . . . The MLS's problem is that it is not the best league and best American players play in European leagues" (Dell'Apa, 2001b, p. E9).

As a result, average attendance has declined 21 percent since 1996 (Frank, 2001). Although the league has investors who are both "patient and rich," progress has still been slow in attracting new investors, expansion, and the construction of team-owned venues more suited to soccer (Dell'Apa, 2001a, p. D7). All told, the league has lost a total of $250 million (Brewington, 2001).

Management Exercise

Although the league has broadcast agreements with ESPN, ESPN2, ABC, and Telemundo, ratings have remained low (0.34 on ESPN, 0.22 on ESPN2, 0.8 on ABC), and the league receives no money up front from broadcasters, but rather shares in any revenues generated. By comparison, NBC pays the University of Notre Dame nearly $7 million a year to broadcast the Fighting Irish's home football games. This supports the notion that people don't always watch what they like to do themselves. High-participation sports like bowling, swimming, bicycling, and freshwater fishing have little TV appeal (Hiestand, 2001a).

Like the NHL, MLS is also considering expansion, even though the league has had trouble attracting investors to take over the league-operated teams in Dallas and Tampa (owners of other local sports franchises have been cited as possible candidates [Dell'Apa, 2001a], which would mirror the ownership model of the Kraft family [which owns the New England Patriots and operates the New England Revolution] and the Lamar Hunt family [which owns the Kansas City Chiefs and runs the Columbus Crew and the Kansas City Wizards]). One company, Anschutz Entertainment, operates five franchises (Chicago, Colorado, D.C. United, Los Angeles, New York/New Jersey), and other investors have been wary of MLS involvement because of the limited amount of control they have over teams (Gruen, 2001).

Several cities, including Houston, Milwaukee, St. Louis, Winston-Salem (North Carolina), Portland (Oregon), Rochester (New York), and Seattle are under consideration as potential expansion sites. The league has stated that an ideal number of teams is sixteen, but that "expansion will not occur at the expense of the quality of play, the dilution of player talent, . . . or without a community that has a proven ability to support major professional sports, including soccer" ("About MLS," 2001, pp. 5–6). In addition, like MLB, the league is considering contraction, with the two league-operated franchises and Miami reported as likely candidates for extinction.

Now here's where things get interesting. You have been given an undisclosed amount of venture capital from a long-lost, recently deceased aunt, which, when coupled with your recent winnings from jai alai from a spring break visit to South Florida, has put you in position to buy into the MLS. But before you do that, you need to apply your understanding of the concepts of strategic management to determine whether this is a solid investment. Here's what you need to do:

1. First, create a mission statement for MLS.

2. Define the general and task environments for MLS.

3. Compose a SWOT analysis for MLS versus the other "Big Four" leagues.

4. Explain which business-level strategy should be implemented in the league's efforts to expand.

5. As the league decides on its expansion site (and the city in which your team will be located), how will the implementing of strategy and strategic control be applied?

6. Finally, for the expansion choices listed above, which, in your opinion, would be the best expansion site?

Abell, D. F. (1980). *Defining the business: The starting point of strategic planning*. Englewood Cliffs, NJ: Prentice-Hall.

About MLS. (2001). Major League Soccer. [online]. Available: http://www.mlsnet.com/about/index.html.

Allen, K. (1999a, April 9). Canadian clubs: Help! *USA Today*, p. C1.

Allen, K. (1999b, May 11). Pittsburgh could lose a winner. *USA Today*, p. 3C.

Allen, K. (2001, January 8). Lemieux takes show on the road. *USA Today*, p. 3C.

Andrews, K. R. (1971). *The concept of corporate strategy*. Homewood, IL: Dow Jones Irwin.

Bernstein, A. (2000, December 25–31). Mario worth $2.9M in Pens' tix revenue. *Street & Smith's SportsBusiness Journal*, p. 1.

Blum, R. (2001, April 5). Welcome to the age of $2 million men. *Boston Globe*, p. C3.

Bodley, H. (1999, April 2). Earnings, salary gap 'most crucial issue.' *USA Today*, p. 13C.

Bouchikhi, H., & Kimberly, J. R. (2000). The customized workplace. In S. Chowdhury (Ed.), *Management 21C* (pp. 207–219). London: Pearson Education.

Brennan, C. (2001, May 8). Talking about a revolution. *USA Today*, p. 3C.

Brewington, P. (2001, March 21). Higher season-ticket sales give MLS a kick. *USA Today*, p. 1C.

Cafardo, N. (2001, May 13). Eagles could take a direct hit. *Boston Globe*, p. F5.

Carlson-Thomas, C. (1992, February). Strategic vision or strategic con: Rhetoric or reality? *Long-Range Planning*, pp. 81–89.

Cohen, T. (2000, April 9). Canada on guard. *Boston Globe*, p. D17.

Collins, J. (1997). It's not what you make, it's what you stand for. *Inc.*, 19(14), pp. 42–45.

Collins, J. C., & Porras, J. I. (1996). Building your company's vision. *Harvard Business Review, 74*(5), pp. 65–77.

Covell, D. (2000). Licensed and branded merchandise. In B. J. Mullin, S. Hardy, & W. A. Sutton (Eds.), *Sport marketing* (rev. ed) (pp. 139–160). Champaign, IL: Human Kinetics.

Dell'Apa, F. (2001a, March 6). Patience is a virtue of MLS owners. *Boston Globe*, p. D7.

Dell'Apa, F. (2001b, April 10). Planting the seeds of soccer. *Boston Globe*, p. E9.

Dupont, K. P. (2001a, January 14). Pro hockey. *Boston Globe*, p. C7.

Dupont, K. P. (2001b). February 1). Canadiens sold—to an American. *Boston Globe*, pp. E1, E3.

Ellick, A.B. (2001, October 3). Pledge of allegiance. *USA Today*, pp. 1C–2C.

Elliott, J. (2001, January 29). The Teflon league. *Sports Illustrated*, p. 31.

Executive organization. (1999). Jacksonville, FL: Jacksonville Jaguars.

Forbes, G. (2001, June 8). '82 strike changed salary dealings forever. *USA Today*, p. 14C.

Frank, M. (2001, March 5–11). Market plan: Fish where the fans are. *Street & Smith's SportsBusiness Journal*, p. 27.

Go figure. (2001, July 30). *Sports Illustrated*, p. 24.

Griffiths, C. C. (2001, August 27–September 2). NHL owners' rookie mistakes turn wealth into heaps of ashes. *Street & Smith's SportsBusiness Journal*, p. 42.

Gruen, D. T. (Ed.). (2001). *Inside the ownership of pro sports 2001*. Chicago: Team Marketing Report.

Guschov, S. D. (1998). *The Red Stockings of Cincinnati: Baseball's first all-professional team*. Jefferson, NC: McFarland Press.

Helyar, J. (1994). *Lords of the realm: The real history of baseball*. New York: Ballantine.

Hiestand, M. (2001a, April 13). WUSA's goals not lofty. *USA Today*, p. 3C.

Hiestand, M. (2001b, May 11). Hype too tough to match. *USA Today*, p. 10C.

Hofer, C. W., & Schendel, D. (1978). *Strategy formulation: Analytical concepts*. St. Paul, MN: West.

Jenkins, C. (2000, June 27). Giants draw fans into web. *USA Today*, p. 3C.

Kaplan, D. (2000a, December 18–24). Private funds, public cheers. *Street & Smith's SportsBusiness Journal*, p. 29.

Kaplan, D. (2000b, December 25–31). Part sports, part entertainment, all empire. *Street & Smith's SportsBusiness Journal*, p. 24.

Kaplan, D. & Bernstein, A. (2001, October 22–28). YankeeNets top brass to call it quits. *Street & Smith's SportsBusiness Journal*, pp. 1, 52.

Kaplan, R. S., & Norton, D. P. (1992, January–February). The balanced scorecard—measures that drive performance. *Harvard Business Review*, pp. 71–79.

Krupa, G. (1999, June 25). With three teams on the way, NHL is growth industry. *Boston Globe*, p. C12.

La Canfora, J. (2001, September 8). NHL's state of flux. *Washington Post*, pp. D1, D6.

Lakers expect taxing time in Philadelphia. (2001, June 7). *USA Today*, p. 8C.

Lee, J. (2001, April 9–15). WUSA's goals within reach. *Street & Smith's SportsBusiness Journal*, pp. 1, 42–43.

Leifer, E. M. (1995). *Making the majors: The transformation of team sports in America*. Cambridge, MA: Harvard University Press.

Lidz, F. (2000, April 17). Up and down in Beverly Hills. *Sports Illustrated*, pp. 63–68.

Lombardo, J. (2001, May 21–27). Taxmen target visiting teams. *Street & Smith's SportsBusiness Journal*, pp. 1, 56.

Lowenfish, L. (1980). *The imperfect diamond: A history of baseball's labor wars*. New York: Da Capo Press.

Masteralexis, L. P. (1998). Professional sport. In L. P. Masteralexis, C. A. Barr, & M. A. Hums (Eds.), *Principles and practice of sport management* (pp. 275–306). Gaithersburg, MD: Aspen.

McDonough, W. (2000, December 30). Not wild about NFL crop. *Boston Globe*, pp. G1, G6.

Meek, A. (1997, December). An estimate of the size and supporting economic activity of the sports industry in the United States. *Sport Marketing Quarterly, 6* (4), pp. 15–21.

Meyers, B. (1997, August 28). Feminine touches planned, but blood and guts remain. *USA Today*, pp. A1–A2.

Mission statement. (1995). Denver, CO: Colorado Rockies.

Much, P. J., & Gotto, R. M. (1997). Franchise valuation overview. In A. Friedman & P. J. Much, *Inside the ownership of professional sports teams, 1997* (pp. 6–7). Chicago: Team Marketing Report.

Mullen, L. (2000, December 4–10). XFL's insurance has experts concerned. *Street & Smith's SportsBusiness Journal*, pp. 1, 28.

Mullin, B. J., Hardy, S., & Sutton, W. A. (2000). *Sport marketing* (rev. ed.). Champaign, IL: Human Kinetics.

Murphy, A. (1999a, June 21). Happy on the inside. *Sports Illustrated*, pp. 55–60.

Murphy, A. (1999b, September 1). NFL landmarks: The '60s. *Sports Illustrated*, p. 57.

NFL team financial performances. (2001, September 3–9). *Street & Smith's SportsBusiness Journal*, pp. 38–43.

Ozanian, M.K. (1998, December 14). Selective accounting. *Forbes*, pp. 124–134.

Pickeral, R. (2000, December 7). Timberwolves' Taylor suspended; McHale on leave of absence. *Knight-Ridder/Tribune News Service*. [online]. Available: http://elibrary.com/s/edumark/getdoc.

Pietrusza, D. (1998). *Judge and jury: The life and times of Kenesaw Mountain Landis*. South Bend, IN: Diamond Communications.

Porter, M. (1985). *Competitive advantage*. New York: Free Press.

Pro Sports Tracker: MLB attendance (final). (2001, October 15–21). *Street & Smith's SportBusiness Journal*, p. 39.

Rofe, J. (2000, December 25–31). Baseball's rich getting richer as economic ills go untreated. *Street & Smith's SportsBusiness Journal*, p. 23.

Sanderson, A. R. (2000, June 22). It just ain't so, Joe. *Chicago Tribune*, p. 5D.

Sandomir, R. (2001, May 1). To live another day in the Arena League. *New York Times*, pp. C15, C18.

Schendel, D. E., & Hofer, C. W. (1979). *Strategic management: A new view of business policy and planning*. Boston: Little, Brown.

Seymour, H. (1960). *Baseball: The early years*. New York: Oxford University Press.

Soccer. (2001). *The SGMA report, U.S. trends in team sports*. Norton Palm Beach, FL: Sporting Goods Manufacturers Association.

Sports salaries rising at a rapid rate. (2001, May 14). *USA Today*, p. 1C.

Sugar, B. R. (1978). *Hit the sign and win a free suit of clothes from Henry Finklestein*. Chicago: Contemporary.

Swift, E. M. (2000, May 15). Sit on it! *Sports Illustrated*, pp. 72–85.

The Arena Football League's Fans' Bill of Rights. (1999). The Arena Football League. [online]. Available: http://arenafootball.com/nets_bill_of_rights.cfm.

Weeks, M. J. (2001, April 13). Introducing the WUSA. *USA Today*, p. 3C.

Weiner, R. (2001a, July 11). Arenaball arrives. *USA Today*, pp. 1C–2C.

Weiner, R. (2001b, July 11). NFL eyes companionship. *USA Today*, p. 3C.

Weisman, L. (2001, September 20). Logo confusion on the sideline. *USA Today*, p. 8C.

White, G.E. (1996). *Creating the national pastime*. Princeton, NJ: Princeton University Press.

Williams, P. (2001, July 9–15). Small-time baseball, big-time success. *Street & Smith's SportsBusiness Journal*, pp. 21, 27.

Willing, R. (2001, June 6). NFL deal benefits veterans, retirees. *USA Today*, p. 1C.

Yashin scores NHL's largest contract ever. (2001, September 6). *Boston Globe*, p. E6.

Yasser, R., McCurdy, J., & Gopelrud, P. (1997). *Sports law: Cases and materials*. Cincinnati: Anderson.

Chapter 7

Operational Planning and Control

PHOTO: © KELLY-MOONEY PHOTOGRAPHY/CORBIS

Purpose: Sport facilities are designed and constructed to support particular sport, entertainment, or civic and private activities or programs. The sport facility is a critical resource that helps the organization realize its mission and goals. It has been argued that sport facilities may anchor area development, particularly in urban areas, and will help drive economic activity. It has also been argued that these facilities, particularly those that require large public contributions, are detrimental to local communities and contribute little to the area's economy.

Stakeholders: Professional sport teams, tour events, sport and entertainment event rights owners, promoters, labor/trade/music unions, private facility management companies, food service companies, security companies, musicians, performers, athletes, guests, sponsors, media, community members, sport governing bodies/agencies, volunteers, vendors, suppliers, the general public, federal, state, and local government.

Size and scope: There are tens of thousands of sport facilities throughout the United States ranging from stadiums and arenas to golf courses, waterfronts, ski resorts, cross-country trails, bike paths, fitness trails, tennis courts to multipurpose grass fields. Convention centers, which feature ballrooms, banquet halls, meeting rooms, and exhibit halls, are often built close to a sport stadium or arena for the purpose of attracting visitors to the area and spurring economic activity.

Governance:
- Federal, state, and local regulation.
- Professional organizations, associations, and trade groups such as the International Association of Arena Managers (IAAM). Sport governing bodies such as the NCAA provide detailed specifications and requirements for facilities utilized by member sport organizations.

Inside Look

Minor-League Ballparks Anchor Downtown Renaissance

Taking a lesson from major-league cities like Cleveland and Baltimore, smaller cities in the United States such as Lansing, Michigan; Harrisburg, Pennsylvania; Dayton, Ohio; and Oklahoma City, Oklahoma, have built new minor-league baseball stadiums to anchor downtown redevelopment projects or reenergize urban neighborhoods. These stadiums have been designed to fit naturally into the surrounding urban landscape so that any area visitor would suspect the park had been there for decades. The new breed of minor-league ballpark is purposely designed to complement local architecture and existing structures. Architects want their designs to be a natural part of the existing landscape rather than to dominate the area. These new structures exude a simple charm and elegance and are combined with high-quality entertainment opportunities that encourage families to make a whole day out of a visit to the ballpark. These parks that seat approximately 12,000 to 15,000 spectators incorporate old-fashioned ballpark features with new technology and amenities that have proven very attractive to fans. In the last fifteen years, more than a hundred new minor-league stadiums have been constructed throughout the United States as a result of the rising popularity of minor-league baseball. In 2000 minor-league baseball attendance surged to 37.7 million as the sport benefited from both the fans' disenchantment with major-league baseball after labor problems in 1994 and minor-league baseball's reputation as reasonably priced family entertainment (Stone, 2001).

Minor league baseball parks, like those in Dayton and Memphis, Tennessee, have been constructed as part of larger downtown area development projects. Whereas the 1970s and 1980s saw the exodus of retail, industry, and service businesses from downtown areas to suburban locations, the 1990s signaled renewed interest in rebuilding downtowns across the United States. Minor-league ballparks have become just one piece of the downtown revitalization puzzle. In Memphis, AutoZone Park, opened in April 2000, was built as a cornerstone property designed to spur both public and private investment in the general area. Older buildings were renovated, and retail and residential space was created. An elementary school was built in the downtown area and public works projects including a boardwalk and improved streets and lighting were completed. The ballpark itself is attached to the Toyota Center, a renovated 220,000-square-foot office building that overlooks the field. The synergy created by the ballpark and surrounding development was enough to create a spirit of excitement about the area and heightened demand for available properties. In fact, the Toyota Center office complex had commitments for all of its available space before construction began. Additional improvements were made to the Cook County Convention Center, and local business officials heightened their marketing efforts to promote tourism. Residents began to return to the downtown area, and retail, restaurant, and professional offices soon followed.

In Dayton, a new minor-league ballpark also served as a cornerstone for local area development. The stadium was designed not only to act as a magnet for business but to spur tourism as well. Through the incorporation of design elements such as picnic areas, playgrounds, and luxury suites and with promotional tie-ins to local restaurants, shopping, and hotels, the facility attracted visitors both during and beyond the baseball season. The new ballpark and baseball franchise, the Dayton Dragons, is credited with breathing new life into downtown Dayton.

In Oklahoma City, a new $34 million Southwestern Bell Bricktown Ballpark has served as a cornerstone of the city's metropolitan area project that also includes the construction of a downtown arena, performing arts center, river walk, and a renovated Myriad Convention Center. The park, part of a nine-piece urban revitalization project, was funded in part by a one-cent sales tax increase that was approved by voters in 1993. Surrounding shops, restaurants, hotels, and entertainment venues have turned the park and the Bricktown area into an entertainment destination for tourists and local residents as well, with visitor counts exceeding four million people a year.

A similar approach was used in Jacksonville, Florida, where public support was given to a "Better Jacksonville Plan," which included construction of a new minor-league baseball stadium, arena, courthouse, and library. The ballpark was just one small piece of the development project that revitalized several neighborhoods and provided for important public services.

Sports facility consultant Rick Horrow suggests that this trend in minor-league baseball sheds light on the future of sports facility construction. Because of the rising costs of sports facility construction—many minor-league ballparks carry price tags over $30 million—facilities will need to be viewed within the context of the surrounding area and their contribution to the entire community.

New facility designs must encompass creative, comprehensive, and integrative solutions (Horrow, 2001) that positively impact both the community and the sports organization. Stadiums, arenas, and recreational sports complexes must be considered as community assets, rather than isolated private projects. They should be viewed as a valuable component and may often serve as the catalyst for the development or revitalization of entire metropolitan or suburban districts. For Horrow, the lesson is clear. Given the rising costs of sports facility construction and the public's hesitancy to fund private development of facilities for professional sports teams, the successful park, arena, or stadium builder must position, present, and deliver a sports facility that will not only spur tangible area growth and economic development, but will complement the character of the surrounding area and contribute to the vitality of the community.

Advocates of this strategy of using sports and recreation facilities to reenergize area development point to the success stories of cities like Dayton, Memphis, and Oklahoma City, but there is a growing backlash against the construction of publicly funded sports facilities throughout the United States. In fact, organized lobbying groups, such as Washington-based FansFirst! and Denver's Citizen's Opposing the Stadium Tax (COST), claim these publicly funded stadiums and arenas are a drain on the local economy. They argue that such facilities are overpriced and never deliver promised economic impact. New sports facilities actually reshuffle or redistribute current spending rather than generating new revenues to the community. Opponents of publicly funded facilities point to the fact that few new significant jobs are created, area neighborhoods are disturbed, and public subsidy of stadiums and arenas are tantamount to putting public dollars in already rich owners' and players' pockets. For some critics, a sports facility, even one presented as part of an overall economic redevelopment plan, should never be funded with public dollars.

In times when local and state governments are faced with many competing funding priorities such as education, public safety (fire and police), infrastructure improvements (e.g., roads, sewers, bridges), and limited tax dollars, public spending on sports facilities has been criticized as a poor use of public funds. Even when the sports facility is owned by the government (e.g., a municipal golf course or public high school football field), taxpayers express views that sports and recreation facilities are nonessential and therefore should receive no or little consideration for public funding.

Additional evidence of public outcry against private stadium contribution was Senator Arlen Specter's (R-Pa.) 1999 bill that would require team owners to dedicate 10 percent of all television revenues to a stadium construction trust fund. The fund would purportedly help lessen the demand for public funds by professional sports teams. The bill failed, but it brought the debate of public support of sports facilities into the national limelight.

It is likely that the debate over construction of publicly funded sports facilities will continue. Sport facility managers will need to be well versed in funding mechanisms and must be aware of the area's political landscape. As construction costs of sports facilities and quality standards continue to rise, sports managers will need to carefully identify and articulate the arguments for sports facility construction. They will most likely continue to point to cities like Dayton, Memphis, and Oklahoma City as shining examples of why and how the government and the sports organization can partner to successfully bring about area development and downtown revitalization.

Introduction

This chapter introduces sports facility management, an important consideration for sports managers as well as a unique industry segment. Operational planning is discussed because of its special significance to this industry: the manager must be concerned with macro-level operations—how the strategic plan is put into action in the organization—and on the micro level—how facility events are planned and executed on a daily basis. Techniques essential for effective operational planning and control, such as management by objectives and the Balanced Scorecard, forecasting, scheduling, procedures, and budgets are discussed. Because special event management is so critical to facilities management, and because effective event management relies so completely on operational planning, we use this aspect of sport to illustrate operational planning and control in sport management.

Sports Facility Management

Sports facilities have existed for thousands of years. Ancient cultures, including the Egyptians, Greeks, Romans, and Chinese, invested in the creation of sports facilities that were used to promote sport for a variety of purposes including military readiness, entertainment, and physical wellness of their people (Farmer, Mulrooney & Amon, 1996). Contemporary sports managers agree that appropriate facilities are an important component of sport. Certainly, there are many examples of how the management of sports and recreational organizations is influenced by sports facilities. A professional sports team, for example, may be financially dependent on a facility that not only provides the appropriate seating capacity, but also offers revenue generation opportunities such as luxury suites, club seating, retail space, and stadium restaurants. A high school that wishes to field swimming and diving teams may only do so if there is a regulation-size competition pool with diving well available. The sports manager would explain that the sports facility is a critical resource for the organization.

Sport by nature depends on facilities. Just about every sporting activity requires a specific venue, playing surface, or area and most likely some type of equipment. Sports facilities may either be indoor or outdoor and may be naturally occurring—mountains, lakes, rivers, ponds—or manufactured—running tracks, bocce court, golf course, or stadium. Regardless of the type, size, or number of facilities available to the sports organization, the sports manager is actively involved in planning, constructing, financing, maintaining, and operating these facilities.

Sports managers recognize that the facility impacts the organization in many ways. Certainly the number, type, and quality of sports programs and activities are directly influenced by available facilities. Secondly, the quality of the sports facility is a direct reflection of the organization and its programs. Thirdly, the sports facility is a critical asset to the organization that can positively affect or negatively impact revenue generation, brand image, and customer satisfaction.

Most sport management programs require students to take a specific course in sports facility management because of the broad recognition of the importance of facility management to the sports organization. Very specific issues, practices, and skills are related to the management of the sports facility and must be mastered by sports professionals. The body of knowledge related to sports facility management encompasses such topical areas as planning, designing, financing, and constructing facilities as well as scheduling, budgeting, finance, marketing, operations management, box office management, maintenance, building systems operation, feasibility studies, economic impact, food service, security, risk management, loss prevention, inventory control, ticketing, advertising, sponsorship, and quality control systems.

Types of Sports Facilities and Their Management

The most familiar type of sports facility is a public assembly facility (PAF), a large structure created to facilitate the gathering of large groups of people who come together for the purpose of viewing or participating in an event. Stadiums, arenas, and coliseums are categorized as PAFs. Tiered seating, specialized playing or performance surfaces, spectator amenities (such as rest rooms and food service areas), and performer amenities (including locker rooms and training rooms) usually characterize the PAF. These buildings host sporting and entertainment events such as concerts, pro sports team games, trade shows, and family shows (e.g., ice shows, circuses). They are usually designed to accommodate one or more sports team tenants that may include a professional sports team (major or minor league) or a top-level college team.

Convention centers, civic centers, auditoriums, exposition halls, theaters, and concert halls are also PAFs. Although the buildings may not be specifically designed to host sports activities, they are designed for public assembly and for the accommodation of entertainment, professional conferences, shows, and other performances or activities that provide entertainment or education for the community, enhance civic culture, generate tourism, and generally improve the quality of life for residents and visitors alike. Sports facility managers are often responsible for managing multibuilding complexes that include any number of PAFs. However, one standard combination is the sports arena or civic center and the convention center.

www.iaam.org

Other sports facilities are designed primarily to accommodate individual or smaller groups of users rather than large audiences of viewers. Such facilities might include a mountain ski resort, sports hall of fame, tennis court, golf course, gymnasium, municipal soccer field, state park, natatorium, equestrian course, or health and fitness club. This segment of the industry is clearly the largest, yet the larger PAFs usually receive the most attention in the study of the sports facility industry. Stadiums, arenas, and convention centers, because of their affiliation with sports teams and the entertainment industry, capture public attention because they receive daily media coverage, whereas the smaller user-oriented facility operates in virtual obscurity. Although there are thousands of PAFs across the United States, there are many more small participant-oriented facilities. Virtually every state and town, high school, recreation department, college and university, military base, YMCA, and health and fitness club regularly manage a variety of different sporting facilities and host numerous sports and entertainment events and activities at those facilities. These facilities usually operate on a much smaller scale than the large PAFs, but their managers are faced with similar responsibilities, issues, and challenges.

There are many different types of ownership and management of sports facilities. Some facilities are owned by governmental entities such as cities, towns, counties, states, or the federal government. Nonprofit organizations or private interests, such as private management companies, pro sports teams, individuals or corporations, own others. Sports facilities are not necessarily owner managed. Most facilities owned by a nonprofit organization or a governmental entity such as the state or the city utilize some type of advisory board or commission to act as an agent or representative of ownership. The board or commission may serve as a policy-making body or may be responsible for oversight and control of the facility. The commission is ultimately responsible for selecting an appropriate management team to operate the facility.

Sports facilities may be owner managed in a model called *in-house management*. Historically, universities, states, and cities chose to manage their own buildings. However, when buildings failed to meet owners' expectations, other management alternatives were considered. For some organizations, in-house management created a variety of problems related to inexperience; political patronage; burdensome public regulation and policies; and lack of resources to attract events, meet customers' needs, and purchase needed equipment, technology, or supplies. In these cases, owners have considered the private management alternative.

Several private companies specialize in managing sports and allied facilities. These management groups promise to deliver more efficient operations and expect to reduce the facilities' operating deficit. Relying on their expertise and connections within the sports, tourism, hospitality, recreation, and entertainment industries, they are usually able to create a more comprehensive and more high-quality schedule, hire more skilled managers, and negotiate better deals with sponsors, promoters, and suppliers. The facility owners secure a private management company through a selection process that begins with a *request for proposal*, or *RFP*. This comprehensive document provides an overview of the current state of the building and its operations, and it details the owner's expectations for new management (Mulrooney & Farmer, 2001). The RFP is then sent to all major private management companies, and a notice of the availability of the RFP is posted in trade publications. Interested parties then express their interest in the facility by preparing a bid within the time limit specified in the RFP. Bidders are provided with the opportunity to tour the facility and discuss the RFP with the facility's owner or governing body representatives. The private management company/bidder may then wish to review the RFP in more detail and are allowed to submit additional materials to supplement their original bid proposal. Once all proposals that have been received by the posted deadline are reviewed, finalists are chosen and are asked to make a personal presentation to the building owner or representatives. Once presentations are completed, a top choice is selected and both parties enter into contract negotiations. The signing of the contract by both parties signals the official completion of the RFP process.

The RFP process is an important one to facility managers because many critical functions in the facility are outsourced in a similar way. Food service, security, maintenance, parking, and other functions can be outsourced. Utilizing private companies to provide these services allows the facility manager to acquire specialized expertise and is often seen as an efficient way to carry out functions that might otherwise be a very expensive and ineffective use of limited internal resources.

The Role of the Sports Facility Manager

Sports facility managers are essentially responsible for two functions: (1) the operation of the building itself, and (2) the planning and execution of events or programs within the building.

Managerial tasks related to the operation of the building include building systems management, maintenance, and the hiring of building administrative staff. A good sports facility manager has a working knowledge of the internal mechanical systems of the building including heating, ventilation, and air conditioning (HVAC), electrical, plumbing, and refrigeration. A facility manager must also be aware of issues related to building design and construction including weight-bearing capacity of the roof, accessibility, and building material composition. A facility manager must understand the building's structure and equipment and also be able to coordinate a sound maintenance plan that assures the building is not only in top condition, but is safe for users, employees, and spectators alike. The sports facility manager need not necessarily be an expert in mechanical engineering, but he or she must understand how the building works.

Other responsibilities that come under the heading of managing the building may include scheduling and booking events; marketing the facility to promoters, travel coordinators, and convention planners; budgeting; human resource management; public relations; marketing; and ticket, advertising, and sponsorship sales.

The second responsibility of the facility manager is event management. This function is commonly called operations, or "ops" management, but we use the term *event management* here to represent this function. Event management consists of the planning and execution of the wide variety of functions and activities that take place in a sports facility every day. Depending on its size and accommodations, a large public assembly facility might host as many as seventy different events in one month, including concerts, family shows, meetings, and professional sports contests. A local recreation sports complex may host thirty softball games, a youth sports banquet, and an instructional clinic in one weekend. A college field house may host a faculty reception, intramural floor hockey game, karate class, men's and women's basketball practice, cheerleading tryouts, and a racquetball tournament in one evening. Regardless of the size or configuration of the sports facility, most sports facility managers suggest the bulk of their time is spent scheduling, planning, and executing events.

Most PAFs have an entire department or unit with an events manager or operations director who is designated to oversee event management. The operations director/event manager is responsible for coordinating all needed services to support each event. He or she purchases supplies, maintains equipment, and hires appropriate staff to guarantee the event goes off as planned. The event manager/operations director may directly oversee laborers, stagehands, electricians, musicians, security, food service, customer service, medical staff, transportation, parking, ticket takers, concession workers, and other part-time workers. The event management function includes managing most of the behind-the-scenes staff that is responsible for planning and executing an event. Event staff works closely with event producers to ensure that all the physical requirements for the event are in place, the equipment is available and functioning properly, and the building is configured and set up appropriately for the event. To summarize, the event management function encompasses preparing the building for each event according to specifications, ensuring the event goes off smoothly and then cleaning up after the function.

For the purpose of our discussion, it is best to think of event management as *micro-level operations management*. That is, the day-to-day activities of the building, carrying out its schedule of events, and hosting programs represents only one level of operations management within a sports facility. The other level of operations management takes place on a macro or strategic organizationwide level. At this level, management translates its selected strategy into action steps or plans in each of the organization's key functional areas, a process referred to as *operational planning*.

This distinction is an important one because operations management in sports facilities varies significantly from what is traditionally considered operations management in most businesses (Mulrooney & Farmer, 2001). For most nonsport organizations, operations management consists solely of what we refer to here as operational planning by which strategy is translated into action across the organization. For sports facilities, the challenge is not only how to put the strategic plan into action, but how to plan and execute hundreds of events, programs, and activities every year. Sports facility management experts Peter Farmer and Aaron Mulrooney suggest the difference is that "operations management in a sports facility focuses on *how* services are produced, rather than the production of those services; this is the traditional definition of operations management" (Mulrooney & Farmer, 2001, p. 274).

For example, a sports business such as professional sports team is interested in producing a high-quality team that repeatedly wins championships. Their manager is focused on the game, the winning, and the team. A concert promoter is interested in securing talented performers who attract ticket buyers. In each case, management is focused on the product. The sports facility manager, however, has a different focus. He or she is keenly interested in how the game or concert is presented or produced. Pertinent issues for the sports facility manager include the sound system, the lighting, cleanliness of the rest rooms, proper ordering and preparation of food, safe parking lots, clear walkways, and clean locker rooms.

To better understand the difference between the traditional definition of operations management and event/operations management in the sports facility business, consider both the business and corporate-level strategies of Callaway and how they are implemented. At the business level, Callaway follows a product differentiation strategy for its golf division. It provides high-quality merchandise, and it has sold more golf clubs than any competitor at the highest prices in the industry because of high-tech oversized equipment that is considered superior by the customer. To achieve this success, Callaway followed a basic marketing strategy, spending most of its marketing budget on televised golf events and on print publications and pro tour promotions (Stogel, 2000). At the corporate level, Callaway followed a growth through diversification strategy by creating a separate Callaway Golf Ball Company. This subsidiary was started from scratch with the construction of a manufacturing plant, the hiring of hundreds of employees, and the development of the Callaway golf ball, positioned at the premium end of the industry. Examples such as these illustrate that coordination among the functional areas of an organization (marketing, research and development, manufacturing, computer systems, and human resources) must occur if strategies are to be implemented successfully.

In essence, once a strategy is formulated or chosen, it must be translated into terms that can be understood and acted on at the operational level. As shown in Figure 7-1, on the macro level, operational planning is part of the implementation stage of the strategic management process.

Contrast this traditional definition of operations management with operations or event management in the sports facility industry. Consider another golf-related example—the golf course where the golf operations manager oversees the production of various events and programs at the course. He or she would be responsible for coordinating tee times, scheduling tournaments, and providing high-quality customer service.

We might think that once goals are set and operational plans are in place both on the macro and micro level that management's responsibilities would largely be complete. However, management is responsible for monitoring performance and for ensuring that actual performance is consistent with the organization's standards or goals. This is the control function of management, and it requires that performance be monitored and action taken to solve problems and find ways to improve performance on an ongoing basis (see Figure 7-1). Control is equally important on the macro and micro level of the organization. Sports facility managers must be concerned with how the organization is carrying out its strategy and also with how it is meeting its daily business objectives in planning and executing events.

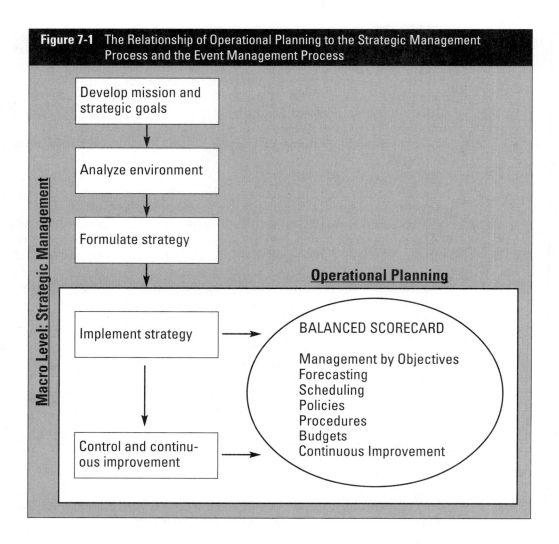

Figure 7-1 The Relationship of Operational Planning to the Strategic Management Process and the Event Management Process

Macro Level: Strategic Management

Develop mission and strategic goals

Analyze environment

Formulate strategy

Implement strategy

Control and continuous improvement

Operational Planning

BALANCED SCORECARD

Management by Objectives
Forecasting
Scheduling
Policies
Procedures
Budgets
Continuous Improvement

Operational Planning

Operational plans differ from strategic plans in several ways. First, operational plans tend to be drawn for a shorter period than strategic plans. For example, the strategy for diversifying the arena food service function into the production and service of in-house beer and arena-branded cigar products might be a five-year plan. In contrast, the construction of a microbrewery and cigar lounge within the arena might be a nine-month plan. Another distinction is that operational plans focus more on the organization than on the external environment. As we discussed in Chapter 6, strategic plans are developed based on projected societal trends, national and regional economic forecasts, and technological factors, for example. The owner of the sports facility who seeks to diversify the food service function through the production of in-house branded beer and cigars seeks to capitalize on forecasted trends that the popularity of microbrewed beer and cigars will continue. This strategic initiative is clearly based on societal trends within the environment and an expectation that such expansion will be profitable for the organization.

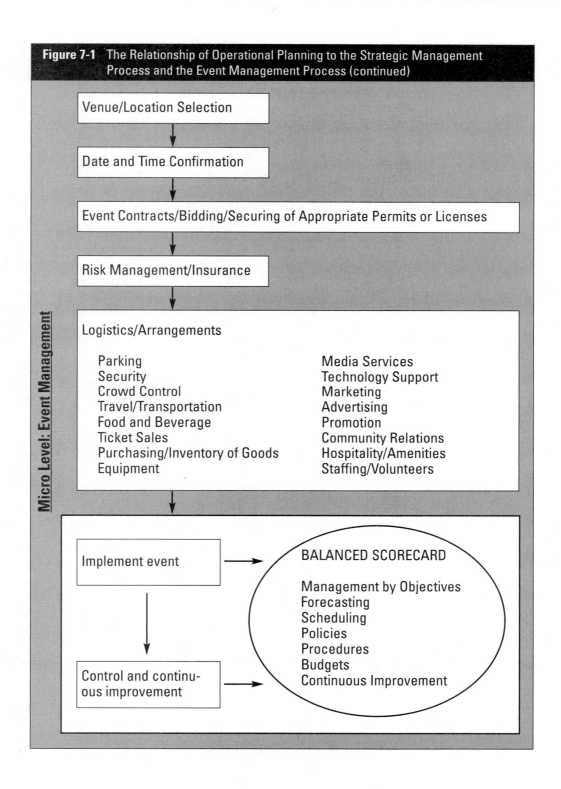

Figure 7-1 The Relationship of Operational Planning to the Strategic Management Process and the Event Management Process (continued)

Micro Level: Event Management

Venue/Location Selection

↓

Date and Time Confirmation

↓

Event Contracts/Bidding/Securing of Appropriate Permits or Licenses

↓

Risk Management/Insurance

↓

Logistics/Arrangements

Parking	Media Services
Security	Technology Support
Crowd Control	Marketing
Travel/Transportation	Advertising
Food and Beverage	Promotion
Ticket Sales	Community Relations
Purchasing/Inventory of Goods	Hospitality/Amenities
Equipment	Staffing/Volunteers

↓

Implement event →

Control and continuous improvement →

BALANCED SCORECARD

Management by Objectives
Forecasting
Scheduling
Policies
Procedures
Budgets
Continuous Improvement

Operational plans, in contrast, are internally based and involve keeping the company running efficiently. Because the focus is on internal operations, planning techniques such as management by objectives and the Balanced Scorecard, forecasting, scheduling, policies, procedures, and budgets ensure that every department's actions mesh with the larger strategies of the organization. In the case of the construction of a new microbrewery within the arena, the production of in-house brand cigars, and the development of a cigar lounge and club within the arena, operational-level planning would involve the coordination of the construction projects, creation of marketing and sales materials, the development of an advertising campaign, the hiring of the staff to work in these areas, and the ordering and purchase of necessary supplies and equipment to set up and maintain both the microbrewery and cigar lounge. Techniques utilized in operational planning are the topic of the next section.

Management by Objectives and the Balanced Scorecard

Peter Drucker developed the concept of management by objectives (MBO) as a system of goal setting and planning to help individuals and departments be more productive, and it proved to be the first framework for converting intangible mission statements into a unified system of interrelated performance measurements (Drucker, 1954). His examples are relevant today. A church's mission of "saving souls" is intangible, but church attendance is measurable. The objective of bringing, for example, two-thirds of the young people of the congregation into the church and its sports programs is easily measured.

Similarly, the mission of a professional baseball team to provide the highest level of baseball entertainment is intangible. However, tallying the level of customer satisfaction is by no means intangible and can be measured based on surveys and the number of fans' visits.

The MBO approach involves sequential steps and starts with top managers identifying their objectives. Through negotiation and agreement, unit heads then establish objectives for their units. A cascading of objectives takes place as the process moves down the line to subordinates. Action plans are defined, and performance reviews are conducted at agreed-upon intervals.

Although MBO remains a popular management technique for linking management and subordinate objectives, the concept of the Balanced Scorecard is designed to take this one step further and create strategy-focused organizations (Kaplan & Norton, 1993, 1996). The Balanced Scorecard is a framework in which groups and individuals develop and closely monitor performance based on customer measures, internal processes, human resource measures, and financial measures—all tied directly to a specific strategic objective. The Balanced Scorecard framework consists of four steps or processes that separately and in combination contribute to linking strategic objectives with operational actions.

1. *Translate the vision.* Despite the best intentions of those creating the organization's mission or vision, statements to deliver "quality baseball entertainment" or "the best sports arena in its class" do not translate easily into operational terms. Like MBO, for people to act on words in mission and strategy statements, top management must agree on the specific objectives and measures that will be the drivers of success. Typically, these are the larger financial and customer objectives.

2. *Communicate and link the objectives to the next levels in the organization.* Although the first process ensures that ten or so individuals in the organization now understand the strategy better than ever

before, it is critical that the next levels of subordinates formulate internal-business processes and human resource or employee learning objectives. For example, if satisfying customers' expectations for immediate access to event tickets via phone or Internet is a major company objective identified by top management, the next level of subordinates would identify several internal business processes (such as installing new equipment, conducting training sessions, constructing new order-processing forms, and establishing guidelines for order preparation), in which the company has to excel. This may involve retraining frontline employees and improving information systems available to them. The group sets up performance measures for these critical processes and measures for staff and systems capabilities.

3. *Business planning.* Some organizations develop a strategic plan and then separately create their budgets for each year. Which document is discussed at monthly and quarterly meetings? Usually, it is only the budget, because a comparison of actual to budgeted figures is based on specific items, such as supplies, cost of goods sold, and so on. The strategic plan is often only discussed or reviewed closely when the next major strategic planning effort occurs. Integrating these two important planning tools (strategy and budgets) is the purpose of this phase of the Balanced Scorecard approach. The budget's short-term financial framework is not changed; however, those developing it now allocate resources based on objectives and plans that are linked to the organization's larger strategies.

4. *Feedback and learning.* In this aspect of the process, companies engage in strategic learning, much like a learning organization. With the Balanced Scorecard and the company's strategy at the center of its management systems, employees can monitor or control short-term results from the perspectives of financial performance, customers, internal business processes, and human relations, as shown in Figure 7-2. Because of this feedback, companies can modify strategies to reflect real-time learning.

In summary, although the Balanced Scorecard approach has many characteristics similar to MBO, it requires managers, teams, and individuals to develop and closely monitor performance based on customer measures, internal processes, human resource measures, and financial measures, which are all tied directly to a specific strategic objective. This deliberate linkage of strategic objectives with operational actions distinguishes the approach from its older cousin, MBO, and is designed to build a strategy-focused organization.

Forecasting

In order to create the specific measures required by the Balanced Scorecard approach, it is important to develop accurate *forecasts*, the predictions, projections, or estimates about future events that are the basis for determining the levels of business in each department. To illustrate, if the manager of Madison Square Garden projects that the Stars on Ice show will sell out weekend evening performances, but not afternoon matinees, this forecast would form the basis for the number of concessions stands opened, employees hired, and level of spending for a marketing campaign.

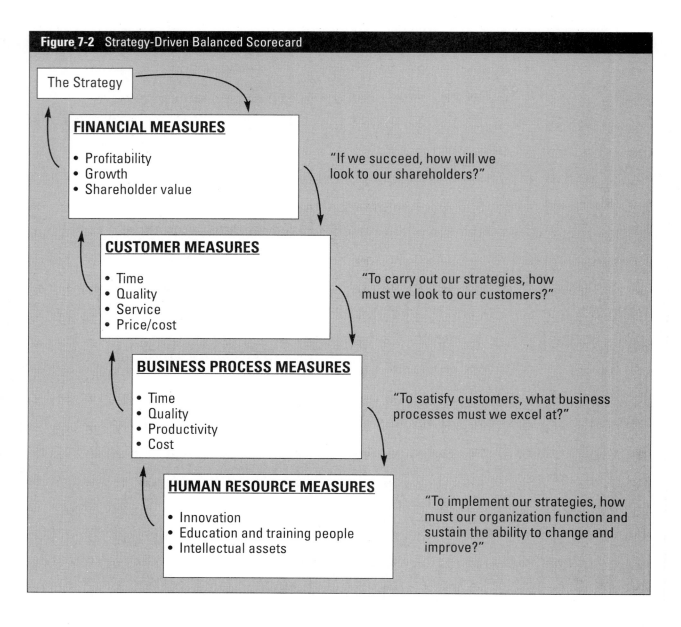

Figure 7-2 Strategy-Driven Balanced Scorecard

The Strategy

FINANCIAL MEASURES

- Profitability
- Growth
- Shareholder value

"If we succeed, how will we look to our shareholders?"

CUSTOMER MEASURES

- Time
- Quality
- Service
- Price/cost

"To carry out our strategies, how must we look to our customers?"

BUSINESS PROCESS MEASURES

- Time
- Quality
- Productivity
- Cost

"To satisfy customers, what business processes must we excel at?"

HUMAN RESOURCE MEASURES

- Innovation
- Education and training people
- Intellectual assets

"To implement our strategies, how must our organization function and sustain the ability to change and improve?"

Forecasts typically fall into two categories: quantitative and qualitative, or judgmental. Although these forecasting techniques are described separately here, managers often use them in combination to help predict future events.

Quantitative Forecasts

Quantitative forecasts use numerical data and mathematical formulas to project information about future events. This type of forecasting is based on the assumption that the past is a good predictor of the future.

Time series analysis. One method of quantitative forecasting using a historical approach is *time series analysis*, which estimates future values based on a sequence of statistical data. For example, organizations often base their sales forecasts on how much was sold during a similar period in the past. Figure 7-3 shows a time series analysis of merchandise sold by an arena retail shop. Assuming the future will be much like the past, the forecast in Figure 7-3 is that sales are expected to increase 17.5 percent in 2002 over 2001 (40,000 to 47,000). Based on this method of predicting future sales, an organization implementing a growth strategy would be able to plan at what rate to hire more workers, to order supplies, or to expand the retail shop.

Linear regression. Another quantitative method of forecasting is *linear regression*, which predicts how changes in one variable might be related to changes in another variable. Suppose a private facility management company has determined that sales of beer at the stadiums and arenas it manages depend highly on the number and type of events scheduled at the facility and the demographics of fans attending the events. Using a mathematical equation and sales information from various facilities, managers can forecast sales at a new building based on the number and type of events scheduled for the facility and the demographic profiles of fans for each event.

Qualitative Forecasts

Qualitative methods of forecasting consist mainly of subjective hunches. For example, an experienced sports facility executive might predict that the previous year's winning season by the facility's prime tenant will create greater demand for luxury and club seating. These predictions rely more on individual or group judgment or opinion to predict future events, rather than on mathematical or statistical analysis.

The *Delphi method* is one such qualitative technique, in which input is solicited from a variety of experts who provide opinions on an individual basis. Their separate opinions are then gathered, evaluated, and summarized to form the basis of a forecast.

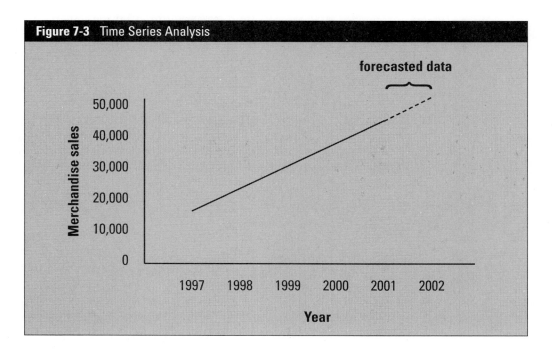

Figure 7-3 Time Series Analysis

Suppose a college is planning to build a new on-campus ice arena. Funding for the building likely will be secured within five years. The athletic facility manager is interested in building a state-of-the-art arena, but is unsure what technology will be available in five years and what players and fans will expect in terms of locker rooms, training facilities, and scoreboard. The sports facility manager is interested in forecasting what new technologies will be available and should be integrated into design and construction plans. For this situation, participants in the Delphi forecast might include experts in refrigeration and scoreboard technology, sports facility architects, executives in the hockey industry, and market researchers. The experts are asked anonymously to predict what the hockey rink of the future will be like and when new technologies will become available. Persons coordinating the Delphi group collect the responses, average them, and ask for another opinion. Those experts who provide predictions in the first round that are significantly different from the others are asked to justify them. When the predictions get more and more similar, the average prediction is taken and becomes the group's forecast.

Other qualitative techniques for forecasting future events include opinion surveys of executives, sales force feedback, and information from consumers. In each case, individual judgments are combined to generate information about the timing and other details of future events, and about conditions in the environment essential to the organization's strategy.

As noted earlier, frequently qualitative and quantitative forecasts are combined. When this occurs, forecasting begins with a quantitative prediction, which provides basic data about a future trend. Next, the qualitative forecast is added to the quantitative forecast, as a validity check. Then the quantitative forecast is adjusted according to the subjective data. Whether companies rely more on quantitative, qualitative, or a combination of both types of forecasts, the challenge is to develop approaches that are continuously monitored by management to determine if improvements are necessary (Fisher et al., 1994).

Scheduling

Scheduling is the process of formulating a detailed charting of activities that must be accomplished to attain objectives with timetables for completing the activities. A visit to a company organized around a Balanced Scorecard process would reveal these charts tacked on walls so functional departments, teams, and individuals can closely monitor the progress of scheduled projects. One might also expect to see these charts in event management offices, where sports facility event managers and their teams carefully plan and execute literally hundreds of events and activities every year.

In the sports facility business, scheduling also refers to the creation of a calendar of activities or events for the building or facility. For example, a political breakfast might take place on Friday morning in the exhibition hall, a rehearsal for a dance competition might take place on the arena floor on Saturday afternoon, a basketball game will be played on Saturday evening, and the circus might begin to move in and set up on Sunday morning for a Wednesday opening performance. Similarly, a YMCA director would schedule activities for space within the building by allocating and reserving appropriate time and space for each program or event; a municipal recreation director might create a master schedule of games, practices, or other activities at each of the city's parks and fields. Sports facility managers often manually create a master schedule for the entire building and all of its available spaces. It is not unusual for a major PAF to maintain a five- to ten-year working calendar. Specialized computer software programs are now available to assist the sports manager in maintaining a facility schedule. Because most sports facilities have several spaces available for hosting events, the task of managing the multiple events that take place in multiple spaces is complex. Not only must the manager consider the time and space requirements of the event, but he or she must also consider setup and breakdown time as well. Facility managers must plan for building changeovers and must provide appropriate labor and equipment to assure that the appropriate building configuration is achieved for each event. Building changeovers—especially those that involve a new playing surface (e.g., basketball court to ice surface) or a new seating configuration (addition of floor or end zone seats)—require careful planning and coordination to achieve the changeover in a timely manner. The goal for the facility manager is to create and maintain a schedule that maximizes the use of the facility while avoiding conflicts between events.

The *booking* process, different than scheduling, involves negotiating terms and conditions for the use of the facility on an event-by-event basis. Booking involves signing a contract that details all event requirements and the guidelines, policies, and procedures for using the facility. Therefore, a facility manager would book individual events to create a schedule or calendar of events for the facility.

Once the calendar is set, the event or project manager would create a plan for executing all activities needed to produce the event. This event schedule serves a critical tool for the operations/event director. It helps him or her assure a timely and coordinated plan for carrying out all of the activities needed so the event goes off as planned. For example, an event manager planning for a weekend flower show recognizes that literally thousands of tasks are associated with the event ranging from show setup, electrical and water hookups, printing of the event program, coordinating media coverage, arranging for food service, and distributing VIP passes. Each event represents thousands of details that must be identified, delegated to appropriate staff members, coordinated, executed, and controlled.

Three popular techniques for scheduling and tracking activities in the sports facility business are Gantt charts, the program evaluation and review technique (PERT), and the event script.

Gantt Charts

Gantt charts are one of the most commonly used graphic scheduling tools. Developed by Henry L. Gantt, these charts show the significant activities required to meet an objective or to complete a project, with the events arranged in chronological order and the amount of time allotted for each activity. Gantt charts are particularly important in event management because of the myriad tasks involved in event preparation and the very specific time frame in which the sports manager must prepare in order for the event to be hosted successfully.

Although simple in concept and appearance, Gantt charts are used widely, from coordinating large projects to scheduling everyday activities. Figure 7-4 illustrates

Figure 7-4 Gantt Chart for Tennis Tournament

	xxx	completed
	////	planned

	September			
	Week 1	Week 2	Week 3	Week 4
ACTIVITIES	1 2 3 4 5	8 9 10 11 12	15 16 17 18 19	22 23 24 25 26
1. Invite players	xx			
2. Establish brackets	xxxxxxxxxxxxxxxxxx			
3. Write press releases	xx		xx	xxx
4. Secure sponsors		xxxxxxxxxxxxxx		
5. Order equipment		xxxxxxxxxxxxxx		
6. Arrange security			xxxxxx	
7. Write staffing plan			xxx	
8. Print program				xxx///
9. Set up stands/tents				xxxx///////
10. Set up courts				xx//////

a sample Gantt chart for a tennis complex hosting a local youth tournament. The shaded areas indicate completed activities. Managers can use Gantt charts for progress reports. In Figure 7-4, note that steps 8 through 10 are yet to be finished.

These charts require analytical thinking because they reduce projects or jobs to separate steps. They have the additional advantage of allowing planners to specify the time to be spent on each activity and are especially useful for scheduling activities that happen sequentially.

PERT Charts

The main weakness of the Gantt chart is that it does not contain information about the interrelationship of tasks to be performed. There is no way of telling if one task must be performed before another. The *PERT chart* (program evaluation and review technique), in contrast, is designed to show the interrelationship of tasks in large and complex projects.

Figure 7-5 displays the activities involved in creating goody bags for participants in a college fun fest held at the campus field house. Note the time estimates for

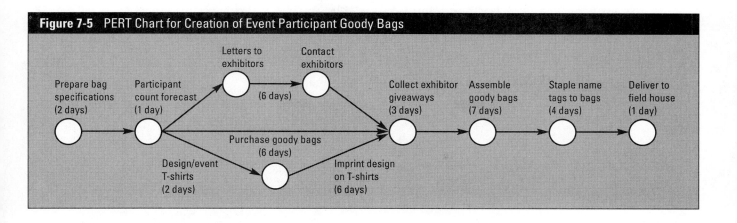

Figure 7-5 PERT Chart for Creation of Event Participant Goody Bags

each PERT activity. Planners pinpoint the critical path, or most time-consuming chain of activities and events in the network. The longest path is the most critical because any delays will cause a delay of the entire project. In Figure 7-5, the longest path is twenty-four days. Any delays in that path will affect the scheduled completion date of the project.

This example is intentionally simplified for instruction purposes. PERT charts are actually most often utilized for projects with numerous activities. The charts allow managers, teams, and individuals to predict resource needs, identify potential problem areas, and assess the impact of delays on the overall project completion time. In this way, they provide valuable information about whether objectives will be achieved and what modifications may be necessary.

Event Scripts

Event scripts, one of the most important tools available to sports facility managers, provide an outline of every activity that occurs in the production of a particular event much as a script details the dialogue of a play. The event script usually begins to detail event activity about two hours before the event and then concludes with the completion of the event. The script provides timed direction to all the event staff participating in the production of the event. For example, the script details when the doors of the facility open, what music is played at what time, what the announcer will say, when the teams will be announced, and so on. The script provides an outline for what will happen during every step of the event. It not only helps the manager plan out in detail how the event will be executed and what will be needed to assure that the event runs smoothly, but it also keeps the staff informed and prepared for what will happen next. A sample of a portion of an abbreviated event script is presented in Figure 7-6.

Computer Software

Computer software packages that can be loaded on a personal computer are making the job of forecasting and scheduling easier. Examples of applicable software are as follows:

Figure 7-6	Excerpt of Event Script of High School Football Game
5:45	Gates open
5:50–6:20	Pregame Warm-Ups—Teams on field
6:15	Color Guard and band assemble in north end zone
6:20	Teams return to locker rooms
6:31	Presentation of colors
	Announcer: *Ladies and Gentleman, please join me in welcoming the District 5 Color Guard and the state champion Littleton High School Band as they present our nation's colors.*
6:33	Announcer: *Please rise as we honor America with our national anthem.*
6:33	Sound Technician: Switch sound feed to field microphone. Return to booth microphone when anthem complete.
6:38	Announcer: *Good evening, ladies and gentlemen, and welcome to this evening's contest featuring the Rowley Bears versus your Argyle Eagles! Officials for this evening's game are John Paul and K. M. Broyles.*
	Sound Technician: Play "Get This Place Jumping." Fade as officials move to field; switch sound system to referee's microphone.
6:40	Referees move to center of field for coin toss.

Forecasting techniques	DecisionPro 3.0 (Vanguard Software); IMA FORECAST (PowerFlex Software Systems, Inc.) Spreadsheet programs can also be used to make forecasts.
Gantt charts	Milestones, Etc. is a project management, planning, scheduling, and Gantt charting program (KIDASA Software, Inc.).
PERT diagrams	PERT Chart EXPERT; Project 98 (both distributed by Microsoft Project)

Guidelines for Operational Planning

Organizations frequently have guidelines for ensuring actions will be consistent with organizational objectives. For example, an organizational policy relating to human resources might be that the organization "strives to recruit only the most talented employees." This policy statement is very broad, giving managers a general idea of what to do in the area of recruitment. Nonetheless, the policy emphasizes the importance attached to hiring competent employees, and it provides a framework for developing actions and plans that support the organization's strategy.

Policies

Policies serve two purposes. First, decisions in the organization must be consistent with the organization's strategic objectives. Strategies heading in one direction, when combined with decisions reflecting a different course, are a disaster for an organization. For example, private sports facility management companies support their strategy of developing highly committed facility management experts by moving employees into positions of increasing responsibility and authority in different buildings managed by the company. In this way, they know their executives will be placed in situations where they can learn all aspects of the business in different settings and can develop mentor relationships with other employees. This policy allows the company to achieve the strategic objective of a highly committed and skilled team of facility management experts.

The other purpose of policies is to ensure a reasonable degree of consistency throughout the organization in the ways decisions are made. In Chapter 5 we made the point that decisions tend to reflect the personality, values, and experience level of the decision maker. Policies can offset this built-in idiosyncratic tendency by establishing guidelines to ensure consistency regardless of who is making the decision. Policies increase the likelihood that decisions will reflect the larger strategic objective of the organization, rather than just the personality or individual objectives of the decision maker. For example, sports facilities provide detailed policy statements about ticketing. One common policy is that lost tickets will not be replaced. This policy assures that all ticket buyers are treated fairly, and it also supports the facility's goal to eliminate problems associated with having two different groups of people showing up to an event holding tickets for the same seats. This policy also helps deter the illegal sale of tickets when one ticket holder sells his or her first set of tickets and then seeks to replace them, claiming they were stolen.

Another policy that most sports fans are familiar with is the policy at professional baseball parks that any fan entering the playing field will be ejected. This policy guarantees uniform treatment for unruly fans, helps deter inappropriate behavior, and supports the organization's larger goals of protecting both the spectators and the game participants.

Procedures

Procedures are guidelines for how tasks in the organization are to be performed. In general, procedures outline more specific actions than policies do. A well-developed set of work procedures can serve as a kind of road map guiding the efforts of individuals throughout the organization. Concession workers, for example, follow a specific set of procedures in serving alcoholic beverages at a sports facility. Workers receive vigorous training in alcohol service and often participate in formal alcohol service training programs. These programs help workers understand alcohol service procedures so they not only become more efficient servers but can help protect the safety of the patron and limit the liability of the facility. Alcohol service procedures might include having the server check the patron's identification or requiring patrons to secure a plastic wrist bracelet at an ID checking station.

Although policies and procedures or work rules and guidelines point managers and employees in the right direction, they should leave room for creativity and judgment in terms of the details of how to get there.

Budgets

Budgets are guidelines indicating how an organization intends to allocate its financial resources. One technique used to ensure that budgets reflect the most current strategic objectives is called zero-based budgeting. In the traditional approach to budgeting for an upcoming year, managers begin with the existing budget, justify any changes that might be needed, and then add or subtract from the existing budget amounts. But in zero-based budgeting, managers start each year from zero and justify each expenditure based on Balanced Scorecard measures from the customer, internal processes, and human resource perspectives.

The budgeting process involves keeping track of revenues and expenses and then comparing them in a summary statement. Figure 7-7 shows this type of statement for a hypothetical sports event. Although this statement shows budgeted and actual figures at the end of the event, it is not unusual to list actual figures against budgeted figures on a daily, weekly, or monthly basis to identify expense overruns or revenue shortages early in the operation.

Figure 7-7 Statement of Revenues and Expenses

Sports Expo
Statement as of December 31, 2001

Revenues	Budget	Actual
Admission	$120,000	$ 72,000
Booth sales	120,000	82,000
Goods sold inside	270,000	162,000
Mailing list sales	2,500	(a)
	$512,500	$316,000
Expenses		
Rental	40,000	40,000
Labor (security)	2,500	2,500
Production	18,000	30,000
Cost of booth sales	62,500	77,500
Cost of selling goods inside	135,000	81,000
Talent	0	8,000
Marketing	80,000	376,000
	$338,000	$ 615,000
Surplus (Deficit)	$174,500	($299,000)

(a) Mailing list sales were not offered, as intended.

The hypothetical example in Figure 7-7 shows an extreme condition. Budgeted revenues were forecasted higher in every category. Reasons for the shortfall in revenues can be overoptimistic forecasting or unforeseen circumstances, such as severe weather conditions that typically reduce attendance more than expected. Also, ticket prices may have been set too high. In the expense area, marketing spent over four times the budgeted amount, a primary expense causing the $299,000 deficit for the event.

The Control Function

Traditionally, *control* has been defined as the process of ensuring that actual performance and results are consistent with performance goals. Control is the process of monitoring performance to ensure that performance goals are being achieved. The steps of the control process are shown in Figure 7-8. Each of these steps represents a challenge to the sports organization as it seeks to ensure that performance is on target.

Establish Performance Standards

Clearly defined goals of the kind described in Chapter 4 are the first step in the control process. Besides serving as a target for performance, every type of goal within the organization—from strategic to operational goals, from benchmarks to budgets, from team to individual performance goals—also becomes a standard against which performance can be measured.

For example, a box office manager may set the goal of providing high-quality service to all patrons utilizing the facility. The manager may believe that quality service is tied to the amount of time it takes to process one order and sets the goal of processing ticket orders from walk-up patrons at three minutes or under. Although this goal sets a target for ticket window staff, it also provides a standard by which the performance of each ticket seller can be measured.

Difficulties with Establishing Standards

The problems with establishing performance standards are the same as the problems with defining effective goals. Obviously, the standards cannot be vague or general; they must be specific enough to be measurable. This presents a special challenge to sports organizations and performance units involved with providing services rather than products. The initial goal of high-quality patron service is too broad. It leads to

Figure 7-8 Steps in the Traditional Control Process

- Establish/identify performance goals or standards.

- Monitor performance.

- Compare actual performance to the standard or goal.

- Take corrective action.

the immediate issue of determining what the standard for good box office service is. Even if a ticket window representative is able to process the patron's order in three minutes, does this mean the patron received good service or was satisfied with the transaction? It is likely that quality box office service is tied to more than speed.

Establishing clear and appropriate standards, then, is the first step in the control process. Without clear standards there is nothing against which to measure performance, no well-defined basis for determining whether existing levels of performance are acceptable. Our box office manager might expand the performance goals to include fewer than twenty complaints a month and decrease processing errors by 5 percent.

Monitor Performance

Once performance standards are set, management must gather data over time to determine the actual level of performance. Management must continuously track performance so accurate information is available about what is being accomplished.

The performance standards defined in the first step of the control process determine which factors or variables will be measured. If standards are set in terms of quality, cost, and speed, for example, then those are the variables that will be monitored and measured. The key decisions of the second stage of the control process involve not which areas of performance will be monitored, but when, where, and how often to inspect or monitor key performance areas. For example, if a facility concessions manager is interested in decreasing waste by 10 percent, he or she must then determine how and when to monitor progress toward these goals. Should individual concession stands be monitored, or should all concession stands be treated as one unit? Should evaluation be completed on a by-event basis, weekly basis, or monthly basis? Should all stands be inspected or just a random sample of stands? Facility managers who are interested in monitoring performance effectively do so by creating well-thought-out and systematic evaluation methods. The performance data collected is only as good as the evaluation process employed by the manager.

Compare Performance to the Standards

The third step in the control process involves an evaluation of actual performance against the goal or standard. Performance goals are set, performance is monitored or measured, and now it must be determined whether a significant gap exists between the goal and the reality.

An important concept in the evaluation stage is the issue of *critical deviations*, any gaps or differences between goals or standards and actual performance that critically impact the success of the process. For example, suppose a sports facility sets the staffing goal or standard of 8.0 security personnel per entry gate (the national average of coverage for facilities and events of this type and size is 10.0 security officers). The facility then monitors its own actual staffing levels and discovers that it only employs 7.0 security personnel members per gate, a rate 30 percent lower, rather than 20 percent lower, than the benchmark national average. This gap between the goal of 10.0 and the actual level of 7.0 represents a critical deviation in management's judgment. The 30 percent deviation suggests that the facility may be drastically understaffed, which may in turn result in unnecessary risks to patrons and to the facility itself.

Defining which performance deviations are critical to the overall success of a process or to the success of the organization is an essential task for managers. Even in a small organization, there will be numerous deviations or gaps between actual performance and the goal or standard. If management attempted to respond to every performance deviation, there would be little time left to do anything else. The manager's task is to determine which performance deviations are genuinely critical and to focus on these.

One strategy for focusing management energy and attention is to identify and focus on a limited number of goals or standards. Limiting the number of critical goals not only facilitates the control process, it also tends to focus the attention and effort of everyone involved in pursuing those goals, which in turn tends to improve performance.

Take Corrective Action

If the level of actual performance reveals that performance standards are being met, the organization knows enough to continue what it is doing, because it is working. If performance is not at a level consistent with goals, and if this gap represents a critical deviation, the organization knows it needs to take action to improve performance. This is called *corrective action*.

For some municipally owned sports facilities, the decision to seek private management is a corrective action. Particularly for those facilities that are running large deficits, falling into disrepair, failing to attract a prime tenant, and remaining vacant or "dark" for too many days of the year, the decision to secure private management brings in venture capital, managerial expertise, and professional clout that can be helpful in securing events and sponsorships.

Regardless of the form it takes, corrective action is the action management takes to put performance back on track in terms of meeting goals and performance standards.

Continuous Improvement

There has been a dramatic shift in recent years in the focus and scope of the control process. It is no longer enough merely to find and fix problems that occur. To compete effectively where quality, innovation, and service are what sells, the focus of control must extend beyond merely monitoring performance, finding mistakes, and taking corrective action. In a world where everyone is looking for a competitive advantage, control is increasingly becoming the process not just of problem solving around critical deviations, but also of learning how to continuously improve performance even when there are no problems.

The search for never-ending improvements involves a Plan-Do-Check-Act circular cycle (Sashkin & Kiser, 1993) shown in Figure 7-9. Management, teams, and individuals plan a change, make the change, check the results, and depending on the outcome, standardize the change or begin the cycle of improvement again with the new information.

The improvement process also involves considering how things would be done if one were to start all over from scratch. The term *reengineering* has been applied to this process of improvement (Hammer & Champy, 1993). Reengineering means that management, teams, and individuals rethink and redesign operations that

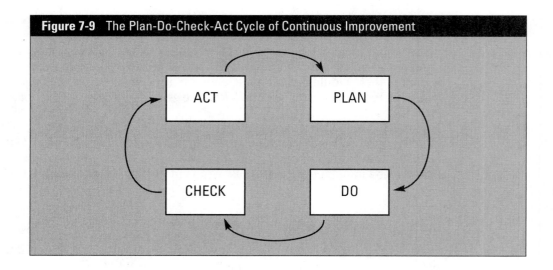

Figure 7-9 The Plan-Do-Check-Act Cycle of Continuous Improvement

have become antiquated and do not add value. For example, a college soccer field has been used for over ten years for local youth soccer games on Sundays. The grounds crew and maintenance staff have been awarded one-hour overtime each week to prepare the field for use by the youth group. The maintenance team has traditionally lined the field, set up additional goals, and erected eight additional sets of portable bleachers that are then removed on Monday mornings. The facility manager, who was recently hired and has a daughter old enough to participate in the league, attends the weekend games and learns that during the course of the season, only three sets of bleachers are used, the extra soccer goals are never used, and the soccer league relines the field to accommodate its own rules and field specifications. The facility manager recognizes that the university's grounds crew's preparations are no longer effective and do not serve the purpose of the league. For the facility manager, continuous improvement means rethinking the field preparation process for the Sunday youth league games. The manager may now call together his grounds team, plan a new preparation process, carry out the process, check to see that the new preparation plan is meeting the needs of the league, and then act on any changes that need to be made.

Like the other responsibilities of management, controlling and managing continuous improvement are demanding tasks but are essential to the success of the organization. An effective control process ensures that critical deviations in performance are identified and responded to well before they threaten the organization's ability to achieve its goals and mission. An effective process of continuous improvement ensures that the organization will continue to satisfy the expectations of its customers and keep pace with competition.

Service Quality

Sports facility owners and managers agree that at the heart of the facility's ability to succeed is the organization's commitment to continuous improvement and to service quality. In fact, SMG, considered to be one of the premier private sports facility management companies in the world, suggests they have successfully turned around underperforming buildings because they operate facilities as entrepreneurial businesses that focus on the best interests of their clients and communities. SMG emphasizes improving operational efficiency, operating cash flow, and

fiscal accountability while delivering high-quality event activity and high levels of customer service. SMG, which operates over fifty-five distinct building operations including stadiums and arenas around the world (ranging from the 2,000-seat theater in Mobile, Alabama, to the 76,000-seat Superdome in New Orleans, Louisiana) has articulated a corporate philosophy which states that successful facility operation and financial performance are linked directly to effective marketing and quality management.

Sports facility managers understand that their business is highly dependent on their ability to attract and retain customers. Although offering a schedule of attractive events and activities is certainly an important factor in filling the building night after night, there is a broader recognition of the importance of how events are presented and how fans are treated. Customers are likely to return when they are pleased by their experience at the facility. Therefore, stadium, park, and arena managers must constantly focus on finding new ways to delight their customers. Sports facilities of today are designed and constructed with the users in mind. Prime tenants and performers are considered in the design of locker rooms, meeting rooms, training facilities, dressing areas, media and production space, loading docks, and private visitor and family lounges. Spectators are considered in myriad ways ranging from the design of the seats (padded with cup holders) to unobstructed sight lines, to handicapped accessible seating areas to plush luxury and club areas to a wide array of food offerings. A visit to any stadium or arena or to a major facility website illustrates the lengths to which designers are willing to go to attract and keep fans. Today's facilities are entertainment complexes where it is not unusual to find an art gallery, retail store, upscale restaurant, concourse games, museum, picnic area, children's playground, or hot tubs integrated into the stadium or arena design.

Amenities, however, are only one piece of the service quality puzzle. Sports facility managers recognize that they must emphasize service excellence in order to create loyal fans who will return to the building for event after event. At the Fleet Center in Boston, for example, managers have adopted the *FISH!* Program. The *FISH!* Program has its roots in the world famous Pike Place Fish market in Seattle, Washington. *FISH!* is a philosophy of organizational operation that creates an environment where exceptional customer service is the key to creating remarkable and unforgettable experiences for customers (Lundin, Paul, & Christensen, 2000). *FISH!*, according to John Wentzell, vice president for operations of the Fleet Center, "is more than a program of customer service, it's an attitude, it's an environment, it's a spirit that energizes the organization and results in a workplace where people are energetic and excited about their work . . . where work is fun and employees create meaningful and remarkable experiences for our customers" (Wentzell, 2001). The core values of *FISH!* are sales, service, and speed. Employees are trained, encouraged, and rewarded for engaging in activities that promote a fun, productive, and fan-friendly workplace where fans are treated as guests and a visit to the Fleet Center is elevated to a remarkable and delightful experience for all.

Management theorist and author Ken Blanchard supports this approach to service quality. For Blanchard, having satisfied customers is not enough. The successful organization must deliver exceptional customer service in order to create "raving fans" whose unwavering loyalty will result in astounding bottom-line results (Blanchard, 1993). The sports facility business is above all else a service-oriented enterprise. Managers must not only present a high-quality product supported by creative, interesting, and attractive amenities, but they must constantly strive in the spirit of continuous improvement to find new and better ways to delight and surprise their spending customers.

Summary

Operations management as it pertains to sports facilities takes place on two levels: a micro level that involves the management of events conducted within the facility and the macro level where the organization's strategy is translated into action. Operational plans are different from strategic plans in two ways: they cover shorter time periods and are, for the most part, internally focused.

The Balanced Scorecard, a current version of management by objectives (MBO), is a system of setting objectives and identifying measures within four categories or perspectives. Managers, teams, and individuals develop and closely monitor performance based on customer measures, internal processes, human resource measures, and financial measures, all tied directly to a specific strategic objective. This deliberate linkage of strategic objectives with operational actions distinguishes the approach from its older cousin, MBO, and is designed to build a strategy-focused organization.

In order to create the specific measures and objectives required by the Balanced Scorecard approach, forecasting and scheduling become critical activities for understanding and planning the conditions and activities necessary for implementing strategy. Forecasting generates predictions and projections that form the basis for determining the levels of business in each department. Scheduling ensures the effective identification and sequencing of key activities within the organization. Computer-assisted forecasting and scheduling make both of these processes even easier and more effective.

Policies, procedures, and budgets are important tools for ensuring that behavior throughout the organization is consistent with the organization's mission and strategies. Policies are guidelines for decisions; procedures are guidelines for action; and budgets are guidelines for allocating financial resources.

Control is the process of ensuring that actual performance is consistent with the organization's goals and standards. Performance must be monitored to ensure that progress is on track, and action must be taken to solve performance problems and to continuously improve performance.

The sports facility business is above all else a service-oriented enterprise. Managers must provide a high-quality product supported by a wide variety of amenities in an environment where the fans are treated as guests rather than customers. The organization must be imbued with a spirit of continuous improvement combined with a commitment to excellent service quality.

Hoop Hysteria

The sport management Association at your college has decided that a campuswide three-on-three basketball tournament would be a good way to raise funds to support the club's activities. Taking on a project of this magnitude would also allow sport management students to gain hands-on experience in sports event management.

1. What operational planning tools would be most helpful in planning the event? Explain your answer.

2. What information, resources, and authorizations will you need on your campus to proceed with planning and executing the event? Identify the various tasks and challenges that will be faced by the association. How will this work be accomplished?

3. Divide into groups and create templates or examples of important operational planning documents.

Management Exercise

References

Blanchard, K. (1993). *Raving fans: A revolutionary approach to customer service.* New York: William Morrow.

Drucker, P. F. (1954). *The practice of management.* New York: Harper & Bros.

Farmer, P., Mulrooney, A., & Amon, R. (1996). *Sport facility planning and management.* Morgantown, WV: Fitness Information Technology, Inc.

Fisher, M. L. et al. (1994). Making supply meet demand in an uncertain world. *Harvard Business Review, 72*(3), pp. 83–89.

Hammer, M., & Champy, J. (1993). *Re-engineering the corporation: A manifesto for business revolution.* New York: HarperBusiness.

Horrow, R. (2001). Sharing the cost. *Stadia, 7,* pp. 56–60.

Kaplan, R. S., & Norton, D. P. (1993). Putting the Balanced Scorecard approach to work. *Harvard Business Review, 71*(5), pp. 134–147.

Kaplan, R. S., & Norton, D. P. (1996). Using the Balanced Scorecard as a strategic management system. *Harvard Business Review, 74*(1), pp. 75–86.

Lundin, S., Paul, H., & Christensen, J. (2000). *FISH!: A remarkable way to boost morale and improve results.* New York: Hyperion.

Mulrooney, A., & Farmer, P. (2001). Managing the facility In B. Parkhouse, (ed.), *The Management of Sport* (pp. 272–295). Boston: McGraw-Hill.

Sashkin, M., & Kiser, K. J. (1993). *Putting total quality management to work.* San Francisco: Berrett-Koehler.

Stogel, C. (2000). Driving the Big Bertha. *Brandweek, 41*(5), pp. 30–35.

Stone, D. (2001). Urban thrills. *Stadia, 9,* pp. 39–42.

Wentzell, J. (2001). *Sport Facility Management: The Old Boston Garden to the New Fleet Center.* Presentation at the Fred Brown Executive Lecture Series, Western New England College, Springfield, MA.

PHOTO: © PHOTODISC

Part 4

Organizing for Performance

Chapter 8

Organization Design and Sports Agency

Purpose: To help clients find the best outlet for their talent and to help them derive the greatest financial and life benefits from their professional relationships.

Stakeholders: Professional athletes, agents, player unions, coaches, individual franchise management personnel, individual franchise employees, franchise owners, league management personnel, league employees, tour management personnel, tour employees, intercollegiate athletes, intercollegiate athletic management personnel, broadcast networks, franchise, league, and tour sponsors, franchise, league, and tour advertisers, sports broadcast, print, and online media, fans.

Size and scope:

- In 1967 the average salary in MLB was $19,000, and the league minimum was $12,000. In 2001, the average had ballooned by 118 times to $2,264,403, and the minimum was $200,000. By comparison, the average U.S. household income that year was $54,842 (Blum, 2001).
- During the 1990s the average salary in the NHL grew 517 percent to $1.4 million; the NBA's average salary grew 429 percent to $3.53 million, and the average NFL salary increased 279 percent to $1.2 million ("Sports Salaries," 2001).
- In the 2001–2002 season, twenty-two Division I-A football head coaches made $1 million in salary and bonuses (led by University of Florida's Steve Spurrier at $2.1 million). Seventeen Division I men's basketball head coaches earned at least that much, with the University of Louisville's Rick Pitino slated to earn $2.2 million following his banishment from the Boston Celtics (Wieberg, 2001).
- At the height of his career, golfer Tiger Woods earns $50 million a year in endorsements alone, including a five-year $100 million deal with Nike.

- SFX Sports, the player representation segment of large-firm SFX Entertainment, owned by Clear Channel Communications and operated by David Falk and Arn Tellem, represents Michael Jordan, Kobe Bryant, Andre Agassi, and Brandi Chastain. SFX is also a huge presence in the concert and theater industry, promoting and/or producing in 1999 by their count 7,800 music events (including the Rolling Stones, Britney Spears, and Ricky Martin), 13,300 theatrical shows (including David Copperfield and Riverdance), 1,400 family entertainment shows, and 500 specialized sports and motor racing shows (including the U.S. women's World Cup soccer team victory tour and monster truck shows). SFX also owns and/or operates 120 live entertainment venues in 31 of the top 50 U.S. markets, including Avalon in Boston, the Bi-Lo Center in Greenville, South Carolina, the Cincinnati Music Hall, the Corel Centre in Ottawa, and the Fillmore in San Francisco ("About SFX," 2001).

Governance: Player unions certify all player agents, as do many individual states. Unions also serve to negotiate basic agreements with leagues, limit the percentage of compensation agents can charge for contract negotiation, and help players and agents access information that will aid them in preparing for negotiations. Courts and arbitrators also serve to regulate agents by voiding contracts that are illegal or unfair.

Inside Look

Being Matt Kinney*

Compared to those in the big leagues, the home team locker room at Hammond Stadium in Fort Myers, Florida, the spring training home of the Minnesota Twins, is wholly unremarkable. The room has wall-to-wall carpeting, and each player has a roomy wooden locker and a padded folding chair, but it is by no means posh or fancy. In the entryway between the players' area and the trainers' room are plain cork bulletin boards with bus departure and daily workout schedules tacked on them. On the cinder block wall above these is a simple, equally unremarkable plaque, much like any to be picked up at a local trophy shop. The plaque is placed there to fuel the current Twins' All-Star dreams by paying homage to the former Minnesota stars whose numbers have been retired: Harmon Killebrew (3), Tony Oliva (6), Kent Hrbek (14), and recent Baseball Hall of Fame inductee Kirby Puckett (34). There is no "51" on the plaque. In the spring of 2001, that number belonged to Twins pitcher Matt Kinney. As you read this, Kinney could be pitching his way to the Hall of Fame in Cooperstown, New York, back in his hometown of Bangor, Maine, just another small-town guy who had a shot at "The Show" and didn't make it, or, most likely, somewhere in between.

Like most kids who grow up loving baseball in Maine, Matt Kinney rooted for the Boston Red Sox, idolized former BoSox star Roger Clemens, and dreamed about the chance to pitch in Fenway Park. However, Maine kids who play baseball in Maine start the season working out in the school gym and are lucky to get outside by mid-April. When they do, they play much of the season in weather more conducive to snowmobiling and ice fishing than pitching, hitting, and fielding. As a result, Kinney was far less experienced than prospects from California, Florida, and the rest of the Sun Belt. Said Kinney, "the good players in the North are as good as the good players in the South, but they don't have as many at bats or pitch as many innings."

But against the odds, the right-handed Kinney lived out part of his dream in 1995 when he was drafted by the Red Sox. Drafting Matt Kinney, like drafting any kid from Maine, was a long-term proposition and a long shot as well. But scout Buzz Bowers convinced the club it was worth risking a sixth-round pick. After the draft, Kinney signed and was sent to the Red Sox rookie league team in Florida, and the next year he pitched for the Lowell (Massachusetts) Spinners, the Sox's affiliate in the short-season Class A New York-Penn League. After progressing through the Sox's system with successful stints at Michigan of the Class A Midwest League (8–5, 3.53 ERA) in 1997, and Sarasota of the Class A Florida State League (9–6) the next year, Kinney was traded to the Minnesota Twins in July 1998 as the Red Sox looked to acquire proven major leaguers to shore up their wild card playoff run.

Once drafted and signed, Matt was now a professional. He was going to make his living from playing baseball. "The second I left high school, I was down here competing. You have to get over the first part of being overwhelmed," said Kinney of this adjustment. "It's not just the talent. It's all a confidence thing. But until you get to that point, you're thinking, wow, everyone here's pretty good, now I have to prove that I'm good. There's that little bit of tension between everybody, because we're all trying to get the same goal. That's a

*Matt Kinney, personal communication, March 13, 2001.

tough adjustment from high school where it's all a team thing."

Like all professional athletes, Kinney needed an agent. But what does an eighteen-year-old kid from Maine, drafted a few days before his high school graduation, know about picking an agent? And what kind of bargaining power does a raw recruit like Kinney have? Shouldn't he just be grateful to sign any contract the club puts in front of him? Does he really need an agent? And what kind of agent is interested in representing a long shot like Kinney, anyway?

These are the questions that drive the engine of the sport agency business. We saw in Chapter 6 that player salaries are the most significant expense for professional sport organizations. Salaries for all sport organizations have steadily, and in some cases, dramatically increased since the 1970s. So what sparked these increases? As we reviewed in Chapter 6, much of this increase came with the advent of free agency following the Andy Messersmith arbitration ruling in 1975. Marvin Miller, executive director of the MLB Players' Association during this time, viewed that event in these terms: "Qualified people have told me that decision and the labor agreement which was signed the following summer resulted in more money changing hands from an owner group to an employee group than any other decision or negotiation in his-

tory" (Bodley, 2000, p. 10C). This includes not just sports labor history, but the history of all labor negotiations everywhere. The advent of free agency, spurred by strong labor unions and an ever-increasing appetite for sport consumption from fans, has created an atmosphere in many sport organizations where there was plenty of money to be had, and the negotiating expertise of a skilled agent could secure it.

As the sport and entertainment industry has grown, so too has the sport agency segment. As we see in this chapter, the individual negotiating skills of a single agent are only part of the sport agency business. There is also the dimension of sport agency that deals with extensive and lucrative product and service endorsement agreements and has meant great wealth for many players and coaches. However, these benefits have come at a cost. The expectations of managing and investing this wealth, negotiating contracts, and securing endorsement deals pose significant managerial challenges for one single sport agent. In response to industry growth, all sport organizations have sought to improve performance by improving the definition and coordination of the units that do the work necessary for organizational success. We examine the most recent efforts of sport agency organizations to organize for performance, but first some background information is necessary.

Introduction

This chapter describes the creation and coordination of the various work units necessary to implement sports agency organizational strategies, including the various departments necessary to do the work these organizations perform—player representation and player marketing, for example. The chapter also discusses in detail the elements of these organizational design responsibilities and traces how sports organizations in general and sports agency organizations in particular have sought to design their structures in response to the continually emerging performance challenges they face.

Sports Agency Defined*

There is an unquestionable lure to being a sports agent. Why? Is it the desire for big money? For fame? For power? To be like Scott Boras, a former St. Louis Cardinals minor leaguer who represents Texas Rangers shortstop Alex Rodriguez (who has a quarter-billion dollar ten-year contract), Kevin Brown, and Bernie Williams? Or maybe Jeff Moorad, who negotiated Manny Ramirez's eight-year $160 million deal with the Red Sox in 2000? Or how about David Dunn, who negotiated quarterback Drew Bledsoe's ten-year $103 million deal with the New England Patriots (the richest in NFL history—so far), David Falk (who represents Patrick Ewing and Michael Jordan), or the Hendricks Brothers (who represent Clemens)?

www.nflpa.org

But the business is cutthroat and competitive. The big-name firms have the lion's share of the players. For example, similar to all unions that certify agents, the National Football League Players' Association (NFLPA) has approved approximately 1,100 agents, but only about 250 players will be drafted each year (Layden, 2001), with others signed as free agents. This makes it a buyer's market from the players' perspective.

There is also the issue of what it takes to be an agent. A student like you who is reading this text as you prepare for class could be an agent right now, because essentially all you need to be an agent is a client. Many individual states have certain certification standards that seek to curb aggressive recruiting of college players, such as giving them cash and threatening their amateur status, but there is no uniform nationally approved certification (although each players' association has some requirements). Even the big-name agents battle with each other for clients. In 2001, two years after receiving a $2 million bonus to stay with the firm (with allegedly agreeing to a noncompetition clause that he would not take clients and start his own firm), David Dunn left Assante Corporation, founded by Leigh Steinberg and Jeff Moorad, and brought (or as Assante claims, stole) 80 percent of the firm's top NFL clients, including Drew Blesdoe, Corey Dillon, Darren Woodson, and Amani Toomer. Assante then sued Dunn in California state court (Borges, 2001).

So money, power, fame, making the big deals. And what's even more alluring about this job is that it could really happen right now. Because all an agent needs is a client. But that's also the problem with the sports agency business. The competition for clients is fierce. Lots of people out there feel *they* can be the next Boras or Moorad; they just need to find the next A-Rod or Manny. It is a wide open market, but that also means the competition is virtually unlimited and can come from anywhere and at any time. So even once an agent has a promising client or two, Boras, and all of the other "Boras wannabees" out there, will be working to steal them away.

Dan Weinberg, personal communication, February 20, 2001.

The job of a sports agent is certainly high profile, but what precisely does he or she do? A sports agent is a personal manager/representative who finds the best outlet for a client's, also referred to as a principal's, talent. A sports agent's biggest responsibility is negotiating contracts, those agreements between players and coaches and sports and business organizations, as described in Figure 8-1.

In the case of players and coaches, the items that can be negotiated include guaranteed income, bonuses, and the length of the agreement. For example, when Japanese star Ichiro Suzuki signed his three-year $12.14 million contract with the Seattle Mariners before his breakout 2001 season, as part of the deal his agent also negotiated numerous benefits such as English lessons and an interpreter, moving and housing allowances totaling $88,000, a sport-utility vehicle, and four round-trip tickets between Japan and Seattle twice each year (Bodley, 2001).

Contracts and clauses for college coaches have also become quite lucrative. Virginia Tech head football coach Frank Beamer gets $200,000 if his team is selected to a Bowl Championship Series (BCS) game (Rose, Sugar, Fiesta, Orange), University of

Figure 8-1   Agency Law and Contracts

Under the tenets of agency law, an agent acts on the behalf of a principal (the player or coach) to achieve a specified accomplishment. In an agency agreement, responsibilities known as fiduciary duties are required of both sides. The principal must comply with the terms of a contract, compensate the agent, and reimburse for expenses. The agent has a duty to obey the wishes of the principal, to remain loyal, to notify, and to show reasonable care (Yasser et al., 1997).

At the heart of nearly every financial relationship is a *contract*. A contract is defined as a written or oral agreement between parties that is enforceable under the law, which must contain a promise to do something in the future. A contract typically consists of the following elements:

* An *offer*: A conditional promise in which one party agrees to act if the other also acts

* *Acceptance*: The agreement to the promise on the part of the party to whom the offer is made

* *Consideration*: The concept of the exchange of value, that one party must give something in return for the other's doing the same

Contracts are not valid if they are illegal (for example, if they include the promise for an act that is illegal, such as murder), or if the party to whom the offer is made lacks the *capacity* to understand the contract due to impairments, or is under age 18. The failure to perform a duty imposed under the contract is referred to as a *breach of contract*. The remedies for a contractual breach are monetary compensation, or specific performance, which means that the party responsible for the breach performs the duties the contract stipulates (Berry & Wong, 1993).

Iowa head basketball coach Steve Alford receives a bonus of $300,000 if he stays at the school through the 2003–2004 season, and University of Kentucky head basketball coach Tubby Smith has the use of two late-model cars, gets twenty tickets to each home basketball game, eight tickets to each home football game, and a country club membership. The terms of a specific contract help illustrate the various negotiable elements, as shown in Figure 8-2 with the terms of Clemson University's head football coach Tommy Bowden. Much of the growth for coach compensation is due to the impact of agents in the negotiating process, with half of the coaches at the power conferences employing agents (Wieberg, 2001). After the terms of the contract are finalized, agents must then make sure that all terms and payments are upheld (Greenberg, 1993; Lester, 1990).

The next most important duty for sports agents is marketing the athlete or coach and helping the principal secure endorsement and sponsorship agreements. This is a key factor for both agents and principals, because it is an additional and potentially significant source of income. The final important duty is assistance with financial planning.

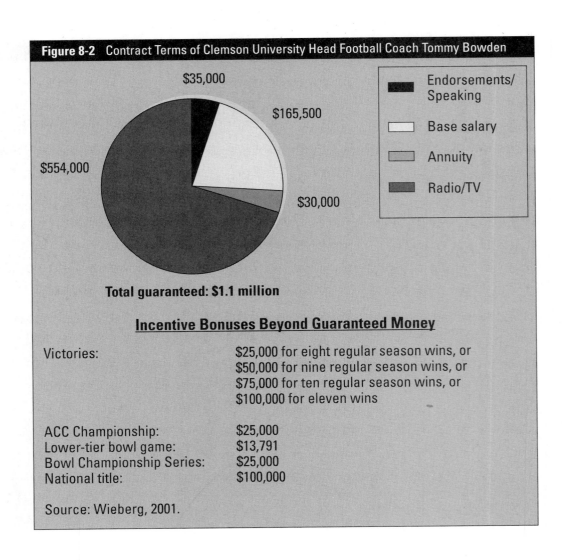

Figure 8-2 Contract Terms of Clemson University Head Football Coach Tommy Bowden

$35,000

$165,500

$554,000

$30,000

Endorsements/Speaking

Base salary

Annuity

Radio/TV

Total guaranteed: $1.1 million

Incentive Bonuses Beyond Guaranteed Money

Victories:	$25,000 for eight regular season wins, or $50,000 for nine regular season wins, or $75,000 for ten regular season wins, or $100,000 for eleven wins
ACC Championship:	$25,000
Lower-tier bowl game:	$13,791
Bowl Championship Series:	$25,000
National title:	$100,000

Source: Wieberg, 2001.

Consider the story of Dan Weinberg. He is marketing manager for the golf division at Woolf Associates, a Boston-based sports agency and marketing firm founded by influential sports agent Bob Woolf. Says Weinberg, who joined the firm in 1999 straight out of college, "I realized my junior year in college that I didn't want to work in finance, or go work for a mutual fund company, or in the financial sector. I wanted to work in sports. Being inside the ropes was what I wanted to do. I wanted to work with professional golf.

"For everything that's said about how difficult an industry this is to get into," said Weinberg, "I feel very, very fortunate. The reality of professional sport is that it's a very closed world. As big as professional sports are, the actual world is small, and you're either an insider or an outsider. I consider it equal parts luck, equal parts being in the right place at the right time. But also, none of this would have happened if I hadn't worked hard. I'm lucky that I got this fantastic break, but if I hadn't been busting my hump, I wouldn't have been able to step through the doors that were opened for me.

"I came on as a contract employee. I wasn't even full time. I remember when I first started working here, one of my bosses asked me to send off some golf bags to someone via FedEx. But we didn't have any boxes that could hold these golf bags. So I had to build boxes. And it was something so small and irrelevant, but the truth was, because I was able to step up to that challenge, the guy could see I could think creatively and could find solutions, whereas I could have just weaseled out of it. You prove yourself gradually. It's not like you're going to step in your first week on the job and start negotiating contracts. You start from the bottom."

After Dan Weinberg's successful bout with the golf bags at Woolf, he sought to move into the area of player representation in golf. "I had a good relationship with Bruce Fleisher (at the time on the PGA Tour) and got to know him and his family. I had caddied for him at a tournament in 1998. Being inside the ropes was the absolute rush of a lifetime. I played golf all throughout high school and college, and worked at The Country Club in Brookline, Massachusetts (the host site of the 1999 Ryder Cup) all through high school and college, and I loved the game and the atmosphere of professional golf. The common bond for everybody that works here is that they are truly passionate about sports."

On a day-to-day basis, Weinberg is involved with a variety of responsibilities. "I am one of two main contacts between Woolf and the professional golfers that we represent," which includes "maintaining contact with them, searching out opportunities for them, everything from soup to nuts. The great thing we have going here is that I'm part of a team. There might be some misconceptions out there that being an agent is all about (yourself); it's not the case. I have to rely on people.

"I really fall under athlete marketing, because golf is unique," says Weinberg. "There are no guaranteed contracts, there's no draft. If you're out there on the PGA Tour, it's because you earned it. You didn't come out of high school drafted by the NBA and get a guaranteed fat contract regardless of how you play. If you go out there [in golf] and have a bad year, you're probably not going to be out there the following year. The professional golfer has to pay for his taxi to the airport. He has to pay for his flight to California to play at Pebble Beach. He has to pay for his hotel, pay for his caddie. I would estimate the cost of a single guy traveling on the PGA Tour for a full season would be close to $100,000."

The key in this selling process, according to Weinberg, is "doing things the right way, having good values, treating your clients the way they deserve to be treated, creating profitable business relationships, and doing it the honest and respectable way. If you watch 'Arli$$' on HBO, agents are portrayed as evil, money-sucking scumbags. That's a tough reputation to get away from. Part of what a agents do is look after the best interests of their clients. That can mean anything. Trying to find them the right team to play for, trying to get them more money under a certain contract to help them provide for their family. One of my main responsibilities is to find marketing opportunities for them, to create endorsement relationships, sponsorship agreements, to put money in their pockets. My division is not going to be profitable unless I make money for our golfers, and we get paid for doing it."

But selling can be tough. "There's nothing worse than having a client you can't provide for, but sometimes that's the reality of the situation," says Weinberg. "Sometimes your players lose their marketability. They might fall out of favor with the public, or they're just not playing at a level where they're going to command endorsement dollars."

Agents usually make more money when their clients make more money because most agents earn income based on the percentage of their clients' income. Other methods of earning income include working for a flat fee or an hourly rate (McAleenan, 1990). The risk in the percentage approach is that there is no guarantee of what the agent will make. It is contingent on what he or she can negotiate on behalf of the client, and the agent can't get paid until the client gets paid. In professional league sports, agents are limited by the unions on what percentages they can charge, which is no more than 6 percent (Greenberg, 1993). And the agent is paid this percentage only on the amount over which the contract exceeds the league minimum. However, agents can earn more when negotiating contracts for endorsements and other agreements and for coaches and nonunionized clients because these are not subject to union oversight. Most firms have standard percentages for marketing services, the highest reaching the 30 percent range.

Agents also provide their expertise so athletes can focus on their game performance without distractions. Says Weinberg, "It's become such a high-stakes game. You need to have somebody out there looking out for your best interests, whether it's searching for opportunities, turning down opportunities. There's so much going on that it would be tough to handle everything and still keep focused on the actual task of playing golf. The more you can reduce your outside concerns, the easier it's going to be to play good golf. That's why I'm here. If you have a couple of million dollars in endorsements waiting for you, there's pressure to show that you're earning those endorsements, but that's a little bit different pressure than knowing that if you don't make the cut this week, you might not be able to afford taking a flight out to your next week's event. That's the harsh reality of golf: you're not getting paid unless you're earning it."

In summary, then, sports agency is about selling. An agent must sell to the client, whether that client is a player, a team, or a potential sponsor. The products vary, but the premise is the same. Competition is fierce, but the potential payoffs are great. It's not for the faint of heart.

Historical Influences

Although the history of sport in North America is replete with astute business-people, colorful promoters, and dubious hucksters alike, three key figures stand out as having exhibited particular influence on the development of the sports agency business: Charles C. Pyle, Christy Walsh, and Mark McCormack. Pyle, also known as "Cash and Carry," was a theater owner and stage producer when he met University of Illinois running back Harold "Red" Grange, the "Galloping Ghost," in 1925. Pyle became Grange's manager, negotiated his professional contract with the Chicago Bears of the fledgling NFL (which stipulated that Grange receive 50 percent of the Bears' home game ticket revenues—of which Pyle got half), and organized many of Grange's endorsement deals and postseason barnstorming tours. Grange's drawing power was so strong that he is credited with saving the inchoate NFL, although Pyle and Grange also organized a short-lived competitor league in the late 1920s (Carroll, 1999).

Sportswriter Christy Walsh served as agent and representative for two of the early twentieth century's sports colossi, New York Yankees outfielder Babe Ruth and University of Notre Dame head football coach Knute Rockne. Like Pyle, Walsh negotiated barnstorming tours and endorsements for Ruth, and lucrative deals for ghostwritten syndicated newspaper columns, endorsements for coaching schools and sporting goods, and speaking engagements for Rockne. Ruth had no real contract bargaining power with the Yankees due to the reserve clause, but Rockne faced no such restrictions. Walsh also helped Rockne use job offers from schools such as Columbia, Southern California, and Loyola Marymount (California) to leverage substantial salary raises and football facility construction and improvements from Notre Dame. At the height of his popularity before his death in a plane crash in 1931 en route to California (to make a film of his life story, for which he was to be paid $50,000), Walsh helped Rockne earn $75,000 a year, a sum that would not be reached by another coach until the 1970s (Sperber, 1993).

Mark McCormack established the basis for the modern sports agency and marketing firm in the early 1960s when he secured endorsement deals for golfing legend Arnold Palmer. McCormack used these skills to found the International Management Group (IMG) in 1960, which remains one of the most powerful agency and event marketing firms in sport. Since the formation of IMG, other firms have moved into prominence, such as Octagon and SFX. These large firms have come to dominate the sports agency business.

Ethics and Sports Agency

In the sports agency business, there are few restrictions as to who can become an agent. This lack of formalized approval and the significant closeness and potential dependence between players and agents mean that this segment is particularly vulnerable to unethical, illegal, and dishonest actions by agents. Perhaps the most well-known recent case of this problem involved sports agent William H. "Tank" Black.

Black, who had a tryout with the NFL's Atlanta Falcons in 1979, was a former assistant football coach at the University of South Carolina in the late 1980s.

According to a former colleague, Black left to become a sports agent because he wanted the opportunity to make big money. By 1999 Black's firm, Professional Marketing Inc. (PMI), represented more than thirty-five NFL players, including Jacksonville Jaguars running back Fred Taylor (who called Black "Pops" and described him as his second dad), New York Giants wide receiver Ike Hilliard, Tennessee Titans defensive end Jevon Kearse, as well as Toronto Raptors guard and Jordan heir apparent Vince Carter. Black attracted these talents to PMI because he would call his clients at all hours, express care and concern, and give them expensive gifts. The firm grew by developing a system of runners on college campuses and paying prospective clients. Black offered under-the-table payments to University of Florida players in 1999, such as $600 a month for Johnny Rutledge; and he leased a $133,500 Mercedes S600V for Kearse, in violation of NCAA amateurism rules and the many state agent regulations. But as Black got more capital, he spent more on recruiting. The more he invested in recruiting, the more players he landed, and the more players he landed, the more capital he had at his disposal (Wertheim, Yaeger, & Schecter, 2000).

However, in 2000 federal investigators from the Securities and Exchange Commission claimed Black was involved in the biggest case of agent fraud in the history of sport. Black was accused of defrauding clients and mismanaging approximately $15 million. Fred Taylor lost his entire $3.6 million signing bonus, which Black had invested in a pyramid scheme that promised a 36 percent annual return on loans made to people who used their car titles as collateral. Black actually promised 20 percent and skimmed 16 percent for himself, and he charged an additional fee for administering the funds. Some players liquidated legitimate stock portfolios to invest in this, although Black was never licensed as an investment adviser. He also encouraged his clients to invest stock in a company that Black himself had ties to, received a consulting salary, sold them shares they were supposed to receive free, and charged them a commission for it. Black also allegedly laundered millions of dollars for a Detroit drug trafficking ring through an offshore account in the Cayman Islands, with connections in Colombia, for which he made a 25 percent commission (Wertheim et al., 2000).

Black thrived on his clients' lack of knowledge of fiscal and financial matters, and instead of educating them, he exploited this lack of knowledge. His PMI brochure actually read: "A successful athlete simply does not have time to research, study, compare and negotiate every opportunity that arises. Too often the result is a missed opportunity or a hasty decision that results in a less than fair deal" (Wertheim et al., 2000, p. 69). Black has denied all allegations, but all of his clients have left him for other agents, and the NFLPA has decertified him.

This one example of agent fraud and exploitation illustrates for clients the importance of choosing an agent and staying informed on the agent's dealings. The design and structures of sports agency firms also impact their overall efficiency and effectiveness. The better the design and oversight in a firm, and the more attention on the part of the client, the less opportunity for Black-like misdealings.

Organizational Design and Sports Agency

It is the choice of whether to sign with a large sports agency firm or to sign with an individual sports agent that is the key decision for emerging professional athletes. Their choice is not a simple one. The next section outlines the essential elements of organizational design and how they impact these two basic models of the sports agency business.

The Essential Elements in Organizational Design

Edgar Schein (1985), a prominent organizational theorist, suggests that four essential elements must be present for an organization to function effectively: common goals, division of work, coordination of effort, and authority structure. According to Schein's model, if any of these elements are missing or poorly designed, the organization is likely to be unsuccessful in implementing its strategies and pursuing its mission.

Common Goals

Common goals, as we saw in Chapter 4, provide the sense of direction, the target to aim for, and the basis of cooperation that are critical for the success of any organization. The concept of using academic achievement to determine interscholastic athletic eligibility is implemented to encourage academic performance. Without goals as a focus for its efforts, the energy of the organization would be wasted on random activities toward no particular end. The emphasis on academic performance sends the message that schools place primary importance on educational activities.

As we saw in Chapters 6 and 7, planning is the process of developing goals and strategies to achieve the organization's mission. Schein's point is that you have to know where you are going (as defined through an organization's mission and goals) and how you're going to get there (using what strategy) before you can design a structure to take you there. Recall that under agency law, the agent is bound to represent the client's wishes. In the case of the sports agency industry segment, a client seeks an agent who can represent his or her interests the most effectively. A prospective agent, therefore, must show that he or she has the ability to produce a plan for clients to achieve their financial, professional, and personal goals. But the goals of the client also impact the goals of the agent.

The organizational design, therefore, must enable the agent to serve the client in the most effective manner and must aid the agent in serving the best interests of the client. Thus the first essential element in designing an effective organization is shared or common goals—from mission to strategic goals to policies and procedures. In the case of sports agency organizations, this means a mission, strategic goals, policies, and procedures consistent with the goals of the athletes the agencies seek to serve.

Division of Work

Common goals alone, however, are not enough. Once the organization's mission and strategic and operational goals are clear, the work necessary to achieve those goals must be divided up in the most productive way possible. Managers have struggled with this question for over a century: how to group and divide the tasks of negotiating contracts, securing endorsements and sponsorship agreements, and producing plans for clients to achieve financial goals. Following this overview of Schein's four key elements of organizational design, much of this chapter focuses on how organizations in the sports agency segment have chosen to divide up work for maximum effectiveness.

Coordination of Efort

Logically speaking, if the work of an organization is divided among separate units or departments, coordination is critical to ensure that the work being done within each unit is consistent with the overall goals of the organization. Also, these units must not work at cross-purposes with one another. Consider a sports agency organization with a mission to provide clients with financial stability combined with a consideration for a client's personal values. The contract department focuses on negotiating the highest rate of compensation regardless of the location of employment, but the client might be content with less money if he or she could be located in an area closer to home and family. The sponsorship unit might be seeking only the most lucrative endorsement agreements, but the client might be unwilling to represent certain products that he or she doesn't use or feels are unhealthy or destructive (such as alcohol). In essence, these units are working at cross-purposes and need better coordination to ensure the organization's mission is achieved and the organization satisfies the client's goals.

As we will see, these factors are complicated in larger sports agency firms. A comprehensive network of goals serves as a starting point for this type of coordination, but goals are not enough. A steady flow of communication among the various units of an organization ensures that the coordination of efforts is continuous and effective. We discuss how sports agency firms attempt to achieve and maintain effective coordination later in the chapter.

Authority Structure

The fourth of Schein's elements of effective organizational design is authority structure. *Authority* is often defined as the right to guide the actions of others (Weber, 1947). Organizations, as we have said, are collections of individuals who share common goals. However, sharing common goals does not mean they will also agree on what must be done to achieve these goals or on who must do what. For this reason, authority—the right to direct the actions of others—is a key element in designing the organization. For an organization to succeed there must be an authority structure, what Henri Fayol would call a "chain of command," to define the goals, to divide the work, and to require coordination to the extent that others will accept and follow this direction. An organization without an effective authority structure is like an individual without discipline or an agent who does not follow the rules of agency law: the goals and plans may be clear and in place, but without the ability to require action, the desired actions will not be performed.

For most of the last century, authority was assumed to be most effective when it rested in the hands of managers at the top of the organization, the so-called executives. It was assumed that only the people at the highest levels of the organization had the education and information necessary to exercise authority responsibly.

Decentralization

The overall trend in organizations has been toward greater decentralization: authority to make decisions is distributed throughout the organization so decisions can be made more quickly and with more focus. Management thinkers David Conklin and Lawrence Tapp (2000) refer to the organizational structures that are emerging in response to decentralization as creative webs, because changing environments and technological innovations require "that all parties interact on an ongoing, extended basis. . . . If there is a free exchange of information and communication, all parties benefit" (p. 221). The creative web focuses on creating change, continual collaboration, and ongoing mutual dependence. Such webs may be created between separate organizations as well.

Another expert, Mick Carney (1998), points out that today's organizational structures need to achieve trust while undergoing decentralization and diffusing power. Trust and communication are especially key factors in the agent-client relationship and must be emphasized in any sports agency firm. The firms that emphasize these aspects must cede to their individual agents the authority to make decisions in the best interests of their clients in today's heightened atmosphere of real-time communication.

From the perspective of clients, this communication, and related services, are important. After Matt Kinney started to have success in the minors, other agents began to try to woo him away from Woolf. Kinney was contacted by dozens of suitors and weighed several offers seriously, but he decided to stick with Woolf's Jack Toffey, because he had been there with him from the start and had been faithful to him.

After that, however, the large sports agency and marketing firm Octagon (formerly Advantage, a full-service sports marketing agency and the second largest company of its kind in the world) bought out Woolf's baseball division. "Octagon was the company that had the guy I was going to switch to, so now I work with [Toffey and Greg Clifton, formerly of Woolf], and there are two other guys that run the baseball division," said Kinney. "They all help you out, but if I ever need anything I talk to [Toffey and Clifton]. The other guys also work for you, but they work with their own clients more. Sometimes they talk about packaging a deal with me and Joe Mays [another Twins pitcher also represented by Octagon], because we both work with them. It works out good for all of us." For a look at the business operations of Octagon, see Figure 8-3.

So how does this Octagon expansion, this change in organizational design, impact new clients like Matt Kinney in meeting their own personal goals? Does it mean that Kinney will no longer get the direct service from his agent now that he's part of a much larger organization with many more clients, and with potential conflicts in communication, coordination of effort, and common goals?

"It's easier for [Octagon] to get more [endorsement] deals for you," said Kinney. "When you're first starting out, when you don't really have any deals and you might need a little bit more attention, you need a smaller firm. But the guys who have always been with me, they ask me what I want. They ask me, 'Do you want to talk to me every week?' I don't really need someone to be my best friend or call me all the time. My big thing is if I need something [such as issues with equipment suppliers such as Nike] and I call, I need them to call me back. When they say they're going to call me, they do it. As you get older and move up, you don't need them to help you with the little things.

Figure 8-3 An Overview of Octagon

- Founded as Advantage in 1983 by A. Lee Fentress primarily as an athlete representation organization. Fentress also founded ProServ, another management company, in 1976.

- Athlete representation is a vital component to the company. Current clients include: NBA stars Grant Hill, David Robinson, Sam Perkins, and Jerry Stackhouse. Professional tennis standouts Martina Hingis, Zina Garrison Jackson, Jana Novotna, Todd Martin, Michael Chang, Richard Krajicek, Mark Philippoussis, and Anna Kournikova. Professional golfers Sandy Lyle, Mark McCumber, and J. C. Snead. Olympic medalist speed skater Bonnie Blair and swimmer Matt Biondi.

- The company is also an international leader in event management for corporate clients such as American Express, British Petroleum, *Black Enterprise* magazine, Lexus, *Time* magazine, Kraft General Foods, Downtown Athletic Club (Heisman Trophy Association)

- Managed events include the Disney U.S. Men's Clay Court Championship, the Senior PGA Tour Cadillac NFL Golf Classic, the LPGA JAL Big Apple Classic, the Continental Grass Court Championships, the Gravity Games

"The biggest thing with an agent is you need them to explain everything that's going on. They worked out the contract [with the Twins], they have to explain the [contract] rules, the taxes, because you have to file taxes in thirteen states. They do a lot and try to make your baseball life as enjoyable as possible by taking care of all the off-the-field stuff. Once you find someone you're comfortable with, it makes everything easier."

The expansion of Octagon has not hurt Kinney's relationship with his agents. The organization clearly has dealt with design issues such as decentralization effectively. However, decentralization can pose challenges in the areas of coordination and consistency. In response to this challenge, many organizations are highly centralized in setting goals for the organization's many units, but decentralized when it comes to deciding how these goals are achieved (Peters & Waterman, 1982). The key to developing an effective authority structure is balance: authority must be centralized enough to ensure consistency and coordination and decentralized enough to provide for timely and focused decisions and action by managers in the various units of the organization. In sports agency organizations, this means it is management's responsibility in designing the organization to ensure that this balance in terms of authority is effectively achieved and maintained.

A Fifth Element of Design: Structure Follows Strategy

Clearly, Schein's four elements of organizational design are essential for the success of an organization. Without common goals, effective division of work, coordination of effort, and authority structure, an organization is unlikely to achieve its purpose. In a sense, Schein's elements are like a chain that is only as strong as its weakest link.

So these four elements are essential, but more is needed to ensure that the design of an organization will be effective. Based on his study of successful U.S. corporations, management historian Alfred D. Chandler suggests what might be termed a fifth element of effective organizational design: structure follows strategy. Chandler (1962) found that successful organizations were designed by management to pursue specific strategies, and that when they changed their strategies they also changed their structures.

Structure Follows Strategy in Sports Agency

A few large firms represent the bulk of professional athletes. But what does this mean, this distinction between large and small? According to Berry (1990), three basic organizational design models operate in the sports agency business: the freestanding sport management firm, the law practice, and the law firm/sport management firm affiliation. Each of these designs also has a strategic advantage.

The large freestanding sport management firm, like IMG, SFX, and Octagon, offers a wide range of services to athletes. These firms serve their players' needs in the areas discussed earlier, but also serve corporate clients interested in sport-related sponsorships and sport-related event management. Firms designed in this way can offer advantages for clients who can benefit from these various activities. These firms seek to serve all the clients' needs in these areas and can make more money from these services, increasing potential revenue sources. The larger firms are also usually more established and have a higher profile because of their other prominent clients. For example, SFX Sports, the player representation segment of large-firm SFX Entertainment, owned by Clear Channel Communications and operated by David Falk and Arn Tellem, represents many star athletes, including thirty current NBA players. This can help generate positive influence by association for an up-and-coming player. SFX is also a huge presence in the concert and theater industry and also owns and/or operates 120 live entertainment venues in 31 of the top 50 U.S.

markets ("About SFX," 2001). SFX also runs an affiliated but autonomous corporate consulting and client service under the CMI brand, which, according to general manager David Paro, is a "marketing services company that really focuses on . . . lifestyle pursuits such as entertainment and music and sports." The continued melding of these entities was evidenced when NBC chose to show a live concert by the Irish rock band U2 during halftime of game 1 of the 2001 NBA Finals. Said NBC's head of NBA production David Neal, "[we] provided more entertainment. . . . I'm comfortable trading [game] analysis [by NBC commentators Ahmad Rashad, Kevin Johnson, and P. J. Carlesimo] for the quality programming of U2" (Martzke, 2001, p. 2C).

Larger firms also can benefit clients because of their extensive resources. For example, IMG runs a predraft camp for their NFL prospects in Bradenton, Florida, where players train and are coached by former NFL staffers to increase their draft value. Such a program worked for quarterback

Charlie Batch, who was little known when he came out of Eastern Michigan University, but improved his draft status sufficiently to be chosen early in the second round by the Detroit Lions, ahead of national champion University of Michigan's Brian Griese, selected by the Denver Broncos (Layden, 2001).

But size and growth can be problematic for these large firms. The Dunn–Steinberg dustup at Assante illustrates that many clients at large firms feel underserved and believe these large firms are more focused on other marketing and property deals than in serving them. This makes them ripe for being snapped up either by outside agents or by agents who work for the firm and want to strike out on their own, like Dunn. Said one agent involved with the dispute, "under Assante's bottom-line approach we were forced to adopt led to the neglect of clients" (Mullen, 2001, p. 40). If size and offerings become an impediment to client service, the large firms will suffer.

Consider the following as an example of the variety of activities of a medium-sized sports marketing firm. According to Dan Weinberg of Woolf, his organization, like its larger competitors, is comprised of the following elements: athlete representation of the team sports athletes in negotiating contracts with teams; athlete marketing (finding endorsement opportunities for athletes, including those, like Lawyer Milloy of the New England Patriots, who do not use Woolf for contract negotiations); event management (running events such as golf tournaments); and sponsorship sales and corporate consulting (working with companies such as Verizon [telecommunications], John Hancock [financial services], and EMC to create sports marketing strategies). Before moving into athlete representation, Weinberg worked as an event coordinator specifically for Woolf's account with technology company EMC, in organizing forty-four golf skills challenge tournaments around the world. The tournaments were, said Weinberg, "a tool used by EMC for their salespeople to get out to their customers and clients to get an entire day on the golf course. EMC was targeting high-end courses and high-end clients and going after the real decision makers, the "C"-level [CFOs, CEOs, COOs, CMOs] executives. It's part hospitality, part entertainment, but you do that to help drive sales by leaving a positive impression on decision makers around the world. I was on a team here at Woolf that would do the pre-event coordinating with the golf courses getting everything set up, getting all the materials out there, and then the actual on-site execution, making sure everything was taken care of, making sure the guests of EMC were provided for and that they were happy."

Weinberg describes Woolf's advantages as a medium-sized firm this way: "it starts with the top, with the leaders of the organization. Why is [hockey Hall of Famer] Bobby Orr in this firm? Bobby Orr could be playing golf every day. But Bobby likes working with the athletes, and having been deceived by a former agent, he isn't going to let that happen to anybody else. It's very real, and it's a frightening prospect." (Orr had wanted to end his career with the Boston Bruins, but his agent, Alan Eagleson, who had a personal relationship with the owner of the Chicago Blackhawks, disregarded an offer from the Bruins that would have made Orr a part owner of the Bruins to accept a deal with Chicago. Eagleson was later convicted of defrauding many of his clients [Conway, 1995]).

"Athletes put a lot of trust into their advisers, and to betray that trust is the worst thing you can do. When you're that intimate with their lives, you're leaving people extremely vulnerable. There are a lot of athletes who are very in touch with what's going on in terms of understanding the complexities of contract negotiations and understanding finances. But there are just as many athletes who aren't familiar with what is involved with representation. Bob Woolf [who became Orr's agent] built the business on being honest and fair and treating people the way they deserved to be treated. Our selling point is that we're steeped in tradition, we have a tremendous amount of experience. I can rely on the experience we have here on our teams. We have so many talented people who work here. I can use them as a resource."

But when compared to IMG, SFX, and Octagon (whom he calls "the big dogs"), Weinberg says, "we're more of a niche firm. We're the 'Goldilocks' firm. Not too big, not too small, just right. One of the common complaints from athletes is that they can't get in touch with their agents. They can't get calls returned. We pride ourselves on that. We're big enough that we can be a major player in the industry, but we're small enough where we can maintain extremely tight relationships with our athletes and our clients. For me, that's what this industry is all about: communication. The game you play is how many clients can you take on and still communicate with them the same as you did before." So the strategy that follows the middle-sized design for firms like Woolf is to provide a range of services with big-firm resources while maintaining solid client contact.

So what about the smaller firms, where one or two agents work on behalf of fewer clients? What are the strategic advantages of these firms? Heightened levels of attention and personal service are generally recognized as the major benefits of this organizational structure. Consider Keith Glass, the "anti-Falk," who represents non-marquee and marginal NBA players, giving them a life beyond the short-term ten-day contract under which many initially make it into the league. Glass represents players like Jamie Feicks (a forward for the New Jersey Nets who played for seven other pro teams before signing a six-year $15 million deal), guard Matt Maloney (who signed a seven-year $17 million deal with the Houston Rockets), Anthony Avent, and Ira Bowman. Glass, who calls general managers to bug them about playing time and contract extensions for his clients, says his advantage is knowing the game and knowing his players. Why can't a bigger firm do this for these players? If you are Ira Bowen, and you are a Falk client, are you as high a priority as Jordan? If you call Falk the same time as His Airness, whose call will get returned first? This smaller simpler structure provides for the contact and communication that players desire and a successful niche for agents like Glass.

So to Schein's four elements of effective organizational design, we add a fifth: to be effective, organizations must be structured to implement their strategies. The relationship between structure and strategy can be thought of this way: structure *follows* strategy, structure *reflects* strategy, structure *implements* strategy, structure *supports* strategy. We next consider the model of organizational design consistent with these five elements.

Traditional Models of Organizational Design

Functional Structure

Like many organizational changes, the next major advance in the design of organizations came in response to the changes in the internal and external environment. Remember, most large organizations at the beginning of the twentieth century were business organizations involved with some form of mass production. Typically, this involved the operation of a large facility filled with a variety of machines, employing large numbers of people to perform many specific and relatively simple tasks. To ensure that a steady flow of products from these factories was being matched by a steady supply of customers, sales became an important function. Sales work was different from manufacturing, and yet the sales tasks were essential to the success of the organization.

"Sales are important in the sports agency business," says Dan Weinberg, "where you learn about sales, how to sell people. I wish I had more practice in college. I wish I had known I was going to need to do it. I always told myself, 'I don't want to be in sales.' Well, I've got news for you. I'm in sales in a big way, whether it's selling one of my athletes to a company that we're trying to create a relationship with, whether it's trying to sell Woolf to a client we're trying to recruit, whether it's me trying to sell myself to my bosses. I'm constantly selling. I'm selling what I believe in, my thoughts and my ideas. I'm always selling." A similar pattern of specialization can be seen for marketing for accounting and finance, and for the other kinds of work that become essential in all agency organizations.

But as Dan Weinberg told us, no individual or group of individuals could be expected to perform all the different kinds of work that needs to be done in all organizations. Different people now specialize in specific areas. The organizational structure that emerged to implement this specialization strategy is called the *functional structure*. Under this framework, the organization is divided into units, with each unit performing one of the specialized functions essential to the operation of the business.

Organizational structures are usually shown on organizational charts. The chart of a sports agency organization designed according to the functional model is shown in Figure 8-4. The functional model is most effective for organizations producing a single product for a single market, and in the case of sports agencies, the basic units of the organization are contract negotiation, athlete marketing, and financial planning.

Although functional structures have an ever-increasing number of units as organizations become more complex, the basis for dividing the work remains the same: a separate unit or department of specialists is created to perform each function essential for achieving the organization's goals.

Division Structure

In the *division structure*, the work of the organization is divided according to the kind of products or services being provided, the type of customer being served, or

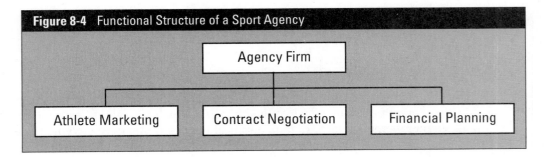

Figure 8-4 Functional Structure of a Sport Agency

Agency Firm

Athlete Marketing   Contract Negotiation   Financial Planning the geographic area in which the organization competes. Woolf has separate divisions for ice hockey representation, for golf, for football, and so on. At Octagon, there are separate divisions for player representation, for events such as the Gravity Games, and so on, and the same for SFX.

For many large and complex sports agency firms, which provide a wider range of financial and marketing services for clients, an organization's structure might actually combine the functional and divisional models. Separate divisions are created to focus on the organization's different types of customers or products, and functional departments provide services to these various divisions. For a firm like this, this mixed divisional and functional structure might look like the model in Figure 8-5.

In each of the preceding examples we see a common thread: the organization is divided into separate units to focus more effectively on the factor most essential to the organization's success. The divisional model allows the agency organization to respond more effectively to the special needs and requirements of different kinds of clients or markets, whichever of these factors is the focus of its strategy.

Conglomerate Structure

The 1980s saw a significant increase in what came to be known as the conglomerate structure. As shown in Figure 8-6, organizations with a conglomerate structure have separate divisions operating in entirely different industries. SFX, which operates entertainment events and venues, as well as its agency business, fits this type of description. The conglomerate structure allows organizations like SFX to expand into many types of entertainment activities, and it uses these separate yet similar divisional operations to the benefit of the company. In the case of SFX, the expertise used in representing athletes can translate into representing music artists, and the expertise in running sport-related events translates well into running concerts and other performances.

Problems with Traditional Models of Organizational Design

Virtually every successful organization that emerged during the twentieth century was bureaucratic in design. Whether the design of the organization was functional, divisional, conglomerate, or some combination of all three, the model was organization by rules with a fully developed chain of command (authority structure) to ensure that the organization's decisions followed the rules, which is

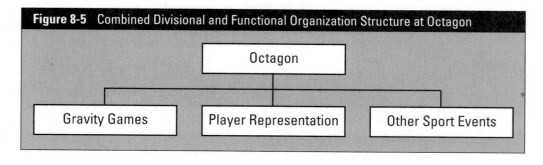

Figure 8-5 Combined Divisional and Functional Organization Structure at Octagon

Octagon

Gravity Games | Player Representation | Other Sport Events

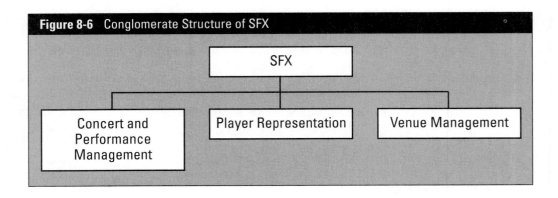

Figure 8-6 Conglomerate Structure of SFX

exactly what is meant by the term *bureaucratic*. And for most of the twentieth century, bureaucratic organizations, because of these qualities, were impressive in terms of their efficiency and effectiveness.

Recently, however, the bureaucratic design has begun to show signs of ineffectiveness. The bureaucratic model seems to work well when the environment changes very slowly, because the rules can be gradually modified to reflect these changes. As the rate of change begins to speed up, however, changes in rules begin to fall behind changes in technology, the competition, and customer demands. At some point, the rules and structure intended to make the organization more efficient become obstacles that impede the organization.

Recall endorsements, the important source of revenue for athletes and agents. Endorsements are complicated by three factors that are notoriously unpredictable and uncontrollable: injuries, performance, and personal behavior. Companies seek to sign athletes who embody the personal skills and abilities that potential customers admire so the company will benefit from the endorsement association, but these can be blunted or obliterated when an athlete gets hurt, plays poorly, gets arrested, or some combination of the three. When the 2001 major-league baseball season began, three of the game's most recognized and prolific stars—Nomar Garciaparra, Ken Griffey, Jr., and Mark McGwire—were either disabled or played sparingly for months. Therefore, the many companies that paid these three to endorse their products, including adidas, Amtrak, Dunkin' Donuts, DirecTV, General Mills, Nabisco, Nike, Pepsi, and Starbucks, were not getting the most from the investment, even though the three players earned over $20 million combined for these endorsements. Said Bauer-Nike Hockey's director of sports marketing Jim Geary of his company's association with oft-injured NHL star Eric Lindros, "We don't get the value on the ice. We don't get the day-to-day value of the player going up and down the ice with the products on" (Brender, 2001, p. 27). There is also the specter of athlete behavior. In 1999 Callaway Golf dropped the mercurial PGA Tour pro John Daly and his $3 million endorsement agreement after his well-publicized bouts with drinking and gambling reemerged.

To be responsive to these kinds of sudden, uncontrollable changes, according to Rosabeth Moss Kanter and John D. Buck (1985), leading management scholars and consultants, "The organizations now emerging as successful will be, above all, flexible" (p. 6). To be effective in the changing environment, organizations must now satisfy an additional requirement for effective organizational design. In addition to common goals, division of work, coordination of effort, and authority structure, the design of the organization must also be flexible. A structure that enables an agency firm to react quickly and to deal with the changes in the environment described here, and to respond rapidly to new opportunities, is an additional requirement of organizational design.

Flexible Models of Organizational Design

Matrix Structure

One of the earliest forms of flexible models of organizational design was the *matrix structure*, in which specialists are assigned to a specific project or product or customer account. In a traditional agency organization, for example, marketing specialists work only with other specialists in their own department. In a matrix agency organization, these specialists work directly with specialists from other areas such as event management as part of an ongoing group or team assigned to a long-term project or to develop a new project. Figure 8-7 shows a matrix structure for a sports agency organization.

One such new project area in the agency segment is the growth of new and emerging sports. As new women's professional leagues like the WNBA and WUSA emerge, as women's intercollegiate athletics continue to grow, and as more lucrative opportunities develop for women in traditional areas such as figure skating, golf, and tennis, agency firms need to be in position to capitalize on these market changes. Ty Votaw, commissioner of the Ladies Professional Golf Association (LPGA), reinforces the value of female endorsers and the associated market opportunity for agency firms: "We have in women's professional sports the most accessible, approachable, appreciative, accommodating professional athletes in the world today. That's an enormous signal to corporate America and the youth of our nation that there are huge positives to be had in bringing the positive attributes of women's sports into their lives" (Brennan, 2001, p. 3C).

www.lpga.com

In addition, as America's Baby Boomers age, a new "old" market for endorsers has emerged, featuring retired standout sports figures. According to Fred Fried, president of SFX's Sports Group Marketing, these figures are more available to companies because they do not have to work around their playing schedules and are

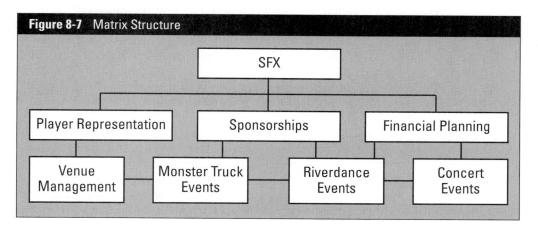

Figure 8-7 Matrix Structure

attractive because "there is the credibility and trust factor. Older athletes have more credibility. . . . As we get older, our heroes get older, so that absolutely has an impact." Fried also stated that retired athletes' earnings do not decrease once they retire (Bhonslay, 2000, p. 36). So we see retired luminaries such as Willie Mays, Bill Russell, Gordie Howe, and Barry Sanders touting Coors Beer (as active players are usually barred from promoting alcoholic beverages) and the images of baseball legends Lou Gehrig and Jackie Robinson promoting technology products and automobiles. The agency firm CMG Worldwide specializes in representation and licensing agreements for retired and deceased athletes and coaches, including Vince Lombardi, Olympic gold medalists Mark Spitz, Florence Griffith-Joyner, Jesse Owens, and Jim Thorpe, tennis great Arthur Ashe, and boxer "Sugar" Ray Robinson.

These emerging markets mean that matrix agency firms with specialists from each functional area can focus their expertise on a specific project or product area, such as the emerging endorsement market for female athletes. Another advantage is that it facilitates communication and coordination among specialists. Instead of having to communicate through channels, specialists communicate directly with each other, dramatically increasing their ability to respond quickly to challenges and opportunities.

Finally, the matrix structure also increases an organization's flexibility and speed by allowing it to create a new group of specialists drawn from existing departments to respond to a crisis or to a rapidly developing opportunity. For example, when CMG Worldwide seeks out endorsement agreements for a client like the late tennis legend Arthur Ashe, the firm needs to target those companies that want to benefit from the association with Ashe's pioneering status as an African American in a predominantly white sport and as an AIDS sufferer (contracted through a surgical procedure) who chose to publicize dealing with the disease, as well as his demonstrated excellence as a competitive athlete. A project group made up of specialists from all the functional areas would enable CMG Worldwide to maximize the expertise and coordination around this project to target the optimum client-company endorsement match with maximum speed in this fast-moving and highly competitive field.

One weakness of matrix organizations is that the authority structure can be confusing. Most who work in a matrix organization have two managers to answer to instead of the one superior prescribed by Henri Fayol's unity of command principle described in Chapter 1. Workers are then responsible both to the manager of their functional department (accounting, sales and marketing, finance, etc.) and to the group manager in the area or project to which they are assigned. When an individual's managers fail to communicate and coordinate with one another, it can lead to conflicting demands being made on the worker and can leave the worker in the middle, not knowing which manager's directions to follow. One of the keys to an effective matrix structure in sports agency firms, then, is to train managers in effective communication and coordination skills, so important in dealing with relaying information to clients, to enhance their ability to provide clear and unified direction to workers in the firm.

Network Structure

A second design option for meeting the organization's need for speed and flexibility is the network structure (Snow, Miles, & Coleman, 1992). The *network structure* is a temporary alliance of organizations that come together to take advantage of a strategic opportunity. Most organizations do not have all of the in-house expertise needed to respond to every opportunity and challenge—and by the time they develop the necessary expertise, it may be too late to take advantage of the opportunity. The network organization brings together independent companies with different areas of expertise to function as temporary organizations. Figure 8-8 shows a network structure where organizations come together for a specific project and then disband after the project has been completed.

Many large sports agency firms that also perform event management functions often work in a network with companies that seek to create brand identity and sales opportunities. When ESPN created "B³, the Bikes, Blades, and Boards Tour" as an action-sports broadcast complement to their X Games competition, they employed Octagon to run the competition and sell sponsorships while ESPN handled all the broadcast elements. Octagon, in turn, employed several other smaller companies to run certain aspects of the actual sports competitions (Covell, 1999). ESPN eventually expanded to take over all aspects of the event, but Octagon was then able to take its expertise gained from B³ to combine with new partner NBC and produce the Gravity Games, a competition similar to the X Games.

The potential weaknesses of the network model of organizational design are in three of the areas identified by Schein: common goals, coordination of effort, and authority structure. Obviously, in an organization consisting of several different independent companies, the management will have to take great care to define common goals and an authority structure, and to develop effective means of coordination. And even if all these challenges can be worked out, there is still an increased number of handoffs and consequently increased potential for disconnects when more than one company is involved in manufacturing a product or providing a service.

Still, it is clear that when managed effectively, network organizations give their constituent organizations more speed, expertise, and flexibility than each possess individually. For Octagon, NBC provided significant expertise in broadcast production and access to media outlets. For NBC, Octagon provided knowledge of the action-sports segment, access to potential sponsors, and a demonstrated ability to pull off such an event. With such success stories, we can expect a steady increase in the number and variety of sports organizations moving into network structures.

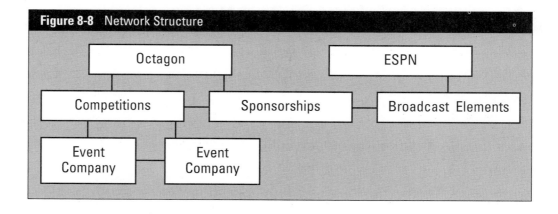

Figure 8-8 Network Structure

Epilogue

Once Matt Kinney became a professional, and after his trade to the Twins, he began to see baseball differently. "People ask me, 'Don't you wish you were still with the Red Sox?' To be honest, it hurt at first when I was traded, because I wasn't going to be a Red Sox. But at the same time, somebody's trading for you. They want you. I came over here, and I have a great opportunity to maybe get to the big leagues faster. Now I look back and I think that was the best thing that ever happened to me, but at the time I was pretty upset. You meet friends, and you play with them for three years, and you want to be a Red Sox player. It's beaten into your head that that's what you're going to do, and all of a sudden, boom, it's not. And I pitched against them two weeks later, and I thought, this doesn't feel right, but now I'm glad I got traded."

After beginning the 2000 season with the New Britain (Connecticut) Rock Cats, the Twins' Double-A minor-league affiliate in the Eastern League, Kinney was promoted to Triple-A in June. After a strong showing there, he jumped to "the Show" in August, five months short of his twenty-fourth birthday. He pitched 6.1 innings in his major-league debut against Toronto and notched his first big-league victory at Seattle on September 8. Kinney had eight starts at the end of the 2000 season, winning two of his four decisions, with an ERA of 5.13. Things were looking good for him to earn a spot in the Twins' starting rotation the next season.

But after strong spring training performances by Brad Radke, Eric Milton, and others on the Twins' pitching staff, Kinney was sent to Edmonton, Alberta, Minnesota's Triple-A Pacific Coast League affiliate, to begin the 2001 season. He spent the whole year there and compiled a record of 6–11, with a 5.07 ERA. "Once you get up to the majors, you find out how much of a business it is. People get sent down because they have options [which allow teams to demote some players while preventing them from demoting others without other teams claiming them]. Before, there was none of that." Sport is a business. It's a lesson for all of us.

The organizing responsibility for sports agency firm managers is to implement the company's strategic direction effectively. The design of a sports agency's structure is a critical factor in how effectively it will achieve its strategic goals and satisfy its various clients.

Edgar Schein has suggested four elements that must be present for the design of an organization to be effective: common goals, division of work, coordination of effort, and authority structure. The careful development of each of these elements is essential for the organization to function effectively.

A number of models for designing organizations have emerged since the late nineteenth century. Each of these models is bureaucratic in the sense that each is designed around rules, plans, and policies to ensure efficiency and objectivity in decision making. The functional, divisional, and conglomerate models are all bureaucratic, and each has specific advantages.

As the rate of change has accelerated in sports agencies, firm managers have been challenged to develop organizational designs that are faster to respond and more flexible than the traditional bureaucratic models. Firm structures based primarily on plans and policies can be slow to adapt to rapidly developing threats and opportunities in the environment. Matrix and network structures have emerged to give sports agency organizations greater flexibility for adapting to the realities of changing environments.

It is highly unlikely that the bureaucratic organizational structure will ever disappear. Within every sports organization there are difficult tensions. On the one hand, there is the need for the kind of rules and clear authority structure that bureaucracy provides. On the other, there is the need for speed and flexibility. It is management's responsibility to recognize both these needs and to exercise creativity and judgment in structuring the organization for optimum performance and for effective response to change.

Summary

Who for Drew?*

New Year's Day, 1969. Lyndon Johnson was president, Woodstock (the first one) was still six months away, and the Purdue football team was playing in the Rose Bowl. It would be more than three decades until a Boilermaker team would return.

In the 2001 Rose Bowl, led by senior quarterback Drew Brees, who completed 23 of 39 passes for 275 yards, Purdue fell short, losing to the University of Washington, 34–24. The game would be the last collegiate contest for Brees, who had been Purdue's starting QB for three seasons. Over his career, Brees set Big Ten conference records for career passing yards (11,792) and touchdown passes (90), and thirty-two other school, conference, and NCAA marks. Only three other college quarterbacks had amassed more total yards. Given all that, Brees finished third in the 2000 Heisman Trophy voting, behind winner QB Chris Weinke of Florida State.

Following the Rose Bowl, Brees set his sights on the upcoming NFL draft, and, as a budding professional, he needed to select his representation. Agents had been chasing Brees since his successful sophomore year, but his parents, both attorneys, had kept them at bay. But as successful as Brees was, no one assumed he would be the top pick in the draft. In fact, since highly touted Virginia Tech sophomore Michael Vick had declared his eligibility for the draft, it was a lock that Brees wouldn't even be the first quarterback picked and would probably not be selected until the second round, although there were few other strong QB prospects in the pool.

So why would such a prolific passer be passed over? Many NFL scouts had their doubts about Brees. At only 6 feet tall, he was considered too small to survive in the league. He was also considered too slow, even though he had rushed for 891 yards at Purdue. They questioned his ability to throw the "deep ball," the long downfield passes that lead to the big play strikes on which NFL offenses rely. Draft cognoscenti also felt that Brees's college stats were inflated and misleading, because Purdue's offense was geared toward passing. Their book on Brees: good head, decent feet, average arm.

At the NFL scouting combine in Indianapolis in late February, where hundreds of NFL scouts measure the size, speed, strength, and skills of prospective draftees, Brees did not perform well. He was particularly shaky in the quarterback drills portion of the workout, where many of his passes were under- or overthrown. As a result, Brees's draft stock fell significantly, so much so that he needed to schedule a private workout session at Purdue with several interested NFL clubs the next month. At that session, Brees excelled, but one scout said, "He's a solid guy. . . . Just very, very efficient." Hardly effusive.

A few days before the draft, the Atlanta Falcons traded with the San Diego Chargers to obtain the first pick overall. On draft day, the Falcons wasted little time in selecting Vick. With the fifth pick (obtained from the Falcons), the Chargers, who signed veteran QB Doug Flutie in the off-season, chose Texas Christian running back LaDainian Tomlinson. As the day wore on and the teams continued to pick, Brees went unchosen. He moved the phone in front of the TV as he

Information used for this case is cited in Layden, 2001.

watched the draft. "Ring, baby, ring!" he shouted. A half hour later, the Chargers called. The club selected Brees with the first pick of the second round (thirty-second overall). The thirty-second choice of the 2000 draft, wideout Dennis Northcutt, signed a seven-year $5.3 million deal with the Cleveland Browns, with a $1.5 million signing bonus. As a QB, Brees should get more, but can he?

As soon as the Rose Bowl was over, Brees had to make his choice for representation. The pool was reduced to three: Tom Condon of large multipurpose IMG (who also represents NFL QB Payton Manning), Leigh Steinberg (the main player for a middle-sized firm that specializes in representation who negotiated the rookie contracts for NFL QBs Drew Bledsoe, Ryan Leaf, and Jake Plummer), and Vann McElroy, a smaller football-focused agent.

1. You have been enlisted to advise Drew Brees on his choice of representation. Explain to him Schein's four elements of an effective organization and how each of his three choices might exhibit them.

2. Explain to Brees how the bureaucratic structure of these firms will protect him from the fate suffered by Fred Taylor and Tank Black's other clients.

3. Explain to him how these firms exemplify functional, divisional, and conglomerate structures, and why it is important for him to understand these distinctions.

4. Explain how each of these firms demonstrate matrix and network structure characteristics.

5. Finally, using all this information, along with the concept of structure follows strategy, explain which of the three choices would be best for Drew.

References

About SFX. (2001, March 28). [on-line]. Available at: http://sfx.com/publish_static.asp?page = aboutSFX.

Berry, R. C. (1990). Representation of the professional athlete. In American Bar Association Forum on the Entertainment and Sports Industries (Ed.), *The law of sports: Doing business in the sports industries* (pp. 1–6). Chicago: ABA.

Berry, R. C., & Wong, G. M. (1993). *Law and business of the sport industries: Common issues in amateur and professional sports* (vol. 2, rev. ed.). Westport, CT: Praeger.

Bhonslay, M. (2000, October 9–15). Sponsors find new ways to use old stars. *Street & Smith's SportsBusiness Journal,* pp. 36–37.

Blum, R. (2001, April 5). Welcome to the age of $2 million men. *Boston Globe,* p. C3.

Bodley, H. (2000, December 22). Free agency: One of the best things in baseball players' lives. *USA Today,* p. 10C.

Bodley, H. (2001, July 13). Give bad-timing award to Selig for game break. *USA Today,* p. 2C.

Borges, R. (2001, June 2). Bledsoe agents in tug of war. *Boston Globe,* p. G9.

Brender, M. (2001, May 7–13). Injuries can deliver wallop to endorsers. *Street & Smith's SportsBusiness Journal,* p. 27.

Brennan, C. (2001, May 8). Talking about a revolution. *USA Today,* p. 3C.

Carney, M. (1998). The competitiveness of networked production: The role of trust and asset specificity. *Journal of Management Studies,* 35(4), 460–478.

Carroll, J. M. (1999). *Red Grange and the rise of modern football.* Champaign: University of Illinois Press.

Chandler, A. D. (1962). *Strategy and structure.* Cambridge, MA: MIT Press.

Conklin, D., & Tapp, L. (2000). The creative web. In S. Chowdhury (Ed.), *Management 21C* (pp. 220–234). London: Pearson Education.

Conway, R. (1995). *Game misconduct: Alan Eagleson and the corruption of hockey.* Toronto: MacFarlane, Walter, & Ross.

Covell, D. (1999). B³: The Bikes, Blades and Boards Tour. In M. A. McDonald & G. A. Milne (Eds.). *Cases in sport marketing* (pp. 195–208). Sudbury, MA: Jones and Bartlett.

Greenberg, M. J. (1993). *Sports law practice.* Charlottesville, VA: The Michie Company.

Kanter, R. M., & Buck, J. D. (1985). Reorganizing part of Honeywell: From strategy to structure. *Organizational Dynamics,* 13, pp. 6–20.

Layden, T. (2001, April 30). Hang time. *Sports Illustrated,* pp. 56–66.

Lester, P. (1990). Marketing the athlete; endorsement contracts. In G. Uberstine (Ed.), *The law of professional and amateur sports* (pp. 23-1–23-36). Deerfield, IL: Clark, Boardman, and Callaghan.

Martzke, R. (2001, June 8). NBC struggles to find balance in halftime show. *USA Today,* p. 2C.

McAleenan, G. (1990). Agent-player representation agreements. In G. Uberstine (Ed.), *The law of professional and amateur sports* (pp. 2-1–2-85). Deerfield, IL: Clark, Boardman, and Callaghan.

Mullen, L. (2001, July 23–29). Big agency problems raise tough questions. *Street & Smith's SportsBusiness Journal,* pp. 1, 40.

Peters, T. J., & Waterman, R. H., Jr., (1982). *In search of excellence*. New York: Harper & Row.

Schein, E. H. (1985). *Organizational psychology* (3rd ed.). Englewood Cliffs, NJ: Prentice-Hall.

Snow, C. C., Miles, R. E., & Coleman, H. J., Jr., (1992, Winter). Managing 21st century network organizations. *Organizational Dynamics*, pp. 5–20.

Sperber, M. (1993). *Shake down the thunder: The creation of Notre Dame football*. New York: Henry Holt.

Sports salaries rising at a rapid rate. (2001, May 14). *USA Today*, p. 1C.

Weber, M. (1947). *The theory of social and economic organization*. (A. M. Henderson & T. Parsons, Trans. and Eds.). New York: Free Press.

Wertheim, L. J., Yaeger, D., & Schecter, B. J. (2000, May 29). Web of deceit. *Sports Illustrated*, pp. 67–80.

Wieberg, S. (2001, August 3). Top dollar, top coaches. *USA Today*, pp. 1A–2A.

Yasser, R., McCurdy, J. R., & Gopelrud, C. P. (1997). *Sports law: Cases and materials* (3rd ed.). Cincinnati: Anderson Publishing.

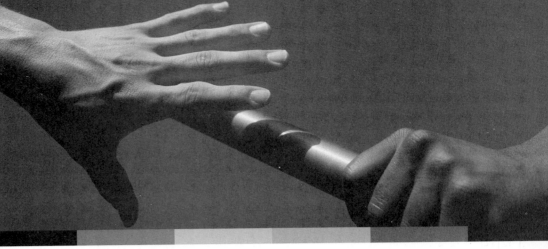

Chapter 9

Recreation and Work Design

Purpose:
To promote the constructive use of leisure time for the purpose of facilitating individual goals and outcomes such as personal health and fitness, therapeutic benefits, socialization, relationship building, education, and skill development. To enhance the quality of life for individuals and communities by providing leisure opportunities supported by a wide variety of park and recreation facilities. Some organizations within the industry segment are particularly interested in conserving natural resources and promoting environmental protection efforts.

Stakeholders:
Public sector recreation organizations (municipal recreation department, community center, and national park service), nonprofit recreation organizations (police athletic league, church recreation center, Little League, and Young Women's Christian Association [YWCA]), commercial recreation organizations (Club Med, ski resort, and private golf club), professional organizations, general public, recreation employees and instructors, coaches, volunteers, board members, recreation facility designers, equipment suppliers, media, federal, state, and local governments.

Size and scope:
The recreation and tourism industry may be the largest of all the sport segments. Millions of people participate in recreation daily whether through organized leagues or classes or informally through activities like walking, gardening, or card playing. Most cities and towns have a park and recreation department. Schools, colleges, religious, and social organizations sponsor recreation programming as do the military and the federal government. There are millions of recreational facilities in the United States, ranging from local bowling alleys, to golf courses, summer camps, and national parks.

Governance:
- Federal, state, and local regulation.
- Professional organizations and trade groups including American Alliance for Health, Physical Education, Recreation and Dance (AAHPERD), National Recreation and Park Association (NRPA), Resort and Commercial Recreation Association, and National Intramural and Recreational Sports Association (NIRSA).
- Individual sport-specific or group-specific professional organizations such as Amateur Softball Association (ASA), U.S. Golf Association (USGA), American Volleyball Association (AVA), and National Youth Sport Coaches Association (NYSCA).

Inside Look

Tightening the Belt

José Martinez, director of the Augustine Recreation Department, had carefully prepared his budget request for the mayor and city council. He waited patiently to present his proposal to the budget subcommittee and listened to preceding requests. First, there was the fire department. The police department went next. He nervously shifted in his chair in the council hearing room as he listened to the senior center director present her request for a 20 percent budget increase. He tried to read the faces of the budget committee members to gauge their reactions to each budget request. Despite his best efforts to read their minds, he just wasn't quite sure what they were all thinking.

As the evening progressed, he felt increasingly anxious. Each department head had carefully presented his or her budget and provided strong arguments for increases in funding. The fire department had requested money for new thermal-imaging equipment that would help locate fire victims in burning buildings. The police department requested additional funding for a community policing program, a drug resistance education initiative, a new cruiser, and two new officers for the gang intervention and anti-crime unit. The senior center director's budget request left two of the budget committee members shaking their heads. José noted that this was the first visible reaction to any budget report that evening. The senior center director explained how the center's van was over fifteen years old and in such need of repair that the senior meals-on-wheels program had been virtually shut down. She also explained that previous budget cuts had forced the center to discontinue the sponsorship of monthly health programs including blood pressure screenings and flu shot clinics.

The recreation department budget request hearing was last on the agenda. José was less than optimistic. Although he felt confident his requests were necessary and would greatly improve recreational opportunities for Augustine citizens, he had learned from previous experience that the recreation department was a low funding priority. José rose and addressed the committee. He detailed his budget requests that included a state-mandated increase in minimum wage for park workers, recreation supervisors, and park gate attendants. He also noted that health care costs for his workers had increased by 5 percent. José then requested funding for capital improvements, safety personnel, and a new program that his staff had agreed would be very important to the community they serve.

The capital improvement request was for $10,000 to repair lights at the athletic field. José explained that the lights on the city's only lighted athletic field were in dire need of replacement. On many poles, only two or three of the light fixtures worked. The lighting system was over forty years old and with over eighty teams registered for the summer softball league, demand for the field was at an all-time high.

José then explained his request for additional lifeguards at city pools. Last summer had been extraordinarily hot and the community pools had been filled to capacity. Parents were utilizing the pools as day-care facilities, and lifeguards reported that carloads of youngsters would be left at the pool for the day with no adult supervision. As a result, lifeguards were reporting that the conditions at the pools had become chaotic, and they were concerned that without additional staff, a tragedy would inevitably occur.

José completed his presentation with a request for a new recreation program for elementary-aged children. He presented a comprehensive plan for the center that would help keep school-aged children engaged in productive recreational activities. The recreation department would use existing school facilities, although there would be some cost for additional recreational supervisors and some new equipment and supplies such as arts and crafts materials, computers, and basketball nets and balls. He explained how this new recreation program would help families with needed after school day care, offer tutoring space, and would support police antigang and youth at-risk programs.

The committee chair thanked José for his report and asked him to explain his current staffing levels and program offerings. José then presented the information in Figure 9-1.

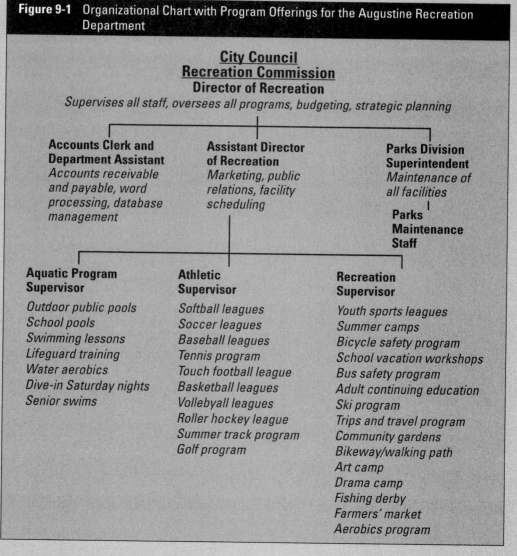

Figure 9-1 Organizational Chart with Program Offerings for the Augustine Recreation Department

City Council
Recreation Commission
Director of Recreation
Supervises all staff, oversees all programs, budgeting, strategic planning

Accounts Clerk and Department Assistant
Accounts receivable and payable, word processing, database management

Assistant Director of Recreation
Marketing, public relations, facility scheduling

Parks Division Superintendent
Maintenance of all facilities

Parks Maintenance Staff

Aquatic Program Supervisor

Outdoor public pools
School pools
Swimming lessons
Lifeguard training
Water aerobics
Dive-in Saturday nights
Senior swims

Athletic Supervisor

Softball leagues
Soccer leagues
Baseball leagues
Tennis program
Touch football league
Basketball leagues
Vollebyall leagues
Roller hockey league
Summer track program
Golf program

Recreation Supervisor

Youth sports leagues
Summer camps
Bicycle safety program
School vacation workshops
Bus safety program
Adult continuing education
Ski program
Trips and travel program
Community gardens
Bikeway/walking path
Art camp
Drama camp
Fishing derby
Farmers' market
Aerobics program

The committee commended the recreation department staff for the wide variety of programs and services offered to the community but explained that only some departments' budget requests would be granted. The committee chair announced that because the city budget was tight, each department would be asked to tighten its belt. Each department head would be asked to prepare a new budget with a 5 percent decrease from last year's funding level and present the adjusted budget to the committee in two weeks. Lastly, the committee chair explained the city would implement a hiring freeze for the next six months. Because of a projected budget shortfall for this year as well, no new positions would be added and vacant positions would remain unfilled until the beginning of the new fiscal year.

The meeting was adjourned and José carefully slid his budget request report back in his briefcase. "Oh well," he thought. Maybe next year he would be able to use all the information he had gathered in preparing his requests that he now knew would very likely go unfulfilled. Then suddenly, the full impact of what had just happened hit him. Just that afternoon, his recreation supervisor had handed in her resignation. She had taken a new job as a recreation and intramural sports director at a local college. The Augustine Recreation Commission was deeply committed to all of the department's programs and to providing quality recreational opportunities to the citizens of Augustine. He suspected the commission would not take any cuts in services or programs lightly. They knew that any cuts in programs and services would negatively impact the citizens of Augustine. As he drove home, he realized the new elementary after-school center might be even more important now than ever before. With across-the-board budget cuts in other city programs, things were going to change, and certainly not for the better, he feared. It was at that moment that José realized he faced a serious managerial challenge in work design.

Introduction

An effective organizational structure provides the framework for the pursuit of the organization's strategic goals. Once the units—the divisions, departments, or work groups—have been established, it is the manager's responsibility to design the work assigned to employees. Managers must organize the work so employees can be as productive as possible. They must consider the work environment as well as those factors that motivate workers to do their best. This chapter introduces work design, the process by which the manager strives to create jobs and work assignments that will not only contribute to the strategic mission of the organization, but will be meaningful to the worker and facilitate high levels of productivity.

We introduce concepts related to work design against the backdrop of examining the recreation industry segment. Recreation is often considered the largest and broadest segment of the sports industry. In fact, recreation is seen as the necessary counterbalance to work, and under those terms, almost all humans engage in some form of recreational activity.

The Recreation Industry

The recreation industry is often considered the largest segment of the sports industry because of the sheer scope and complexity of activities that may be defined as recreational. It is difficult if not impossible to measure the vast number of people who are engaged in recreational pursuits every day and to count the number of volunteer coaches, recreational equipment manufacturers, retailers, and recreational facilities in operation on any given day. Recreation is commonly defined in terms of constructive use of leisure time or a diversion from work (Guillion, 1998; Mull, Bayless, Ross, & Jamieson, 1997; http://www.activeparks.org, 2001). Most everyone engages in some sort of recreational activity, whether it is a walk in the park, competing in an organized sports program, playing backyard volleyball, or taking a swim at the beach. Recreation has come to include not only the more traditional sports activities such as tennis, baseball, basketball, golf, and hockey, but also extends to more nontraditional sporting or leisure activities such as game playing, hunting, fishing, gardening, dance, drawing, arts and crafts, music, and yoga. The recreation industry seems to have unlimited boundaries in that people engage in infinite numbers of activities during their nonworking or leisure hours. It is also a very fragmented industry with a very wide variety of activities, service providers, and facilities functioning sometimes collaboratively, but frequently in isolation.

People participate in recreation for a variety of reasons. For some people, recreation is physical activity and therefore a means to reach personal fitness objectives (see Chapter 5). Recreation programs can foster physical skill improvement such as hand-eye coordination or balance. Recreation can also aid in rehabilitation and wellness (weight loss, stress reduction, flexibility, recovery from injury or illness). Recreation professionals suggest that recreational programming not only meets a variety of physical needs, but meets social, emotional, and intellectual needs as well. Participants can learn new things, interact with others, develop leadership skills, learn how to work as part of a team, and create personal relationships. Managers of recreational sports programs encourage people to become involved in recreation as a lifelong personal lifestyle choice. They suggest that involvement in recreation not only provides many immediate benefits such as physical fitness and personal enjoyment, but that long-term benefits are even more important. Lifelong participation in recreation enhances quality of life by bringing about personal wellness and meaningful involvement in the community.

The recreation industry may be further understood by examining its various segments (see Figure 9-2). These segments include municipal or community-based recreation programs, commercial recreation, therapeutic recreation, military recreation, college or university/educational recreation, and sports and recreation tourism.

Another useful way of looking at the recreation industry is to examine program focus areas. Each of these areas represents types of programs based on anticipated outcomes or program goals. For example, social programming is intended to bring participants together for the purpose of interaction and relationship building. Such programming may take the form of an organized weekly card game, dance, gardening club luncheon, or travel club. Certainly other benefits of participation such as physical fitness or intellectual stimulation will accrue to participants engaged in these activities. However, social interaction may be a primary objective of the recreation programmer. It is inappropriate to suggest that participants gain one finite benefit from involvement in any one recreational activity, but examining these program focus areas provides additional insight into the scope and breadth of the industry.

www.ymca.net

Program focus areas include social programming, cultural programming, sports programming, special events, games, therapy, and fitness/wellness. For an overview of these focus areas, see Figure 9-3.

Recreation activities, in general, tend to offer a wide variety of benefits. The challenge of the recreation manager is to assess the needs of the service population and provide appropriate activities and facilities to meet those needs. An infinite number of recreation activity options are available ranging from skeet shooting to parasailing, and managers often pride themselves on creating a diverse menu of recreation options for their constituents so there is literally something for everyone.

Practitioners may organize their program and service menus based on a variety of variables. Programs may be identified as indoor versus outdoor recreation or as sport specific (e.g., aquatics programming, tennis programming). Programs may be further defined by their intended target audience, (e.g., youth programming,

Figure 9-3 Recreation Program Focus Areas

Social Programming: Bridge, travel, hobby, and garden clubs, dances, mixers.
(Focusing on social interaction, relationship formation, community building)

Cultural Programming: Woodworking, arts and crafts, dance, drama, music.
(Focusing on creativity; fine arts; related to aesthetics and cultural activity)

Sport Programming: Leagues, tournaments, sport skill instruction.
(Focusing on individual and team sport participation; sport skill development and practice)

Special Events: Easter egg hunt, fall festival, craft fair, Halloween costume party, summer concert series in the park.
(Focusing on seasonal, annual, onetime programming that often emphasizes celebration of the human experience)

Games: Checkers, chess, puzzles, dodgeball, capture the flag, hide-and-seek.
(Focusing on cooperative and competitive play, mental acuity, physical skill, social and emotional component)

Therapy: Play therapy; music and art therapy; dolphin therapy; horseback riding therapy; aquatics therapy; movement therapy programs delivered through hospitals, wellness centers, correctional facilities, independent living centers, psychiatric facilities.
(Focusing on social, emotional, physical, and mental well-being, rehabilitation, and encouragement of personal growth and realization of individual potential)

Fitness/Wellness: Walking club; weight loss program; yoga; strength training; aerobics.
(Focusing on improving and maintaining physical health and well-being)

teens-at-risk programming, senior programming). Recreation is certainly a very dynamic, complex, and multifaceted industry.

In the last several years, the recreation industry has come to encompass a growing sports tourism segment as well. As the population has become increasingly mobile and disposable income has risen, sports tourism has become a more prevalent leisure-time option. Individuals and families alike have taken advantage of opportunities to spend leisure time away from home. They have chosen to make recreation away from their local community a priority. Sports tourism opportunities abound. One may travel to a state park for a camping trip, to a seaside resort to water ski, or to a famous sports or recreation venue such as the Baseball Hall of Fame in Cooperstown, New York. Sports and recreation tourism may also include a trip to play soccer in a regional or national tournament, to witness the Olympic games, or to view a NASCAR event. It may also be a vacation to a historic site or natural attraction such as the Grand Canyon or Niagara Falls.

Sports and recreation tourism has come to represent a catchall category in the sports industry that encompasses many different sports and recreation activities designed to attract visitors or tourists either as spectators or as participants. The sports and recreation tourism segment is logically attached to the recreation industry because tourism involves the use of leisure time. Sports and recreation tourism has become the subject of increasing attention by sports managers because of the amount of money brought into a host community by visitors/tourists who participate in that community's recreational/sports offerings. Many areas have created sports commissions or tourism boards that become allied with the local chamber of commerce. Their sole purpose is to attract major sporting/recreation events or construct facilities for the intent of generating business activity and positive economic spin-off for the community. The measurement and documentation of the economic impact of sports and recreational tourism has been central to the securing of public funds to support the activities of sports commissions and their efforts to construct and renovate sports and recreation facilities such as arenas, stadiums, and parks.

Recreation professionals' interest in constructing and maintaining recreation facilities is not new. In fact, in the early 1900s the American Institute of Park Executives was one of the first organizations in the United States interested in maintaining open public space. Public parks were seen as a way to keep a sense of nature and wilderness as part of the urban landscape. They provided a safe place for urban citizens, especially children, to engage in safe and wholesome physical play. Play, recreation, and open space have long been thought of as crucial elements of American life. In fact, the federal government established and entrusted the National Park Service of the U.S. Department of the Interior and the National Forest Service of the U.S. Department of Agriculture with the management of the 374 national park areas and 119 national forests in the United States.

The Financial Challenge for Public Parks and Recreation

One of the many challenges, however, for government on the federal, state, and local level is to find the financial resources needed to sponsor recreation programs and maintain park and recreation facilities (*Dateline*, 2001). Politicians have repeatedly suggested that although they are in favor of parks and recreation facilities and programs, no public money is available to support them (Crompton, 2001). Competing funding priorities such as education, public services, and infrastructure improvements have left public park and recreation officials with diminishing public financial support. As a result of the funding shortfall, public park and recreation department and facility managers throughout the country are faced with the challenge of finding new sources of revenue to support their activities. Some managers have created public and private partnerships, engaged in fundraising, taken on corporate sponsors, and/or passed on costs directly to users through fees and charges.

Military recreation programs throughout the country and abroad have faced similar financial hardships. Military programs are designed to foster the fitness and readiness of armed service personnel, and they are also targeted toward families of military personnel. With the downsizing of the nation's military and closing of bases throughout the United States, military recreation programs have been receiving ever-decreasing federal support. In an attempt to counter the negative effects of declining federal support, some military recreation programs are being opened to the general public. At Fort Knox, Kentucky, where the base had lost over six thousand troops, the fort opened its facilities including a $4.4 million aquatics facility to the general public. The effort has resulted in wonderful base–community relations, and the facilities are now generating adequate use and revenue to support the facility's primary purpose of serving soldiers and their families (Sherman, 1998).

Task Specialization

As recreation professionals continue to face the challenges of shrinking financial resources, assessing and meeting constituents' needs and managing a complex network of programs and services, their success becomes dependent on their ability to effectively and efficiently organize the work that needs to be done in the organization. Designing an effective organizational structure is one-half of the organizing responsibility of management. The other half has to do with the design of the work itself. Once the units—the divisions, the departments, the teams—have been created that are needed to perform the essential work of the organization, it is management's responsibility to organize how the work will be done within those units to make it as productive as possible.

Adam Smith was one of the early commentators on the design of work. Writing in the late 1700s, Smith chronicled the advantages of task specialization. In his classic example of pin making, he described how breaking complex work into smaller, simpler tasks and having each worker perform only one of the separate tasks resulted in the work being many times more productive than when each worker performed all of the tasks required to complete the finished product. Task specialization allows each worker to focus only on a single part of the overall work and to become a specialist at that task.

Two advantages result from the task specialization model of work design. First, usually very little training is required to perform each of the various tasks. Because the tasks are broken down to be relatively simple, it is easy to learn how to perform them. Second, focusing on a single task usually allows the worker to perform the task more quickly. An individual repeating a specific task can work faster than an individual moving from task to task to complete the overall product or service. For both of these reasons, task specialization is an extremely effective work design for work that can be divided into simpler subtasks. For example, a grounds crew of three men are assigned by the recreation director to prepare twenty-four ball fields for play each day during the summer months. One crew member specializes in removal of trash and debris at each field. Another member focuses on raking the field, and the third member has become a specialist at lining the diamonds. They move from field to field, each performing their specific task and in doing so are able to efficiently and effectively accomplish their work within their eight-hour workday.

Whereas Adam Smith recognized the power of dividing work into simpler subtasks, Frederick Taylor focused on how the work should be divided and how each task should be designed. Taylor is credited as the first person in history to study the design of work systematically (Drucker, 1973). Taylor's scientific approach to the study of management involved observing workers in action and experimenting with work design in an attempt to make workers as productive as possible. In many ways, the dominant design of work for most of the twentieth century has been task specialization. Recreation organizations, for example, have engaged in task specialization on many levels. From the administrative standpoint, there is accounting work, marketing work, public relations work, and so on. In the area of program delivery, task specialization is also evident. A typical recreation organization has divided work on the basis of program areas (e.g., aquatics work, health and fitness work, senior programming, sports leagues, and summer camps). Specialists who are highly trained and qualified for their assignment then perform each subtask. The task specialization model has been so effective, it is the most common work design in every kind of organization, from businesses to colleges to hospitals and government organizations. In every case, work has been made more productive by dividing it into ever more specialized tasks. In many ways, the tremendous economic advances during the twentieth century in the United States, Western Europe, Japan, and the Pacific Rim countries, and most recently Mexico, are striking testimony to the power of task specialization to make work more productive. The incredible growth of the recreation industry in the last century may also be attributed in part to task specialization as individuals have become interested in a wide variety of recreational activities. The industry has responded by developing more specialized recreational programs, equipment, facilities, and services, thereby fueling the growth of the industry as a whole.

Problems with Task Specialization

As effective as task specialization has been as a work design, it is not without problems. One is worker boredom. Taken to the extreme, task specialization can result in work that consists of tasks so simple and repetitive that the person doing them has no sense of meaning or satisfaction. Return for a minute to our example of the ball field grounds crew. Imagine being the member of the crew whose sole responsibility is picking up trash and emptying waste barrels. It is likely that by the end of the first week of work, this crew member is bored with his work, daydreaming while performing his task, and developing a negative attitude about his summer job. Over forty years ago, management researcher Chris Argyris reported that workers assigned highly specialized tasks exhibited signs of boredom, were likely to daydream, be absent, have a negative attitude, and be less productive (Argyris, 1957). Obviously, this would not be a problem for professional staff members who specialize in a particular area. A manager would not expect to find these same results with workers assigned to a specialized golf program, adventure program, or hockey instructional camp. Yet for people who are on assembly lines, entering data, stuffing envelopes, selling entry tickets, checking member identification cards, and so on—for people on the front lines in manufacturing and service industries, there is a point at which task specialization can actually result in less productivity. As the general level of education in a society rises, worker dissatisfaction increases when tasks are so simplified and repetitive that they become boring and meaningless. At that point, task specialization becomes part of the problem in terms of task design instead of part of the solution.

Job Satisfaction

Frederick Herzberg's two-factor theory provides a framework for better understanding the relationship between work design and worker satisfaction (Herzberg,

1966 and Herzberg, 1968). Herzberg's research suggests that two kinds of factors influence how people feel about their work. One category of factors is called *hygiene factors*, and the other is called *motivators*.

Hygiene Factors and Motivators

When Herzberg surveyed workers in the 1960s about the things they didn't like about their jobs, he noticed an interesting pattern in their responses. People generally talked about different aspects of the workplace, or the conditions surrounding the job, rather than about the job itself. Examples of these working conditions or hygiene factors, as Herzberg calls them, are shown in Figure 9-4.

For Herzberg, hygiene factors are important primarily because if workers are not satisfied with these basic conditions in the workplace, productivity will suffer. A good example of the importance of hygiene factors in the recreation industry relates to seasonal recreation employees. Seasonal employees are part-time staff members hired for the duration of a particular program or service. They are often frontline staff members who work directly with the public. They may be sports instructors, summer camp counselors, lifeguards, or gate attendants, for example. Given the nature of recreation jobs, these staff members often work outside and are directly affected by weather conditions. A gate attendant who works alone at an entry gate selling admission tickets and checking for vehicle entry stickers at a

Figure 9-4 Hygiene Factors and Motivators

Hygiene Factors

- Working conditions such as temperature or lighting

- Interpersonal relations with other workers

- Company policies relating to vacations, sick time, and benefits

- Effectiveness of superiors as supervisors

- Basic wage or salary

Motivators

- Sense of achievement

- Sense of recognition

- Sense of responsibility

- Opportunity for advancement

- Sense of personal growth

public beach is very directly affected by the hygiene factors related to the job. Recreation managers take steps to improve the hygiene factors related to the job. They may provide a shelter or attendant booth that protects the employee from the elements such as excessive temperatures and a blazing sun. They may offer an hourly rate that exceeds minimum wage or may assign attendants to work in pairs so staff members can enjoy some level of social interaction at their stations.

For many recreation seasonal employees, hygiene factors are of paramount importance. Often these employees are college or high school students who consider these jobs a way to make money to pay for school expenses. They often have other commitments such as classes or sports team participation. For these employees, salary is critical as is flexibility. A college or high school student looking to make money for school is apt to seek out the summer job that offers the best salary. In fact, many recreation organizations find themselves competing with retail, restaurant, and fast-food businesses for part-time employees. In order to fill seasonal positions, recreation managers must offer not only competitive wages but flexibility as well. It is not unusual for a recreation manager to design seasonal jobs so employees can honor other commitments. For example, a recreation director might allow summer camp counselors to leave early in the afternoon to attend a summer course or play in a competitive sports league. The director might also give employees a chance to work extra hours during weekend special events. For many college students employed as seasonal recreation employees, it is important that their job allows them the flexibility to return to their campus either for classes or fall sports practices in August despite the fact that the traditional summer recreation season extends to Labor Day or beyond. Recreation directors who recognize the importance of these considerations are able to design hygiene factors that are attractive to these types of seasonal employees. Without an understanding of the importance of these hygiene factors, the recreation manager might have a very difficult time recruiting and keeping qualified seasonal employees. Notice that hygiene factors are not directly related to the design of the work itself but do relate to the conditions or terms of employment and the work environment.

The factors more closely related to the design of the work itself are what Herzberg calls *motivators*. He uses this term for the kinds of factors people mention when they are asked about what motivates them to do a better job. The list of motivators that emerged from Herzberg's research is also shown in Figure 9-4. Unlike hygiene factors, motivators can increase someone's satisfaction with the work he or she is doing. A recreation tennis instructor, for example, might consider opportunities for increased responsibility, advancement within the organization, and a sense of personal growth to be a very important part of her job. She may be very interested in utilizing her advanced degree in recreation management and improving her abilities so she might one day qualify for a recreation director's job. For her, the chance to move beyond providing daily tennis lessons to becoming more of a program coordinator who organizes tournaments, schedules maintenance of the courts, and attends professional development seminars may motivate her to achieve excellence in her current position. For her, the work and its relationship to her sense of personal and professional accomplishment, what Herzberg has identified as motivators, is most important. Motivators, unlike hygiene factors, are strongly affected by the design of the work itself. It is important to recognize that although both hygiene factors and motivators affect employee productivity, the degree of importance of both varies on an individual basis. Where one employee might be most affected by hygiene factors, another may be more compelled by motivators.

The Herzberg model provides a theoretical explanation of why task specialization is sometimes less effective as a work design. Doing extremely simple and repetitious tasks makes work so routine and boring that it lacks the motivators necessary to allow the individual to be productive. Task specialization may fail to provide workers with the opportunity for a sense of achievement, recognition, responsibility, and personal growth.

For years, it was acceptable for organizations to focus on hygiene factors in the workplace, on eliminating or at least minimizing those things which were sources of worker dissatisfaction. In an increasingly competitive environment and the changing workplace, it is no longer enough to minimize people's dissatisfaction with the work they are doing. Now it is essential to design work to allow people to be as productive as possible. The challenge for management is to move beyond task specialization to work designs that incorporate Herzberg's motivators—to design work so it yields the sense of achievement, growth, responsibility, and recognition that can lead to better job performance.

Job Redesign

Job redesign is the term used to describe the effort of organizations to improve job satisfaction by improving the way work is designed or organized. It recognizes that most jobs have traditionally been divided into simpler subtasks, and for this kind of work to become more satisfying it is necessary to redesign how the work is done. Two redesign options that have emerged in this effort are job rotation and job enlargement.

Job Rotation and Job Enlargement

Job rotation is the practice of periodically moving individuals from task to task within a work area. For example, at a golf resort, an individual might move from working in the snack bar, to taking inventory in the pro shop, to scheduling tee times. Or at a national park, rangers might change stations, one day working in a tourist information center and the next day checking campsites. The intent of job rotation is to increase the variety of tasks any one person is performing and to reduce the boredom that occurs from doing the same thing over and over. Job rotation can also increase the individual's sense of achievement, because it requires the mastery of a variety of skills rather than the constant repetition of a single skill.

Rotating among a variety of tasks has the added advantage of giving each individual an increased understanding of how the various tasks of the organization fit together. Even managers and other professionals seem to gain a greater sense of the overall operation of the organization when they rotate through a variety of managerial or professional positions or tasks, moving from marketing to finance to strategic planning, for example. In fact, in some recreation organizations, job rotation is a necessary component of operation. Because of the seasonal nature of recreation—sports and other program offerings change on a regular seasonal basis—recreation employees engage in a somewhat mandatory job rotation. That is to say that they rotate from basketball program coordinator to tour club coordinator to football program coordinator to bicycle club coordinator to community gardens program director. In fact, many recreation professionals suggest it is the ever-changing nature of their job that they find most rewarding. For many recreation employees, the most stimulating and challenging part of their work is that every day brings something new.

Job enlargement goes beyond job rotation to combine simpler tasks into a larger series of tasks, all performed as part of one individual's job. The ball field grounds crew we introduced earlier in the chapter might benefit from job enlargement. Rather than having each member of the crew perform one routine task such as lining the fields, cleaning the dugout or raking the infield, each member of the crew could take on all of these tasks and complete the preparation of a ball diamond independently. In the past, where the crew of six would all work on one field at a time, each performing his or her own subtask, the crew could now be split into groups of two with each person taking on an enlarged job. With job enlargement, two-person crews would now take on all of the various tasks involved in preparing a field.

A manager at a public park might use job enlargement to give some of the employees relief from selling and collecting attraction tickets all day. The manager might decide that she wishes to have each of the attraction staff members spend no more than 60 percent of his or her time collecting tickets. Jobs might be enlarged to involve some administrative work such as database management, ordering supplies for the attraction, creating weekly staffing schedules, and developing promotional advertising materials as well as maintenance activities such as feeding zoo animals, tending to flower beds and landscaping, and sweeping guest waiting areas. By combining tasks, job enlargement attempts to improve worker satisfaction and performance by increasing the variety of tasks performed as well as the sense of achievement that can come from mastering a variety of tasks. The park manager then instituted an attraction-of-the-week program and announced she would be honoring the employees of the attraction that operated most effectively and efficiently each week. The manager expects this approach will give her employees a sense of what it takes to operate each attraction and become more meaningfully involved in the overall task set. The manager expects that job enlargement will encourage park employees to take more pride in their work and to take greater ownership for the operation of their attraction.

Both job rotation and job enlargement are intended to improve performance by improving work design, but the results are not always positive. This is especially true when the initial tasks being redesigned have been extremely simplified. (Is it enough to have attraction ticket takers sweep, pull weeds, and pick up trash in their area?) Herzberg himself questions why anyone would be more motivated just from rotating through a variety of low-skill jobs or just from having the job enlarged to include a larger number of low-skill tasks. Both these approaches may represent steps in the right direction, but for genuine improvement in terms of work design, Herzberg suggests a redesign approach he calls job enrichment.

Job Enrichment

Job enrichment is the redesign of work to incorporate as fully as possible an increased sense of achievement and responsibility as well as expanded opportunities for growth and recognition. The definitions of job rotation, job enlargement, and job enrichment are summarized in Figure 9-5. It seems that our park manager was not only enlarging ticket takers' jobs, but enriching them as well. Because she provided ticket takers with an opportunity to develop marketing materials, order and manage inventory, and create staffing schedules, she enriched the jobs by providing employees with more responsibility and expanded opportunities for growth and recognition. She had enlarged the jobs by bundling simple tasks such as ticket taking, flower bed maintenance, trash collecting, and sweeping, but had enriched the jobs by giving employees more complex and important tasks. In Herzberg's view, giving workers not only different tasks to perform, but also varying levels of responsibility, produces the motivators that can result in improved performance.

The recreation industry faces some very interesting issues when it comes to job enrichment. Many recreation organizations rely on volunteers to assist with operations. Volunteers serve as coaches, officials, club organizers, league supervisors, and board members. Successful recreation managers have learned to utilize Herzberg's theory of job enrichment to skillfully engage volunteers. Savvy recreation professionals recognize that volunteers are most committed to their work when they feel their efforts are valuable, recognized, and a critical part of the organization's success. By giving volunteers fully enriched jobs, they are likely to become not only advocates and supporters of recreational programs and services but very productive extensions of the recreation staff. Although there are many issues related to volunteer management including volunteer training and control (see Chapter 11), recreation managers need to understand that those people who give generously of their time and energy to the recreation program are usually not fully engaged when they are repeatedly assigned to mundane and low-skill tasks. Most volunteers expect that they will occasionally be required to take on a simple task, but long-term quality commitment only comes when volunteers are provided with the sense of achievement and responsibility with an opportunity for recognition that comes from enriched jobs.

Job Characteristics Model

Management theorists Richard Hackman and Greg Oldham (1980) have suggested a model of work design that actually expands and clarifies Herzberg's definition of job enrichment. They call their model the job characteristics model. This model

Figure 9-5 Job Redesign Definitions	
Job rotation	Periodically moving individuals from one simple task to other simple tasks within a work area.
Job enlargement	Combining simple tasks into a larger series of tasks performed as part of the job of one individual.
Job enrichment	Redesigning work to include not only core tasks but other significant functions as well.

Figure 9-6	Five Characteristics of Fully Enriched Jobs
Skill variety	The job requires or involves multiple skills, activities, and abilities to complete the work.
Task variety	The job allows the completion of an identifiable "whole" rather than just a very minor part of a much larger task.
Task significance	The job is important enough to have a substantial impact on the lives or well-being of others.
Autonomy	The people doing the job have the authority to make decisions on how to organize and do the work.
Feedback	People doing the job receive clear and regular information about how well they are performing.

suggests that more can be done to improve work design than just giving workers some of the planning, problem-solving, and inspection responsibilities. The five key characteristics of fully enriched jobs are shown in Figure 9-6.

According to the job characteristics model, these five elements—skill variety, task identity, task significance, autonomy, and feedback—greatly enhance Herzberg's motivators—the sense of personal growth, of achievement, of recognition, and responsibility. According to Paul Fawcett, the coordinator of the aquatics minor program at Ball State University, keys to maintaining an effective lifeguard staff are found in the job characteristics model. Fawcett suggests that managers must conduct thorough and proper training and orientation for aquatic staff members so they recognize the significance of their responsibilities and they have the multiple skills necessary to perform competently the variety of lifeguarding and aquatics facility management tasks required (Fawcett, 2001). Guards should be prepared to take on the responsibility of organizing and managing their own work and making decisions that can protect the safety of patrons. Providing feedback to aquatics staff is also important. Fawcett advocates that the aquatics manager be regularly visible and on hand not only to provide immediate input to the employees about their work, but also to assist workers with problem solving (Fawcett, 2001). By designing lifeguard jobs that include the characteristics identified by Hackman and Oldham, aquatics directors can expect to improve significantly the performance of their lifeguarding staff (Fawcett, 2001).

Difficulties with Job Redesign

Full-scale job enrichment is not the answer in every situation. Not every worker is ready for the kind of expanded responsibilities that job enrichment offers. Not everyone possesses the skills necessary for planning and inspecting his or her own work or for dealing directly with customers. Some workers might also prefer not to participate in the decision-making responsibilities. Our part-time college student seasonal employee, for example, may not be interested in being involved in managerial decisions. Instead, he or she may be only interested in collecting a check to contribute to the payment of the tuition bill.

For these reasons, the job characteristics model is actually a contingency model. The effectiveness of job enrichment may depend on the workers' need for growth and personal development. In fact, Hackman and Oldham specifically suggest that job enrichment is more appropriate in situations in which workers have a strong desire for increased opportunities for growth, responsibility, and achievement. The theory is that workers with greater personal growth needs are likely to respond more positively to the increased opportunities afforded by enriched jobs. Workers with greater security needs (such as our college students) are likely to feel more threatened by what they view not as increased opportunities but as increased demands. For this reason, research on the relationship between job redesign efforts and performance has revealed mixed results (Reif & Luthans, 1972).

Task or redesign tends to be extremely difficult. Change does not come easily to organizations that for decades have been designed around task specialization. Job redesign is not simply a potentially better way of organizing work; it can also represent a drastic change in the way an organization does business. Like all such changes, job redesign of any kind can be extremely threatening to an organization that has been operating in a certain way for generations. The resistance to this kind of change can be a critical factor in the success or failure of efforts at job redesign. Yet, despite resistance and mixed results, sports organizations continue to press forward in their search for improved work designs. The challenges of global and industry competition require that designs be developed to make work and workers even more productive.

Teamwork

One approach to job redesign that has become increasingly important is work teams. A *work team* is a designated group of individuals who together are responsible for a significant unit of work—a product or service delivered to a customer either inside or outside the organization. Work teams are known by various other names, including autonomous work groups and self-managing teams. Work teams are more like departments than they are like project teams, because the members of the teams work together on a long-term day-to-day basis. In its most advanced form, the work team essentially replaces the manager by taking on responsibility for most of the tasks traditionally performed by management: planning and scheduling the work, hiring and training team members, and providing discipline and resolving conflicts among team members and with other teams. Organizations have discovered that by bringing skilled individuals together on teams, and by eliminating the need to go to management for every decision, the speed of virtually every process in the organization could be increased significantly. Besides increased speed, the other advantages of work teams include increased productivity and improvements in service quality.

One municipal recreation agency began its foray into self-managed teamwork design by creating a team to establish a municipal employee recreation, fitness, and wellness program (*Northampton, MA. Recreation Department Annual Report*, 2001). The team consisted of recreation staff members, school officials, public

health officials, city human resource managers, health care agency representatives, and employee union officials. The team has not worked together every day, but has met biweekly to develop and manage a municipal employee recreation and fitness program. The team has been able to identify necessary resources, create promotional materials for city employees, conduct an employee needs assessment, and organize a program kickoff wellness fair. It may be argued that this team began as a project-based team, but the team has evolved into a long-term work team that will manage the employee recreation and fitness program for the future. The city recreation director found that this team approach has resulted in a very high-quality program that was developed and established in an extraordinarily short period of time.

Making Teams Work

The potential effectiveness of the team-based work design is clear. But making a team design work effectively can be a challenging task for management. Team design is very different from traditional methods of job design, and therefore many people are unfamiliar with or uncomfortable with the concept. People are usually very resistant to try something new because humans tend naturally to resist change.

One strategy for reducing resistance to team-based work is training. If people feel they possess the skills to be successful in the new team environment, they are more likely to be willing to stay with the transition to teams. But even with training, some workers are likely to leave for a work situation that is less demanding. Management consultant Michael Hammer states the issue clearly: "getting people to accept the idea that their work lives—their jobs—will undergo radical change is not a war won in a single battle. It is an educational and communications campaign that runs from reengineering's start to its finish" (Dumaine, 1994). Even with an effective campaign of worker education and training, a period of time will probably be required for an organization to allow less willing employees to leave and to recruit new workers who are more comfortable with the demands of working in teams.

Individual workers are not the only source of resistance to the work team design. Organizations designed around highly managed departments of experts can have great difficulty learning how to function as self-managing teams. Issues of chain of command (who reports to whom) and channels of information (who tells who what) take time to redefine. Organizations, like individuals, often require a period of training and education to learn to do their work through teams.

Self-Managed Teams

Research suggests that self-managed work teams can be involved in a wide variety of management activities and tasks, including those listed in Figure 9-7. Not every team design includes responsibility for all the tasks shown in Figure 9-7, but it is reasonable to suggest that any truly self-managed work team will perform a significant number of these responsibilities. One of the key challenges for management, then, is to provide team members with training in each activity for which they are responsible. Some of this training will be technical, in the areas of accounting and finance, for example, or statistical quality control or inventory management. Much of the training must be managerial and in the areas of planning, organizing, providing feedback, group decision making and problem solving, managing conflicts, and so on. Work teams will be effective in managing themselves only if their members possess managerial skills and understanding.

This is an important point. Henri Fayol suggested that to improve performance, management must be trained in the functions of the manager; managers must be provided with the training and skills needed to manage effectively. In the work team design, teams share in the responsibilities that are part of management. For teams to fully achieve their potential, work teams must receive the kind of training they need to allow them to perform their management responsibilities effectively.

Teamwork: The Bottom Line

Teams enhance the speed of work processes in the organization; they have the potential to increase quality and productivity; and where workers are motivated by growth needs, teamwork can increase job satisfaction. The barriers to effective teamwork are also apparent. They include the natural human resistance to major change; the inherent difficulty of organizations learning to operate in new ways; and the need for work teams to develop the skills necessary to manage themselves efficiently.

Figure 9-7 Activities Often Performed by Self-Managed Teams

- Recording quality control statistics

- Making scheduling assignments

- Setting group or team goals

- Resolving internal conflicts

- Solving technical problems

- Assessing group or team performance

- Delegating assignments to team members

- Preparing a budget

- Training members

- Selecting new members

- Allocating pay raises for members

Management's task is to have the patience and commitment necessary to develop a work force and an organization capable of achieving the improved performance that team-based work design makes possible. An important part of this task is understanding what it takes for teams to be effective. If team members have the necessary training and the organization has the required commitment and patience, management still needs to ensure that conditions are in place for teamwork to be effective.

Conditions for Effective Teams

McKinsey & Co. consultants Jon R. Katzenbach and Douglas K. Smith studied the differences between teams that perform well and other groups that don't. They interviewed hundreds of people, on fifty different teams in thirty organizations, from Motorola and Hewlett-Packard to the Girl Scouts. Based on these interviews, Katzenbach and Smith have established this definition for high-performance teams (Katzenbach & Smith, 1993): "A team is a small number of people with complementary skills who are committed to a common purpose, set of performance goals, and approach for which they hold themselves mutually accountable." Complementary skills, common purpose, common performance goals and approach, and mutual accountability: these appear to be the essential conditions for teamwork to be effective (Figure 9-8).

Complementary Skills

Team sports such as basketball and softball require collective effort. Katzenbach and Smith point out that these kinds of collective efforts are likely to be most effective where team members possess complementary skills—that is, where each team member contributes some of the skills needed for the team's success. Just as a baseball team benefits from having pitchers, hitters, and fielders, work teams benefit when team members contribute different skills and when their skills are complementary to the group. It is not essential that each member possess all of the skills required for the work of the team. It is essential that the team members possess together all of the skills required for their work to be performed well.

Figure 9-8 Conditions for Effective Teamwork

Complementary skills	Each team member contributes some of the skills needed for the team's success.
Common purpose	The team commits to a shared mission or purpose.
Performance goal	The team sets specific targets for its performance.
Mutual accountability	The team has a sense of shared responsibility for the team and its work.

Common Purpose

The second key ingredient for successful teamwork is the commitment of team members to a common purpose. Without this shared commitment, groups are likely to be little more than collections of individuals each performing independently. With shared commitment to a common purpose, groups become genuine teams. Anyone who understands how a sports team functions will recognize the importance of team members sharing a common purpose. Despite the fact that a basketball team, for example, has five very talented and complementarily skilled athletes, if they are all not committed to a common goal of winning, the team will not be successful. In some cases, members of the team are committed to individual goals such as personal statistics or handling the ball as much as possible. The player driven by an agenda other than the team success is likely to be more of a detriment than an asset to the team's productivity regardless of that player's talent. On sports teams, just as in organizational teams, it is the responsibility of management (the coach) to set the mission or goal for the team.

In essence, management is often the source of the group's initial purpose. The most effective teams, however, are continuously involved in refining and reshaping that initial purpose. For example, the recreation department's recreation and fitness team may have been brought together by management simply to create a municipal employee recreation and fitness program. However, the team will refine this mission and its purpose to create a *model* municipal employee recreation and fitness program that would be admired and adapted by other cities in the state. As the team works together, their excitement for the project increases and they begin to explore new and creative programming options. They continue to broaden their purpose and to reshape their initial charge to include wellness program components, municipal employee discount promotions, motivational speakers, social outings and educational and professional development opportunities as well. In effective teams, the emphasis seems to be on expanding the assigned purpose to one of greater meaning or significance.

Performance Goals

Complementary skills and strong commitment to a meaningful common purpose are just the starting point for effective teams. The best teams translate their common purpose into specific goals. Such goals might be defined as creating a certain level of awareness in the community of the programs or enrolling 60 percent of city employees in the program. Such goals provide a clear target to aim for as well as an opportunity for feedback. It is the combination of shared purpose and clear performance goals that is essential. According to Katzenbach and Smith, "clear performance goals help a team keep track of progress, while a broader purpose supplies meaning and emotional energy" (Katzenbach & Smith, 1993, p. 114).

Mutual Accountability

The final ingredient in the recipe for effective teams is a sense of shared responsibility for the team and for its work. In the best teams, members hold themselves accountable for the team's performance. They may receive their initial direction from management, but the most effective teams eventually define their own purpose and their own goals, and they hold themselves responsible for achieving them. Because management is responsible for performance, it should not be surprising that the most effective teams are self-managing—that is, they take responsibility for their own performance.

Katzenbach and Smith (1993) found that the sense of mutual or shared responsibility produces a unique satisfaction for team members. "What we heard over and over from members of effective teams is that they found the experience motivating in ways that their normal jobs never could match" (p. 116).

Although effective teams are powerful tools for improving performance, teamwork is not necessarily the right work design in all situations. For tasks in which individual talent or insight or intuition is the most important element, a team-based design might only complicate or undermine productivity. The task for managers is to recognize the kind of work that can best be done by teams and in those situations to create and support the conditions necessary for teams to be effective.

Continuous Improvement in Job Design: The Learning Organization

Sports organizations now recognize that effective work design can bring a critical competitive advantage. Sports managers have learned that well-designed work will not only affect employee performance but will lead to better service delivery and ultimately enhanced customer satisfaction. There is also an emerging consensus that teamwork offers a potentially effective alternative to traditional task specialization. However, sport managers have also realized that simply taking the same work and redesigning it for teams may not be enough. Examining how a task is designed or how it is being done is always valuable, but the more important question is whether the task needs to be performed at all. Managers must be committed to continuously assessing and examining what work is done in the organization and how it is done. Those organizations that continuously engage in such self-assessment are learning organizations in that they continually and systematically seek to examine themselves and better their operation through the insights gained in self-evaluation.

For example, a new intramural sports director at a university inherits an intramural program that provides a menu of over fifty different sports programs and recreation opportunities each semester. The new director is concerned that the current program is ineffective and inefficient as she examines her department budget and program participation numbers. Staff members report they are overworked and spread in too many directions. They also suggest that there is never enough money to do everything that needs to be done to offer fifty quality activities per semester. The new director asks all staff members to put together a report that details each of their program supervision responsibilities and the tasks they currently perform. Three days later, the new director reviews her staff's reports and is dismayed to learn that many program supervisors are spending much of their time collecting and processing student registrations, scheduling student workers, and writing nightly program reports. She also learns that the intramural department has over two hundred student workers who are responsible for more than 60 percent of her department's human resource costs.

The new intramural program director begins immediately to reengineer her department. First, she eliminates all of those tasks she decides are superfluous such as writing nightly reports when one end-of-program final report will suffice. She also decides to look closely at program offerings and determines that any program that did not have consistent student participation of at least ten students per semester for the last three years ought to be temporarily discontinued until greater student interest is demonstrated. In reviewing student payroll sheets, she sees that often students are assigned to tasks in groups of four when one or two students can handle the job assigned. She decides to eliminate some student work positions. By beginning to examine her department, the intramural director is likely to utilize resources (both human and financial) much more efficiently.

The self-assessment just described was taken on voluntarily by the manager, but that is not always the case. In many recreation organizations, executive management forces reevaluation for the purpose of realizing cost savings. As we discussed earlier in the chapter and in the discussion case, many recreation organizations are faced with diminishing funding, and therefore self-evaluation becomes necessary to the survival of the organization. It is not unusual for a municipal recreation department or national park to be faced with budget cuts every year. Managers of these organizations must then look closely at what they do and how they do it so they may adapt their operation to available funding. In some cases, this means that evaluation results in severe cuts to programming, service quality, or personnel.

As might be expected, self-evaluation is a difficult process for any organization to undertake. Managers and employees understandably are reluctant to involve themselves wholeheartedly in a process that can result in the elimination of their own jobs. Still, the questions posed in the process of becoming a learning organization are important. To achieve success, does an organization really need to do everything it is currently doing? Might performance even be improved by eliminating some of these tasks? Another interesting question is at what point does self-evaluation result in such excessive expansion of job responsibilities that it threatens to overwhelm the individuals and teams performing the work?

Recall the case of the Augustine Recreation Department at the beginning of the chapter. With the resignation of the recreation supervisor and a hiring freeze in place, how will the director continue to carry out the programs currently managed by the recreation supervisor? One solution might be to eliminate all programs currently managed by the recreation supervisor. Another solution might be to split the programming responsibilities between the two remaining managers. Is it likely that the level of service quality will remain constant now that the two managers are doubling their responsibilities? This case demonstrates one of the negative consequences of self-evaluation: it often results in fewer and fewer people doing more and more work. Similarly, if our new intramural director eliminates ten programs per semester and then cuts her student work staff by 50 percent, undoubtedly each of the remaining staff and managers will be left with significantly greater responsibilities than they had previously. This kind of increased workload can have a negative effect on workers' attitudes and performance.

Research suggests that when self-evaluation results in significant downsizing of an organization's work force, potential is increased for stress and morale problems. A survey of managers by the American Management Association found significantly increased levels of stress and widespread erosion of morale at companies where major job cuts have left employees who have kept their jobs with no choice but to cope with the overwhelming amount of work still remaining (Hammonds, Kelly, & Thurston, 1994). Sports managers must recognize that self-assessment is an important process and a necessary part of an organization's efficiency. Organizations must engage in continuous evaluation of their operations for the purpose of continuous improvement. However, managers must also be concerned with just how far they can go with reshaping their organizations as a result of such evaluation and still sustain the benefits in terms of performance over the long run. Once again, the challenge for management is one of balance. The key in self-assessment and reshaping is to identify and maintain the tasks essential to the organization's success and at the same time maintain a work force large enough to perform those tasks well. This balance will probably be achieved only as organizations gain more experience with the continuous improvement process and its consequences.

Technology and Job Design

Recreation professionals, like other managers in the sports industry, have become increasingly affected by the revolution in technology. Especially in the area of information management, recreation practitioners are finding the way they do their jobs is dramatically changed. The development of technology impacts the work of both administrative and frontline staff. New computer software that assists the recreation staff member in managing program participant registration, scheduling facilities, and setting up league schedules or tournament brackets is just one example of how technology is constantly reshaping the work of recreation professionals. New technologies that take advantage of automation are also changing how recreation professionals work. For example, many pools are now equipped with automated filtration and chemical delivery systems, relieving the pool operator of the daily task of measuring out chemicals, treating the water, and making filter adjustments.

The advent of improved communication technology such as 24-hour recreation telephone hot lines and websites make it easier for consumers to gather up-to-date information about their favorite recreation program or facility. Recreation managers have found these new advances to be very helpful in their efforts to market their programming, reach new markets, and communicate directly with program participants. Another example of how benefits are delivered to consumers through the use of technology is the computerized Professional Golf Association (PGA) handicapping system. Golfers at some courses are now able to return to the clubhouse upon completion of their round, enter their score into an online PGA computer, and then have their official handicap calculated and recorded with the PGA. Another interesting technology at the center of much debate in golfing circles has been the introduction of the GPS, or global positioning system to the game. The system allows the golfer to utilize technology to identify more accurately the location of the ball on the course and its position in relation to the cup. The system gives the golfer a distinct advantage by allowing him or her to determine precise yardage to the hole and select the appropriate club more accurately.

Technological developments such as the GPS continue to affect the way Americans recreate. Automated timers in swimming and track and field, for example, have made measurements of performance much more precise. Advancements in medical and fitness-related technology have greatly changed therapeutic recreation models as well as health and fitness programming. Increasingly sophisticated workout equipment and health-monitoring devices have raised the standards for health and fitness and recreation providers. One marriage of technology and fitness/recreation programs that has been utilized by recreation program managers has been the adaptation of video monitors to treadmills and stationary bikes. The video monitors, attached to the front of the exercise apparatus, show videotapes that provide the user with a virtual recreation experience of biking through the countryside in Ireland or along a trail in the Grand Canyon, for example. Some of this equipment is designed to integrate the operation of the exercise apparatus with the image on the video monitor so as one appears on the screen to be biking up a mountainside, pedaling resistance increases. Such technological advancements are likely to continue to improve the recreational experience for the consumer and provide the recreation professional with powerful new tools to engage constituents. In any case, as technology continues to grow and expand throughout the recreation industry, such changes will have a significant impact on the design of work and how people do their jobs.

Summary

The recreation industry may be the largest segment of the sports industry. Its segments include municipal or community-based recreation programs, commercial recreation, therapeutic recreation, military recreation, and college or university/educational recreation.

Recreation is best defined as constructive use of leisure time or a diversion from work. A variety of activities can be considered recreational. They range from traditional sports to games, to art and dance, to hunting and fishing, to aerobics, karate, and yoga classes. Each activity falls into one or more recreation program focus areas that include social programming, cultural programming, sports programming, special events, games, therapy, and fitness/wellness. Recreation professionals suggest that recreational programming not only meets a variety of physical needs, but meets social, emotional, and intellectual needs as well.

One of the many challenges, however, for recreational professionals, especially those employed in the public sector, is to find the financial resources needed to deliver quality recreation programs and maintain park and recreation facilities. Given the complex scope and nature of the recreation industry, combined with shrinking resources, intense competition within the industry, and consumers' demand for quality programs and services, recreation managers have become increasingly concerned with how to organize work so workers can be as productive as possible.

The earliest and most enduring work design was task specialization, the process of breaking down a large, complex task into a series of simpler tasks. When individuals within a group each focus on a single task they can be significantly more productive than when each individual must master and perform all of the tasks required in the production process. Task specialization becomes a problem, however, when tasks become so simple that they are meaningless to the people performing them. At this point, the workers actually become less productive.

Job redesign is the name for the overall effort to counteract the negative effects of task specialization. One form of job redesign is job rotation, which allows people to move among a number of tasks to avoid the boredom of performing the same task indefinitely. Another form of job redesign is job enlargement, which combines a number of similar tasks to allow the individual worker to complete a more significant portion of the overall task. A third form of job redesign is job enrichment. In job enrichment, teams are formed and are given both greater freedom and greater responsibility in determining how the work will be completed.

Recreation organizations have begun to place a greater emphasis on teamwork and on understanding the conditions for effective teamwork. Complementary skills, a commonly shared purpose, specific performance goals, and a sense of mutual responsibility are all essential for team-based work to be effective.

Beyond teamwork, organizations must engage in continuous improvement by systematically evaluating their own operation. They must evaluate the work they do and how they do it. Such organizations that are committed to self-assessment are learning organizations. The process of self-examination and reshaping has been suggested as a process not only for improving the way tasks are performed, but for evaluating which tasks are essential to the work of the organization and which tasks have become extraneous and should be eliminated altogether. All of these approaches to improving the design of work, including self-evaluation and continuous improvement, have been supported and enhanced by the application of new technology that affects both how recreation is managed and how it is experienced.

Practice in Job Redesign

Exercise I. This exercise is designed to familiarize you with Herzberg's hygiene factors and motivators and to give you experience in applying Hackman and Oldham's job characteristics model.

1. Identify a job you have held in the sports industry, or if you have not yet had a job in sport or recreation, think of a job with which you are familiar—one that you or someone you know has had. Make a list of hygiene factors and motivators that pertain to the job. How did the hygiene factors and motivators affect your performance? Why?

2. Using the scale provided, rate this job on each of the five following core job dimensions:

    7 = very high

    6 = high

    5 = somewhat high

    4 = moderate

    3 = somewhat low

    2 = low

    1 = very low

Core Factors

Skill Variety	Consider all of the skills required for this job including technical, mental, physical, social, and so on.	_____
Task Identity	Does the job allow for the completion of a specific product or service (high) or just a small portion of the completed product or service (low)?	_____
Task Significance	How important is the performance in this job to the satisfaction of the customer or to the overall success of the work unit?	_____
Autonomy	How much control does the person doing this have? How much freedom to make decisions about how the job will be done?	_____
Feedback	How much feedback is there from the job itself, from customers, peers, and superiors?	_____

3. Using your ratings of the five core job dimensions and the following formula, calculate the "motivating potential score" of the job you are analyzing.

$$\text{Motivating Potential Score} = \frac{\text{Skill Variety} + \text{Task Identity} + \text{Task Significance}}{3} \times \text{Autonomy} \times \text{Feedback}$$

A score higher than 200 suggests a job with a high motivating potential. A score below 100 suggests a job that would benefit significantly from redesign.

4. Develop a plan for improving the motivating potential of this job by listing specific suggestions for improving the rating on each of the five core job dimensions.

Exercise II. In the discussion case, José Martinez suggests he is faced with a work redesign challenge. Is his interpretation correct?

1. Assume you are the assistant recreation director of the Augustine Recreation Department. What job redesign strategies might you suggest to the director? What additional information would you need to suggest work redesign alternatives?

2. How might Martinez utilize a teamwork strategy to establish a new teen center? Devise a plan that would require no additional staffing positions.

References

Argyris, C. (1957). *Personality and organization*. New York: Harper & Bros.

Crompton, J. (2001, May). The impact of parks on property values. *Park & Recreation*, pp. 91–95.

Dateline. (2001, February). Gale Norton: Support goal of LWCF full funding." Public Policy and Legislation Newsletter of the National Recreation and Park Association.

Drucker, P. (1973). *Management: Tasks, responsibilities, practices*. New York: Harper & Row.

Dumaine, B. (1994, September 5). The trouble with teams. *Fortune*, pp. 86–92.

Fawcett, P. (2001, February). Managing lifeguards effectively. *Park & Recreation*, pp. 73–75.

Guillion, L. (1998). Recreational sport. In L. P. Masteralexis, C. A. Barr, & M. A. Hums, (Eds.). (1988) *Principles and practice of sport management*. Gaithersburg, MD: Aspen.

Hackman, J. R. and Oldham, G. R. (1980). *Work redesign*. Reading, MA: Addison-Wesley.

Hammer, M. (1990, July/August). Reengineering work: Don't automate, obliterate. *Harvard Business Review*, pp. 104–112.

Hammer, M., & Champy, J. (1993). *Reengineering the corporation*. New York: Harper Business.

Hammonds, K. H., Kelly, K. & Thurston, K. (1994, October 17). Rethinking Work, *Business Week*, p. 84.

Herzberg, F. (1966). *Work and the nature of man*. Cleveland, OH: World.

Herzberg, F. (1968, January/February). One more time: How do you motivate employees? *Harvard Business Review*, pp. 53–62.

http://www.activeparks.org (2001).

Katzenbach, J. R., & Smith, D. K. (1993, March/April). The discipline of teams. *Harvard Business Review*, p. 112.

Mull, R. F., Bayless, K. G., Ross, C. M., & Jamieson, L. M. (1997). *Recreational sport management*. Champaign, IL: Human Kinetics.

Northampton, MA. Recreation Department Annual Report. (2001). City of Northampton, MA.

Reif, W. E., & Luthans, F. (1972, Fall). Does job enrichment really pay off? *California Management Review*, pp. 30–37.

Sherman, R. (1998, January) School of Hard Knox, *Park & Recreation*, pp. 26–28.

Part 5

Improving Performance

Chapter 10

Motivation and Leadership

PHOTO: © DUOMO/CORBIS

Purpose:

www.olympic.org

According to the International Olympic Committee (IOC), the purpose of the Olympic movement is to create international goodwill through sport and "to contribute to building a better world by educating youth through sport" ("The Olympic Charter," 2000).

Stakeholders:

Athletes, coaches, governing body personnel, politicians, government and diplomatic personnel, citizens of all countries that participate in the Olympics, organizations that purchase Olympic-related sponsorships.

Size and scope:

- At the 2000 Summer Games in Sydney, Australia, over 10,000 athletes from more than 200 countries participated. Over 3,400 hours of coverage were broadcast to 220 countries, with a cumulative global TV audience of 22.6 billion ("Recent Olympic," 2000).
- The 2002 Winter Games in Salt Lake City had a proposed budget of $1.313 billion (of which $222 million went for venue construction), which was to be covered with revenues from sponsorships ($600 million), broadcast rights ($445 million), ticket sales ($180 million), and merchandise and other sources ($88 million) (Powers, 2001a).
- Olympic marketing, composed of broadcast rights, sponsorships, licensing, ticket revenue, and coin and philatelic programs, generated $5.5 billion between 1997 and 2000 ("Olympic Marketing," 2000).
- Current members of The Olympic Program (TOP), the IOC's corporate sponsorship group, include Kodak, McDonald's, and Samsung. Each of ten members pays $55 million in cash and value-in-kind (Brockinton, 2001).

Governance:

International Olympic Committee (IOC)
- The IOC, headquartered in Lausanne, Switzerland, is the ultimate ruling body of the Olympic Games. The IOC decides where the games will be held and in which sports events will be held. There are currently 122 IOC members from 79 countries. The IOC itself does not organize the competitions in the various sports; that is done by the national organizing committees (NOCs) in conjunction with the international sports federations (IFs).

National Organizing Committees (NOCs)

www.usoc.org
- NOCs such as the United States Olympic Committee (USOC) serves "to recruit, supervise, and certify" Olympic hopefuls (Senn, 1999, p. 11). The IOC certifies one NOC per country, which are supposed to be independent of governments. Although the IOC states that the Olympics are open to the youth of the world, without NOC certification, no athlete can compete in the Olympics.

International Sports Federations (IFs)
- The IFs (such as FIBA, the international basketball governing body, and FIL, the International Luge Federation) set the rules and hold the competitions at the Olympics, and the NOCs supply the athletes ("The Olympic Charter," 2000).

Olympic Organizing Committees (OCOGs)
- The OCOGs prepare the site of the Games for competitors and spectators.

Chapter 10: Motivation and Leadership

Inside Look

"Do You Believe in Miracles?"*

Friday afternoon at five? For the biggest Olympic event ever? On February 22, 1980, in the Adirondack Mountains resort village of Lake Placid, New York, the U.S. Olympic men's ice hockey team was about to take the ice against the best team in the world. Just a few weeks earlier, the Americans' opponent that day, the squad from the former Union of Soviet Socialist Republics (USSR), had soundly beaten them 10–3 at an exhibition in New York City's Madison Square Garden. The Soviets had dominated international ice hockey for two decades and had captured each Olympic gold medal since 1960, when the Americans had triumphed at the Squaw Valley Games. The 1980 U.S. team, coached by Herb Brooks, head coach at the University of Minnesota (ironically, the last player cut from the 1960 U.S. Olympic team, one day before the Games began), was comprised of twenty amateur collegiate players mostly from the regional hockey hotbeds of Massachusetts, Michigan, and Minnesota. The experts predicted the Americans, the youngest and most inexperienced team in the Games, would finish behind the Soviets, the Czechs, the Swedes, the Canadians, the Finns, and the West Germans and not win a medal.

The highly skilled and veteran Soviet team was stocked with members of the USSR's Red Army, and although technically not professional players, their military duties consisted solely of training and playing hockey. The team remained in training camp away from their families for nine months a year and practiced three times a day. Paced by goaltender Vadislav Tretiak and forward Boris Mikhailov, they were at the very least on par with their NHL counterparts and generally acknowledged to be the best team in the world and a lock to win the Olympic gold again.

But it didn't happen that way. Brooks hastened team bonding by making himself, not the Soviets, the enemy and the focus of the players' ire, and he drove the team hard. A common Brooks rebuke: "You're playing worse and worse every day, and right now you're playing like next month!" After a loss to the Norwegian team in a tune-up game in 1979, Brooks kept his team on the ice, putting the team through punishing skating drills for an hour. The session continued even when the rink staff turned out the lights. Once the games neared, however, Brooks began to chip away at the mystique of the supposedly invincible Soviets, stating that the team was overconfident, he didn't like the way they were playing, and that "somebody's going to beat those guys."

Once the Games began, the U.S. team, led by forward and captain Mike Eruzione and goalie Jim Craig, came back from a late 2–1 deficit to tie Sweden in the opening game, then ran off big wins against Czechoslovakia, Norway, Romania, and West Germany. The Soviets cruised through their qualifying games, including routs of Japan and the Netherlands by a combined score of 33–4, setting up a match with the United States in the first game of the medal round.

On top of all the on-ice factors, the U.S.–Soviet medal round game was also impacted by a generation of Cold

*Unless otherwise noted, content for this introduction is based on information in Hyland, 2001.

War tensions between the two nuclear superpowers. In the decades following World War II, any athletic contest between the two countries, be it boxing, basketball, or canoeing, became an allegorical battle between capitalism and communism, and for many served as a measuring stick of the comparative effectiveness and success of the democratic and oligarchic political systems.

The U.S. players fully grasped the perceived ideological conflict. Said Eruzione, "It was us against them. Freedom versus communism." As Bill Cleary of the 1960 gold medal team said, "I looked down at the 'USA' on my jersey, and I'll never forget the feeling. I could have won 100 Stanley Cups, and they wouldn't have equaled it" (Swift, 2001, p. 44).

Months earlier, the game had been scheduled for a Friday afternoon at five, because it was expected the Soviets would be dominating, the Americans would be long gone, and popular interest in the United States would be nil. The heightened interest in the U.S. team's fortunes led to consideration of moving the start time of the game to generate a larger TV audience, but the Soviets refused. So the game was not carried live, but taped and broadcast at 8 P.M. on ABC. Before the game, Brooks told his team, "You were born to be a player. You were meant to be here. This moment is ours. It's our turn." The Soviets struck first, however, and looked poised to take a 2–1 lead into the first intermission when forward Mark Johnson slipped behind the flat-footed Soviet defense, gathered in a long rebound, and beat Tretiak to knot the score with one second left in the period. Soviet coach Victor Tikhanov then pulled Tretiak in favor of backup Vladimir Myshkin, hoping to fire up his club. The move worked

for a while as the Soviets notched another goal against Craig early in the second stanza, outshot the United States 12–2, and held the Americans scoreless for the period. But midway through the third, forward Dave Silk fed Johnson for the tying marker, and eighty-one seconds later, Eruzione corralled a bouncing puck and whistled a wrist shot past a screened Myshkin. The United States now led 4–3, and the rink was bedlam. The Americans fought to hold on through the final ten minutes, with Craig making several big saves. As the last seconds ticked away, ABC commentator Al Michaels punctuated the upset with his now famous exclamation, "Do you believe in miracles? Yes!" The United States had beaten the best team in the world.

The gold medal game was, for many, an afterthought. But not for Brooks, who told his team straight out before the game, "If you lose now, you'll take it to your graves. To your graves!" A loss to the Finns might also mean no medal at all. But they didn't lose. The Americans erased a 2–1 deficit with three third-period goals, and the Finns fell 4–2. It was the Americans, not the Soviets, who were the best team in the world.

In organizational terms, Herb Brooks created a high-performance environment in which his team was motivated to perform at levels that allowed them to succeed personally while allowing the team to prosper. The 1980 U.S. Olympic men's ice hockey team constituted a high-performance work group. Creating this kind of work force has become an essential management responsibility. Even the most carefully developed strategies and structure are not enough to make an organization competitive unless its people are highly motivated to perform.

Introduction

This chapter reviews the theories and concepts of motivation within the rubric of Olympic sport. It highlights aspects of this industry segment by reviewing the essential steps in creating a high-performance work environment.

We also focus on the indispensable role of leadership for this segment. The chapter reviews the evolution of leadership theory and the increasing importance of more recent leadership forms. Communication, perhaps the most essential component for effective leadership, is also discussed.

Understanding Performance Motivation

For several decades, scientists, researchers, and theorists, primarily in the fields of psychology and organizational behavior, have worked to develop a clearer understanding of the factors that influence and shape individual and group performance. The combination of these factors is called *performance motivation*. The results of these efforts strongly support the view that human performance reflects a highly complex set of dynamics, involving people's needs and goals, their skills and abilities, and the demands and challenges of the task itself.

In this section we consider four different models or theories of performance motivation. Although each of these theories differs in emphasis, each makes an important contribution to our understanding of how to improve human performance in pursuit of the organization's goals.

Goal Theory

As we discussed in Chapter 4, the power of goals is to enhance organizational performance. Effectively defined goals are no less important for individual and team performance. SMART goals provide direction, the basis for decisions on where to invest energy and effort, and the basis for feedback. Each is a key element in performance motivation.

On the playing field or in the arena, specific goals are a natural part of the environment. Competitive or recreational sports almost always include a goal or target outcome. For the 1980 U.S. Olympic men's ice hockey team, the goal for some may simply have been to compete in the Olympics. That goal may have been sufficiently challenging and engaging to allow those individuals to be selected for the team, but it almost certainly would not have been sufficient to enable the team to achieve a medal. For Herb Brooks, from the very beginning, the goal was to win the gold: specific, meaningful, and challenging, to say the least. Brooks's task was to create a situation in which the players believed the goal could be achieved, that it was realistic enough for the players to accept the goal fully and to put forth all the work and effort that achieving the gold would require.

The message from goal theory is that to enhance motivation, managers must establish goals that engage and challenge their people to achieve the levels of performance needed for the organization to compete and succeed.

Reinforcement Theory

A second lens through which to bring performance motivation into focus is reinforcement theory: all behavior is shaped by the consequences of that behavior. Consequences are what happen as a result of that behavior. B. F. Skinner (1953, 1972), perhaps the most prominent reinforcement theorist, describes the four types of consequences shown in Figure 10-1.

For the members of the 1980 U.S. Olympic men's ice hockey team, the positive reinforcers were obvious: the reward of an Olympic medal for the highest performing teams, the opportunity to play at the highest level of international competition, and the greater playing time for individuals who performed well.

There was also negative reinforcement. Remember the statement of Herb Brooks after the U.S. team had defeated the USSR, but still had to defeat Finland to win the gold, in fact, to win any medal at all? Brooks said the team would take the loss to their graves, pointing to the terrible consequence of lifelong regret, of having worked so hard and come so close without achieving their goal, as a threat to motivate his team's performance.

Finally, Brooks also used punishment. As we already mentioned, there were negative consequences of the physical variety, such as the punishing one-hour extended skating drills that followed the game in which Brooks felt his team's effort was poor. And there were Brooks's words: "You're playing worse and worse every day, and right now, you're playing like next month!" Clearly Brooks understood the value of negative consequences as a means to minimize unacceptable performance.

The difference between punishment and extinction is that extinction involves no consequence or type of reinforcement. For the 1998 U.S. Olympic men's ice hockey team, there was no real stake in the winning of a gold medal. They had not trained as a unit like the 1980 squad and thus had no real sense of team identity, there was no ideological gulf between nations as existed in 1980, so there was no sense of "us versus them," as Mike Eruzione said, and because they were already playing against the stars on the other Olympic teams in the NHL, the sense of accomplishment to be had by beating the Czechs (the eventual gold medal winners at the 1998 Nagano Winter Games, when two or three of them might actually be your teammates in the NHL) was minimal at best. There was also the sense that as paid professionals, the current crop of American NHL players were not

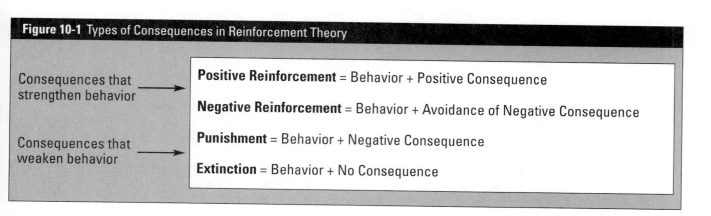

Figure 10-1 Types of Consequences in Reinforcement Theory

Consequences that strengthen behavior →

Positive Reinforcement = Behavior + Positive Consequence

Negative Reinforcement = Behavior + Avoidance of Negative Consequence

Consequences that weaken behavior →

Punishment = Behavior + Negative Consequence

Extinction = Behavior + No Consequence

playing for pay as they did day in and day out in the NHL, and the Olympics were some sort of exhibition hiatus rather than a chance to make a significant statement about their own abilities. So we lost the gold, they might think. So what, we go back to our NHL teams and pick it up where we left off a few weeks ago.

In fact, the U.S. squad felt so little for the Olympic experience that three members elected to wreck their Olympic village rooms before skulking out of Nagano. The culprits were never identified or punished for their actions (supposedly the miscreants feared lifetime Olympic bans, so the team members chose to hide their identities), other than the team's not being invited to the White House with other Olympians (Farber, 2001). Because no punishment or negative reinforcement was forthcoming, there is no reason to believe that this type of behavior will be extinguished.

The message from reinforcement theory for managers is that to build high levels of performance motivation, positive performance must be shaped by a carefully selected set of consequences that reinforce and strengthen that performance.

Needs Theory

A third perspective on performance motivation is provided by needs theory, which suggests that all human behavior, including behavior in organizations, is an effort to satisfy the individual's needs. In other words, people work and perform at a level that will allow them to satisfy their needs.

Some of the most important contributions to our understanding of human needs have come from psychologist Abraham Maslow (1970), who concluded that most of our needs can be grouped into five categories and arranged in levels, as shown in Figure 10-2. Maslow suggested a number of interesting elements about human needs. He began with the assumption that in any given situation human behavior

Figure 10-2 Maslow's Hierarchy of Needs

Self-actualization: The need for the feeling or sense that you are achieving your full potential as a human being.

↑

Esteem: The need for the sense of respect first from others and then self-respect.

↑

Social: The need for the sense of belongingness and acceptance by others.

↑

Security: The need for those things that will allow us to feel physically and psychologically safe.

↑

Physiological: The need for those things that will keep us alive and functioning physiologically.

or performance tends to reflect the particular need level of an individual in a particular situation. For example, Maslow states that different individuals in exactly similar situations might behave or perform in totally different ways depending on their needs at the time. Someone at the esteem-needs level, for example, might work extremely hard to receive recognition. Someone at the social-needs level might only work hard enough to be accepted by the group in which he or she is working. And someone at the security-needs level might purposely perform only well enough to keep his or her job and seek to avoid any attention at all.

The message from needs theory is that managers must recognize and understand the need levels of employees and create opportunities for them to pursue the satisfaction of these needs through what they do.

The 1980 U.S. Olympic men's ice hockey squad also provides an excellent illustration of Maslow's hierarchy of needs in action. The members of the U.S. team would be operating at the social-needs level if they were satisfied simply with being accepted as a member of the team. Although the evidence is strong that these individuals did indeed bond into a highly cohesive group concerned with each other at both the personal and the performing levels, it is highly unlikely that this would be enough to explain the unprecedented level of performance this team achieved.

The team's high level of performance suggests the members were motivated by esteem and self-actualization needs. In terms of self-esteem, this means that Johnson, Craig, Eruzione, and the others who comprised the U.S. team were driven by the need for respect and recognition as hockey players and by the need to avoid the very public embarrassment of playing poorly. In terms of self-actualization, this means these athletes were driven by an intense desire to achieve all they were capable of as hockey players in the most important international competition. From a needs theory perspective, it was the intensity of these upper-level needs that best explains the very rare level of performance achieved by the team.

Expectancy Theory

Developed by Victor Vroom (1964), expectancy theory suggests that the level of effort an individual puts into a task depends on three factors:

1. The strength of the individual's expectation that he or she is able to perform at a level that will result in success. According to Vroom, the more positive the expectation, the greater the likely effort.

2. The strength of the individual's expectation that success will result in reward. Some rewards are extrinsic (e.g., money, recognition, a promotion); others are intrinsic (e.g., learning new skills, sense of personal satisfaction). However, for motivation to be positive, the expectation must be positive that success on a task will result in reward.

3. The valence of the reward, or how much the reward for success is valued by the individual. Just having a reward is not enough. For motivation to be positive, the reward for success must be something valued by the individual.

According to expectancy theory, each of these conditions must be met to ensure a high level of performance motivation. Once again, the 1980 U.S. Olympic men's ice hockey team provides an illuminating illustration of theory. There can be no question of the extent to which the members of the U.S. team valued the reward for success in the Olympics. The reward included the personal satisfaction of winning the gold medal, the recognition and respect that comes with that kind of achievement, and the professional and financial opportunities that accompany being a member of a world championship team.

There can also be no question that the members of the team knew that if they were successful with their task, they would be assured of receiving these rewards. The only uncertainty in this equation was whether they could expect their best level of effort would in fact result in success. And it is this expectation that Coach Brooks worked hardest to establish and strengthen.

First, consistent with expectancy theory, he simply demanded more of the team in terms of its performance than anyone else, including the players. Second, he provided greater direction and feedback in terms of his coaching. And finally, he made success seem more possible by making sure his players weren't being unnecessarily pessimistic about the difficulty of the task. Talking about the supposedly unbeatable Soviet team, Brooks said he didn't like the way they were playing, that "Somebody is going to beat them." All the evidence suggests that by the time the U.S. team met the Soviets, they genuinely believed they were capable of defeating them.

The lesson from expectancy theory for the manager is the importance of creating strong links between success and rewards that people value, and of creating the strongest possible expectations that high levels of effort will lead to performance.

Theory into Practice: Creating a High-Performance Work Environment

The true value of these theories of performance motivation is that, taken together, they provide clear direction on how to structure the work environment for high levels of performance. Four key factors support and enhance performance motivation.

Engaging, Challenging Goals

High levels of performance motivation clearly begin with a set of fully developed goals and standards that define exactly the performance target. These goals and standards provide the basis for focus, challenge, and feedback, all essential for high performance.

Training

High levels of performance motivation also require high levels of skill. Expectancy theory makes clear that workers must be confident that the skills they possess will allow them to achieve the performance goals. Training is the critical means for ensuring that people have the skills they need to meet the performance challenge. As we show in Chapter 11, training—effectively provided and continuously updated—is essential for ensuring the levels of confidence and competence necessary for high levels of performance motivation.

Performance Incentives: Creating a Stake in Achieving Success

A third key element in creating a high-performance environment is *rewards*, also known as *incentives*. Both expectancy theory and reinforcement theory emphasize creating a clear link between high levels of performance and incentives or rewards for achieving performance goals. Needs theory helps the manager understand the needs level of her or his people and also helps determine the types of incentives that will be most valued. Thus a third key element in creating a high-performance work environment is a clear link between achieving performance goals and the assurance of highly valued rewards for pursuing and achieving those goals.

Involving Employees: Sharing Responsibility for Performance

A fourth key element is directly involving employees in problem solving and decision making. This strategy of employee involvement has most recently been called *employee empowerment* (Conger & Kanungo, 1988; Manz, 1992). Even the most effective goal and incentive systems are almost always part of an overall management effort to more fully involve people in the responsibility for their own performance.

Empowerment strategies are certainly consistent with needs theory. More specifically, sharing responsibility for performance responds directly to people's esteem and self-actualization needs. Empowerment represents a significant form of recognition of employees' judgment and skills, as well as an opportunity for employees to test and develop their own potential. This combination of recognition and opportunity for development results in an enhanced level of performance motivation.

High-Performance Motivation: Grasping for the Rings

Stories abound of managers in sports organizations aligned with the Olympic movement who have employed goals, training, incentives, and involving employees to achieve organizational success. Consider the Herculean task of staging the Summer Olympic Games. The IOC has the power to determine sites for each set of Olympic Games and makes its decision seven years in advance of the scheduled Games. In 2001 the IOC prepared to decide from among Beijing, Istanbul, Osaka, Paris, and Toronto which city would host the 2008 Summer Games. These and other prospective host cities had to submit a formal application, and the list was whittled to ten in February 2000 and then to the final five that August. Members of the IOC then visited each city in February and March 2001.

But why seek to hold the Games in the first place? The city of Atlanta reported spending $7 million alone just in its winning bid for the 1996 Centennial Olympics (selected from among Athens, Belgrade, Manchester, Melbourne, and Toronto).

Atlanta was chosen in large part because of its location in the eastern time zone of the United States, which allowed for higher American television revenues because of the number of events that could be broadcast live during prime time (a factor that hurt the TV ratings for the 2000 Sydney Summer Games because NBC chose to show most key events on a tape-delay basis). Atlanta sought the Games for several reasons: as an opening to world business and tourism, as an economic boom for the surrounding area, and for the resulting benefits from related construction and improvements. The city had to commit millions toward constructing Olympic venues, including $170 million for the Olympic stadium (later reconfigured for use by the Atlanta Braves as Turner Field), $30 million for a field hockey venue (later given to Morris Brown College and Clark Atlanta University), and $17.5 million on an aquatics center (later given to the Georgia Institute of Technology), and the city was later criticized for overly commercializing the Games through a plethora of sponsorships to cover costs.

But why go through all this, especially considering the financial woes of the Montreal Summer Games in 1976, where due to graft, labor strikes, poor planning, and design problems, Quebec taxpayers were saddled with $1.3 billion in debt that will be retired in 2005 ("A Legacy," 2001)? All these flaws were blatantly evident for years when one visited Olympic Stadium to watch an Expos' game. This trend was reversed when for the 1984 Los Angeles Summer Games organizing committee head Peter Ueberroth negotiated huge increases in TV rights' fees and sponsorship dollars and used 50,000 volunteer workers so the LA Games turned a profit of $222 million on revenues of $718 million (Helyar, 1994).

Recall that the U.S. Olympic Committee (USOC) is the American national organizing committee (NOC) that serves "to recruit, supervise, and certify" Olympic hopefuls (Senn, 1999, p. 11). The IOC certifies one NOC per country, which are supposed to be independent of governments. Although the IOC states that the Olympics are open to the youth of the world, without NOC certification no athlete can compete in the Olympics. The USOC, like all NOCs, allows national governing bodies (NGBs) in each sport to focus on preparing athletes for Olympic competition (Senn, 1999).

The USOC is also responsible for certifying which U.S. city will make the official bid to the IOC to host an upcoming Olympiad. The USOC makes its decision on the basis of how each city meets each of nineteen areas, including security, medical and health services, accommodations, transportation, current available venues, past sports event hosting experience, and most importantly, a financial guarantee to cover any shortfalls that develop in preparing to host the Games. (However, in the case of the 2002 Salt Lake City Games, the federal government spent $1.5 billion to help support the Games, including $25 million for buses for spectator transportation, $11 million for infectious disease monitoring, $1 million for weather forecasting, and $500,000 for planting new trees [Bartlett et al., 2001].) In 2002 eight U.S. locales (Cincinnati, Dallas, Houston, Los Angeles, New York, San Francisco, Tampa/St. Petersburg/Orlando, Washington, D.C./Baltimore) sought selection by the USOC as the U.S choice to bid for the 2012 Summer Games. From this group the USOC pared the potential sites to Houston, New York, San Francisco, and Washington, D.C./Baltimore.

The Bay Area Sports Organizing Committee (BASOC), San Francisco's organizing committee, anticipates costs of at least $2 billion to prepare for the Games (much of which comes from IOC and USOC funding sources), excluding $2 million

needed for its initial bid efforts, and when chosen by the USOC, another $3 million to be used in the next bid stage (Leuty, 2000). In terms of the Bay Area's bid, many of the needed venues are already in place, including Stanford Stadium in Palo Alto (for track and field, modern pentathlon, and the opening and closing ceremonies, with a capacity of 85,000), the 1.2 million-square-foot Moscone Center in San Francisco (for team handball, fencing, table tennis, tae kwon do, and indoor volleyball), San Jose's 17,773-seat Compaq Center (gymnastics), and 11,200-seat Raley Field in Sacramento (for baseball). However, a major drawback for the BASOC bid to overcome is that these venues are widely spread geographically.

The pot of gold at the end of this process? To attract 800,000 visitors who would spend a total of $937 million, which would create 70,000 jobs, for a total potential economic impact of $6 billion (Byrd, 2000). However, University of South Florida economist Philip Porter, based on research from data from the 1996 Atlanta Games, noted that the Olympics push as many people out of town as they bring in and made no noticeable difference from a typical Atlanta summer (deMause, 2001). ACOG, Atlanta's Olympic organizing committee, with a budget of $1.7 billion, ultimately broke even on the Games (Senn, 1999). However, the 2000 Sydney Games added about $4 billion (at a total cost of $3 billion to stage the Games) to the economic output of Australia, and for the upcoming 2008 Summer Games in Beijing (see later), the Games will lead to $32 billion in economic growth in China between now and the start of the Games, including billions from foreign corporate investment (Landler, 2001). In addition, monies spent on the Games can greatly enrich local landowners, as was the case with the 2002 Salt Lake City Games. The $15 million spent to upgrade roads leading to resort land owned by Charles C. Myers increased the assessed value of the land from $3 million in 1990 to $48 million, as well as land owned by the Church of Jesus Christ of Latter-day Saints. Said the head of Utah's department of transportation, "We are, without shame, using the Olympics to try and get federal funds" (Bartlett et al., 2001, p. 90).

But the pursuit of the Olympic rings is a process that takes over a decade and involves numerous workers, both paid and volunteer. The issue here is how BASOC CEO Anne Warner Cribbs, an Olympic gold medal swimmer and advertising and public relations firm head, will lead people in such a huge and all-encompassing task, and how she could use goals, training, incentives, and empowerment in this pursuit.

In terms of goals, they are clear for Cribbs and BASOC: to convince the USOC first, and then the voters in the IOC, that the Bay Area has the venues, infrastructure, and each of the other required elements in place to host the world's largest athletic event. In terms of training, Cribbs must train a wide variety of paid staffers and volunteers in the areas of preparing and presenting the information required to sway voters and to work with local businesses and government organizations to help generate local support for the bid. In the area of incentives, although the goal may be to win the Games for the Bay Area, the incentive is the potential economic boom the region could experience from the Games.

However, the early empirical research on empowerment in organizations as a means for success has not been definitive. Some reports question whether empowerment promises more in terms of performance improvements than it can actually deliver. In 2000 USOC CEO Norman Blake (former CEO of the Promus Hotel Corporation) resigned from the post after trying to push through changes that gave employees more control while holding them more accountable. Blake had been hired after the USOC spent $500,000 on an organizational study following the Salt Lake bidding scandal (see later), which stated that the USOC CEO should have experience running a large corporation (Lloyd, 2001). However, Blake's move to limit the input and control of the many volunteer groups on which the USOC had relied backfired, and his lack of employee input on a strategic plan led to his resignation (Woodward, 2001). Another study suggests that empowerment works best only in companies that are already achieving high levels of performance. Lower performing organizations often lack the training resources to make empowerment work (Bleakley, 1993; Fuschberg, 1992).

This last point suggests that the problem may not be with the empowerment strategies themselves, but with implementing them (Mathes, 1992). It is often difficult for managers to give up or even to share the authority and responsibility that has defined the essence of management for over a century. In addition, not all workers in organizations are eager to take on even part of the responsibility for the problems surrounding their work, especially when they do not feel they will be given the authority to make real changes or improvements (Heifetz & Laurie, 1998). When Norman Blake took the USOC CEO job, he was told he had complete authority, and he made decisions to cut staff and to centralize fund-raising efforts on that basis (Woodward, 2001). It is not surprising that some of these actions were seen as not empowering.

Many critics note that his replacement, former Maytag chairman Lloyd Ward, will fare no better than Blake because of the conflicts between USOC's traditional members, and the executive committee who was seeking a proven executive that could bolster the organization's revenues (Powers, 2001f). It seems that Ward will have difficulty determining which group to empower.

To summarize, the four essential conditions for creating a high-performance work environment are well-defined goals and standards, continuous training in high-level skills, performance-based incentives, and employee empowerment. To be effective, these conditions must be implemented through a coordinated set of systems and programs designed specifically to create and to develop a high-performance workplace. These systems and programs represent a special responsibility of management known as human resource management (see Chapter 11).

The Leadership Factor

Beyond performance motivation, leadership has emerged as one of the most critical ingredients for success in all organizations, not just in sports organizations. All organizations are in a seemingly never-ending quest to define leadership and to seek those with the abilities to lead effectively. A quick check of the business and management sections in the local bookstore will reveal dozens of titles devoted to the study of leadership in organizations. In one such book, *Leaders* by Warren Bennis and Burt Nanus (1985), the authors emphasize the crucial importance of leadership: "A business short on capital can borrow money, and one with a poor location can move. But a business short of leadership has little chance of survival" (p. 20).

Think about this: are the definitions for the terms *manager* and *leader* interchangeable? Do we expect managers to be leaders? Most of us probably do. However, management scholar John Kotter (1988) identifies an important distinction:

Management is about coping with complexity. Its practices and procedures are largely a response to the emergence of large complex organizations in the 20th century. Leadership, by contrast, is about coping with change. Part of the reason [leadership] has become so important in recent years is that the business world has become more competitive and more volatile. More change always demands more leadership. (pp. 37–38)

Because of this element of change (especially as sports organizations look toward international expansion), leadership is a crucial component for every kind of organization. Leadership in organizations is the process of directing and supporting others in the pursuit of the organization's mission and goals. From this perspective, leadership is as much every team member's responsibility as it is the highest level managers' and CEO's responsibility. Everyone is a potential leader, capable of contributing to the direction and support of others as he or she pursues the mission and goals of the organization.

The question for all sports organizations is how best to provide the kind of direction and support people need to be productive. The answer to the question is not a simple one. It has been evolving and ever changing as research reveals more about the leadership process, and the very nature of leadership has altered to meet the realities of the contemporary workplace. Our discussion of leadership begins with a review of some of the early research and theories, which focused on the personality and characteristics of effective leaders, and then highlights how individual leaders influenced the development of the modern Olympic movement.

The Psychology of the Leader

The early research on leadership focused on the leader as a person, on the personality traits of the effective leader, on the leader's attitudes and assumptions, and on leaders' expectations of their followers. The underlying assumption was that if research could determine the kind of person who would be an effective leader, organizations might be better able to identify and select people with the greatest leadership potential.

Leadership and Personality

The initial leadership research focused on determining whether specific personality traits are common to effective leaders. For many years, the results from this research did not substantiate that premise, and little or no evidence supported the concept of a particular leadership personality. By the 1980s, however, expanded research identified at least five personality traits consistently associated with effective leaders (Kirkpatrick & Locke, 1991). The personalities of those considered effective as leaders might vary in other ways—whether they were shy as opposed to outgoing, for example, or reflective versus immediately reactive. But most effective leaders were found to possess many of the five traits listed in Figure 10-3 on page 284.

Recognizing the key personality characteristics of effective leaders can assist organizational efforts to identify potential leaders. It can also aid in efforts to develop

Baron Pierre de Coubertin (IOC president, 1896–1925): The establishment of the modern Olympic movement had much to do with the efforts of Coubertin, a French aristocrat with passions for physical and sport education as well as classical history. Coubertin based his concept of the modern Olympics on those held in ancient Greece, which were first held in 776 B.C. Coubertin was not an internationalist, meaning he did not necessarily see the value of the Olympics as a way to bring countries together, but rather saw the competition as a way for his native France to promote sport and physical fitness for the betterment of the nation's military. Coubertin also believed that the games should be open to amateurs only, as professionalism supposedly tainted the ideal of participation for its own sake (this was not in line with the ancient Olympics, whose winners received prizes for their victories). The most notorious enforcement of the amateurism rules was in 1913, when American track star Jim Thorpe was stripped of the medals won at the previous summer's games in Stockholm when it was discovered he had played summer semi-pro baseball for pay in 1909 and 1910 ("*The Outlook*'s," 1997).

The first modern games were held in Athens, Greece, in 1896: 311 male athletes (11 women would compete in the Paris Games in 1900) from 13 nations competed in 9 sports, and the Greek team won the most medals (49, 10 gold) (Senn, 1999). Coubertin had arranged for an international congress two years before to establish the event and had spent several years before that trying to convince students and educators in Europe and the United States of the merits of his ideas.

Although Coubertin was criticized for misinterpreting the ancient Olympics as restricted to amateurs, which led to claims of Olympic class elitism and to decades of conflicts within the Olympic movement, he was the person most responsible for the establishment of the modern Olympics.

Avery Brundage (IOC president, 1952–1972): After the leadership of Coubertin, the presidency of the IOC fell first to Henri Baillet-Latour of Belgium (1925–1942) and then to J. Sigfrid Edstrom of Sweden (1942–1952). However, Senn (1999) writes that the former USOC head Avery Brundage was the real key to power in the IOC during this time. As IOC vice president, Brundage played a major role in the reconstruction of the Olympics after World War II (none was held in 1940 and 1944), was elected to the presidency in 1952, a position he would hold for two decades, and marshaled the Olympics through the political machinations that resulted from conflicts of the Cold War. Brundage worked to reincorporate the Germans and admit the USSR to the Olympics, and he struggled to keep the Olympics free of the political contexts in which the Games were inevitably imbued (Senn, 1999). Brundage served a sort of apprenticeship under two IOC presidents, and he developed the skills needed to manage the reemergence of the Olympics through a particularly difficult political period.

In the context of Brundage's leadership of the IOC, many involved with the Olympic movement after World War II were against the readmission of the Germans into the Games, and Brundage himself was initially opposed to the inclusion of the USSR. In addition, Brundage felt that the inclusion of team sports seriously threatened the Games' amateurism code, that too many sports had been added (the numbers of competitors in the 1960 Rome Summer Games had increased by 60 percent from the Melbourne Games four years earlier), and that because women did not compete in the ancient Games their events should be eliminated or at least reduced (Senn, 1999). The majority of IOC representatives (who are chosen by the existing IOC members from "active athletes and (NOC) presidents or senior leaders of the IFs and NOCs" ["The Olympic Charter," 2000, p. 1], the total of which may not exceed 115) did not agree with Brundage, so he decided not to push for his reform ideas. Brundage understood the political motivations and needs of the IOC members, and he chose to heed them.

Lord Killanin (IOC president, 1972–1980): Michael Morris, Lord Killanin, an English-Irish nobleman, succeeded Avery Brundage as IOC president after the tragedy-marred Munich Games. Formerly the IOC vice president, Killanin was considered a pragmatist in relation to Brundage's idealized perspectives on amateurism and competition. Killanin also offered a more inclusive management style, involving more IOC members in the consulting process, but retained ultimate control over the Games. Killanin was far more willing to hold general meetings and work with subcommittees. Through his conferring style Killanin made peace with ambitious members of the IFs and the NGBs and formally incorporated this deliberative style into the Olympic structure. His successes also included a liberalization of eligibility rules, which would allow Killanin's successor, Juan Antonio Samaranch of Spain, to finally include openly professional athletes (Senn, 1999).

However, Killanin's eight-year term was beset with boycotts and the threats of boycotts—including the U.S. refusal to participate in the 1980 Summer Games in Moscow and the Soviets' reciprocal refusal to take part in the Los Angeles Summer Games four years later. Killanin also dealt with the financial woes of the Montreal Summer Games in 1976, and Denver's failure to meet its promise to host the 1976 Winter Games after Colorado voters chose not to support the Games in 1972 due to environmental concerns (Senn, 1999). Despite Killanin's inclusive style, he was unable to handle these challenges successfully.

Juan Antonio Samaranch (1980–2001): As with all of the IOC presidents, Samaranch had to face significant problems as well. The specter of performance enhancing drugs, which had lingered in the Olympic background for decades, came center stage after Canadian sprinter Ben Johnson was stripped of his gold after testing positive at the 1988 Seoul Summer Games. The most difficult issue faced by Samaranch was the bribery scandal surrounding the awarding of the 2002 Winter Games to Salt Lake City, Utah. After losing out to Nagano, Japan, in a bid for the 1998 Games, members of the Salt Lake Organizing Committee (SLOC) offered bribes of cash and other gifts, including all-expenses-paid ski weekends, snowmobile tours, and Christmas Eve carriage rides totaling $7 million (Michaelis, 2001b, 2001c; Bartlett et al., 2001), to IOC members in exchange for favorable votes for the awarding of the 2002 Games. After the scandal broke, 10 of the IOC voting members were expelled or resigned, and criminal fraud, conspiracy, and racketeering proceedings were initiated against several SLOC staffers (Michaelis, 2001a). The fact that the bribes had been going on for years from many bidding cities was blamed on the self-regulating and closed nature of the IOC, and on Samaranch as well, who was seen as responsible for "allowing a runaway brand of corruption that threatened to derail the entire Olympic movement" (Michaelis, 2001c, p. 3C). However, after the scandal the IOC did adopt a more open managerial and membership process, and it instituted ethics-based reforms. Said Samaranch of the changes, "It was not easy to convince our members it was time to change. Our organization was not up to date. We convinced them after the crisis in Salt Lake City" (Michaelis, 2001d, p. 8C). Although Samaranch was able to transform the IOC on several levels, he was unsuccessful in dealing adequately with the drug and bribery challenges.

Figure 10-3 Personality Traits of Effective Leaders
• Drive, ambition, energy, tenacity, initiative
• Desire to lead
• Honesty and integrity
• Self-confidence
• Intelligence

leadership potential among employees who are not yet in leadership positions. An individual who possesses drive and initiative, for example, as well as the desire to lead, honesty, and integrity, might be provided specific training and assignments to improve self-confidence, which is also associated with effective leadership. Developing these traits is also possible, as Avery Brundage demonstrated during his tenure as vice president of the IOC, which then enabled him to assume the role of IOC head in 1952. This is a common path for subsequent IOC heads, as with the current head, Jacques Rogge (see later).

Identification of key personality traits is an important contribution to solving the leadership puzzle. Understanding the assumptions of leaders is another.

Leader Assumptions

Management researcher Douglas McGregor (1960) studied a different aspect of the leader as a person, focusing on leaders' assumptions about which factors are most important in motivating people at work. McGregor's research suggested to him that leaders' assumptions about worker motivation tended to fall into one of two categories, which he called Theory X and Theory Y. The difference between these two sets of assumptions is shown in Figure 10-4.

One of McGregor's concerns as he considered his research findings was that Theory X might represent an inaccurate set of assumptions about what motivates most people at their work. He felt that as·the educational level of the work force continued to rise, people would become less motivated by the security needs that are the focus of Theory X and more motivated by the higher level needs of acceptance, esteem, and self-actualization that are more consistent with Theory Y.

McGregor did suggest that in some situations Theory X assumptions may be more appropriate than Theory Y. For example, when people are being asked to perform tasks they would otherwise reject, work is not "as natural as play." In this kind of situation, the security need may become a significantly more important source of motivation, and the leader needs to realize this. From McGregor's perspective, however, an effective leader is one who recognizes that people are looking not just for security in their work (Theory X), but opportunities for growth and development as well (Theory Y).

Figure 10-4 The Difference between Theory X and Theory Y

Theory X	**Theory Y**
• Work is inherently distasteful to most people.	• Work is as natural as play, if the conditions are favorable.
• Most people are not ambitious, have little desire for responsibility, and prefer to be directed.	• Self-control is often indispensable in achieving organizational goals.
• Most people have little capacity for creativity in solving organizational problems.	• The capacity for creativity in solving organization problems is widely distributed in the population.
• Motivation occurs only at the physiological and safety levels.	• Motivation occurs at the social, esteem, and self-actualization levels, as well as at the physiological and safety levels.
• Most people must be closely controlled and often coerced to achieve organizational objectives.	• People can be self-directed and creative at work if properly motivated.

The Power of Expectations

Research on the leader as an individual also suggests a strong direct relationship between the leader's level of expectations and followers' level of performance (Single, 1980). According to this research, not only must the leader's assumptions about followers be accurate, the leader's expectations as to what the followers are capable of achieving must be as positive as possible.

In studying the reasons for strong links between leader expectations and follower performance, researchers discovered that leaders with positive expectations provide their followers with significantly more direction and supervision than leaders with less positive expectations about their followers with:

1. a greater degree of challenge

2. more direction on how to complete the tasks

3. greater feedback on how to improve performance

4. in general, a more positive work climate.

In other words, high-expectation leaders provide much more leadership.

This pattern of effective leaders working hard to help their people succeed is an example of a self-fulfilling prophecy. Positive examples of this pattern can be found in every type of sports organization. The leadership lesson of the self-fulfilling prophecy is this: to influence the performance of their followers positively, leaders must expect the best of them. Only a leader with high expectations is likely to provide the amount and quality of direction and support that his or her followers need to achieve the highest levels of performance.

Recall, for example, that the establishment of the modern Olympic movement had much to do with the efforts of Baron Pierre de Coubertin. Although Coubertin did not necessarily see the value of the Olympics as a way to bring countries together via sport (now stated as the goal of the IOC), and he believed the Games should be open to amateurs only, he worked to make the modern Games a reality. This could only happen if, as Coubertin did, he worked with British, German, Greek, Hungarian, and French governments and physical fitness experts, as well as working hard to raise funds for staging the Games. As he wrote in the booklet for the inaugural Games in Athens, he gratefully acknowledged the efforts of others while highlighting the lofty goals he set for them and the Olympic movement:

> I claim [the Games'] paternity with raised voice and I would like to thank once more here those who assisted me to bring it into well-being; those who, together with me, think that athletics will emerge greater and ennobled and that the international youth will draw from it the love of peace and respect for life. (Cited in Hill, 1996, p. 28)

Research on the personality of the leader, McGregor's Theory X and Theory Y, and the concept of the self-fulfilling prophecy each contribute to our understanding of leadership. Effective leaders do tend to have in common such personality characteristics as drive, intelligence, and integrity, among others, and some of these can be developed through training and experience. Effective leaders like Coubertin clearly and accurately recognize the full range of needs that motivate their followers and have the highest expectations about their followers' performance potential.

Leadership Behavior

A second major focus of the research on leadership has been on the behaviors of the effective leader. In addition to studying the leader's personality, assumptions, and expectations, researchers have attempted to analyze and understand what the effective leader actually does.

In some of the initial work on leader behavior, researchers suggested that leadership could be defined as a combination of two different kinds of behavior: task behavior and relations behavior (Fleishman, Harris, & Burtt, 1955; Katz, Maccoby, & Morse, 1950). *Task behavior* is defined as leader behavior focusing on the design and completion of a specific task. It includes setting goals and establishing priorities, providing direction and instruction, and supervising and monitoring tasks to completion. In contrast, *relations behavior* focuses on satisfying the needs of the people performing the task and includes providing support and encouragement, answering questions, and problem solving with followers. A more complete comparison of task and relations behaviors is shown in Figure 10-5.

Figure 10-5 Differences between Leader Task and Leader Relations Behavior	
Relations Behavior	**Task Behavior**
• Giving support	• Goal setting
• Communicating	• Organizing
• Facilitating interactions	• Establishing time lines
• Active listening	• Directing
• Providing feedback	• Controlling

These studies defined leadership as various combinations of these two kinds of behaviors. The different combinations of leader behaviors are often called *leadership styles*. Defining leadership in these terms was important in that research on leadership could now concentrate on identifying which combination of leader task and relations behaviors, or which leadership style, resulted in the most effective leadership.

Styles of Leadership

Robert Blake and Jane Mouton (1982, 1985) created the "Leadership Grid" to present in graphic form the leadership styles possible from integrating task and relations behavior. They call the task behavior dimension "concern for production" and the relations behavior dimension "concern for people." Based on an extensive review of the leadership research then available, Blake and Mouton concluded that the most effective pattern or style of leadership combines high levels of concern both for people and production. They termed this high task/high relations behavior approach the *team management style* of leadership. According to Blake and Mouton, team management was the leadership style used in over 60 percent of situations reported in the research.

From the Blake and Mouton Leadership Grid point of view (see Figure 10-6), the task of management is to ensure that leaders have the skills necessary to implement the team management approach to leadership effectively. To develop these team management skills, training is the key. Individuals being prepared for leadership positions must be provided with training and work experiences that will enable them to be both high task and high relations in their leadership behavior. For example, as featured in the Olympic leaders' discussion, through a series of IOC positions held since 1952, Killanin observed the workings of the system and of Brundage, and he adjusted his leadership style to include more concern for people as well as production.

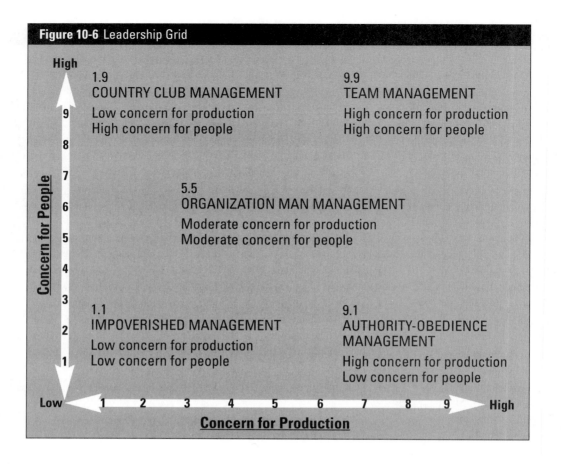

Figure 10-6 Leadership Grid

Concern for People

High

1.9
COUNTRY CLUB MANAGEMENT
Low concern for production
High concern for people

9.9
TEAM MANAGEMENT
High concern for production
High concern for people

5.5
ORGANIZATION MAN MANAGEMENT
Moderate concern for production
Moderate concern for people

1.1
IMPOVERISHED MANAGEMENT
Low concern for production
Low concern for people

9.1
AUTHORITY-OBEDIENCE
MANAGEMENT
High concern for production
Low concern for people

Low   1   2   3   4   5   6   7   8   9   **High**

Concern for Production

The work of Blake and Mouton seemed to have answered the question of which pattern of leader behavior is effective in *most* situations, but the problems encountered by Killanin raise an even more difficult question: How do you determine which leader behavior pattern might be most effective in a *particular* situation, such as handling a boycott or dealing with financial cost overruns?

Contingency Leadership

The contingency theory of leadership claims there is no "one best way" to lead or influence people and that leadership style depends on the situation. Supporters of the contingency view point out that the team management approach represents only 60 percent of the success stories in the research on leadership styles. They say that many situations require leaders who are high-involvement team-manager types, similar to the Olympics under the direction of Coubertin. Others may require a more directive and less personal "boss" approach, as Brundage utilized, and still other situations may require a leader who encourages greater participation by followers in establishing goals and direction, like Killanin. According to the contingency theory of leadership, different leadership styles are effective in different situations.

There are a number of situational or contingency models of leadership. In the situational leadership model, developed by Paul Hersey and Ken Blanchard (1982), the key situational variables for a leader to consider are the competency and commitment of his or her followers. The leader must first determine the level of training, education, and experience of the followers (*competency*), as well as their level of motivation and confidence (*commitment*) to perform the task. These two variables together they called the *readiness level* of the followers. The leader must then match his or her style of leadership to these key follower variables. Hersey and Blanchard's four options in terms of leadership style and the matching degrees of follower readiness are shown in Figure 10-7.

Regardless of the specific aspects on which the situation is focused, all of the contingency models emphasize that different styles of leadership are required for different kinds of situations. The challenge for the sports manager is to be flexible in his or her approach to providing the support and direction needed for high performance.

Transformational Leadership

Most of the research on leadership, including the models described in the previous section, has focused on the leadership of organizations. The emphasis has been on how managers influence subordinates to perform well. Historian James McGregor Burns, in his efforts to understand the essence of effective leadership, took a different approach. Burns reviewed and analyzed the actions of important political and social leaders such as Jesus Christ, Mahatma Ghandi, and Franklin D. Roosevelt. Based on his research, Burns (1978) coined the term *transformational leadership* in relation to those leaders who actually transform or change the beliefs, attitudes, and needs of followers. Traditional models of leadership, as we have said, have been concerned with directing and supporting the performance of followers. These are what have been called *transactional leadership*, because the leader provides rewards, recognition, support, and direction as a part of an exchange for follower performance consistent with the organization's goals. To some degree, each of the four key Olympic leaders made successful transactional leadership moves. Coubertin lauded the stakeholder groups when they worked together to establish the Games, as did Brundage when he heeded the call to keep women in the Olympics. Killanin broadened the power of individuals within the IOC, and Samaranch worked with stakeholders to shore up the IOC financially. Samaranch moved to help the IOC generates more revenues to be redistributed to OCOGs, NOCs, and other sports organizations through the creation of the Olympic Program (TOP), which generates sponsorship dollars from corporations. In addition, the IOC currently reaps more than $1.3 billion from global TV rights (Burton, 2001).

The transformational leader, in contrast, endeavors to transform the belief system of his or her followers to enable them to achieve new and significantly higher levels of performance. Each of the IOC's presidents has faced significant transformational challenges. Coubertin had to work to convince stakeholders of the need for the Games. Brundage brought the Games back after the tumult of World War II, but Killanin inherited problems stemming from political protests and controversy. Notable cases included when American 200-meter medalists Tommie Smith (gold) and John Carlos (bronze) raised their black-gloved fists and bowed their heads

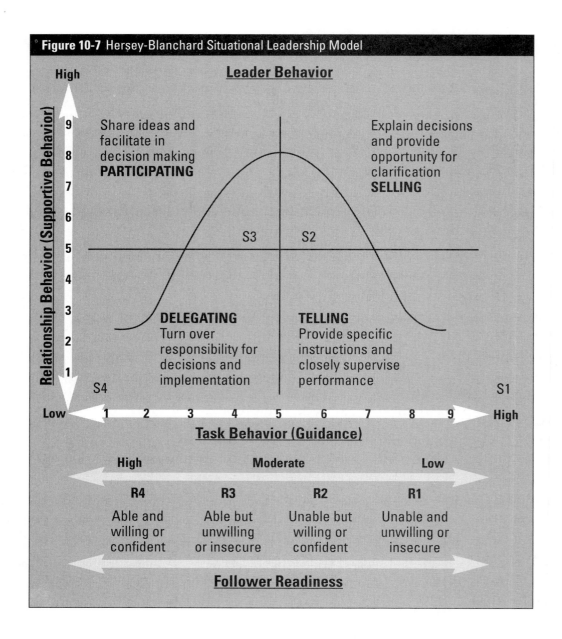

Figure 10-7 Herşey-Blanchard Situational Leadership Model

Leader Behavior

Share ideas and facilitate in decision making
PARTICIPATING

Explain decisions and provide opportunity for clarification
SELLING

S3   S2

DELEGATING
Turn over responsibility for decisions and implementation

TELLING
Provide specific instructions and closely supervise performance

S4   S1

Relationship Behavior (Supportive Behavior)

Task Behavior (Guidance)

R4	R3	R2	R1
Able and willing or confident	Able but unwilling or insecure	Unable but willing or confident	Unable and unwilling or insecure

High — Moderate — Low

Follower Readiness

during the playing of "The Star-Spangled Banner" at the 1968 Mexico City Summer Games to raise awareness of the discrimination faced by African Americans (Webb, 2001). At those same games, the Mexican government brought out troops to quell protesters who criticized the expenditures for staging the games while millions of Mexicans lived in poverty. The troops fired on protesters, killing hundreds (Hessler, 2001). In addition, Killanin had to deal with the aftermath of the 1972 Summer Games in Munich, Germany, when terrorists took nine Israeli athletes and coaches hostage and demanded the release of Palestinian prisoners in Israel. The siege, broadcast live during ABC's coverage of the Games, ended after an attack by German police at a nearby airfield. In all, nine hostages and five terrorists were killed. In spite of calls for the Games to then be canceled, Brundage allowed them to go on (Reeve, 2000). Killanin also had to deal with the related political issues of boycotts. In response to the Soviet army's invasion of Afghanistan in 1979, President Jimmy Carter moved to keep U.S. Olympians from competing in the 1980 Summer Games in Moscow. The Soviets had considered matching the boycott and sitting out the Lake Placid Games, but finally opted to send their athletes. However, the Soviets and aligned nations responded and stayed away from the 1984 Summer Games in Los Angeles. The political matters facing him were indeed thorny, and Killanin ultimately proved unable to overcome them and act as a transformational leader.

Samaranch built on the efforts of Killanin to open the Games to all competitors and stabilized the IOC and Olympism financially, but he failed in efforts to stem the tide of doping and was scarred by the bribery issues associated with the host site bidding process. As former Olympic gold medallist Carl Lewis remarked offhandedly recently, "The weight guys (shot put, discus, hammer), they're all on drugs" (Deford, 2001, p. 58). The newest head of the IOC, Belgian Jacques Rogge (named in July 2001), will face the challenge of becoming a transformational leader and leading the Olympic movement into the twenty-first century.

In recent years, as interest in achieving continually higher levels of performance has increased dramatically, a number of researchers and theorists have focused their efforts on identifying what the essential elements of transformational leadership might be. Researchers James Kouzes and Barry Posner (1987, 1990) identified five behaviors common to transformational leaders (see Figure 10-8).

Figure 10-8 Characteristics of a Transformational Leader

1. **They inspire a shared vision.** They have a mission in which they passionately believe, and they tirelessly enlist others to share in that mission and to help make it happen.

2. **They challenge the process.** They are unwilling to accept things as they are, they push for change, and they risk mistakes to find better solutions.

3. **They enable others to act.** They emphasize cooperation and collaboration. They build teams and empower their followers.

4. **They model the way.** They live their beliefs. They communicate their vision through the consistency of their actions.

5. **They encourage the heart.** They dramatize encouragement, reward performance, and celebrate winning. They love their people, their customers, their products, and their work.

Leadership and Communication

Effective leadership requires effective communication. Virtually all the leader behaviors, practices, and skills presented in this chapter involve communication. Every leadership task—from providing direction, support, and encouragement to providing inspiration and meaning—can be accomplished only through effective communication.

The Conditions for Effective Communication

Scholar Howard Gardner (1996) took an approach similar to Burns in seeking to understand the nature of leadership. In studying significant social, political, religious, and business leaders, Gardner identified four factors that he cites as crucial to the practice of effective leadership, each of which relates to the key function of communication.

A tie to followers. Gardner states that the relationship between leaders and followers must be ongoing, active, and dynamic, and leaders and followers must take cues from each other. Leaders and followers, says Gardner, must work together to build organizations that embody their common values. This type of connection and collaboration cannot occur without communication. Jacques Rogge (pronounced "rahg"), an orthopedic surgeon, has been an IOC member since 1991, an executive board member, and served as the president of the European Olympic Committees and chairman for the coordination committee for the highly successful 2000 Sydney Games. This tie to the many facets of Olympic activities should help Rogge, who is also a former world champion in yachting and competed in the 1968, 1972, and 1976 Games, as the identified symbolic leader of the Olympic movement.

A certain rhythm of life. Gardner states that a leader must be in regular contact with his or her followers while maintaining a sense of his or her own mind, thoughts, values, and strategies. Opportunities for reflections are important for preserving these personal attributes. Like all IOC heads, Rogge will be challenged to meet these expectations, keeping contact with the many stakeholder groups while sustaining his own individual concepts of what is important for the success of the IOC. Communication with these groups will be critical to maintaining this regular and constant contact. One symbolic way Rogge sought to do this was to elect to stay in the Olympic village during the Salt Lake City Winter Games. During a tour of the venues and the village several months before the Games, he sat on one of twin beds in the spartan quarters and said, "It's all I need—no more" (Michaelis, 2001f, p. 2C).

An evident relation between stories and embodiments. Gardner argues that leaders exercise their influence through the stories and messages they communicate and through the traits they embody. To Gardner, these stories grow out of life experiences and are naturally embodied in the presentation of the self. Rogge's story is one of long and dedicated service to the IOC and Olympism in many important organizational facets, so he is uniquely and well qualified to serve in the IOC's top post. Rogge also has the image of being uninvolved with the Salt Lake City bribery scandals that plagued the IOC. Rogge's capabilities thus become his story, one he can communicate to followers and stakeholders to hasten the achievement of IOC goals.

The centrality of choice. To Gardner, effective leaders are those who are chosen by followers, rather than those who take power by means of brute force or instruments of terror. The mechanisms of the IOC are organized in such a way that the president is chosen by the current IOC membership. Candidates to the post are permitted to lobby for election, but the ultimate choice remains with the membership and is presumably based on the merits of each candidate. Rogge was selected by his colleagues over Richard Pound of Canada (who had appeared to be the most qualified candidate because he had headed the IOC's anti-doping organization, negotiated the IOC's TV deals, and headed the investigation of the Salt Lake City bribery scandal); Un Yong Kim of South Korea (the former head of that country's CIA); Pal Schmitt of Hungary; and American Anita DeFrantz. He was chosen because of his specific abilities, which serve to legitimize his path to leadership. However, Rogge will also have to overcome the perception that Samaranch wanted Rogge as his successor so he could continue to influence the IOC and was able to engineer his election because many of Samaranch's cronies in the IOC had come to despise Pound because of the post–Salt Lake City scandal expulsions ("IOC Image," 2001, McDonnell, 2001b).

Epilogue

So was the success of the 1980 U.S. Olympic men's ice hockey team a miracle or something else? True, Herb Brooks created a high-performance environment where his team was motivated to perform at levels that allowed them to succeed personally while allowing the team to prosper. The 1980 U.S. Olympic men's ice hockey team constituted a high-performance work force, and creating this kind of work force has become an essential management responsibility.

However, even the most carefully developed strategies and structure are not enough to make an organization competitive unless its people are highly motivated to perform. As noted earlier, at the 1998 Winter Games in Nagano, Japan, a team of American NHL stars, including Brett Hull and Mike Richter, came into the games with dreams of winning the gold. The entire NHL season had been put on hold for over two weeks to allow NHL players from all nations to participate. However, the U.S. team underperformed and failed to qualify for the medal round. The Czech team, led by NHL stars Dominek Hasek and Jaromir Jagr, won the gold, and the U.S. players trashed their Olympic village rooms before returning to America. Interestingly, only a few players on the 1980 U.S. team (notably Ken Morrow and Dave Christian) had significant NHL careers. Winning a gold medal apparently meant little to the American NHL stars in 1998, but certainly meant something to the Czech NHLers.

But was the win in Lake Placid truly a miracle? Two decades later, goaltender Jim Craig reflected, "A bunch of talented, dedicated guys who believed in one goal, and took all their personal satisfactions away to achieve it. If that's a miracle, I believe in that." In an effort to capture the magic of 1980, Herb Brooks was named to coach the team for the 2002 Winter Games in Salt Lake City.

Creating a high-performance workforce has become an essential management responsibility, particularly with the increased level and intensity of global competition that sports organizations face. Four theories help managers understand the factors that influence and shape individual and group performance. First, goals provide the direction and feedback to engage and to challenge people toward high levels of performance. Second, reinforcement theory provides the basis for shaping behavior through a carefully selected set of consequences. Next, needs theory suggests that managers must understand the needs level of employees and create opportunities for them to pursue the satisfaction of their needs in the workplace. Lastly, expectancy theory emphasizes the links between success and the rewards that people value.

Reflecting ideas from this range of theories, sports organizations increasingly are focusing their efforts in four areas: (1) defining tasks in the most challenging and specific terms possible; (2) providing continuous training to ensure the competence and confidence required for high performance; (3) empowering employees by sharing responsibility with them for decisions and problem solving around their own performance; and (4) providing employees a stake in the success of the organization, a reason to pursue high performance.

Leadership is the process of directing and supporting others in pursuit of the organization's missions and goals. With the competitive pressure of the changing international sports environment, leadership is more important than ever as sports organizations seek to develop high-performance work forces.

One focus of the research on leadership has been on the leader as a person, on the psychology of the leader. This research has resulted in identifying a number of personality traits that are associated with effective leaders. Two sets of assumptions that leaders have about their followers—Theory X and Theory Y—have also been identified, which emphasize the importance of leaders' having accurate assumptions about worker motivation. Additionally, in terms of the psychology of the leader, the importance of leader expectations has been documented.

Research has also examined the behaviors of effective leaders. Initially the focus was on identifying the one most effective leadership style. Subsequent research resulted in developing contingency models of leadership that emphasize the importance of matching leadership style to the needs or demands of the situation. Most recently there has been interest in the transformational leader, the leader who succeeds in changing the beliefs and attitudes of followers to enable them to achieve unprecedented levels of performance.

Communication is the tool through which the leader provides support and direction. Effective communication requires an understanding on the manager's part of followers' needs and concerns. For this reason, effective communication relies on a leader's tie to followers as each takes cues from the other, a certain rhythm of life where leaders stay in regular contact with followers, an evident relation between stories and embodiments, and the centrality of choice.

The leadership responsibility in all sports organizations is a critical one. In many ways, leadership represents the connection between the sports organization and its people. Understanding how to develop most effectively and to maintain the leadership connection is a significant challenge, to say the least. Some IOC presidents met different aspects of this challenge, proving that high performance is a difficult goal to achieve in such a complex set of organizational relationships, but possible when the leadership connection works.

Chapter 10: Motivation and Leadership

Summary

Beijing 2008—The Great Leap (and Sprint and Throw) Forward or Backward?

As noted earlier, IOC president Jacques Rogge has identified a number of challenges for the IOC and associated organizations and stakeholders. One major concern Rogge inherited was the bureaucratic delays and snafus plaguing the city of Athens as organizers struggled to meet the venue and infrastructure construction requirements necessary to host the upcoming 2004 Summer Games (Lynch, 2001), as well as the increasing concern over security issues for the Salt Lake City Games that arose in the wake of the September 11, 2001, terrorist attacks. Rogge will also be expected to review and rescind the IOC's ban on visiting host cities, instituted after the SLOC bribery scandal, in time for IOC members to visit cities bidding for the 2010 Winter Games in 2003. These visits would be paid for and managed by the IOC rather than the bid cities (Michaelis, 2001b). There is also the issue of webcasting and real-time Internet video broadcasting, which the IOC banned during the 2000 Sydney Games to protect the television broadcast audiences (the octogenarian Samaranch later admitted he was truly uncertain about what to do with these technologies [Burton, 2001]), but the use of these technologies will be unavoidable in subsequent Games.

www.beijing-2008.org

Another challenge, which came just three days before his election, was the selection of Beijing as the host city for the 2008 Summer Games. The Chinese capital, which lost by two votes (cast by secret ballot by the IOC members) to Sydney in its bid for the 2000 Games in 1993, was chosen over bids from Toronto (which had 70 percent of the necessary venues already in place), Istanbul, Osaka, and Paris. To land the Games, Chinese officials hired Western public relations specialists (who enlisted Chinese martial arts star Jackie Chan for a promotional video aimed at swaying IOC voters). The Chinese also stated that they would spend between $20 and $30 billion to modernize Beijing's airport and other infrastructure, build the required thirty-seven competition venues (most of which are to be located in Olympic Park on the northern outskirts of the city), and clean up its pollution and environmental hazards (the city, with a population of 12 million, is one of the world's most polluted capitals) (Liu, 2001; Powers, 2001c, 2001e).

According to many in China, the country lost the bid in 1993 because of human rights concerns and sought to win the Games to improve the world's view of China, even though the concepts of competitive sport as practiced in the West (and virtually all Olympic sports) are practically unknown there (Hessler, 2001). However, one young prospective Chinese table tennis athlete gushed, "Having the Olympics here will let foreigners see what a great and powerful country this is" (McDonnell, 2001a).

Even so, to many, the bid of the former runner-up would have been a slam dunk had it not been for China's longstanding poor record on human rights, as evidenced by the Tiananmen Square antidemocracy crackdown in 1989, an Amnesty International report that alleged China executed more people in three months in 2001—1,781—than the rest of the world had in the previous three years (Nichols, Michaelis, & Wiseman, 2001), and the 2001 standoff with the United States over the Chinese detainment of a U.S. spy plane and its crew after a midair collision with a Chinese fighter plane off China's Hainan Island. After the affair, the U.S. House of Representatives' Committee on International Relations approved a nonbinding resolution urging the IOC to deny Beijing's bid (Michaelis, 2001e). The European Parliament also passed a similar resolution a week before the decision, citing China's "disastrous record on human rights" that made it "an unsuitable venue" (Powers, 2001d, p. E1).

Many critics also point out that the authoritarian communist leadership of China will impose its will on its people to meet the demands of hosting the Games, and many people will lose homes and land without input or compensation.

After the House committee action, then-IOC vice president Richard Pound warned the United States that its political machinations could be damaging, saying, "The U.S. should be cautious, particularly if it is going to have a candidate in the field for 2012" (Menez, 2001, p. 27). Even the four American IOC members, including failed IOC presidential candidate Anita DeFrantz, who had been unable to compete at the 1980 Games because of the U.S. boycott, did not support penalizing the Chinese because of political concerns. Supporters of the Beijing bid hoped the awarding of the Games to China would push the country toward more cultural and political reforms, although commentator Frank Deford pointed out that countries should be rewarded after they make reforms (it didn't make the Nazis change in 1936 or the Soviets in 1980), not in anticipation of them, and that those who feel politics should not be a factor in choosing sites often contradictorily state that the Games would push recalcitrant countries toward political reforms (McDonnell, 2001b). Two former U.S. ambassadors to China agreed, as Jim Sasser, ambassador during the Clinton administration, wrote, "The focus of the world's media on the Olympics will bring further liberalization of the Chinese press and accelerated restraints on the police" (Sasser, 2001, p. 11A). However, Congressman Tom Santos (D-Calif.) complained that the IOC's decision "would allow the Chinese police state to bask in the reflected glory of the Olympic Games despite having one of the most abominable human rights records in the world" (Powers, 2001e, p. A1).

It is clear that the United States had neither the clout nor the commitment from its IOC members to block Beijing's bid, but Rogge must still be wary of any changes in the political climate that may occur between now and 2008. Another spy plane incident or another U.S. military exercise with Taiwan could prompt the USOC to take its own actions in response to public pressure in the United States and could thrust the IOC back into the boycott vortex of the 1980s. And this could hurt the IOC financially, because most of their revenues come from broadcast deals with NBC ($3.6 billion for the rights to all Games through 2008). No U.S. team in Beijing, and NBC's ratings plummet. No one in the United States is going to tune in to watch a tape-delayed broadcast of the 50-meter freestyle women's swimming event with Australians, Chinese, Germans, but no Americans. Plus, what about all the TOP corporations that shelled out millions to reach potential customers?

1. As we noted earlier, in supporting high-performance work teams, the focus of the leader's energy and activities shifts from the team members to the organization surrounding the work team. Jacques Rogge's task is to reduce or eliminate the barriers and interference that might hinder the team's performance and to assist the team in securing the resources it needs to achieve its goals. Which teams are we talking about? Which organizations? What barriers and interference? What resources?

2. Can Rogge's behaviors in response to China-U.S. conflicts influence the performance of followers and other stakeholder groups? How might he affect them positively? How might he affect them negatively? What specific leader behaviors would you recommend to solve Rogge's challenge? Cite models or concepts from this chapter to support your recommendations.

3. How can Rogge become a transformational leader for the IOC?

A legacy to forget. (2001, July 16). *Montreal Gazette*, p. B2.

Bartlett, D. L., Steele, J. B., Karmatz, L., & Levinstein, J. (2001, December 10). Snow job. *Sports Illustrated*, pp. 78–98.

Bennis, W., & Nanus, B. (1985). *Leaders*. New York: Harper & Row.

Blake, R. R., & Mouton, J. S. (1982, February). How to choose a leadership style. *Training and Development Journal*, pp. 38–45.

Blake, R. R., & Mouton, J. S. (1985). *The managerial grid III*. Houston, TX: Gulf.

Bleakley, F. R. (1993, July 6). Many companies try management fads, only to see them flop. *Wall Street Journal*, pp. A1–A6.

Brockinton, L. (2001, February 26–March 6). Live TV events, fewer profiles on NBC. *Street & Smith's SportsBusiness Journal*, p. 26.

Burns, J. M. (1978). *Leadership*. New York: Harper & Row.

Burton, R. (2001, August 20–26). IOC's new emperor takes stock of his realm. *Street & Smith's SportsBusiness Journal*, p. 34.

Byrd, A. (2000, December 11–17). Jumping through hoops in search of Olympic rings. *Street & Smith's SportsBusiness Journal*, pp. 1, 34, 35.

Conger, J. A., & Kanungo, R. N. (1988, July). The empowerment process: Integrating theory into practice. *Academy of Management Review*, pp. 473–474.

deMause, N. (2001, April 10). Preening, pride, & a pyrrhic prize. [online]. Available: http://www.sportsjones.com/sj/35.shtml.

Deford, F. (2001, August 6). Time bandits. *Sports Illustrated*, pp. 56–62.

Farber, M. (2001, December 17). The village idiots. *Sports Illustrated*, p. 60.

Fleishman, E. A., Harris, E. F., & Burtt, H. E. (1955). *Leadership and supervision in industry*. Columbus: Ohio State University Bureau of Business Research.

Fuchsberg, G. (1992, October 1). "Total quality" is termed only partial success. *Wall Street Journal*, pp. B1–B9.

Gardner, H., with Laskin, E. (1996). *Leading minds*. New York: Basic.

Heifetz, R. A., & Laurie, D. L. (1998). The work of leadership. In *Harvard Business Review on leadership* (pp. 171–197). Boston: Harvard Business School Press.

Helyar, J. (1994). *Lords of the realm*. New York: Ballantine.

Hersey, P., & Blanchard, K. H. (1982). *Management of organizational behavior: Utilizing human resources* (4th ed.). Englewood Cliffs, NJ: Prentice-Hall.

Hessler, P. (2001, May 7). Great sprint forward. *The New Yorker*, pp. 38–44.

Hill, C. R. (1996). *Olympic politics: Athens to Atlanta 1896–1996* (2d ed.). Manchester, England: Manchester University Press.

Hyland, B. (Producer). (2001, April 9). *Do you believe in miracles? The story of the 1980 Olympic hockey team*. Los Angeles: Home Box Office.

IOC image takes a pounding. (2000, July 17). *Montreal Gazette*, p. 87.

Katz, D., Maccoby, N. M., & Morse, N. (1950). *Productivity, supervision, and morale in an office situation*. Ann Arbor: University of Michigan Institute of Social Research.

Kirkpatrick, S. A., & Locke, E. A. (1991). Leadership: Do traits matter? *Academy of Management Executive*, 2(5), p. 49.

References

Kotter, J. P. (1998). What leaders really do. In *Harvard Business Review on leadership* (pp. 37–60). Boston: Harvard Business School Press.

Kouzes, J. M., & Posner, B. Z. (1987). *The leadership challenge: How to get extraordinary things done in organizations*. San Francisco: Jossey-Bass.

Kouzes, J. M., & Posner, B. Z. (1990). The credibility factor: What followers expect from their leaders. *Business Credit, 92*, pp. 24–28.

Ladler, M. (2001, July 14). The bill for these Games could exceed $20 billion. *New York Times,* pp. B16–17.

Leuty, R. (2000, December 11–17). Bay Area bid unites disparate interests, from Monterey to Sacramento. *Street & Smith's SportsBusiness Journal,* pp. 45–46.

Liu, M. (2001, July 16). All that glitters . . . *Newsweek*, pp. 30–32.

Lloyd, J. (2001, August 14). USOC president renews backing for interim CEO Blackmun. *USA Today,* p. 10C.

Lynch, D. J. (2001, February 14). Rising out of the ruins? *USA Today,* pp. 1C–2C.

Manz, C. C. (1992, July–August). Self-leadership . . . the heart of empowerment. *Journal for Quality and Participation*, pp. 80–85.

Maslow, A. (1970). *Motivation and personality* (2d ed.). New York: Harper & Row.

Mathes, K. (1992, March). Empowerment: Fact or fiction? *HRfocus*, pp. 1, 6.

McDonnell, E. (Executive producer). (2001a, July 11). *Morning edition*. Washington, DC: National Public Radio.

McDonnell, E. (Executive producer). (2001b, August 15). *Morning edition*. Washington, DC: National Public Radio.

McGregor, D. T. (1960). *The human side of enterprise*. New York: McGraw-Hill.

Menez, G. (2001, April 23). Five-ring circus. *Sports Illustrated*, p. 27.

Michaelis, V. (2001a, February 8). Leaders: Focus will be on stars, not trial. *USA Today*, p. 2C.

Michaelis, V. (2001b, May 15). Bids for 2008 Games low-key. *USA Today,* p. 3C.

Michaelis, V. (2001c, July 9). Samaranch era flickering out. *USA Today*, p. 3C.

Michaelis, V. (2001d, July 10). Bidders hold on to hope. *USA Today,* p. 8C.

Michaelis, V. (2001e, July 11). Top candidates take Baldwin remark in stride. *USA Today*, p. 10C.

Michaelis, V. (2001f, August 8). Pound doubts reform's hold in IOC. *USA Today*, p. 2C.

Nichols, B., Michaelis, V., & Wiseman, P. (2001, July 9). Why China is likely to land the Olympics. *USA Today*, pp. 1A–2A.

Olympic marketing revenue distribution. (2000). The International Olympic Committee. [online]. Available: http://www.olympic.org /ioc/e/facts/finance/fin_mark _intro_e.html.

Powers, J. (2001a, February 15). Light their fire. *Boston Globe*, pp. C1–C2.

Powers, J. (2001b, April 12). Solid field poised to replace Samaranch. *Boston Globe*, p. C9.

Powers, J. (2001c, May 26). Rights, wrongs collide in '08. *Boston Globe,* p. G9.

Powers, J. (2001d, July 13). Beijing looks to win Games. *Boston Globe*, pp. E1, E7.

Powers, J. (2001e, July 14). Beijing gets nod for 2008 Olympics. *Boston Globe*, pp. A1, G6.

Powers, J. (2001f, October 22). Ex-Maytag exec named USOC CEO. *Boston Globe*, p. B3.

Recent Olympic Games broadcast coverage has achieved unparalleled success. (2000). International Olympic Committee. [online]. Available: http://www.olympic.org /ioc/e/facts/marketing/mark_broad_ cover_e.html.

Reeve, S. (2000). *One day in September*. New York: Arcade.

Sasser, J. (2001, July 13). Olympics would spur change. *USA Today*, p. 11A.

Senn, A. E. (1999). *Power, politics, and the Olympic Games*. Champaign, IL: Human Kinetics.

Single, J. L. (1980). The power of expectations: Productivity and the self-fulfilling prophecy. *Management World, 19*, pp. 37–38.

Skinner, B. F. (1953). *Science and human behavior*. New York: Macmillan.

Skinner, B. F. (1972). *Beyond freedom and dignity*. New York: Knopf.

Swift, E. M. (2001, June 11). Going out with a shout. *Sports Illustrated*, pp. 44, 46.

The Olympic Charter. (2000). The International Olympic Committee. [online]. Available: http://www .olympic.org/ioc/e/facts/charter /charter_intro_e.html.

The Outlook's dismay with Indian sportsman Jim Thorpe and the forfeiture of his Olympic medals. (1997). In S. A. Reiss (Ed.), *Major problems in American sport history* (pp. 281–283). Boston: Houghton Mifflin.

Vroom, V. H. (1964). *Work and motivation*. New York: Wiley.

Webb, R. (2001, April 10). "If these boys are serious . . ." Sportsjones [online]. Available: http://www .newcitycgi.com/sj.

Woodward, S. (2001, January 1–7). Blake: USOC at risk without changes. *Street & Smith's SportsBusiness Journal*, pp. 1, 32.

Chapter 11

Human Resource Management

Purpose: To present and promote sport competition through single events and series.

Stakeholders: Tour athletes, tour facilities, facility designers, maintenance and equipment providers, host communities, spectators, sponsors, media, sport governing bodies/agencies, volunteers, media, general public, federal, state, and local government.

Size and scope: Thousands of professional and amateur sport events and series throughout the United States. Includes traditional tour sports, outdoor adventure/extreme sports, and sport entertainment enterprises.

Governance:
- Federal, state, and local regulation
- Professional organizations, associations, and trade groups such as the United States Golf Association (USGA), Professional Golf Association (PGA), United States Tennis Association (USTA), International Jet Sports Boating Association, American Speed Association, Gravity Games, Professional Rodeo Cowboys Association (PRCA), Harness Tracks of America (HTA), X Games, and Bass Anglers Sportsman Society (BASS).

Inside Look

Can Rob Get a Job?

Rob Warinski has just completed his senior year in college and will graduate in two weeks. Much like Dan Weinberg, the agent for Woolf Associates profiled in Chapter 8, Rob has been an avid golfer all his life. He received his first set of clubs from his parents for his tenth birthday and spent time at his local golf course during just about every spare moment. He secured his first part-time job at the course on the grounds maintenance staff when he was fourteen. For the next eight years, Rob spent summer vacations, holidays, weekends, and after-school time working at the course in a variety of capacities. He worked in the pro shop, at the snack bar, at tournaments, and on the course itself. Rob was eager to learn everything he could about the golf business and was happy to take on any job that came his way. Rob scheduled tee times, took inventory in the pro shop, resolved customer complaints, met with golf equipment sales representatives, fixed golf carts, assisted the pro with junior lessons, helped with landscaping, and even cleaned the rest rooms.

During Rob's college years, he participated on the university golf team, and as part of his sport management curriculum, he completed an internship with Titleist. He also volunteered at the annual United Way Golf Tournament, assisted with the intramural golf program, and worked three nights a week as an assistant manager of the golf department at a large retail sporting goods store. Rob also volunteered to help with the university athletic department golf tournament. He coordinated student volunteers and managed golfer registration. At the tournament, Rob was able to work directly with corporate sponsors and had the opportunity to meet and become friends with many of the university alumni including several alums who work in sport. In fact, it was through one of these contacts that Rob was able to secure the internship at Titleist. At Titleist, Rob was invited to attend several Professional Golf Association (PGA) and Ladies Professional Golf Association (LPGA) tournaments. At each event, Rob effectively networked as his supervisor introduced him to PGA and LPGA officials, golf course managers, sponsors, members of the media, and some players. At the end of his internship, Rob felt a new enthusiasm for his major and felt for the first time that he really had a good idea of what he wanted to do with his passion for golf.

As the last few months of his undergraduate program and his final season of collegiate golf began to wind down, Rob scheduled an appointment with his college adviser to discuss his postcollege plans. He knew he wanted to work in the golf industry and was particularly interested in tour events. He was eager to explore his options. What should he do? Where should he look? How should he start? Looking over the resume he developed with the university's placement counselor, Rob felt good about both his experience and his education. He knew he was ready to start his professional career and fully expected to realize his lifelong dream of working in tour sport. More than anything else, Rob wanted a job that involved professional golf.

Introduction

Human resources are considered the sports organization's most important asset. People, in essence, are the organization. Their skills, their knowledge, and their abilities dramatically shape the organization and have a critical impact on the organization's ability to carry out its mission and achieve its goals. In this chapter, we introduce the human resource function through an examination of the tour sports industry. We consider the human resource function within a sports organization both from the perspective of a potential employee and as a manager within the organization who is responsible for the staffing function.

The Tour Sports Industry

The tour sports industry consists of those sports organizations that sponsor and participate in sports competitions at various tour event site locales throughout their season. It may be useful to look at the tour sports industry as consisting of three specific segments: traditional tour sports (e.g., golf, tennis, horse racing, rodeo), outdoor-adventure/extreme sports (e.g., skateboarding, fishing, ski surfing, mountain climbing, log rolling), and commercial sports entertainment (e.g., WWF and Harlem Globetrotters) (see Figure 11-1).

The typical tour sports event features a number of individuals or teams that compete in a tournament-type format. Results of individual events may or may not be compiled and recorded as part of a tour series with individual contestants or teams competing for points toward a tour season championship. Such events can take place on a single day or may be held over a period of days. Among the sports currently being offered through the tour sports system are tennis, rodeo, golf, volleyball, speed-boating, mountain biking, cyclo-cross, running, bicycling, skiing, motocross, skateboarding, kayaking, fishing, and white-water rafting.

Traditional tour sports include golf—the PGA, LPGA, Senior PGA, and Buy.com tours; tennis—ATP Tour; and auto racing—NASCAR, IRL, CART tours. One of the best known international tour events is the Tour de France in which cyclists from around the world compete both individually and in teams. Traditional tour sports have gained great popularity in the last decade with professional golf and auto racing accounting for much of the new and heightened interest in this segment of

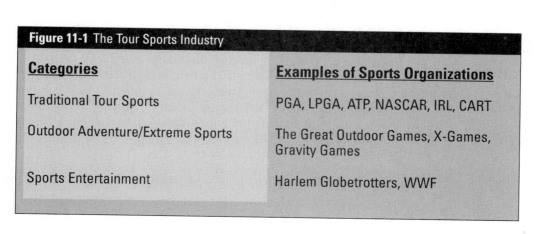

Figure 11-1 The Tour Sports Industry

Categories	Examples of Sports Organizations
Traditional Tour Sports	PGA, LPGA, ATP, NASCAR, IRL, CART
Outdoor Adventure/Extreme Sports	The Great Outdoor Games, X-Games, Gravity Games
Sports Entertainment	Harlem Globetrotters, WWF

Chapter 11: Human Resource Management

the tour sports industry. Once thought to be a regional interest sport for blue-collar fans, professional stock car racing continues to capture the attention of sports fans throughout the country. Television ratings attest to the increasing population of NASCAR. In 2001 races on Fox network drew an average of 19.9 million viewers and a total of 278 million viewers for fourteen Winston Cup events, more than double the 133 million viewers for the first half of the previous season when the broadcasts were distributed across several networks (King, 2001, p. 4).

The second category of tour sport includes outdoor adventure/extreme sports. These events feature an amalgamation of competition or contests. Some of these tour events encompass nontraditional sports activities that have been identified as adventure sports or extreme sports because they are characterized as rebellious and high risk. Some people even suggest that part of the attraction is that these sports are inherently dangerous and athletes are constantly pushing the limits as they attempt to jump higher, go faster, and add new twists and elements that have never been done before. Participation in extreme sports events requires a high level of skill and a willingness to push both the human body and the sports equipment to the limit. Extreme sports events feature competition in nontraditional sports such as motocross, freestyle skiing, and skateboarding. The emphasis is frequently on the performance of the individual athlete rather than a team.

Extreme sports are particularly identified with young athletes who have created the extreme sports culture to counter what they have viewed as a conservative and excessively commercial traditional sports industry. The Gravity Games, created in 1997, and X-Games, which began two years before, are examples of tour sports competitions based on extreme sports. These events are targeted to young extreme sports athletes and their fans, an audience that corporations often identify as a highly desirable demographic group. It is also a group that has money. Extreme sports enthusiasts ages ten to twenty-four are estimated to have a total discretionary income of $250 billion, and as a segment will grow to 64 million by 2015 (Krantz, 2001). This is a consumer group that many companies covet. For the 2001 X Games in Philadelphia, EPSN sold out its entire inventory of sponsorship packages weeks before the event for a total of $30 million. The highest level event sponsorships, which require a minimum $2.5 million investment, included significant organizations and manufacturers of major products such as Mountain Dew, Taco Bell, Pontiac, 1-800-CALL-ATT, and adidas, all five of which renewed sponsorships from the previous year (Brockinton, 2001b).

Interestingly enough, it may be argued that in the creation of these extreme sports events and competitions, extreme athletes and their fans have begun to adopt some of the trappings of highly organized traditional sports (corporate sponsorship, endorsements, television deals) that this countersport culture had previously criticized. In effect, sport that had been considered a fringe or niche sport comes into the mainstream through the formal organization of tour events and the subsequent popularization of extreme sports competition. This is even more significant because research shows that more and more young people are less apt to be involved with traditional team sports, even the de rigueur ones such as soccer and lacrosse, and are more likely to gravitate toward individual pursuits like the so-called extreme sports (Putnam, 2001).

Other tour sports events in this category offer outdoor adventure activities rather than extreme sports. Adventure-type tour sports also feature activities or sports events that have been characterized as being out of the sports mainstream. For example, the Great Outdoor Games, created by ESPN, features twenty-one events in four competition areas that include fishing, target sports, timber events, and sporting dogs. The event draws more than three hundred competitors and is nationally televised on both network and cable television (Brockinton, 2001a, p. 15).

The third category of tour sports may be defined as sports entertainment. Sports entertainment events are commercial in nature and may or may not have a predetermined outcome. The sports event is often tightly scripted, and comedy or drama is played out within a sport context. The most well-known examples of sport entertainment include the Harlem Globetrotters and the World Wrestling Federation (WWF). Both of these sport organizations offer sport entertainment as part of a tour or series and have been very successful in playing to full arenas throughout the country. Other tour sports entertainment organizations include the Harlem Wizards (basketball) and King and His Court (softball). Tour sports exhibitions such as those found in figure skating or gymnastics may also be included in this category. Some tour sports entertainment teams travel from city to city and often arrange to play a home team made up of local all-stars or celebrities as an exhibition or fund-raising event. A portion of the proceeds is usually designated to a local charity or the sponsoring organization.

Another interesting feature of the tour sports industry is its dependence on sponsorship because of the high cost involved in putting on these events. Partnerships with corporations, media, or businesses may bring a host of benefits to the event including equipment, volunteers, operations capital, media opportunities, and prize money. ESPN has actually created tour events as a way to develop compelling programming and attract specific target audiences. Fox Sports Net has created the new Alternative Sports World Cup, a competition intended to draw extreme athletes from more than twenty countries (Brockinton, 2001, p. 13). Athletes compete individually and for their countries as they participate in extreme events such as street luge, mountain biking, and motocross. David Hill, CEO of Fox Sports Television Group, argues that "alternative sports make great television. . . . I think that maybe in 15, 20 years, they could well be just as powerful and have as big a fan base as the major sports now" (Brockinton, 2001a, p. 13).

Sponsors may be secured on the tour series level, the individual event level, and on the athlete level. For example, NASCAR's championship series is known as the Winston Cup Series, and Western clothing manufacturer Wrangler is the title sponsor of the professional rodeo tour. One of the best examples of individual event sponsors is the professional golf tour where events often carry title sponsors such as the *Canon* Greater Hartford Open or the *Buick* Open.

As we discussed in Chapter 8, individual athletes who participate in the tour sports system often rely on sponsorship as well. Golfers, tennis players, cyclists, skateboarders, runners, surfers, and drivers often utilize corporate partnerships to help pay for entry fees, travel, equipment, lodging, food, clothing, and living expenses. Tennis players or golfers, for example, may sign a deal with a sneaker or equipment manufacturer. They may agree to use the particular brand of equipment in competition in return for free equipment or cash. A sponsor need not necessarily be obviously related to the particular sport. However, the corporate sponsor always seeks an appropriate fit with the property (series, event, athlete) and the fan base. LPGA Tour player Pamela Kerrigan, for example, is sponsored by Fiskars Consumer Products, best known for making orange-handled scissors. Although scissors may seem to have little to do with golf, Fiskars has determined that the fit with the LPGA player and LPGA fans makes their sponsorship an effective one because it helps facilitate the achievement of their business goals. Kerrigan carries a Fiskars golf bag and wears Fiskars-branded golf apparel while playing tour events and making public appearances.

The National Thoroughbred Racing Association and Breeders' Cup partnership has sought sponsorship on the event level. They have been selling sponsorships to various races and divisions in the Breeders' Cup Series. Bessemer Trust will be the title sponsor of the Breeders' Cup Juvenile, a race for two-year-old colts and geldings at the Breeders' Cup at Belmont Park and will also be the title sponsor for the Juvenile Challenge, a series of seven races to air on national television (A. Bernstein, 2001). Bessemer, a New York–based banking company and investment specialist will receive commercial spots, onsite advertising, and hospitality in return for its estimated $1 million-plus financial commitment to the National Thoroughbred Racing Association and Breeders' Cup.

Certainly NASCAR has deservedly received recognition as the most effective and efficient organization in utilizing corporate sponsorship in the tour sports industry. The Winston Cup series, along with NASCAR's other tours such as the Busch Grand National and the Craftsman Truck Series, has long since broken out of its good ol' boy, moonshine-runnin' roots to reach fans and markets across the United States. It enjoys increasing TV ratings in cities like San Diego and Detroit, track attendance at races in nonsouthern locales such as Loudon, New Hampshire, Las Vegas, and metro Chicago, and the recent appearance of pop music star Britney Spears giving the starting call of "Gentlemen, start your engines!" at the 2001 Pepsi 400 at Florida's Daytona International Speedway (Cruz, 2001), notable in that Spears also performs in a series of TV ads for Pepsi. In a similar vein, comedian and motor sports enthusiast Jay Leno served as the pace car driver for the 2001 Brickyard 400 in Indianapolis. NBC, which broadcast the race, sought to leverage its involvement to a broader segment of its viewers by featuring Leno, the host of NBC's *The Tonight Show*. These efforts by Pepsi and NBC show that corporations invest and become involved in NASCAR in part because of its broad national appeal, but also work in conjunction with NASCAR to broaden this appeal further.

NASCAR is the sports organization that has most successfully leveraged sponsorships on the tour, event, and athlete level. Fans and media alike refer to cars not solely in terms of their drivers, but also in conjunction with the car's main sponsor. It isn't Mark Martin's #6 car, it's Mark Martin's #6 Viagra Ford Taurus. Pfizer, the pharmaceutical manufacturer of the product, spends approximately $2 million annually for the prominent hood, rear quarter panel, and back panel locations and the de facto naming rights for the car. Pfizer and the makers of nonautomotive products and services like Home Depot (that sponsors Tony Stewart), Miller Lite (Rusty Wallace), Tide (Ricky Craven), and UPS (Dale Jarrett), along with companies that make automotive products like Citgo (Jeff Burton), Interstate Batteries (Bobby Labonte), and Pennzoil (Steve Park), make these investments because they know, as we discussed in Chapter 1, that fans identify strongly with the drivers. In addition, they know that fans can identify and recall their sponsorship activities and that they make purchasing decisions in part based on these sponsorships. Recent research shows that nearly three-quarters of NASCAR fans buy products to support their favorite drivers (Hagstrom, 1998). Simply put, if a fan likes Ricky Craven, then he or she is nearly 75 percent more likely to buy Tide because of Tide's support of Craven.

Sponsors will continue to turn to tour sports organizations to promote and sell their products and will become increasingly creative in developing mutually beneficial sponsorship partnerships. A sponsorship package developed jointly by ESPN, Comcast, and video game maker Konami may provide insight into future directions of tour sports sponsorship. The three organizations came together to promote sales of the X Games and a new video game called ESPN X Games Skateboarding made by Konami (Brockinton, 2001b). Comcast and ESPN will sponsor a video-game playing tournament (featuring Konami's recently released ESPN X Games Skateboarding game) called the X Gamers Challenge. Qualifying tournaments will be held in Philadelphia, corporate headquarters to Comcast and home to the First Union Center, which is owned by Comcast. Philadelphia is also the site of the Summer X Games. Metro-area tournament winners will compete in the first ever Summer X Games video-game playing tournament where the contest has been sanctioned as an official X games event. ESPN has agreed to cover the tournament as part of its regular X games broadcast. A marketing campaign for the video game available on PlayStation2 and GameBoy Advance will prominently feature the competition, and media buys include television and print advertising in ESPN-owned magazines.

Human Resources in Sports Organizations

The challenge of securing a position in the sports industry can be daunting to any graduating sport management student. Although competition for jobs in sport is intense, many opportunities are available to a skilled student who is willing to work hard, be persistent, and consider the full spectrum of segments that make up the sports industry. For students and nonstudents alike seeking to secure a job in sport, it is important to understand how the human resource function works in sport.

There really are two different tracks or types of human resource development in sports organizations. One is the athlete, performer, or "talent" track. It may be useful to think of this track as being the "on-field" side of human resource management. It is the means by which sports organizations secure athletes or other highly skilled specialty performers for their organization. In professional sport, for example, this area is called *player development*. The player or talent development side of the sports business is distinct in that a variety of unique systems and practices have been developed to assure the organization is able to find, develop, and secure player "talent."

Components of this system are controlled on the league level for the express purpose of managing the on-field side of human resources. For example, the league sets forth the terms and conditions for acquiring players either through the draft or by trades. Leagues through basic labor agreements with players unions may also set minimum salaries, requirements for free agency, and other important policies and guidelines for the management of player talent. Leagues, owners, agents, and player unions have a vested interest in influencing how player talent is managed. Leagues and owners are particularly interested in the distribution and management of player talent and its effect on league operations. For example, the draft system has been seen as a mechanism by which competitive balance among teams can be created—teams that have finished poorly in any year have better draft positions and theoretically are able to improve their teams by bringing in new young talent. As discussed in Chapter 8, players unions are focused on establishing and protecting players' interests, and they influence policies and procedures related to the treatment of players through the collective bargaining process.

A variety of systems are related to player development. They include scouting, drafts, developmental leagues, coaches, trainers, and instructional leagues. Sports organizations that depend on the performance of player talent create divisions or departments that focus specifically on player development. The player development division, for example, is likely to include player talent specialists including scouts and instructors, whose sole focus is on the identification, evaluation, and acquisition of appropriate player talent. On the collegiate level, the player development function rests within the athletic department, and specifically with the individual sports program. Coaches and their staffs are responsible for identifying, recruiting, and developing player personnel. In college sport, player development is controlled not only through institutional oversight, but through the NCAA or other governing bodies that establish rules and guidelines pertaining to the recruitment and treatment of the student athlete.

This first track of sports human resource management includes coaches as well as players. Coaches, in fact, are the second critical component of the on-field talent equation. They are an important on-field asset because of the unique abilities, personality, and skills they bring to the sports organization. The professional team and Division I college sports coach may rise to celebrity status, and some sports organizations view the acquisition of a marquee coach as more important than the acquisition of a star player. Because of the coach's role in managing player talent and making critical game decisions, the coaching positions are vital to the performance of the sports organization.

Although this first track of human resource management in sports organizations has predominantly come to mean players and coaches as on-field talent, the category also includes top-level sports broadcasters in the sports media industry segment. These broadcasters are performers who work in a high-profile environment of "on-air" rather than "on-field." For example, sports media personalities such as college basketball analyst Dick Vitale, ex-Oakland Raiders coach and NFL analyst John Madden, and FoxSports' Jim Rome are distinct talents who are unique assets to their sports organizations. They fall into this first track of human resource management because like coaches and players, they are specialty talents. They are highly skilled and have reached the highest level of success within their profession. Like the player and coach, they are at the center of public attention and provide the talent that directly shapes the sports organization's product and, ultimately, its success.

Most sports organizations, however, are predominantly engaged in the second track of sports human resource development, the "off-field" side of human resource management. This area deals with those employees who are not athlete performers, coaches, or media personalities, but are actively engaged in administrative, managerial, or service delivery components of the organization. For example, professional tennis player Andre Agassi, professional figure skater Michelle Kwan, and NASCAR driver Jeff Gordon provide the "talent" and are sports athlete-performers, and the concessions manager, marketing director, arena manager, sports information director, athletic trainer, equipment manager, aerobics instructor, lifeguard, park attendant, and ticket taker are the other half of the human resource equation for sports organizations (and would be where most college students who major in sport management would fit in).

In this chapter, we emphasize the "off-field" side of human resource management because the majority of human resource management in the sports industry occurs in this area. For students studying sport management, a general understanding of human resource practices for the off-field side is most important. Because students themselves are potential off-field employees and because someday they will be involved in managing others, an understanding of off-field human resource management track is relevant. Clearly, the majority of sport management students will pursue careers in sports that focus primarily on managing off-field rather than on-field or on-air personnel.

Additionally, relatively few segments of the sports industry are extensively involved in on-field human resource management. Most sports organizations including recreation departments, sports facilities, sporting goods manufacturers, and fitness clubs, for example, are predominantly engaged in the management of off-field staff. It may be argued that on–field personnel management is, in fact, a specialty of human resource management in sport. Those few students who pursue careers in sport that involve the on-field side of human resource management can build on their academic preparation in the specialty of on-field human resource management through an appropriate internship and professional experience in that area. There are unique issues in "on-field" personnel management including agency (as discussed in Chapters 6 and 8), drafts, salary caps, injured reserve lists, player unions, and collective bargaining. Some of these issues are addressed in other chapters throughout the text and to a limited degree in this chapter, and thorough examination of this topical area can be found in a good sports law or sports labor law text or course.

As students begin their job search in sport, they are often most concerned with personal issues. How does my resume look? Who would hire me? What do I want to do? How much will I be paid? What type of benefits can I expect? Where do I want to live? Am I qualified for a job in this industry? What can I expect in an interview? All of these questions are important to the job seeker, but it is also very valuable to look at the job search from the sports organization's perspective as well. What is the sports organization looking for? Where will they find good candidates? How will they know they are hiring the right person for the job? By looking at the human resource function in sports organizations from management's perspective, sport management students can not only gain insight into the job-seeking process, but can also develop critical knowledge and skills they can then put to good use as employees of a sports organization.

The Importance of Human Resource Management

The sports industry is a growing enterprise that requires sports managers to find and develop the right people with the right skills to move their organization forward. Clearly, the success of the organization hinges on management's ability to secure necessary human resources. In this way, sports organizations are not all that different from other nonsport organizations. In a poll of American managers several years ago, they identified the most significant barrier to the success and growth of their businesses as "attracting and holding on to the people with the right attitudes and the right skills" ("The Worried Rich," 1994). Overcoming this barrier is the challenge of human resource management.

For much of the twentieth century, whether the job involved processing paperwork or producing products, most work was organized in an assembly line approach.

Each worker was responsible for performing fairly simple tasks and for then passing the work on to the next person to continue the process until the job was completed. Training for this kind of work was fairly simple and long lasting, with the technology involved in performing these tasks changing very little over the years. In this approach, the worker is really just an element in the production process, and with just basic education and a good work ethic could perform the typical job quite well.

During the past twenty-five years, however, all of that has changed dramatically. The work to be done has become progressively more complex and demanding. Teamwork is now the basic approach, requiring interpersonal and problem-solving skills that simply weren't necessary on the product or paperwork assembly line. Competency in computer and other information technologies is essential, and increasingly, individuals and teams share in the responsibility for managing performance and promoting and sustaining quality throughout the organization. Ensuring that the organization is attracting and holding on to people with the right attitudes and the right skills is the challenge of human resource management.

The function of human resource management may be defined as "a strategic, integrated collection of employee-centered activities and processes whose objective is to help the organization meet its short and long term goals" (Linnehan, 2001, p. 111.) Some sports organizations have their own human resources department or staff; other smaller organizations often rely on executive management to carry out this function.

Some sports enterprises, including many tour sports organizations, have the complex human resource challenge of not only working with paid staff, but also many volunteers. Volunteers can be a critical resource for many sports organizations, particularly those that require a great deal of labor to carry out their activities. For example, thousands of volunteers work for golf and auto racing tour sports organizations every year. They serve as hosts, course marshals, parking attendants, concessions workers, members of the set-up and clean-up crew, and so on. Sports organizations need volunteer coaches, field maintenance staff, game officials, and scorekeepers. The list of possible event jobs is endless, and event organizers and sports programmers readily admit their reliance on volunteer assistance. The effective performance of volunteers is frequently an important component of successful sports events or sports programs. For this reason, sports managers "must understand volunteer motivation and their satisfaction with the volunteering experience in order to respond effectively to management needs in the areas of recruitment, retention and daily operations" (Farrell, Johnston, & Twynam, 1998, p. 288), so they are able to develop and maintain a strong volunteer corps.

Sports organizations must also rely on volunteers to serve as board members or trustees. As board members, volunteers play a critical role in setting the mission, creating a strategic plan, establishing policy, facilitating community relations, and securing resources for the sports organization (Inglis, 1997). Volunteer board members can bring expertise, experience, and other critical resources to the table.

Human Resource Management Systems and Planning

Progressive and successful sports organizations treat all employees and volunteers as valuable resources. Providing appropriate human resources for the organization involves a series of areas or systems essential to a high-performance work force (see Figure 11-2). With these systems in place, management can recruit, develop, and retain the highly skilled people needed for an organization to pursue and achieve its goals.

As with virtually all management responsibilities, the human resource management process begins with planning. The human resource planning process actually flows naturally from the strategic management process. Once the organization is clear on its mission and on its strategy for pursuing that mission—whether it's a growth or a retrenchment strategy—it becomes essential to ensure the organization has the right number of people with the right skills to accomplish the work necessary for the organization to achieve its strategic goals. For example, at the Tournament Players Club (TPC) at River Highlands, the home of the Canon Greater Hartford Open, managers set forth very specific goals for each year in the areas of administration, accounting, golf course maintenance, golf shop and outside operations, food and beverage, and marketing (see Figure 11-3) based on their mission and strategy. These goals are then analyzed on the basis of staffing needs and requirements in order to achieve the goals.

Job Analysis: Assessing Current Capabilities

Once the manager has determined human resource needs by examining the strategic plan and reviewing goals for the organization, the next task is to look closely at what the organization is currently doing and how this work is being carried out. At this point, the manager should have a thorough understanding of the type of work required for the organization to achieve its goals. He or she must assess current capabilities against these needs in order to construct a human resource plan.

Good managers recognize that an effective human resource plan begins with a clear and comprehensive understanding of all of the types of work the organization is currently capable of performing. Job analysis is the process of determining the skills and other requirements of each of the jobs performed in the organization.

Figure 11-2 A General Model for Human Resource Management

Human Resource Management Systems and Planning

Staffing

Training and Development

Performance Evaluation

Compensation

Employee Wellness

Employee Relations

Figure 11-3 Sample Goals with Objectives and Projected Staffing Needs for the TPC at River Highlands

Golf Course Maintenance

- Improve aesthetics of the course

    1. Be more proactive with trees, shrubs, and landscape beds in decline

    2. Implement large tree replacement program

    3. Continue large tree pruning programming

    4. Rebuild all tee beds

    5. Continue improvement plan for mulch hill

    6. Clean and weed native rough on weekly basis

    (Staffing: hire three new maintenance staff; one with expertise in tree management)

Golf Shop

- Limit merchandise shrink to $200 for year

    1. Improve management of consignment pieces

    2. Develop return authorization form

    3. Continue training employees on asset protection

    (Staffing: one additional clerk; secure intern for golf shop)

Typically, this analysis is performed by individuals who are specifically trained in evaluating and categorizing the range of skills and personal characteristics required for effective performance in each job.

Position Description

The product of this job analysis process is a job or position description, which is a clear and concise summary of responsibilities, skills, and other key elements required in each job. Figure 11-4 provides a sample job description for the position of a banquet manager for a sports facility that sponsors recreational play and hosts a tour sports event.

In many ways, the position description provides the foundation on which much of the rest of the human resource management process is built. The position

Figure 11-4 Sample Job Description

North Beach Tennis Club Banquet Manager

The North Beach Tennis Club banquet manager, under the direction of the director of the North Beach Tennis Club, carries out the administrative, managerial, and service work related to the successful operation of the North Beach Tennis Club banquet facilities. The North Beach Tennis Club banquet manager will function as a critical part of the club's management team. Responsibilities are carried out with latitude for independent judgment and action, subject to the requirements of applicable laws, rules as established by the North Beach Tennis Club board of directors, and established North Beach Tennis Club policies. Individual will also work closely with the North Beach Tennis Club food service division, maintenance division, accounting division, security division, and marketing and member service division. Responsibilities may include, but are not limited to the following:

- Gives tours of the banquet facility with prospective clients

- Establishes room layouts for various types of functions

- Establishes and reviews informational packet for clients

- Maintains schedule for banquet facilities

- Handles contracts for sales, clients, bartenders, cleaning services, and other outside contractors as necessary

- Collects deposits and balances due from clients and patrons at each function, coordinating financial management with accounting division

- Schedules and hires all necessary event staff

- Orders all necessary supplies and materials for functions

- Maintains accurate inventory

- Develops equipment and facility maintenance schedule with maintenance division

- Serves as liaison with outside tour event management and staff in the area of hospitality

- Performs other related duties as assigned.

The North Beach Tennis Club banquet manager will have demonstrated expertise in the area of food service and event management. The individual will need to have the ability to plan, organize, and execute high-quality events that are in keeping with the mission and goals of the club. The banquet manager must demonstrate excellent communication skills because he or she will be required to represent the club before community groups, private clients, media, members, and other key constituents. A high level of professionalism is expected of the banquet manager at all times. A bachelor's degree in hospitality management, sport management, or related field is required with five years progressive experience highly desirable.

description plays a major role in shaping the staffing, training and development, performance evaluation, and compensation elements of that process.

Understanding Strategic Requirements

Once the organization is clear on its current capabilities, the next task is to compare the current level of human resource capabilities with the demands of the organization's strategy. As sports organizations increasingly attempt to adapt themselves to the Internet and other information-based technologies, for example, they may require a level of capability—in terms of both numbers of people and their level of expertise—beyond what is currently available in the organization.

The same would be true in a case where changes in strategy require changes of levels in capability in areas such as marketing, finance, customer service, or even human resource management itself. The development of position descriptions allows the manager to look at all of the jobs currently being performed and the required skill and expertise within the context of the entire organization. In this way, the manager can see what existing workers have to offer. Once the manager has assessed the skills of existing employees, he or she is ready to identify and understand any gaps in terms of human resource requirements that now exist because of changes in the organization's strategy.

For example, recall the position description for the banquet manager of the North Beach Tennis Club. Let us assume that an outside company had previously handled the food service function at the club. Club trustees decided to adopt a growth strategy by taking over their own food service, thereby entering an industry they had not competed in previously. The club chose not to renew their contract with the private food service company and then built a new food service building complete with snack bar and banquet facility. It was their plan to provide all elements of club food service. The club's general manager was then faced with the challenge of staffing the facility. In writing position descriptions for food service employees, he was able to identify what skills, experience, and expertise would be needed for the club to carry out its strategy. Once the manager examined the requirements for this new position in the context of existing positions and their requirements, he recognized these skills were not available within the organization. The manager realized it would be necessary to do something to bring the requisite skills to the organization to move forward successfully with the new strategy.

Formulating and Implementing Human Resource Management Strategy

It is at this point that the club's general manager must devise a strategy to ensure the organization's human resource needs are met. The goal of this phase of the human resource planning process is to ensure that effective systems are in place to support a high level of performance by current employees, and to recruit and select new employees with the skills and other characteristics needed to achieve the organization's strategic goals.

At the North Beach Tennis Club, the general manager was faced with an important decision. Once he had determined that the skills, experience, and expertise needed to manage the new banquet facility were not currently available to him through the existing staff, he identified two alternatives for securing the skills needed to run a new banquet facility. He realized he could either train an existing employee to fill the new position or he could conduct a search to hire someone who already possessed the requisite skill needed to manage the banquet facility.

Once a manager has developed and examined position descriptions and reviewed available human resources within the organization, the next task is to formulate and implement a strategy not only for filling positions but for developing systems, policies, and procedures that will facilitate optimal performance by employees.

Staffing

The process by which an organization brings new employees into the organization is called the *staffing process*. In recent years, this process has become increasingly challenging. As the workplace requires ever increasing ranges and levels of skills, and as economic growth has resulted in ever-greater competition for people with the right skills, the task of staffing has become significantly more difficult. In the sports industry, one of the major challenges for sports managers is to sift through the ever-increasing numbers of applicants for jobs to find the individual who has the right skills and personal attributes that will allow him or her to contribute to the success of the organization.

Sports jobs often attract hundreds of applicants who believe that because of their interest in a particular sport, knowledge of relevant sports statistics, or because they have either played or followed the sport all their lives, they would be perfect for the job. Sports managers are not unfamiliar with candidates who profess their love for the game, their status as a die-hard fan (of baseball, gymnastics, weight lifting, or soccer, for example), and their reputation as being people oriented. These personal attributes may be interesting to a particular sports employer, but they are not always significant. Sports managers generally assume that *all* candidates have knowledge of the game, enjoy the sport or activity and possess people skills. What they are really interested in are individual skills, experiences, ideas, and personal abilities that will benefit the organization. Prospective employees of sports organizations should think about what makes them stand out from the crowd of literally hundreds of applicants for any sports position.

Recruiting New Employees

Once it is clear that additional employees are needed to implement the organization's strategy, the first step in the staffing process is to notify potential employees of job openings and encourage them to apply. This is called *recruiting*. In the past, most sports organizations recruited new employees primarily by means of word of mouth (employees telling colleagues and associates, family and friends about job openings) or industry or trade paper advertising. Historically, the word-of-mouth approach in sports organizations led to patterns of nepotism and/or political hiring in sport. Critics still suggest that an old boy or old girl network in sports dictates hiring of friends, associates, and/or colleagues. Career counselor Virginia Goldsbury suggests that in sport, personal connections are critical:

> The truth is, it's not who you know, it's who knows you. Having a degree is simply not enough. In the sport industry, as much or perhaps more than in just about any other industry, people hire someone because of a personal recommendation from someone else. The importance of networking cannot be overstated. (Goldsbury & Hums, 1998, p. 478)

A candidate may learn of a job through a colleague or friend, and several trade or industry magazines are used for the placement of sports job advertising. For example, college sports jobs are usually listed in the classified section of the *National Collegiate Athletic Association (NCAA) News* or *The Chronicle of Higher Education*. Individual segments of the industry have trade magazines, papers, websites, or newsletters that list job openings. There are also several commercial electronic sports job services that require job seekers to pay a registration fee for access to sports job classified websites. Some sports organizations such as the PGA offer a resume bank service (of PGA-trained professionals) designed to help sports organizations identify qualified candidates. Sports job seekers need to acquaint themselves with the variety of sport-related employment vehicles available and should make it a habit to subscribe to and read these publications and visit sport-related job websites.

For the most part, the sports industry may be described as a hidden industry because most sports organizations do not broadcast job openings through general employee recruitment vehicles such as daily newspapers or general employment websites. Sports managers tend to be much more targeted in their staffing efforts and focus on those recruitment strategies that are efficient in that they are cost effective and most likely to provide them with a viable candidate pool.

Word of mouth, trade advertising, and internal promotion are utilized by sports managers because they are targeted strategies. In an attempt to attract only legitimate qualified candidates, sports organizations focus on recruiting employees through sport-specific vehicles. Sports managers recognize that any general broad announcement of a sports position is likely to result in hundreds of resumes. In fact, many sports organizations receive hundreds of unsolicited resumes a year. For the human resource manager, processing these resumes is a laborious task that is neither an efficient use of time nor particularly productive. That is why sports managers have consciously devised recruitment strategies that are most likely to yield a finite pool of legitimate candidates.

As position requirements become greater and more specialized, the search strategy usually becomes more narrowed. That is, whereas staffing of entry-level positions usually is done through a more broad-based approach such as general or trade industry advertising, top-level executive management searches are much more focused on strategies related to industry networking. For example, a municipal golf course manager looking for a new head pro would be more likely to network with industry colleagues and use golf industry trade magazines and associations to identify potential qualified candidates than to advertise the position in a general newspaper or on a general employment website.

Although this approach to human resource recruitment in sports organizations has been productive, it is not without its problems. A targeted approach to recruitment may fail to identify strong candidates who exist outside of the scope of the search. For example, Rob, the young man introduced at the beginning of the chapter, has developed a good network within the golf industry and reads trade publications, but as a college student, he might not be aware of certain positions in the industry that are advertised through word of mouth among industry professionals. The reality is that the word-of-mouth strategy has its limitations. There is no guarantee that individuals will pass along the appropriate information to good candidates. This approach is clearly unsystematic and relies on a busy network of colleagues who may or may not subjectively help identify quality candidates. Another problem with the targeted recruitment approach is that it tends to perpetuate existing hiring patterns. Most people find it easy and comfortable to build relationships and network with people who are similar to one's self; however, for the sports industry to grow and take advantage of the skills and talents of a diverse population, it is necessary to broaden recruitment strategies so opportunities in sport will be available to all (Goldsbury & Hums, 1998).

All sports managers must be aware of their organization's policies and practices that pertain to staffing. Public sports organizations and sports programs in educational institutions are required to follow the human resource policies of their directing or sponsoring agency. For example, the city's general human resource department could carry out the human resource function for a municipal golf course. If there were a city policy that all jobs are to be announced in the local paper and published in a municipal employee newsletter, this would be done even though the golf club manager may believe it would be unlikely to reach qualified candidates in this fashion. Similarly, a college athletic department may be required to post a job internally for a new soccer coach even though the athletic director believes there is currently no qualified internal candidate for the job.

It is important, however, not to overlook existing employees. Internal promotion has historically been a successful recruitment strategy. Sports organizations, like other businesses, often emphasize job advancement. As discussed in Chapter 10, career growth can be a powerful motivator for improving human performance and retaining talented employees.

More recently, as sports organizations have needed to extend their recruitment horizons to find the right people with the right skills, they have had to broaden and become much more innovative in their recruitment strategies. Figure 11-5 lists some of the approaches now being used.

Thus it is often no longer sufficient just to rely on word of mouth, trade advertising, or internal promotion to identify viable candidates. Attracting the most skilled and talented job applicants now requires creativity and initiative. This is not to say, however, that importance of networking within the industry has diminished. Sports organizations will continue to rely on candidate referrals. At a time when sport management programs are becoming more pervasive and competition for sports jobs is at an all-time high, sports organizations are likely to rely on this strategy to help them hone in quickly on serious candidates.

For example, many sports organizations utilize the internship as a prospective employee-screening program. Through the internship, the sports organization is able to assess effectively the performance of the intern to determine whether or not he or she has the skills and or personal traits the organization deems necessary for success. This strategy has helped sports managers identify highly skilled

Figure 11-5 Recruitment Strategies in Sport Organizations

- Recruiting on the Internet using such sites as prosportjobs.com, sportscareers.com, and others.

- Creating a memorable identity at industry trade shows.

- Sending recruiters to beaches, ski areas, and other recreational locations to hand out T-shirts, Frisbees, and other materials encouraging new applicants.

- Recruiting on college campuses—sending job announcements to faculty of sport management programs.

- Seeking referrals from colleagues or industry peers.

- Holding open houses, sporting events, and tournaments to showcase the organization to potential applicants.

- Using direct mail to target specific categories of people with the desired skills (e.g., professional association members).

- Using sport job head hunting, executive search firms, or industry resume banks.

- Sponsoring internships to create a relationship with students who will soon be entering the work force.

Source: Adapted from Solomon (2001), p. 69.

potential employees while helping the organization avoid making the human resource mistake of hiring someone who looks qualified on paper, but who fails to live up to the organization's performance expectations. For this reason, you must treat the internship seriously and consider it an audition for future work. Any organization is unlikely to hire an intern that performed poorly, and the consequences of poor performance are magnified because of the reliance on industry peer referrals across the sports industry. Sports organizations rely on friends, peers, and associates within the industry to identify qualified candidates. It is not unusual for an intern site supervisor to assist a highly regarded intern in identifying and securing employment with other sports organizations when no position is available within the host organization. Peer recommendations are usually given a great deal of weight by sports managers, and therefore a good word on your behalf can open doors. Conversely, a negative performance appraisal by an internship site supervisor may become an insurmountable obstacle for seeking employment in the sports industry.

To improve your chances of securing a positive reference upon completion of the internship, make every effort to understand and abide by the organization's written and unwritten rules of conduct. Some sports organizations have formal intern handbooks or manuals that detail specific requirements and expectations for behavior. Written guidelines may detail policies for everything ranging from comp tickets to dress code to fraternization with players or clients. Other sports organizations have few written guidelines, and therefore it becomes your responsibility to initiate a discussion of organizational policy related to interns with the site supervisor and the faculty adviser. In all situations, it is in your best interest to ask questions to clarify any concerns you might have about the organization's behavioral standards and performance expectations rather than make an assumption that leads to a mistake with possible long-term negative consequences on your career in sport. As a general rule, always treat the internship as a professional opportunity that serves as a critical building block for a successful career in sport.

The Selection Process

The process of evaluating applicants to determine their fit for the jobs that are available is called the *selection process*. In many ways, this phase of the staffing process has become even more challenging than the recruiting phase. Not only has it become more important than ever that the right person with the right skills is identified for each job, but legal considerations make important additional demands in terms of selection.

Selection and the Law

Several pieces of federal legislation shape and influence the selection process. The first, Title VII of the Civil Rights Act of 1964, guarantees all American citizens equal employment opportunity. This law forbids discrimination on the basis of sex, race, color, religion, or national origin. An organization cannot refuse to hire, train, promote, or transfer employees simply on the basis of any of these characteristics. This means that selection and all other employment-related decisions must be made on the basis of objective standards, such as the actual requirements of the job as indicated in the position description.

Similarly, the Age Discrimination in Employment Act (most recently amended in 1986) and the Americans with Disabilities Act (ADA) of 1990 prohibit discrimination in employment decisions on the basis of age and disabilities, respectively. Enforcement of these laws is the responsibility of the Equal Employment Opportunity Commission (EEOC), which has the ability to accept lawsuits and impose heavy fines against employers with discriminatory practices. For example, golfer Casey Martin recently successfully sued the PGA for the right to use a golf cart while playing tour events. He claimed the ADA protected his right to use the cart as a necessary accommodation in his participation in PGA events. Martin has a degenerative leg disease that makes walking excruciatingly painful. The PGA tour argued that golf is a game of endurance as well as skill, and all golfers should face the same obligation to walk to each hole. However, the Supreme Court ruled that allowing Martin to use a cart was a "reasonable accommodation that would not fundamentally alter" professional golf (D. Bernstein, 2001).

The key for managers, then, is to ensure a selection that focuses both on attaining the right fit in terms of the requirements of the job, but also provides equal employment opportunity to all applicants.

Testing

EEO guidelines define employment testing to include any procedure used as a basis for the employment decision. This means that employment tests, which may be considered as application forms, pencil-and-paper tests, performance tests, interviews, education, or experience requirements, must be administered and used in ways that avoid discrimination. Figure 11-6 summarizes some of the more common employment tests currently in use.

Pre-Employment Screening

In addition to the more formal testing techniques shown in Figure 11-6, reference and background checks are also important elements of most selection processes. In checking references, it is best to request multiple references, to speak with each of the individuals provided, and to focus the discussion on job performance rather than on areas that might be viewed as violating the applicant's rights to privacy.

Pre-employment screening for volunteers has become the subject of discussion in the sports industry, particularly for those segments that deal with children or young adults, specifically youth sports, high school sports, college sports, youth development leagues, and recreation. There have been several documented incidents of sports volunteers, specifically coaches of youth sports teams, physically

Figure 11-6 Examples of Types of Employment Tests

Type of Test	Use
Psychological and personality test	Measures personality characteristics felt to be essential for performance.
Pencil-and-paper honesty test	Evaluates integrity/degree of comfort with risk for engaging in dishonest behavior.
Skills test	Assesses skills in areas such as math, English, written communication skills, and computers.
Assessment center, simulation	Evaluates more complex skill sets such as teamwork, organizational skills, and leadership in a hands-on situation.
Drug test	Checks for the presence of controlled substances through chemical analysis of urine, blood, or hair samples.
Handwriting analysis	Infers personality characteristics.

and sexually abusing players (Nack & Yeager, 1999). Although many states require criminal and sexual criminal offender checks for employees working with children, laws may not extend to volunteers (Lazar, 2000). Sports managers must be extremely diligent in screening volunteers for programs that involve children. Professional associations, parent groups, and politicians are leading the charge to make Criminal Offender Record Investigation (CORI) and Sexual Offender Record Investigation (SORI) checks mandatory for youth sports volunteers.

As the members of our society become more mobile, many sports organizations are now conducting background checks as well as reference checks as a way to receive additional information about potential employees and volunteers. Through services available on the Internet, for example, it is now possible to receive credit reports, criminal conviction records, workers' compensation claims, court judgments, personal address histories, and more (Perry, 1999). Extreme caution must be exercised not to violate the applicant's privacy rights, but the responsible acquisition and use of this kind of information can help ensure that a sports organization does not hire someone who will become a problem for the organization, its employees, members, or clients.

The Job Interview

The job interview is perhaps the most common of all employment tests, but in its most common forms, it is the least valid and least reliable predictor of eventual performance on the job. Most of the problems with the job interview are related to the fact that many managers are not trained to conduct effective interviews. As a result, interviewer bias and inconsistencies in the way interviews are conducted tend to raise questions about conclusions drawn from the interviews.

To reduce the impact of interviewer bias and interview inconsistencies, two techniques are combined. The first is to require structured interviews in which specific interview questions are developed in advance and each applicant is asked the same questions. This is combined with a multiple rater approach in which applicants are interviewed by a team of interviewers (in some cases, the search committee), or by a series of individuals, each of whom asks some of the preselected interview questions. This combination of multiple interviewers using a structured interview format tends to result in an employment test that is both fairer to the applicant and more useful to the sports organization. Many sports managers utilize this type of search committee strategy effectively.

Training and Development

Because of the constantly changing demands of business, training has become an increasingly important human resource management process, not just for new employees but for virtually all employees. Training for a new job's specific skills and/or professional development that contributes to the overall competencies and knowledge base of the employee are the responsibility of the sports organization. Training of the worker does not stop with the initial employee orientation. New employees and volunteers need a basic orientation to the organization, and systematic continuous employee training programs also are critical to the employee's or volunteer's long-term success with the organization.

In previous decades, most training focused on the basic skills needed to perform a specific job such as machine operator or concession worker, and much of that training occurred on the job. A volunteer, for example, might have been assigned the task of court monitor and be sent to the court with the instructions "just figure out what needs to be done and do it." Today's sports organizations have realized that in addition to specific job skill instruction, training efforts must increasingly focus on developing employees at every level including skills in teamwork, problem solving, communication, information systems, and creativity. For example, at the TPC at River Highlands, introduced earlier, one of the organization's goals is creating a "continuous learning atmosphere to promote employee commitment to personal and company growth (TPC Players Club, 1998, p. 31). Club management has instituted several ongoing training activities that focus on helping employees develop customer service, teamwork, and communication skills. Training initiatives include encouraging and supporting management staff's attendance and seminars and industry shows, holding daily, weekly, and quarterly staff meetings that include an education and training session, and continually giving feedback to employees on their progress.

In providing continuous training for all of the organization's employees, there are two critical challenges: selecting the most appropriate approach for the particular type of skill being targeted, and ensuring an overall training design consistent with the fundamentals of how learning can best be facilitated.

Selecting the Most Appropriate Instructional Approaches

In one survey of training practices, organizations were asked to indicate the areas of training they included in their programs and the instructional approaches they used to provide this training ("Industry Report," 1999). A summary of the results of this survey is shown in Figure 11-7.

One significant trend in selecting instructional approaches is the dramatic increase, since the mid-1990s, in the use of computer-based learning technologies. In one national survey of the training practices of some of the most successful U.S. businesses, the percentage of training time spent in instructor-led training formats fell from 80 percent or higher in 1996 to around 60 percent in 1999. Almost all of this decrease was accounted for by an increase in training time spent in technology-based learning formats, from 8 percent or less in 1996 to around 25 percent in 1999 (Bassi & Van Buren, 1999). Part of the key to effective training, however, is to select the training format most appropriate for the kind of learning being targeted. For example, learning about teamwork is likely to be more effective through approaches that include simulations (role plays) in which the trainees are actively involved in exercises designed to enhance teamwork, rather than through an approach involving simply viewing a video on teamwork. But information intended to enhance the employee's understanding of a product or process can be very effectively communicated through video-based instruction. For example, some Craftsman Truck Series team managers utilize a variety of strategies to teach members of the pit crew how to improve their performance. Not only do they provide written instructions, hands-on training, and review sessions but they also videotape pit crew members and guide them through self-assessment of performance.

Figure 11-7 The Top Ten Areas of Training and Instructional Approaches

Most Frequently Cited Areas of Training	Percentage of Organizations
Computer applications	95
Communication skills	88
Management skills/development	85
Customer service	83
Supervisory skills	82
Computer systems/programming	81
Executive development	78
Technical skills/knowledge	77
Personal growth	67
Sales	57

Most Frequently Cited Instructional Approaches	Percentage of Organizations
Classroom programs—live	90
Workbooks/manuals	74
Videotapes	69
Public seminars	56
CD-ROM	54
Self-study (noncomputerized)	39
Role plays	37
Audiocassettes	36
Internet	36
Case studies	33

The most effective training designs match the area of training being targeted with the instructional approach most appropriate for that type of learning. The most effective training often combines two or more instructional approaches.

The Fundamentals of Effective Learning

There is obviously a wide range of options in terms of instructional approaches, but a number of fundamentals for effective learning should be present in every training program, regardless of which approach is chosen. These fundamentals for learning skills (behaviors) or information (understanding) are summarized in Figure 11-8.

Whether the training is instructor led or computer based, whether the training occurs in groups or individually, to be effective there must be clearly defined learning goals, effective presentation of the skill or information, and sufficient opportunity for practice and feedback.

Beyond these fundamentals, the most effective learning occurs when the individual has the opportunity to actually use the new skill or understanding on the job.

Figure 11-8 Fundamentals of Effective Learning

1. **Learning goal(s):** Clearly defined target in terms of what the trainee will be able to do or understand as a result of the learning.

2. **Modeling:** Demonstration of the targeted skill broken down to its key components.
OR
Meaning: Detailed and engaging presentation of the key information.

3. **Practice:** Multiple and varied opportunities to try out the targeted skills or understanding.

4. **Feedback:** Reinforcement and information about performance during practice and beyond.

This means learning is most complete when the individual has the opportunity to continue to practice and receive reinforcing feedback as part of the day-to-day work he or she does (Wexley & Latham, 1981). In other words, it is not enough that skills be practiced and refined in the training setting. For optimal learning, the reinforcement of new skills requires continued practice and feedback as part of the individual's regular work activities. Whether a NASCAR pit crew member, volunteer customer service representative at a rodeo tour event, or professional volleyball tour marketing director, continued professional development is critical to success. All sports managers should assure that their employees consider professional development and training to be part of their regular job responsibilities. Effective sports organizations continue to educate and support their employees long after the initial orientation is complete. By doing so, they ensure that all members of the organization have the skills and understanding required for overall strategic effectiveness. Appropriate training programs then require instruction in the right skills, using the right mix of instructional approaches, delivered the right way in terms of the fundamentals of learning.

Performance Evaluation

Effective staffing and training are two of the core elements of an organization's human resource management system. A third is effective performance evaluation, sometimes called performance appraisal or performance planning and review. It is the formal process of assessing how well each employee in the organization is performing her or his job. Perhaps no tendency in sport is stronger than the tendency to assess performance. In virtually every sport, performance is continuously monitored and statistical measures developed and constantly updated as a way to assess individual, team, or organizational performance.

In professional golf, for example, key performance measures include average strokes per round, percentage of greens reached in regulation, percentage of tournaments in which the golfer made the cut, and so on. In car racing, driver performance is measured in average speed per lap, percentage of finishes in the top ten, number of laps in the lead, and more. For off-field employees, performance is measured in numbers of tickets sold, percentage increase in sponsor renewal, gross sales, number of customer contacts, number of new members, and so on. The point is that in sports, measures of performance have emerged naturally to allow effective assessment of how well individuals or teams are doing their jobs. The challenge is to develop similarly effective means of assessing or measuring the work of everyone in the organization.

Performance Evaluation Formats

A wide variety of formats have emerged to evaluate work performance in organizations. Probably the most common general format involves the use of graphic rating scales. In this approach, employees are rated on a range of different traits (creativity, cooperativeness, initiative, etc.) or behaviors (see the example in Figure 11-9) using a numerical scale indicating the level of performance in this area (1 = low, 5 = high), or the quality of performance (1 = poor, 5 = excellent), or the frequency of performance (1 = never, 5 = always). Figure 11-9 shows an example of a particular type of graphic rating scale, a behaviorally anchored rating scale (BARS). Using the BARS technique, combinations of specific behaviors are used to determine the level of performance in the various areas of performance required in a specific position. In the example in Figure 11-9, the scale shown is for communication skills. Other areas of performance required for the position, interpersonal skills, technical skills, and so on, would have separate BARS allowing evaluation of performance in each of those areas.

Figure 11-9 Sample BARS (Behaviorally Anchored Rating Scale) to Evaluate the Communication Area of Performance

Communication Skills

Presents ideas clearly, responds constructively to others' ideas.

10 = Communicates effectively in writing, one on one, in small groups, and with management.

8 = Communicates effectively in writing, one on one, and in small groups; appears less comfortable communicating with management.

6 = Communicates effectively in writing and one on one; appears less comfortable communicating in small groups and with management.

4 = Communicates effectively in writing; appears less comfortable communicating one on one, in small groups, and with management.

2 = Needs improvement in all phases of communication: written, one on one, in small groups, and with management.

Another common performance evaluation format is the Balanced Scorecard or management by objectives (MBO) approach described in Chapter 7. You will recall that, in the Balanced Scorecard approach, managers work with individuals to define specific performance objectives for the individual consistent with the organization's goals. Some organizations combine BARS and Balanced Scorecard, using the rating scale component for those job requirements that are consistent year to year and the goal-setting component for areas of performance that might be of particular importance in a given year. For example, an advertising sales position in a marketing department of a tour sports organization might be evaluated using BARS for the areas of performance relating to how well the individual deals with existing advertisers, but use a Balanced Scorecard approach for evaluating how well the individual performs in terms of attracting new advertisers or increasing sponsorship revenues for a tour event or series.

Performance Evaluation and Equal Employment Opportunity

Performance evaluation usually occurs annually for each employee, and the results of this evaluation are very often the basis for decisions on whether and how much to increase the employee's pay for the coming year, as well as for decisions relating to the future training opportunities, promotion, and potential reassignment of the employee. Because performance evaluation does provide the basis for so many important decisions relating to pay, future training, and promotion, the federal antidiscrimination legislation discussed earlier in the chapter requires that an organization's performance evaluation process be legally defensible. Although the Equal Employment Opportunity Commission has not defined specific guidelines for a legally defensible performance evaluation process, research on a large number of court decisions on employment discrimination cases suggests four criteria (Kreitner, 2001).

1. A *job analysis* should be used to develop the performance evaluation instrument. Job analysis is the systematic assessment of what skills, personal characteristics, and other qualifications are actually required to perform the job successfully and ensures that the evaluation process is focusing on the actual requirements of the job. It also minimizes the extent to which a manager's bias might result in different evaluation processes for different employees. Every employee with the same job description is evaluated on the same items.

2. The evaluation should *focus on behavior*, rather than on traits or characteristics. This ensures that the actual performance of the individual is being evaluated, rather than the individual's personality or other traits. The problem with evaluating personality or traits—unless they are defined in terms of specific types of behavior—is that judgments on characteristics such as initiative or attitude tend to be very subjective and, for that reason, less consistent. The BARS approach represents the kind of behaviorally oriented format supported by these guidelines.

3. The performance evaluation process should be performed consistent with *specific written instructions*. Written instructions on exactly how to conduct the performance evaluation ensure that every

employee is evaluated using the same system. This reduces the likelihood that managers, for whatever reason, might treat different employees differently in the evaluation process.

4. Managers should *review the results* of the evaluation with their employees. This guideline reflects what the courts have tended to view as one of the characteristics of a legally defensible performance evaluation process. But sharing the results of evaluation with the individual is also good management. If one of the key goals of the performance evaluation process is improved work performance, feedback on work performance to the individual is essential. When conducted effectively, the performance evaluation process provides a valuable opportunity for the manager to recognize and reinforce positive performance and to exchange views and information with the employee about how work performance might be improved.

In summary, each of these criteria for a legally defensible performance evaluation process represents an important guideline for an effective appraisal. Organizations following these guidelines are creating a system of evaluation that is not only more likely fair in terms of validity and reliability, but is more likely also more accurate in the judgments it produces for purposes of pay and promotion, and more productive in enhancing future work performance.

Compensation

The next core element of an effective human resource management system is *compensation*, the rewards that individuals receive for performing the work of the organization. The challenge for sports organizations is to design a total compensation system that (1) allows the organization to attract and retain individuals with the skills and qualifications it needs to be successful, (2) supports a high level of work performance by its members, and (3) allows the organization to remain profitable or financially viable into the future. A number of potential elements can be included in an organization's compensation system.

Base Pay

Base pay is the compensation provided for performing the basic duties required by a given job. Traditionally, salary ranges are established for each position in the organization. These salary ranges set the lowest level and highest level of base pay available for individuals in that position. Employees progress upward through the salary range for their position, most often on the basis of how long they have spent in the position and how well they do their job as determined by their annual performance evaluation.

The salary ranges established by an organization usually reflect industry standards of the going rate for similar positions at other companies in the same geographic area or in the same or competing industries. Organizations research what other organizations are paying their employees in order to ensure that their own pay scales are high enough to allow them to attract and retain good employees and, at the same time, not paying more than the market requires.

Performance-Based Pay

In recent years, as organizations have focused on becoming more competitive by improving their performance, there has been an increased emphasis on compensation systems that reward employees for performance beyond the basic requirements of their jobs. Performance-based pay can include incentive pay, bonuses, or commissions, usually for attaining specific individual or team performance goals in terms of quality, efficiency, or productivity. For example, a sales staff member might be compensated based on a percentage of ticket revenue developed, sponsorship fees collected, or gross premium sales. Similar to this is gain sharing or results sharing in which employees receive additional financial compensation in return for contributing to the organization's overall success as measured by increased profits, reduced expenses, or some other indicator of improved organizational effectiveness.

Another form of performance-based pay is pay-for-skills or pay-for-knowledge, in which additional compensation is awarded to employees who learn and successfully apply new skills or knowledge considered valuable to the organization's success. For example, a sports program supervisor who completes a course in advanced lifesaving or emergency medicine or achieves certification in athletic training may be financially compensated for these new skills. A manager who completes computer network training, an advanced sales training course, or an advanced degree may be awarded a pay increase for the new knowledge or skill.

Actually, some criticism has been leveled at the increasing emphasis on performance-based pay. Critics argue it can be difficult to measure performance in some jobs, such as customer service, or jobs where the focus is on the quality of what is done rather than the number of units produced. Critics also charge that tying pay to performance focuses employees' attention on reaching short-term goals rather than on the kind of problem solving that can use up a lot of time over the short term, but significantly improve performance over the longer term. In an attempt to overcome such possible negative effects, some sports managers have financially awarded creativity or new ideas. Even if the ideas have produced poor results or have failed outright, some managers believe that risk taking and creative problem solving should be encouraged, and to ensure that employees remain committed to trying new things, they provide bonuses for unconventional thinking and creative problem solving.

Finally, unless managed carefully, pay-for-performance programs can result in employees competing with each other to be judged "above average" or "exceptional," rather than cooperating with one another for the greater good (Kohn, 1993). For example, some sports managers create friendly competitions among sales teams in an effort to motivate high performance. One negative outcome of these competitions is that employees assume a win-at-all-costs attitude and may focus on sabotaging other sales teams or employing high-pressure sales strategies that may be detrimental to the organization in the long run. These criticisms represent important warnings to sports organizations as they attempt to use pay to motivate work performance.

Another compensation issue of concern to sports managers and students entering the sports industry is salary scale. There is a general misconception that sports salaries are high. Media stories reporting the gargantuan salaries of professional athletes do not represent compensation on the off-field side. Generally, salaries in sport, particularly starting salaries, are low. Organization type, that is, nonprofit or for profit, often affects salary scale as does industry segment and organization location. Senior-level executives and staff may be well compensated in some sports organizations, but there is little trickle-down effect. Because of the glut of potential employees willing to work for little or nothing just to be in sport, sports salaries are generally deflated. The reality for most sports managers is that they need to pay their dues. They must work long hours—oftentimes on nights and weekends—at pay levels lower than other business enterprises. Success in the sports industry is often about perseverance and dedication. It is possible to move up the ladder within the sports industry and to be well compensated for skills and demonstrated performance. As many sports managers are quick to advise their young employees, "it's not always about the money, but the opportunity." Certainly there are other benefits for those who are passionate about a career in sport that can help compensate for a deflated salary.

Benefits and Other Nonfinancial Compensation

In addition to direct pay, or financial compensation, there are also the nonfinancial forms of compensation. The most common forms of nonfinancial compensation are called *benefits*. Typically, these include medical and life insurance, vacation, holiday, and other paid time benefits, and some form of company-sponsored retirement or savings programs. Most often, the costs of these benefits— which can represent 35 to 40 percent of total compensation expenses—are shared with the employee.

Finally, there are other forms of nonfinancial rewards that can vary from organization to organization. For sports organizations, these types of benefits are particularly useful for compensating poorly paid employees and/or thanking volunteers and cultivating volunteer support. These range from dinners and event tickets to access to athlete performers, company-sponsored trips, golfing privileges, preferred parking, merchandise discounts, and clothing. At many tour sports events, special functions are held specifically for volunteers. They may include concerts, luncheons, and/or receptions with tour athletes.

For employees, other rewards might include additional vacation time and flex scheduling to paying for college courses and other forms of career development opportunities. The key to an effective compensation component is to develop a combination of pay, performance incentives, benefits, and other nonfinancial rewards that will enable the organization to attract and motivate a high-performance work force. The sports manager must also understand employee and volunteer motivation, as discussed in Chapter 10, and design compensation or reward packages that are attractive to employee and volunteer groups.

Employee Wellness

Every year, more than six thousand workers die in the American workplace, and over six million are injured or become ill as a result of working conditions. Most of these accidents and illnesses are in manufacturing organizations, 40 percent are in the service sector (in which sports organizations are included), and over 80 percent of these result in lost work time, medical treatment beyond first aid, loss of consciousness, work restriction, or job transfer (Bureau of Labor Statistics, 1999). Clearly, one of the major challenges of human resource management in sports organizations, especially with on-field talent, is maintaining employee safety and wellness.

NASCAR, its stakeholders, and fans felt the impact of safety and wellness issues to a devastating degree at the 2001 Daytona 500, when on the race's last lap, legendary driver Dale Earnhardt was killed when his #3 GM Goodwrench Service Chevrolet Monte Carlo skidded right and crashed full speed straight into the track's concrete retaining wall. The death of Earnhardt, stock car racing's equivalent of Michael Jordan, followed less than a year after fatal crashes of fellow drivers Kenny Irwin and Adam Petty (grandson of NASCAR legend Richard Petty and son of current driver Kyle Petty)—both at New Hampshire International Speedway—and Craftsman Truck Series driver Tony Roper. Earnhardt's fatal crash was followed by weeks of controversy over whether the death had been hastened by a broken seat belt and legal wrangling over whether Earnhardt's autopsy photos would be made public. Florida governor Jeb Bush eventually signed a bill to keep the photos from public release ("A Look," 2001).

As noted previously, NASCAR's greatest asset is its drivers, and it has rules governing car speed and certain equipment to help protect drivers and ensure close and fair competition. However, in its rule book, the organization states the following:

> Stock car racing is an inherently dangerous sport. Each competitor assumes that risk when he or she participates in an event. The risk of serious injury or death cannot be eliminated and, in fact, will always be present at a high level. Members are required to advise their spouse and next of kin, if any, of this fact. . . . Although safety generally is everyone's concern, NASCAR cannot be and is not responsible for all or even most aspects of the safety effort. (Wood, 2001b, p. 8C)

Regardless of this disclaimer, after the recent spate of fatalities, the organization was roundly criticized for not requiring more precautionary safety equipment, such as the HANS (head and neck safety) restraint device that many experts claim would have saved Earnhardt, Sr. NASCAR claims that the drivers don't want HANS mandated, but some suggest that if the organization requires it, it assumes the legal liability if the device fails, so it leaves the choice to employ the device up to the individual drivers. Says Geoff Smith, president of Roush Racing, one of the teams that races cars in NASCAR, "There is a legal proposition that is built into the sport, . . . that says that [drivers] are responsible for [their] own safety. If I were running a business I'd do it the same way. . . . But there's a public relations awkwardness that goes with a discussion of safety" (Wood, 2001b, p. 8C).

NASCAR, founded in 1948 by William France, is a private family-owned organization (the France family also controls International Speedway Corporation [ISC], a publicly held company that owns twelve racetracks, on which half of the NASCAR races are held [Wood, 2001c]). For decades, the France family has run NASCAR in whatever way they felt was best, but since the sport has boomed in popularity over the last decade (in no small part due to the Frances' savvy business practices), they will find public scrutiny more of a factor in safety and wellness decisions. And unlike many professional league sports, the fact that tour drivers are not unionized means that, unlike major-league baseball, the drivers have not presented a united front to push NASCAR to address these issues. Some experts, like sports marketing guru Bill Sutton, say that NASCAR has said it might have acted differently to prevent the deaths of Earnhardt, Sr., and others, but "now they need to go the rest of the way and say they're sorry . . . that [they] didn't handle it the way they should have" (Wood, 2001a, p. 2C).

Safety and Government

As serious a problem as worker safety is today, more than thirty years ago, the problem was even more severe, with more than fourteen thousand work-related deaths in 1970. In that year, the U.S. government created the Occupational Safety and Health Administration (OSHA) to set health and safety standards for the American workplace and to monitor organizations to ensure work conditions are free from recognized hazards. OSHA requires employers to maintain conditions consistent with federal safety standards, submit to periodic workplace inspections, and record and report all workplace accidents and injuries. Where violations of safety standards are found, OSHA is able to levy penalties of up to $70,000 for each violation, with increasing penalties if the violation is not corrected in a timely fashion.

Critics charge that some OSHA requirements or limitations on employers are excessive and the paperwork can be time consuming and expensive. But there is little question that the effect of OSHA has been both a safer workplace and much greater attention by employers to the health and safety of their workers.

Alcohol and Substance Abuse

The history of alcohol and substance abuse with prominent sports idols is a long and storied one. Babe Ruth was beloved in part because of his profligate lifestyle. Many of the baby boomers who worshipped Mickey Mantle, blissfully unaware of his drinking binges, forgave him for his hard-drinking ways once he came clean and neared death due to liver disease. Modern sport is beset almost daily by stories of drug involvement and alcohol abuse by high-profile athletes and sports personalities.

Clearly, one of the most serious threats to wellness in the sports workplace is the prevalence of alcohol and drug abuse that impacts all of American society. Approximately one in every eight American workers abuses either drugs or alcohol, with significant consequences not only for themselves, but also for their employers and coworkers. For example, employees who abuse drugs or alcohol are ten times more likely to be absent from the job and three times more likely either to have or cause an accident (Castro, 1986). To minimize the impact of this problem, approximately one in every four employers tests employees for alcohol, and nearly half for drugs (Ivancevich, 2001). Legal restrictions place limits on testing employees for substance abuse, however, and the tests themselves are not always reliable, leaving employers open to lawsuits.

In addition to testing, many organizations have taken the route of providing employees with substance abuse and other emotional or behavioral problems access to an employee assistance program (EAP). The philosophy behind the EAP approach is that employees are important to the organization, and every effort should be made to assist employees with problems that affect their performance. Most EAPs include some form of the following (Ivancevich, 2001, p. 465):

1. Employees identified as needing assistance are referred to the program.

2. The employee's problem is evaluated, counseling or options for treatment are discussed—all in a confidential manner—and where appropriate, a referral for treatment is provided.

3. Employees receive professional counseling or treatment, usually by an outside provider or agency.

The EAP approach has actually expanded in recent years to include programming for the full range of employee health and wellness issues that impact workplace productivity.

A Wellness Approach to Employee Health

There is actually a much better reason than OSHA mandates or substance abuse problems for organizations to focus on the health and safety of their employees. A healthy work force is simply more productive than a work force where employees are unable to perform their jobs well as a result of accident, injury, illness, or unhealthful behaviors. Thus employers are increasingly taking a wellness approach to employee health.

A wellness approach focuses on preventing accidents, injuries, or illnesses before they happen. In this approach, employees are encouraged to engage in a range of behaviors and activities associated with better health. These include improved nutrition and regular exercise, stress management training and employee counseling for personal problems, programs for reducing or eliminating use of alcohol, tobacco, and other unhealthful substances, and regular medical examinations. Although definite expenses are associated with supporting a wellness approach to employee health and safety, these expenses are generally found to be much lower than the potential productivity gains from a healthy work force.

Employee Relations

The final challenge of human resource management that we discuss is maintaining a productive and mutually satisfying relation between employees and the organization. Fairness and competency in implementing each of the processes already described in this chapter are essential for positive employee relations. But other challenges exist as well, including unions and collective bargaining, sexual harassment, and government-mandated accommodations for employees.

Unions and Collective Bargaining

Prior to the last few decades, when one out of every three American workers were union members, relations between employers and employees were largely defined by the union contract, more formally known as the collective bargaining agreement. Even though fewer than one in seven U.S. workers now are union members, in several segments in the sports industry, unions play an important role. For example, in the sports facility industry, labor union members may supply critical services such as electrical service, plumbing, construction, sound and lighting, and transportation. Often public sports agencies such as recreation and park departments and educational institutions deal with municipal or state labor unions or professional labor associations. As we discussed earlier, the operation of professional sports industry is widely influenced by players, officials, and labor unions or associations.

Employees usually form unions as a way to improve their ability to have an impact on their working conditions, on how they are paid, how work is scheduled, and so on. The federal government formed the National Labor Relations Board (NLRB) to ensures fair and orderly process for workers seeking to form a union. Employees interested in forming a union must first obtain the signatures of 30 percent of the potential members of the union. Once this is done the NLRB supervises an election in which employees vote by secret ballot whether they support the formation of a union. If a majority of those voting are in favor, the NLRB certifies the union as the employees' official representative in negotiating with management.

Collective bargaining is the process of negotiating a labor contract acceptable to both management and employees. Typically, the labor contract negotiated contains agreements about wages and hours; conditions of employment, promotion, and layoff; discipline; benefits; overtime, vacation, and rest periods; as well as grievance procedures (Griffin, 2000). Union members have the opportunity to accept or reject the terms suggested in the proposed contract by voting for or against it. Again, ratification of a new collective bargaining agreement requires a majority of those voting.

If relations between management and employees are not well managed, the collective bargaining process can become extremely difficult, with employees sometimes resorting to work slowdowns or labor strikes as a way to express their displeasure. As management and unions have learned to cooperate more effectively in the negotiation process, collective bargaining agreements have become an important tool for ensuring positive relations between employees and the organization, and for making workers and the workplace more productive.

Sexual Harassment

A second area of challenge in terms of employee relations is the need to maintain a work environment free from sexual harassment. As more and more women have entered the work force at every level and in every industry, the frequency of complaints of sexual harassment has increased. Sexual harassment is generally considered to include unwanted sexual attention or behavior, either directly toward a specific group or individuals or contributing to an offensive or intimidating work environment.

Sexual harassment is never acceptable, but as a result of the Civil Rights Act of 1964, employers are considered legally responsible for maintaining a work environment free of the conditions that constitute sexual harassment. The consequences of failing to maintain such an environment can be considerable. In 1998 alone, the costs to just two major U.S. corporations of settling sexual harassment suits approached $100 million (Cole, 1999). This is just the legal cost. What is much more difficult to calculate are the costs to these organizations in the increased difficulty of attracting and recruiting skilled and talented workers who will now question working for a company with the reputation resulting from the publicity from these lawsuits.

For all of these reasons, most American businesses now have formal programs to ensure an environment in which sexual harassment is clearly unacceptable. These programs typically include the following elements:

1. A clearly articulated policy on sexual harassment including definitions of unacceptable behavior and penalties for violating the policy.

2. Clearly defined procedures to ensure that employees with complaints in this area can receive a fair hearing without fear of retaliation.

3. Training throughout the organization—for managers, supervisors, and other employees—to ensure widespread understanding of the organization's sexual harassment policy, and of the processes available to employees for registering complaints. (Segal, 1998)

Sexual harassment represents a serious threat to the goal of positive employee relations. Reducing this threat to the lowest possible level will pay off, not only in avoiding costly legal battles, but also in the value of achieving a more productive work environment.

Americans with Disabilities Act

In two other areas the government has intervened to ensure fair treatment of employees. The first is in the area of accommodating the needs of workers with disabilities. In 1990 Congress passed the Americans with Disabilities Act (ADA). This law requires employers to make "reasonable accommodations" for qualified individuals with known disabilities. A qualified individual with a disability has been defined as an individual with a disability who, with or without reasonable accommodation, can perform the essential activities required by the job (Ivancevich, 2001).

In the years since passage of the ADA, court cases have clarified what is meant by reasonable accommodation and known disabilities. As employers' legal responsibilities continue to become clearer in this area, the ability of employers to respond to the needs of workers with disabilities will continue to improve.

The Family and Medical Leave Act

Over the course of the last several decades, the number of women entering the workforce continued to increase, as did the number of single women heading households. The number of families with children under eighteen headed by females doubled between 1980 and 1990, from 2.9 to 5.8 million (Cook, 1992). In response to the need, primarily of women, to balance the demands of work and home, Congress passed the Family and Medical Leave Act (FMLA) in 1993.

With some exceptions, the FMLA requires employers with fifty or more employees to provide up to twelve weeks of unpaid leave to eligible employees during any twelve-month period. The unpaid leave can be for births, adoptions, the care of sick children, spouses, or parents, or for the employee to recover from his or her own illness (Hall & Walker, 1993). Sports organizations that exceed the fifty employee minimum would be required to provide the leave specified in the FMLA.

Title IX

Title IX of the Educational Amendments of 1972 was enacted to end gender discrimination and create gender equity at educational institutions that receive money from the federal government. Application of Title IX has been extended to interscholastic and intercollegiate athletic programs where institutions receive federal funding. The Office of Civil Rights (OCR) has established guidelines for applying Title IX regulations to athletics programs. The OCR is responsible for assessing whether or not an institution is in compliance with Title IX and does so through the application of a three-point standard. OCR looks at how athletic scholarships are awarded. Next, it examines how benefits and opportunities between male and female athletes are distributed. It seeks a standard of equal treatment whereby both male and female athletes are afforded access to facilities, equipment, coaching, and administrative staff, for example. Lastly, it seeks to determine whether or not the institution has historically equally and effectively accommodated the athletic interests and abilities of male and female students. Sports managers in publicly funded institutions must be aware of Title IX regulations and policies not only because of the importance of creating and sustaining an organizational environment that treats athletes and employees equitably, but because of the potential negative publicity and costs associated with a failure to adhere to Title IX and resultant employee complaints and litigation.

Summary

The tour sports segment consists of a single or series of sports competitions at various locales throughout a tour season. They may feature individuals (as in golf) or teams (as in volleyball) that compete in a tournament-type or championship event format either on the basis of one single event or as part of a series. The tour sports industry consists of three distinct segments. The first segment is known as traditional tour sport and encompasses traditional sports competition such as golf, tennis, rodeo, bicycling, or auto racing where individuals and teams may compete in one event and/or as part of a championship event series. The second segment is outdoor adventure/extreme sport that features nontraditional sports activities such as freestyle stunt skiing, sky surfing, log rolling, or skateboarding. Examples of this segment include the Gravity Games and X Games. The third segment is tour sports entertainment, usually commercial in nature, and features sports activity typically scripted to some degree and sometimes with predetermined outcomes. Examples of this segment are the WWF and Harlem Globetrotters.

Human resource management is the responsibility of management to establish and maintain specific programs and systems needed to attract, develop, and support a high-performance work force. The human resource function is directly tied to the organization's strategic initiatives and may be viewed in the context of two separate human resource tracks—on-field personnel management and off-field personnel management. The sports organization must employ a human resource management system that includes job analysis, human resource planning, recruiting and selection, training and development, performance evaluation, compensation and reward systems, and employee safety and wellness. The human resource manager's responsibility also includes complying with organizational policies, legislation, and guidelines established by the sports organization's governing bodies.

Creating a Road Map for Success

1. Imagine you are Rob Warinski, the sport management student introduced in the opening discussion case in this chapter.

   a. How would you go about finding a job in the sports industry?

   b. What jobs might be of interest to you? What jobs in sport are you qualified for?

   c. How would you find out about potential job openings in your chosen sports career area? What employment resources would be most valuable to you?

   d. What special skills, experience, or knowledge would you bring to the sports organization?

   e. Do you think Rob has been successful in preparing for a job in sport? Why? Why not?

2. Develop your own resume. What resources are available on your own college campus to assist you in putting together a professional resume?

3. Research available positions in your chosen sports industry segment. What types of entry-level jobs are available? What skills, education, and experience are necessary to secure an entry-level position?

4. Interview a sport management professional. Write a two-page career analysis. How did they come to hold their present position? What is their educational background? Did they undertake an internship? What types of skills are needed to perform their job? What advice do they give someone just starting out in the sports business?

5. Divide the class into teams of four students. Each group should prepare a job description for a position within the sports tour industry. Detail job responsibilities and requirements. What level of education, skills, and experience are required of the successful candidate? What questions should the committee ask of candidates? Devise several recruitment strategies. Conduct simulated interviews.

Management Exercise

A look back. (2001, July 31). *USA Today,* p. 8C.

Bassi, L. J., & Van Buren, M. E. (1999, January). Examining training practices in U.S. businesses. *Training and Development Journal,* pp. 23–33.

Bernstein, A. (2001, June 25–July 1). Bessemer Trust puts name on Breeders' Cup juvenile race for 2 years. *Street & Smith's SportsBusiness Journal,* p. 11.

Bernstein, D. E. (2001, May 5). Casey Martin ruling is par for the course. *Wall Street Journal,* p. 9.

Brockinton, L. (2001a, June 25–July 1). Great Outdoor Games riding in style with Jeep's new SUV sponsor. *Street & Smith's SportsBusiness Journal,* p. 13.

Brockinton, L. (2001b, August 6–12). Video games join X games. *Street & Smith's SportsBusiness Journal,* p. 6.

Bureau of Labor Statistics. (1999). *Workplace injuries and illnesses in 1997.* Available: http://www.stats .bls.gov/news.release/osh.nws.htm.

Castro, J. (1986, March 17). Battling the enemy within. *Time,* pp. 52–61.

Cole, J. (1999). Sexual harassment: New rules, new behavior. *HRfocus,* pp. 14–15.

Cook, M. F. (1992). Workplace 2000: Prospects and challenges. In *AMA Book for Employee Recruitment and Retention* (pp. 7–17). New York: AMACOM.

Cruz, C. (2001, July 20). The fast crowd. *Entertainment Weekly,* pp. 20–21.

Farrell, J. M., Johnston, M. E., & Twynam, D. G. (1998). Volunteer motivation, satisfaction, and management at an elite sporting competition. *Journal of Sport Management 12,* pp. 288–300.

Goldsbury, G., & Hums, M. (1998). Strategies for career success. In L. Mas-teralexis, C. Barr, & M. Hums, (Eds.), *Principles and practice of sport management.* Gaithersburg, MD: Aspen.

Griffin, R. (2000). *Fundamentals of management,* (2d ed.). Boston: Houghton Mifflin.

Hagstrom, R. H. (1998). *The NASCAR way: The business that drives the sport.* New York: Wiley.

Hall, M., & Walker, B. S. (1993, August 5). Federal family leave act: Provisions at a glance. *USA Today,* p. 2B.

Industry report. (1999, October). *Training 36,* pp. 54, 56.

Inglis, S. (1997). Roles of the board in amateur sport organizations. *Journal of Sport Management 11,* pp. 10–17.

Ivancevich, J. (2001). *Human resource management* (8th ed.), Boston: McGraw-Hill.

Kohn, A. (1993). *Punishment by rewards.* Boston: Houghton Mifflin.

Krantz, M. (2001, August 3). Sponsors get a gnarly idea: Surf sells, dude. *USA Today,* pp. 1B–2B.

Kreitner, R. (2001). *Understanding management.* Boston: Houghton Mifflin.

Lazar, K. (2000, June 11). Law designed to protect kids falls short. *Boston Herald,* p. 17.

Linnehan, F. (2001). Human resource management in sport. In B. Parkhouse (Ed.), *The management of sport: Its foundation and applications.* Boston: McGraw-Hill.

Nack, W., & Yaeger, D. (1999, September 13). Every parent's nightmare. *Sports Illustrated,* pp. 40–53.

Perry, P. (1999, February). Use the web to check out those job applicants. *New England Printer and Publisher,* pp. 34–36.

Putnam, R. D. (2001). *Bowling alone: The collapse and revival of American community.* New York: Touchstone.

References

Segal, J. (1998, October). Prevent now or pay later. *HRMagazine*, pp. 145–149.

Solomon, C. M. (2001, August). Stellar recruiting for a tight labor market. *Workforce*, p. 69.

The worried rich. (1994, December 5). *Business Week*, p. 8.

TPC Players Club at River Highlands. (1998). *Above and beyond: Employee training package.*

Wexley, K. N., & Latham, G. P., (1981). *Developing and training human resources in organizations.* Glenville, IL: Scott, Foresman.

Wood, S. (2001a, July 31). NASCAR follows its own road. *USA Today*, pp. 1C–2C.

Wood, S. (2001b, July 31). Safety concerns are delicate series issues. *USA Today*, p. 8C.

Wood, S. (2001c, July 31). Going behind the scenes. *USA Today*, p. 8C.

Chapter 12

Managing Change in Collegiate Athletics

PHOTO: © JAMES A. SUGAR/CORBIS

Purpose:

To provide opportunities for college students to engage in athletic activities designed to enhance the educational experience and character development of participants; to generate visibility and enhance the reputation of the institution; to attract support to the institution; to create community spirit and to unify the various communities and stakeholders of the institution.

Stakeholders:

Participant athletes, students, parents, coaches, related support personnel (trainers, officials), equipment suppliers, conference/league member schools and administrators, media, alumni, faculty, university administration, national administration officials (e.g., NCAA), licensees, corporate partners, local, state, and federal taxpayers.

Size and scope:

- The NCAA, which oversees the overwhelming majority of intercollegiate athletic programs, has over 1200 members that offer intercollegiate athletic programs for over 320,000 student athletes.
- The NJCCA is currently made up of about 550 junior college intercollegiate athletic programs with over 50,000 student athletes represented.
- The NCAA employs approximately 300 people and has an annual budget of over $30 million.
- Currently, about 50 big-time athletic programs or "power schools" compete at the highest levels and have gained the bulk of national media attention and coverage. They are considered members of an elite inner circle of intercollegiate sport programs.

Governance:

- The National Collegiate Athletic Association (NCAA), founded in 1905, is considered the primary governing organization for intercollegiate sports. Other governing bodies include the National Junior College Athletic Association (NJCAA) and National Association for Intercollegiate Athletics (NAIA).
- Institutions are also governed through conference affiliation (Big East, Big-10, ACC, NESCAC), where member institutions agree on specific policies, procedures, and practices that comply with national association guidelines.
- The intercollegiate athletic program is also governed internally through the institution's own control mechanisms. Presidents of institutions have come together to influence the operation of the intercollegiate athletic systems. The NCAA supports the notion of presidential control of intercollegiate athletics.

Inside Look

In the Wake of the Oneida

August 1852: Although the beginnings of intercollegiate athletics were firmly rooted in higher education long before this date, this was the month it all began. Before Duke–North Carolina, before UCLA–USC, before Auburn–Alabama, before Michigan–Ohio State, before Joe Paterno, Adolph Rupp, Knute Rockne, and Michael Jordan, Doug Flutie, and Doak Walker, there was Harvard and Yale. But the first battle was not in football or basketball, but in crew, or more specifically, rowing. And this seminal tussle took place neither on the Charles River by the gates of Harvard Yard nor in New Haven harbor, but on Lake Winnipesaukee in bucolic New Hampshire, miles and miles from either campus. But why then and why there? Or maybe more importantly, why do it at all?

From its earliest inception at Harvard, American institutions of higher education have sought to integrate all facets of life into the collegiate experience. Turner (1984) noted that Harvard's founders intentionally chose the English collegiate system where students and masters lived, ate, studied, worshipped, and played together rather than the European or Scottish model where students lived and boarded in the community. The choice was based first on academic and religious principles to form a sense of community within the school, in much the same manner as intercollegiate athletics would later be used to build and promote school loyalties. This institutionalizing of nonacademic student life would inevitably give rise to the college's involvement in sponsoring, at least by virtue of its responsibility of in loco parentis, the extra curriculum.

This meant activities beyond classes and required chapel and would soon come to mean athletics. Nearly a century before the advent of intercollegiate athletics, activities such as literary societies, Greek-letter fraternal organizations, and organized on-campus "intramural" athletics were established by students (Rudolph, 1990). Athletic participation was usually decried by faculty, as evidenced as early as 1787, when Princeton faculty forbade students to participate in "shinny," a form of hockey, because it was "low and unbecoming to gentlemen and scholars" (Rudolph, 1990, p. 151). Nonetheless, an annual junior class versus sophomore class game there was quite popular (Sheldon, 1969), and Princeton students also played an early form of baseball as early as 1786 (Seymour, 1989).

In spite of these concerns, students persisted in these athletic pursuits because, as one Amherst College student of the day noted, such activities "served to vary the monotony, and relieve the dryness of college duties" (Cutting, as cited in Smith, 1988, p. 15). Students participated in exercise regimens as a precursor to the gymnasium movement of the 1820s, with colleges opting then to incorporate such programs formally by midcentury. Amherst was the first school to add a Department of Hygiene and Physical Education in 1860, in hopes of channeling student activity into higher purposes (Rudolph, 1990). Soon, though, the movement was perceived by students as "so mechanical, so business-like" (Bruce, as cited in Rudolph, 1990, p. 153).

In response to the disinterest in gymnastics, but a real interest in other forms of physical activity, students chose instead to compete in sports such as baseball, crew, track, and football. As the popularity of sport grew on campuses, students began to look beyond campus boundaries for challenges, as evidenced by the Harvard–Yale crew race. But the offer to support the race financially came from James Elkins, a railroad superintendent for the Boston, Concord, and Montreal railroad. The company believed enough spectator interest existed in an intercollegiate athletic event that it paid for the travel and room and board for the two teams, and the teams looked forward to a "jolly lark" (as cited in Smith, 1988, p. 28). With a thousand or so spectators in attendance, the Harvard crew in their boat *Oneida* won first the 1.5 mile morning race and after a respite of lunch, mineral water, ale, brandy, and cigars, won the two-mile afternoon race as well. With presidential candidate Franklin Pierce looking on, the winners received a prize of a handsome pair of black, silver-tipped walnut oars (Smith, 1988). Commercialization had led to the first intercollegiate athletic contest, but other factors would lead to its establishment and entrenchment into American culture.

Rudolph (1990) aptly summarized that

> For the American college student, the gymnasium, the boat club, the baseball team (and before long the track team, the football team and cricket team) were necessary for the fullest enjoyment of life. They were the institutions in which the student embedded his values, the values of worldly success; institutions in which he clarified the nature of distance that stretched between his view of life and the view that the college purveyed. (pp. 154–155)

A lot has happened since the crew of the *Oneida* won the day. At the beginning of the twenty-first century, nearly a century and a half after the Lake Winnipesaukee duel, American intercollegiate athletics are more popular than ever. This point is succinctly articulated by a former Miami football player who said, "You don't get 70,000 people to watch a chemistry experiment" (Dealy, 1990).

From its humble beginnings as a "jolly lark" for male students to today's multifaceted and broad-based athletic programs for both male and female students, intercollegiate athletics have experienced incredible expansion in size, scope, and purpose. But now that collegiate athletics are inextricably intertwined with higher education, the question that arises is, do we need collegiate athletics? Can colleges and universities get along without them? What do they have to do with higher education?

Introduction

Throughout this book, we have discussed the notion that management is a complex organizational task made even more challenging by the dynamic nature of the sports industry. Change is both the most daunting challenge confronting management and the most promising opportunity. Change threatens to overwhelm the organization, and yet, at the same time, it reveals unprecedented possibilities. New competition, new technology, and new performance standards are just some of the changes that managers must not only anticipate, but must bring about.

Change is inevitable. The question is not whether to accept the challenge of change but how to manage change to make it as productive as possible, to make it a process for strengthening and renewing the organization. This chapter introduces the principles and process of managing change. Lewin's model of organizational change is discussed as a simple theoretical framework for managing change. We identify strategies for overcoming resistance to change and for effectively bringing about change in the organization. Lastly, the concept of the learning organization is introduced.

There may be no better segment in all of the sports industry than collegiate athletics to examine the process of managing change. Intercollegiate athletics have evolved from their beginnings in the 1800s as student-organized and directed activities to multimillion-dollar businesses. Collegiate athletic organizations today are dynamic organizations that must constantly change and evolve to fulfill their responsibilities in support of the institution's mission and stakeholder interests.

The Challenge of Change in Collegiate Athletics

Jeremy Foley, athletic director at the University of Florida, suggests the evolution of collegiate athletic programs into business enterprises has changed the role of the athletic director: "there's no question that with the dollars that are involved and the facilities that are involved and the legal issues that are involved, the person behind this [athletic director's] desk has to understand business—and I mean really understand business" (King, 2000, p. 35). Whereas athletic directors of the past focused on hiring and managing coaches, creating team schedules, and purchasing athletic equipment, today's athletic director must successfully navigate an environment of constant change while securing the necessary financial, human, facility, equipment, and technological resources needed in order to succeed.

The athletic director must develop and manage relationships with a wide variety of stakeholders including student athletes, alumni, faculty, students, administrators, parents, and members of the media. He or she must continually shape the operation of the organization to comply with new rules, policies, and procedures promulgated by the NCAA, the university itself, and other governing bodies. The ultimate challenge for the athletic director is to manage a complex enterprise that includes not only the business functions of marketing, accounting, finance, and information services, but also to create and oversee over twenty individual sports teams that are competitive and operate within the boundaries of NCAA guidelines and the university's educational mission.

University of Arizona athletic director Jim Livengood confirms that the athletic director of today must be a change specialist. Athletic directors must be flexible and possess a broad range of managerial competencies. He or she must not only be a good manager of people, but must also be part fund-raiser, financial analyst, marketer, politician, and lawyer. "There's not a week that goes by that we don't have to think about legal problems," says Livengood. "That means dealing with liability involved with our venues, our coaches, our student athletes, our fans" (Schwartz, 2000, p. 36).

For Foley, the most important change in intercollegiate athletics in the last decade is the increase in the amount of capital required to run a successful athletic program: "it's changed because the dollars have gotten bigger and continue to get bigger every day [and with that] the expectations get bigger every day" (King, 2000, p. 35). The financial pinch is being felt in athletic departments throughout the country. One of the biggest myths in college sports is that all athletic programs make money when, in fact, very few programs make a consistent profit. In the 1999–2000 budget year, Michigan showed a $3.8 million budget deficit; Princeton reported a $6.6 million loss ("College Athletic Programs," *Street & Smith's SportsBusiness Journal*, June 12–18, 2000, p. 32).

Syracuse athletic director Jake Crouthamel explains that internal factors such as an increase in human resource, equipment, and insurance costs are partly responsible for deficits. But changes in the external environment such as population loss and slow, if not stagnant, job growth in the Syracuse area have also negatively affected the athletic department's ability to raise revenue by increasing ticket prices or securing additional corporate sponsorships (Maloney, 2000). Fan and student expectations, the economy, changes in technology, and political interests are just some of the many factors that influence and shape the collegiate athletic department.

Internal factors within the university may also force changes on the athletic department. When university administrators are faced with limited financial resources that must be allocated across the institution, athletic department funding may be seen as a lesser priority. Administrators and faculty may view athletics as unnecessary to the school's educational mission. As a result, in times of institutionwide financial exigency, athletic directors are asked to shoulder budget cuts or may be required to generate whatever money they need to operate. Crouthamel suggests that in times when both institutional funding and state support is tight, the athletic director must be increasingly resourceful in developing new sources of revenue, "we have to work harder . . . without state funding [and] without student fees" (Maloney, 2000, p. 26).

Crouthamel, Livengood, and Foley all suggest the athletic director of the future must not only be able to enhance revenue streams and perform essential management tasks, but they must also be able to understand the dynamic environment of intercollegiate athletics and manage change successfully. Athletic directors are faced with increasing pressure from both within and outside the university not only to run financially solvent programs, but also to win and to run clean programs as well. The Knight Commission, originally launched by the John S. and James L. Knight Foundation in 1990 to examine the operation of and recommend reforms to intercollegiate athletics, serves as one of the most powerful and vocal forces in directing the future of college sports. The commission, made up of a panel of twenty-eight leaders from the education, business, and sports industries, continues to examine critical issues facing intercollegiate athletics and is particularly interested in assessing the influence of money on college sports (Lee, 2001a). Both the Knight Commission and the Collegiate Athletes Coalition, a group of former athletes interested in lobbying the NCAA for policy and rules changes that would favor student athletes (Lee, 2001b), continue to exert pressure on both the NCAA and individual institutions to engage in ongoing reform.

A general consensus is that the role of the athletic director will continue to evolve. Intercollegiate sports managers of the future will need to become better businesspeople. "I think the business has changed pretty dramatically. Notice I used the word 'business' . . . it didn't used to be the business it is now. It encompasses pure business," says Crouthamel (Maloney, 2000, p. 26). Successful athletic directors will not only be those who can successfully wear the many hats of business as strategic planner, fund-raiser, lawyer, politician, and financier, but they will need to be able to anticipate change and innovate as they lead their athletic departments in achieving both on- and off-field goals.

The Intercollegiate Athletic System

The intercollegiate athletic system in the United States is complex with over nine hundred schools competing as members of the National Collegiate Athletic Association (NCAA) at Division I (Division I-A/Division I-AA, I-AAA), Division II, and Division III levels (see Figure 12-1). All schools must offer a minimum number of sports programs, meet specific student athlete financial aid qualifications, and must agree to be bound by NCAA regulations.

Schools petition to join the NCAA as a member of one of the three divisions. Division I schools are usually larger in student population, budget, number of sports programs offered, and staff size. Division I schools offer athletic scholarships, seek regional and national prominence, and focus on producing athletic-related revenues to support the operation of the program. Division I schools have two specific functions that relate to separate constituent groups. NCAA Division I schools must serve both the campus community and the general public by providing entertainment to fans within the broader community. Within Division I, two major subdivisions exist. They are Division I-A schools that offer football at the nationally competitive level and Division I-AA schools that field regionally competitive football programs. In most instances, Division I-A schools are considered on the high end of the intercollegiate athletic program spectrum because they gain the most national media coverage, bring in millions of dollars in sponsorship and television revenue, and generally attract the most athletically gifted student athletes.

Division II schools focus on providing broad participation opportunities in athletics. They seek competitive excellence and provide some scholarship support to athletes, but to a lesser extent than Division I institutions. They are also interested in serving the campus community, but they focus to a lesser degree on creating entertainment value for the general public. Division III schools award no athletically related financial aid and focus primarily on participants and members of the campus community rather than on entertainment needs of the general public. Division III schools also focus on achieving athletic excellence, but their major concern is to support the student athlete and coaches and to assure that athletics support the institution's broader educational mission.

Although NCAA member institutions ascribe to the specific divisional philosophy as adopted by that division's membership, schools vary greatly within each division on how the philosophy is translated into action. Consider, for example, Widener University, a Division III institution in Pennsylvania. Widener has attained national prominence with its athletic programs, secures corporate sponsorships for its highly competitive basketball program, and aggressively seeks television deals for its football program. Clearly, despite the school's designation as a Division III institution, one might argue that its athletic program is exhibiting typical Division I behaviors.

The NCAA is considered the premier association for intercollegiate athletics in the United States, but institutions may choose to join other athletic associations

> **Figure 12-1** Summary of NCAA Division I, II, and III Philosophy Statements

Division I (I-A , I-AA, I-AAA)

Strives for regional and national excellence; believes in offering extensive opportunities in varsity intercollegiate athletic sports programs for both men and women; emphasizes scheduling other Division I institutions; committed to offering one or both of the traditional spectator and revenue-producing sports (football or basketball), focuses on being self-supporting; grants highest number of permissible athletic scholarships, minimum limits for football stadium size, and attendance at home football games. (*An institution may earn a Division I-AA designation by offering a football program that is more regional in orientation and is one step removed from traditional big-time Division IA football programs.*)

Division II

Strives to offer a maximum amount of opportunities in intercollegiate athletics sports programs for as many students as possible; encourages competitive excellence; recognizes the athletics program should serve both the campus and the general public; focuses on scheduling other Division II institutions; grants athletic scholarships but to a lesser degree than Division I.

Division III

Strives to emphasize the importance of athletics on the participants and the student athletes' total educational experience; encourages broad-based participation; focuses on regional in-season competition and conference championships; emphasizes athletics as part of the campus community and focuses on internal stakeholders rather than the general public; grants no athletic scholarships.

Note: All divisions subscribe to principles that encourage sportsmanship, fair play, and gender equity. Additionally, the operation of each program should support the mission and philosophy of the institution as a whole and encourage excellence in both academic and athletic pursuits.

Source: Adapted from *NCAA Manual* (1999–2000).

www.naia.org

including the National Association for Intercollegiate Athletics (NAIA) or National Junior College Athletic Association (NJCAA).

In addition to their voluntary national association with the NCAA, schools may also become affiliated with like institutions through conference membership (e.g., The Big East, Pac 10, Atlantic Coast Conference). Conference membership facilitates scheduling through the provision of available opponents (the conference schedule), provides opportunities for postseason play, and creates opportunities for joint marketing, licensing, or broadcast fee negotiation.

www.njcaa.org

Managing an intercollegiate athletic department is complex. As intercollegiate athletics have become an integral part of campus life at institutions of higher learning throughout the United States and national interest in sport has blossomed, athletic directors in the last decade have faced the challenge of a growth binge in college athletics (King, 2000). For example, Division I athletic programs such as those at Florida, Ohio State, Texas, and Tennessee currently operate with annual athletic budgets of over $50 million a year (Schwartz, 2000); athletic programs such as those at Stanford and Princeton field teams in over thirty sports (King, 2000).

Understanding Change in Sports Organizations

sport management theorist Trevor Slack suggests that sports organizations are in a constant state of change (Slack, 1997). Intercollegiate athletic programs are no exception. Student athletes graduate and new coaches are hired. New facilities are built. Budgets are cut. New sports are added. New training methods and equipment are developed and tried. The list of changes that occur within the life of an intercollegiate sports organization is endless. For the intercollegiate sports manager, the challenge of change is to view it not as a problem for the athletic department to overcome, but rather as a key competency for the organization as it continues to pursue improvement and success.

In order to understand change, we must examine why change occurs. Slack (1997) suggests that change emanates either from external sources or from within the sports organization itself.

External Forces

Impetus for change in the external environment seems to originate from either one of two sources: external stakeholders or external conditions. External stakeholders may include the federal or local government, college sports governing bodies, competitors, parents, media, alumni, boosters, licensees, recruits, conference member institutions, and community members. The Knight Commission and the Collegiate Athletes Coalition, discussed previously, are examples of external stakeholders who are seeking to force change in the operation of intercollegiate athletic programs.

Effects of pressure to change exerted by external stakeholders are easy to identify. For example, the federal government as external stakeholder has imposed several changes on intercollegiate sports programs. Federal mandates including Title IX and the Americans with Disabilities Act have required athletic departments to develop and invest more resources in women's programs and to provide better stadium access to disabled fans, respectively. Certainly the impact of the NCAA on individual athletic programs is of paramount importance to the athletic director. The NCAA virtually controls all aspects of intercollegiate athletics in the United States. Its rules and regulations, pertaining to every aspect of intercollegiate sport including recruitment of student athletes, eligibility of student athletes, length of playing season, championships, sports information, and game management as well as its ability to penalize member institutions and athletes for breaking these rules, continues to shape the daily operation of the athletic department.

Whereas external stakeholders include specific constituent groups, external conditions include general trends, interests, or factors that directly impact the operation of the sports organization. External conditions may include the economy, waning interest or rising popularity of a particular sport, the political, religious, or social climate, and development of new technology.

An example of a change brought about by an emerging environmental trend is the increased popularity of women's ice hockey in the years following the U.S. women's winning of the gold medal at the 1998 Olympics. Young women throughout the country became interested in playing ice hockey ("Boost for Women's Game," 1998). Girls' youth ice hockey programs were developed on the local level, and colleges and universities throughout the country began to evaluate the benefits of adding women's ice hockey to their sports offerings. The link between the women's success in the international arena to growth of women's ice hockey programs in colleges and universities is undeniable.

The advent of new technology is another example of change, and it has resulted in one of the most perplexing challenges faced by intercollegiate athletic department managers. For example, many sports managers agree that cable technology significantly changed the operation of sports organizations. New markets were opened up, new fans were reached, and new sources of revenue were made available. Evidence of the change brought about by cable television can be seen in athletic departments throughout the country: several athletic directors continue to willingly change game schedules and starting times to accommodate the needs and interest of television broadcasters, the popularity of the men's and women's basketball final four is fueled by television coverage, and television rights fees are a significant revenue line item for many college athletic programs.

The Internet has also brought a new dimension to collegiate athletics. Athletic directors now are faced with the challenge of devising strategies to capitalize on Internet technology. The combination of the availability of this technology and demands by parents, prospective students, media, alumni, and fans for instantaneous and comprehensive sports information make it necessary for athletic directors to transform the sports information function within their departments to an electronic platform. For example, at the University of Richmond, the latest sports information including game scores and highlights are now available 24 hours a day through the athletic department's website. Game schedules, profiles of coaches, live game broadcasts, booster club information, online athletic merchandise shops, and on-line ticketing make it convenient for fans to follow the Spiders anytime night or day.

Internal Forces

While external sources exert pressure on the athletic department to change, internal forces lead to change as well. Slack (1997) suggests that an emphasis on service quality, a move to self-managed teams, and the demand for flexible operating procedures have produced pressures for change from within the sports organization. Change may also be triggered by such simple operational activities as the hiring of a new employee, the development of a new policy, or the cutting of a budget item (Slack, 1997).

The construction of a new sports facility is a good example of how change can be driven from within. With the construction of the Mullins Center at the University of Massachusetts, the athletic director, Bob Marcum, had to restructure the season ticket holders' seating plan (Katz, 1993). A priority point system was put in place whereby season ticket holders were awarded points for donations to the athletic department, alumni or faculty status, purchase of other football, basketball, or hockey season tickets, and volunteer contributions to the athletic department. Season ticket holders were assigned seats based on their point total. The system was designed to encourage contributions to the athletic fund and to generate additional season ticket sales for the football, basketball, and hockey programs. The adoption of the new priority point system brought about additional changes in the athletic department operation. New staff members were needed to manage the point system. New computer software was purchased. Staff training programs were initiated, and a new system for processing season ticket applications was developed and instituted.

Categories of Change in Collegiate Athletics

Whether the impetus for change comes from internal or external sources, the manifestation of change occurs in one of four areas within the sports organization: technology, structures and systems, products and services, and people (Slack, 1997).

Technological change refers to a change in production methods, service provision, or equipment based on the development of new technology. Examples would include the adoption of new ticketing software, website development, or creation of a fan loyalty card program that rewards fans for swiping their fan loyalty card at kiosks in the arena so they may accumulate loyalty points to be used to purchase tickets or merchandise.

Structural and system changes encompass those changes to the organization's structural elements including division of labor, reporting structure, or organizational control. The creation of the senior women's administrator position or the development of a private booster club or foundation that exists outside of the university structure and authority are examples of structural and system changes.

Products and services changes reflect changes to operational areas including the basic supply of goods and services, marketing, finance, and facility management. Examples would include the construction of a new arena, moving the hockey program from Division II to Division I, and introducing a new logo and mascot.

Lastly, changes in the people area involve human resource–related concerns. For example, these might include a policy change in recruitment of student athletes, the hiring of a new coach, creation of a captain's council, or initiation of a student athlete life skills program.

The Domino Effect of Change

Although it is useful to examine change on the basis of how it affects each of these areas—technology, structures and systems, products and services, and people—change does not occur in isolation. That is, a change in one area is frequently related to change in another area. In a domino effect for sports organizations, one change brings about subsequent changes throughout the organization.

When the University of Massachusetts constructed its Mullins Center, the creation of the new building not only brought about immediate operational changes, such as how season tickets were distributed, but it resulted in broader long-term changes to the athletic department as well. With the construction of the Mullins Center, a new athletic hall of fame was built and alumni were recognized for their lifetime achievements. The new Mullins Center also made it possible to reinstitute the men's ice hockey program that had been dropped in the 1970s.

This type of network of change is not unusual. In fact, as long as intercollegiate athletics exist, there will be both internal and external pressures to grow, improve, and innovate. For the intercollegiate athletics manager, change is not only inevitable, it is necessary.

Identifying the Change

Regardless of the specific change an organization might pursue, effective management of the change process begins with comprehensive understanding in two areas. First, a vision of the desired change or a comprehensive set of goals is needed that defines the change for the organization. Nowhere is vision more critical than in the process of achieving effective change. Management must develop a comprehensive set of goals that is so specific it will communicate an unmistakable vision of what the changed organization will look like. Second, there needs to be an understanding of the factors and forces likely to influence and shape the change process. The manager needs to assess carefully and consider all possible influences emanating both from the internal and external environment and should necessarily forecast how these factors will shape the change process.

Developing the Vision

Consider the case of University of Connecticut athletic director Lew Perkins and the university's goal of elevating its athletic program to national prominence. UCONN men's basketball coach, Jim Calhoun, describes Perkins as a "good leader, a terrific business man and a true visionary" (Steinbreder, 2000, p. 34). When Perkins was hired in July 1990, he talked with people throughout and beyond the university. He asked people to tell him about their aspirations for the athletic department and to define the future of UCONN athletics. He then began to carefully articulate a vision for the University of Connecticut to all of the athletic department's stakeholder groups. His vision was to upgrade all aspects of the athletic department and its operations, to make the athletic program an integral part of the university, and to have winning teams, but never to the detriment of the student athlete or the university (Steinbreder, 2000). He carefully created a comprehensive set of goals including increasing fund-raising revenues, securing more corporate sponsors, generating more licensing revenue, lobbying state budget decision makers, attaining gender equity, and constructing new sports facilities, including a student recreation center, ice arena, football stadium, and outdoor sports complex field. He also set a goal of running a clean program where there would be no NCAA violations, problems, or investigations under his tenure. His vision for the future of UCONN athletics was not only well conceived, but represented a thoughtful and strategic idea that positively positioned the athletic department for the future. Although there was much work to do, Perkins provided a clear vision and worked with his staff to develop appropriate and achievable goals that would bring about the changes required to realize their vision for the future.

Perkins's actions demonstrate what management expert Noel M. Tichy calls *envisioning*, a process that involves not just management, but the entire organization:

> The visioning process is creative and often chaotic. A vision is a group effort. It is what the group believes to be important. It is also a work in progress, an architectural rendering that constantly gets modified. As many people as possible should be involved, thinking "out loud" and getting feedback from many different stakeholders. (Tichy, 1993, p. 118)

The first responsibility of the sports manager in directing change involves not just stating one's individual philosophy or ideas about what the organization should look like or what changes should occur, but instead, including all members of the organization in the thinking and planning process.

Leadership researchers Warren Bennis and Burt Nanus (1985) come to the same conclusion:

> The leader only rarely was the one who conceived of the vision in the first place. Therefore the leader must be a superb listener, particularly to those advocating new or different images of the emerging reality. . . . Successful leaders, we have found, are *great askers,* and they do pay attention. (p. 492)

In managing change, the sports manager's first responsibility is to "get" the vision, to listen and to "think out loud" in conversations throughout the organization for the purpose of developing a specific set of goals that will define exactly what the change should look like in his or her organization. Through a vision that can be directly translated into clearly defined goals and with a strong and specific sense of exactly what the change should be, the manager then can turn to the next task in the change process. This task involves understanding all the forces and factors that will affect the organization as it pursues the change goals.

Force Field Analysis

Social scientist Kurt Lewin developed a process for identifying and analyzing the forces operating in a change situation that he called *force field analysis* (Lewin, 1951). Lewin suggested that in any organizational change effort, two kinds of forces affect the change operating in any change situation: driving forces and restraining forces.

Lewin defined *driving forces* as forces or factors in the situation that initiate, assist, and support the change. Driving forces include changes in the organization's environment that make change necessary or that represent an opportunity for the organization. They include key individuals and groups within the organization who are in favor of and support the change. They also include the availability of training, technology, and other resources necessary for the change to be effective. Driving forces might also include information or experiences that make clear what will happen if the organization doesn't change.

To understand the effect of driving forces in bringing about change, we need only look at the recent articles reporting the elimination of some sports programs at colleges and universities. In the last decade, many schools have added sports programs, and several schools have decided to drop some sports entirely. In 1997 Boston University announced it was eliminating its I-AA football program. Boston University's decision to drop men's football was a result of driving forces including the need to trim athletic expenses, the lack of attendance at football games, and the school's failure to field a competitive team (Moran, 1997).

Restraining forces are forces or factors working against the change, forces generating resistance at the individual and corporate culture levels. In many ways, restraining forces are the opposite of driving forces. They include opposition from key individuals and groups within the organization, and lack of availability of training and other resources needed for the change to succeed. Restraining forces might also include negative information or experiences relative to the change.

At Boston University, restraining forces working against the decision to drop the school's I-AA football team were alumni, institutions who had depended on a game with Boston University in their schedule, a 100-year-old football tradition, and current football players who felt they had been recruited under false pretenses (Moran, 1997).

A force field analysis for the change from a football-playing institution to a non-football institution at Boston University is shown in Figure 12-2.

Once the decision to drop the football team was announced, the university announced a new athletics plan that detailed increased spending on women's sports programs. Funding for women's programs was increased by $500,000 annually, an additional twenty-three new scholarships were added for women's varsity athletes, and the university identified four priority sports for men and four priority sports for women ("Division I Notes," 1997).

For change to be effective, managers must begin with a careful and complete force field analysis. They must first identify the driving forces in the situation and make full use of them to overcome the obstacles to change. Perhaps more importantly, managers must also correctly identify the restraining forces in the situation and develop strategies to eliminate or minimize them as the change moves forward. At Boston University, there was a clear mandate for the athletic department to address gender equity concerns and to provide more resources for women's programs. Although restraining forces to the change including angry stakeholder groups (football proponents and football alumni) had been vocal in their opposition to the move, the institution recognized that driving forces (including fear of violation of Title IX, lack of student and alumni attendance at football games, proponents of women's athletics, costs associated with football, and paucity of financial resources) supported the change.

Only when this depth and scope of understanding has been achieved is the sports manager ready to begin actually implementing the change process.

Figure 12-2 Force Field Analysis: Boston University Football Program

Should the Boston University athletic department eliminate the football program?

Driving Forces
Reasons for dropping the
football program

Athletic budget red ink
Football program budget deficit
Challenge to compliance with Title IX
Stakeholders lobbying for gender equity
Potential lawsuits for Title IX noncompliance
Lack of fans at home games
Lack of student support of football
Potentially positive publicity
Number of scholarships allocated to football
Noncompetitiveness of the football team
Elimination of associated expenses

Restraining Forces
Reasons against dropping
the football program

Tradition
Football boosters
Football alumni group
Existence of football stadium
Football opponents
Current football players
Parents of current football players
Potentially negative publicity
Backlash from athletic donors
Football friendly trustees
Staff positions lost—unemployed workers

Implementing the Change Process

Once the change goal has been clearly defined and the analysis of the force field relative to that goal has been completed, the sports manager must begin to implement the change plan. Again it is Kurt Lewin who provides a simple theoretical model for understanding how change is brought about within organizations. Several theories that may be useful for the manager in understanding how to manage change, but Lewin's theory provides a good starting point to examine how change takes place within an organization. According to Lewin, a successful change process involves these three stages:

1. The *unfreezing* stage, during which the organization addresses the problems of resistance and prepares its people for change;

2. The *actual change* stage, during which the new beliefs and new behaviors are communicated, modeled, and initiated;

3. The *refreezing* stage, during which the new beliefs and behaviors are supported and reinforced.

To achieve the change goal successfully, the manager must negotiate each of these stages effectively.

Stage 1: Unfreezing—Reducing the Resistance to Change

Change does not come easily, for individuals or for organizations. For reasons we discuss later, both individuals and organizations tend to resist change vigorously. The first stage in the change management process, then, focuses on reducing the resistance to change. This resistance to change in organizations exists at the individual and at the organizational levels. At the individual level, the source of resistance to change appears to be our human nature. At the organizational level, it is the corporate culture that tends to resist change.

Stress: The Human Response to Change

The changes required for organizations to be competitive in today's dynamic environment are not minor. People are being asked to learn and use technology that may not have even existed a few years earlier; to do more work, faster and with greater quality than ever before, and, in the case of sports organizations, to adapt successfully to new rules and regulations that are continuously being promulgated by governing bodies. The natural response to change of this dimension or magnitude has been called the stress response (Seyle, 1976).

The *stress response* is the fight-or-flight response that prepares us for action when we are in danger. Unfortunately, most people view major change as a potential source of danger, and their natural reaction is one of stress. People become anxious about whether they can do what the change requires in terms of using new technology, doing different work than they are used to, and doing more of it, faster and with greater quality. People worry about whether there will still be a place for them in the organization. From a needs perspective, change represents a threat to people's security, and often their natural reaction is to resist and defend against this perceived threat.

For example, as media scrutiny increases on the percentage of athletes in a sport who actually graduate from college, coaches and athletic directors now must worry not only about their student athletes' athletic performance, but about their performance in the classroom as well. And increasingly, this concern has been extended to include the behavior of these young people outside the sports and athletic arena, in the community. For many coaches, the additional task of monitoring students' academic and social performance is outside their comfort zone. They are used to breaking down game films, assessing athletes' skills, and devising game strategies. Monitoring students' academic eligibility, interpreting NCAA regulations, and supervising student athletes' social development is not what they are used to, and they are unsure whether they can be effective with this "new work." In an effort to escape the stress associated with these additional responsibilities, the initial response is often one of resistance. Their view may be that these new responsibilities should be given to someone else. In fact, many coaches have successfully lobbied their athletic directors for the creation of new positions such as team academic adviser, peer adviser, and compliance coordinator to take on the new work of facilitating the graduation of student athletes.

As in this example, the human response to change in organizations tends to be negative. Not only do people question how the change affects them individually, but they also question how the change will affect the organization. Change may be resisted because stakeholders question the outcomes of the change. Will this change be worth the necessary investment of time, effort, and money to bring about the changes? Is this change good for everyone? Will some of us be left behind? Do the benefits of this change outweigh the total costs to the organization and all of the stakeholders? For this reason, effective change must begin with strategies to help people get beyond this initial stress response to enable them to adapt fully to the requirements of the change.

For management change theorist Robert Kriegel, people are the most critical element of successful change: "[P]eople are the gatekeepers of change. They have the power to breathe life into a new program or kill it. If they're excited and positive; it's open sesame. If they're not—and that's most of the time—it's clang! The gate's slammed shut in your face" (Kriegel, 1996, p. 5).

Corporate Culture

The other major source of resistance to change in organizations is *corporate culture*, the term used to describe the set of beliefs, norms, and values that are shared by the members of an organization. These beliefs, norms, and values have to do with the way the organization operates and what is important in that organization.

Researchers Terrence Deal and Allan Kennedy (1982) suggest that corporate culture tends to be created and communicated by the stories an organization tells about itself, by the language it uses, by whom the organization celebrates as its heroes, and by its rituals and ceremonies. College sports are famous for the kinds of stories, language, and rituals that communicate the beliefs and values of sports programs at specific institutions:

- At Indiana University, President Myles Brand oversaw a probe that uncovered a pattern of misbehavior by basketball coach Bobby Knight. Despite proof of Knight's head-butting his players, grabbing a player around the neck, cursing a secretary, and throwing a potted plant at a sixty-four-year-old female university employee, Knight was only initially reprimanded and placed under a no-tolerance policy (Burwell, 2000).

- In the New England Small College Athletic Conference (NESCAC), member institutions do not allow student athletes to participate in postseason play if the games conflict with scheduled student exams.

- NFL player, Dexter Manly, testified before the U.S. Congress that he was still unable to read and write after four years at Oklahoma State (Sperber, 2000).

- The NCAA Executive Committee threatened to cancel future events, including first- and second-round regional games in the Division I Men's Basketball Tournament in 2002, unless South Carolina took action to remove the Confederate battle flags from the state capitol. (Lee, 2000).

In a very real sense, the beliefs, norms, and values communicated through these stories, rituals, and heroes provide a mental road map for the members of a sports organization. They define and reinforce in people's minds what is important in the organization and "the way things are done around here."

Because it requires a shift in "the way things are done around here," change represents the most serious kind of threat to an organization's corporate culture. Change requires a new set of beliefs, new norms, and new values. It not only requires new heroes, new language, and new rituals; change renders the old heroes, language, and rituals obsolete.

Lew Perkins, in his attempts to bring the athletic program to national prominence at the University of Connecticut by upgrading football from Division I-AA to Division I-A, came to experience the restraining power of corporate culture. In 1996 when Perkins announced the men's football program would be moving from Division I-AA to Division I-A, he had hoped to bring about the change quickly. The reality was very different. Not only would he have to change the university's culture, he would have to effectively introduce the change to critical external stakeholders including the state legislature, Big East Conference affiliates (where the school already competed in basketball), alumni, and media.

He was having difficulty changing the university's culture as quickly as he felt it needed to be changed. Even after he had hired a new coach, set a target date for the first Division I-A season, and began to lobby for a new stadium, many students, athletes, faculty members, and coaches did not understand the necessity of upgrading the football program. Both men's and women's teams had been very successful, and some UCONN employees felt the investment required to enhance the football program would create a major drain on the institution's and athletic department's budget. Some people suggested that trying to bring football into the national spotlight might even take away from the nationally competitive men's and women's basketball programs (Rabinovitz, 1997a). Others felt the football team had not been sufficiently successful at Division I-AA to warrant such a jump (Rabinovitz, 1997b). Members of the athletic department staff were wondering what additional work requirements this would mean for them. Great concern was also expressed over the site of a new stadium and the potential negative effects of the traffic generated on game days. But Perkins was trying to change the UCONN corporate culture from a basketball-only emphasis to one that would also rely on football for revenue generation and national attention.

As shown in Figure 12-3, for the process of change to be successful in an organization, management must recognize both the potentially intense individual human resistance to change and the equally intense collective resistance from the organization's corporate culture and utilize the appropriate strategy to diminish their negative effects. The first step in managing change, therefore, is to deal with the reality of this resistance. Management's task in the unfreezing stage is to reduce this resistance to change at both the individual and the organizational level. The resistance must be unfrozen, softened, and thawed to enable the personal and organizational flexibility necessary to accept and embrace the change.

Strategies for Reducing Resistance to Change

John Kotter and Leonard Schlesinger (1978) have identified a number of strategies (shown in Figure 12-3) for reducing individual and organizational resistance to change in organizations. For our purposes, this collection of strategies for unfreezing can be divided into two categories: agreement-oriented approaches and the coercive approach.

Figure 12-3 Strategies for Reducing Resistance to Change

Education and communication	When the source of resistance is a lack of understanding and information.
Participation and involvement	When a higher level of input and cooperation would benefit the change process.
Facilitation and support	Where resistance is primarily the result of difficulty adjusting to the change.
Negotiation and agreement	Where a fuller partnership is required to make the change successful.
Implicit and explicit coercion	Where fast, dramatic change does not permit the time or latitude required for a more participative approach.

Agreement-oriented approaches to unfreezing. Four of the options identified by Kotter and Schlesinger—education and communication, participation and involvement, facilitation and support, and negotiation and agreement—could be described as agreement-oriented approaches to preparing people for change. Each of these four options represents an effort to work with people to help them accept the need for the change before moving forward. As a result, these approaches each have the important advantage of being more likely to maintain the bond of trust between managers and the other members of the organization. The assumption is that resistance to the change will lessen as management takes the time to address people's concerns and to reach agreement about how best to achieve the change.

Lew Perkins effectively utilized several of these strategies at the University of Connecticut. He hired Southeastern Conference (SEC) commissioner Roy Kramer to help devise and write a complete and thorough implementation plan for the upgrade and then secured the services of KPMG, an international marketing and consulting firm, to assist in developing these studies. He then shared these reports with decision makers through educational meetings and receptions with key stakeholder groups including athletic department staff, university personnel, donors, and alumni. He and University of Connecticut president Harry Hartley also worked closely with the state of Connecticut legislature and board of trustees to negotiate support and to involve important decision makers in the process of moving the program to the more competitive Division I-A and securing funding necessary to build a new football stadium. Finally, when the state legislature and governor passed a $770 million proposal to rebuild Hartford's riverfront, which included a $90 million stadium project for the University of Connecticut, senior assistant athletic director Jeff Hathaway pointed to intensive lobbying efforts as making the difference in securing the approval of the bill: "we were there [at the state legislature] more than you can believe through the whole process" (Lee, 2000b).

Perkins had to consider the opinions, ideas, and points of view of internal constituencies such as administration, trustees, faculty, staff, coaches, and students. Through open communication with these stakeholders, Perkins attempted to generate internal buy-in of the change. He solicited suggestions from coaches, faculty, administration, and staff. He openly discussed the plan, integrated internal stakeholder feedback, and encouraged internal stakeholder investment in the plan. He knew the change would come about more easily if internal stakeholders were involved in shaping the change and felt invested in its success. His goal was to facilitate universitywide ownership of the plan.

In some change situations, however, these agreement-oriented approaches to unfreezing may not be possible. For example, it is conceivable that no amount of lobbying, education, participation, facilitation, or negotiation could prepare a sports organization for the kinds of change required when there is an immediate threat to the athletic program, student athlete, or athletic department staff member. This brings us to the second category of unfreezing, which involves a more coercive approach.

Coercion as a strategy for unfreezing. *Coercion* is the process of imposing change on an organization, requiring people to perform new tasks, or to perform their old tasks in new ways, or to perform in conditions that might be dramatically different from what they have been accustomed to, whether they agree or not. Coerced change is not voluntary; it does not involve education or facilitation or negotiation, and it is usually not gradual. Coercion is used when the need for change is too urgent to permit the more time-consuming agreement-oriented option.

Consider the case of the University of Vermont ice hockey team. In September 1999 a freshman ice hockey player notified university officials that a party was planned at which freshmen members of the ice hockey team were going to be hazed. University officials interviewed every member of the hockey team and were assured no such party was planned. Athletic department personnel reminded the students of the university's ban on hazing and encouraged students to think carefully about the ramifications of ignoring the ban. In October the student athlete complained again to university officials that the party had in fact taken place and he described in detail the hazing that had occurred. At that time, the university hired an outside law firm to investigate the student's claim and mandated that all players cooperate with investigators. After reviewing the findings of the interviews, the university placed the team on probation, suspended players for one game each, required all players to attend educational programs about hazing, and ordered the team to perform community service (Lively, 2000).

In January, however, the athletic director and university president learned that some members of the team had lied and conspired to cover up their behavior. The athletic director and president immediately cancelled the rest of the team's season. An immediate departmentwide hazing investigation was launched that examined all athletic programs. All student athletes and coaches were compelled to participate in the self-study and required to attend a mandatory informational session about hazing. The athletic director immediately instituted new policies and practices designed to discourage hazing of any type and to dismiss any student found to have participated in hazing activities. The student athlete involved in the case left the institution and filed a suit in federal court, alleging that several incidents of hazing took place and the university failed to intercede adequately (Lively, 2000).

In this case, the sports managers involved determined that the severity of the incident and the likely irreparable harm to participants and the university were so heinous that coercion to bring about changes to eliminate hazing was the only available option. None of this was voluntary; all of these changes were required of the people at the University of Vermont. The athletic director was convinced the changes could not be participatory. At the very least, there was not enough time for education, participation, and negotiation. These changes were necessary for the athletic program's survival and the safety of student athletes, so the changes were coerced.

Some critics might argue that coercion is not a strategy for reducing resistance to change, but rather is a process of imposing change despite continuing broad-based resistance. There is some validity to this position, but grounds also exist for viewing coercion as a legitimate means to reduce resistance. Based on his research on the relationship between feelings and behavior, Harvard psychologist Jerome Bruner (1973) concluded, "You more often act yourself into feeling than feel yourself into action." According to Bruner, people tend to adjust how they feel about something to the reality of the situation. This suggests that, even if people are forced into change, once they realize they can survive new conditions and may even benefit by them, their resistance to the change may at least be reduced, if not eliminated entirely.

Some experts still question whether coercion might not actually increase resistance among resentful employees over the longer term. They point out that the problem with forcing people into change is that you then find yourself operating an organization with a crushed and battered work force. Defenders of coercion as an approach for unfreezing, in contrast, argue that coerced change can still be implemented in ways that respect the needs and dignity of people. Still others point out that, given the pressure on an organization to change rapidly in response to opportunities and threats, there may be no effective alternative.

Regardless of the outcome of this controversy, the first task of the manager in implementing the change is to unfreeze the organization. Whether through coercion or through one or a combination of the agreement-oriented approaches, the task for the manager is to prepare the people and the organization for change by reducing as much as possible their natural resistance to it.

Stage 2: The Actual Change

Once resistance to change has been reduced to the extent possible, the task for managers is to begin the actual change. The new behaviors, the new approach, the new priorities required by the change must be preached, modeled, and initiated. Pat Williams, CEO of the Orlando Magic, has suggested that in leading change in sports organizations, "your grand vision is worthless if you, as a leader, cannot sell that vision to your team . . . whether you know it or not, if you are a leader, you are a salesman. You've got to sell your vision . . . not as *my* vision for this team, but as *our* vision for success" (Williams, 1997). In other words, you can't expect people to follow you from the old way to the new way until it is clear to them, in the most specific terms possible, just what the new way is, what it means, and that they are an important part of the process.

We have already pointed out that a clear definition of the change goal is essential prior even to beginning the change process. We have also discussed the importance of getting constituents to become invested in the change and take responsibility for the change by participating in the shaping of the vision and resultant change goals. But even the most inspiring vision will not move an organization unless it can effectively be shared. In the second stage of the change process, the challenge for managers is to *communicate* the change both within and beyond the organization through words and actions.

Words

Words are a powerful force in focusing our attention and mobilizing our energies. Anyone who has heard the motivational words of a coach before a big game understands the power of the spoken word. Change is a political process in which the forces for improvement attempt to overcome the forces of resistance and the status quo. Effective change can be viewed as the result of an effective campaign, and words are a potentially powerful weapon in deciding the outcome of that campaign.

We said at the outset that effective change begins with a clear and comprehensive vision of exactly what the change means and looks like for the organization. The challenge in this second stage of implementing the change is to find the words, the phrases, and the stories that will enable the stakeholders of the organization to share the change vision and to begin to act on it. The athletic director must truly be an organizational coach who encourages, motivates, and energizes members of the organization and other constituencies with his or her enthusiasm for the change.

Actions Speak Louder Than Words

As important as an effective change message is, however, all the words in the world will not be as effective as the example of a leader, especially in communicating new behaviors and values. There is often no more effective way to help people understand the change vision than to have "the new way" modeled for them by the manager.

Words can yield a variety of interpretations in terms of the kind of behaviors people *think* they mean. But a manager's actions provide a clear model of exactly the kind of behavior required. In the case of change, imitation is more effective than interpretation. Managers who want people to take a more team-based approach with their people, for example, will almost certainly get better results by taking a more team-based approach themselves rather than just by making a speech on teamwork.

The same is true for sports managers who want to see their staff spending less time in their offices and more time talking and working with their people. If managers want their managers out of their offices and talking with people, the best way to achieve it is to lead by example. The actions of leaders, *if they are consistent with their words,* simply provide a much clearer message about the kind of new behavior required by the change.

Was Athletic Director Lew Perkins able to use both words and actions to help bring about the move from Division I-AA to Division I-A football? Perkins set up receptions at local restaurants and hotels to speak directly to key stakeholders. He addressed local business and civic organizations and traveled to the capital to meet with local legislators. He granted interviews with local media. In each meeting, he provided clear information about what the change would mean to the athletic department and the university. He was able to show a new model of the stadium and detailed projections of expenses as well as revenues produced by the football team. Perkins, a very motivational speaker, spoke about national championships in football and the positive impact that competing on a national level in football would bring not only to the university but to the entire community. He made himself available to discuss the change with the media and regularly updated his staff about progress made. Perkins also included the university president, football coach, and football players in his presentations. Together, they were able to articulate clearly the benefits to the university and its stakeholders and to lobby donors, fans, politicians, and alumni effectively.

Communication in actions and in words is the essential task of the manager in the second stage of the change process. Only through a strongly shared sense of exactly what the change is, expressed compellingly in words and shown dramatically in the leader's actions, will the organization be able to begin to move from where it has been to where the change seeks to take it.

Stage 3: Refreezing/Rearchitecting

Lewin termed the third and final phase of the change process *refreezing,* the process of reinforcing the change, once it emerges, to ensure it endures over the long term. If the new patterns and the new behaviors developed in the change phase are genuinely to take root and prosper, they must become embedded in the very fabric of the organization, and they must yield positive results. This is what Tichy (1993) means by "rearchitecting": designing and building the structures and support needed to sustain the new behaviors and beliefs far into the future.

For change to endure and prosper, the new ways of doing things must become part of an overall positive experience for the people doing them. To achieve this, the refreezing phase requires the elements shown in Figure 12-4. In other words, successful change requires developing an entirely new corporate culture focused on the new behaviors and the new beliefs.

Recognizing Heroes

Successful change requires heroes, individuals, and groups who adopt the new behaviors and run with them. The heroism can take many forms, from the sports information director who works extra hours to prepare a last-minute press release to

---

Figure 12-4 Elements of Refreezing/Rearchitecting

- Recognizing the heroes and champions of change

- Celebrating the successes of the change

- Rewarding commitment to change

---

the booster club member who solicits a major gift from his own company to support the athletic program. Clearly, the successful achievement of change requires the support and dedication of many people. Refreezing the change requires the recognition of those individuals and groups who actively participate in and lead the change.

Sports managers traditionally recognize their heroes through awards and publicity programs. Heroes are awarded trophies or plaques for their contributions as a matter of tradition. However, the celebration of heroes need not necessarily take the form of a certificate of appreciation, university golf shirt, or golden cup. Heroes may be recognized through other positive feedback strategies such as writing a feature story about the hero in the athletic newsletter, appointing the hero to an athletic advisory or booster club board, or recognizing the hero during halftime ceremonies during homecoming weekend. Some sports organizations celebrate their heroes by providing them with premium sports event tickets or inducting them into an athletic hall of fame.

Sports managers must take the time to identify and recognize heroes. In doing so, they not only clarify the direction of the change, but also reinforce the emerging value that views trying the new behaviors as nothing short of heroic.

Celebrations

Celebrations are a powerful way to emphasize and reinforce values and behaviors through a positive social experience. Celebrations are community events that dramatically enrich the experience of the group and the individual. In recent past years, organizations have begun to recognize the power of celebration. Initially during this period, celebrations were organized around employee anniversaries: five years with the firm, ten years, twenty-five years, and so on.

Over time, the forms of celebration in sport have multiplied from informal postgame pizza parties to more formal athletic banquets or sports luncheons. Some athletic directors recognize athletic department staff who have championed change by taking them to celebratory lunches or on an afternoon golf outing.

One of the most well-known and traditional celebrations in sport has been the raising of championship banners to the roof of the arena or the retiring of a hero's uniform number. These types of celebrations are often reserved for those athletes or coaches whose performance on the court or field is worthy of recognition, but they are sometimes extended to include other organizational champions, such as the athletic department volunteer or staff member who has successfully spearheaded and implemented an organizational change. For example, the athletic alumni coordinator who created and implemented a new system for securing corporate contributions may be worthy of a halftime celebration or pregame reception in honor of his or her contributions to upgrading the athletic development program at the institution.

In one sense, even those traditional celebrations of athletic performance such as senior night or the awarding of a rookie of the year or most valuable player may be viewed as celebrations of change heroes in that these individuals play an important role in contributing to the positive change or improvement of a particular sports program. Many institutions and conferences in their efforts to improve graduation rates of student athletes and dispel the myth of the "dumb jock" celebrate those individuals who are bringing about change through their own academic excellence by naming all-academic teams.

The common thread in these celebrations is that they are community events marking community achievement, whether in terms of athletic performance, fund-raising, sales, service, or just completing another productive week. If a change is to become a genuine part of the life of the organization, it must be celebrated as it unfolds and advances. Recognition and appreciation of the achievement of the change goals must be raised to the level of community celebration. Only very reluctantly do we give up our celebrations, so celebrations, in a sense, serve as insurance that the changes will endure.

Reward

As important as recognition and celebrations are for refreezing or reinforcing the new behaviors required by change, pay and promotion remain among the most powerful means of reinforcing behavior in organizations. The ultimate indicators of an organization's priorities are still most clearly reflected in what you get paid for and who gets promoted. Basing pay and promotion decisions on progress made toward adopting the new behaviors sends a powerful signal that the organization is serious about the change.

For example, if a marketing coordinator has been asked to lead efforts to secure new corporate sponsorships for a new arena and a ticket manager is asked to increase season football ticket sales, some significant portion of their compensation should be based on how well they perform in these new areas. Additionally, their success may be rewarded with promotions to the assistant director level.

Designing reward systems that directly reinforce the change priorities of an organization can be difficult. By paying and promoting change champions and change heroes, however, and by rewarding the early adopters of change, the organization is sending a clear message about what matters now through one of the most important channels it has.

Recent experience with change in organizations has made it clear that successfully achieving change in an organization is a marathon, not a sprint. Many managers say that for significant change to be achieved and genuinely to take root will take closer to a decade than a year. Lew Perkins would definitely agree. His hard work and commitment and that of the entire athletic department at UCONN has resulted in the football team's competing at the Division I-A level nearly five years after the change was first publicly announced. The conception of the idea and the laying of the groundwork necessary to accomplish the change began nearly ten years before. After several years of debate over the location and construction of a football stadium and a failed partnership with the New England Patriots, state of Connecticut, and city of Hartford to develop a stadium as part of an urban revitalization project, a new stadium is expected to be built in Hartford and ready for play in the 2002 season ("Lawmakers," 1999).

The message from this section is that effective change should be viewed as a managerial triathlon of three events: unfreezing, the actual change, and refreezing. Only successful performance in all three will enable the sports manager to achieve the "gold" of effective change.

Managing Continuous Change

In the world of the 1950s, any organizational change tended to be viewed as an infrequent event that would likely be followed by a period of stability for the organization. Once a change occurred, the organization would continue in the new direction. However, in today's dynamic environment, change is never ending. Once the three-part change process is complete, it is time to start all over again. It may be argued that change is an ongoing process and management of change is an ever-present concern that must be viewed as a critical responsibility of management.

The "Calm Waters" versus "White-Water Rapids" Metaphors

Management professor Peter Vaill (1989) has used the term *calm waters* to describe the conditions of the 1950s. He compares the organizations of that period to large ocean liners traveling calm waters with a crew that had made the trip together dozens of times. Under "calm waters" conditions, change is usually required only when the occasional storm appears. The "ship" (the organization) makes a change in course to avoid the storm, but once the storm passes, the ship resumes course toward its destination.

As we have noted throughout this book, conditions in more recent times have changed sports organizations into business enterprises. The effects on management and operations are dramatic. According to Vaill (1989), the environment is no longer one of calm waters with only occasional storms, and organizations are no longer like large ocean liners with a veteran crew. In his words,

> The organization is more akin to a forty-foot raft than to a large ship. Rather than sailing a calm sea, this raft must traverse a raging river made up of an uninterrupted flow of permanent white-water rapids. To make things worse, the raft is manned by ten people who have never worked together, none have traveled the river below, much of the trip is in the dark, the river is dotted by unexpected turns and obstacles, the exact destination of the raft is unclear, and at irregular frequencies the raft needs to pull to shore, where new crew members are added and others leave. (p. 89)

In the permanent white-water rapids described by Vaill, organizations need to be not merely capable of implementing an occasional change, but *built* for change, with constant change as one of their fundamental goals.

This approach may result in a successful organization that is constantly innovating and creating change, but a word of caution is necessary. Change, in and of itself, is not always inherently beneficial to the organization. Some managers in an

Figure 12-5 Principles for Creating Innovative Organizations

- Set specific goals for innovation.

- Invest in applications-oriented small projects aimed at innovation.

- Encourage pilots and prototypes of new ideas rather than getting bogged down in detailed analysis.

- Support champions, individuals, and teams committed to innovation.

- Support "perfect failures"—those unsuccessful efforts in which the organization learned or tried something new.

attempt to become bigger, better, faster, more competitive, or more innovative can dramatically increase employee stress levels, drain resources, and diminish the quality and service of existing programs or initiatives. Change can and does fail when an organization tries to do too much all at once, tries to move too quickly, initiates changes that are impractical or impossible (Kreigel, 1996), or fails to fully consider existing resources or potential consequences of the change. Ill-advised organizational change initiatives can create a workplace that resembles a "panic zone" where employees are rushed, stressed out, reactive, nervous, and scared (Kriegel, 1996, p. 299). In this environment, communication breakdowns occur, creativity suffers, good judgment is threatened, and people shift into crisis management mode (Kriegel, 1996). The lesson is that although innovation and change require a certain amount of risk taking, managers must not abandon logic, common sense, and sound business practices when positioning their organization as change leaders. Managers must never forget the people component of change.

Thriving on Chaos: The Innovative Organization

Tom Peters suggests that an organization successfully built to seek out and thrive on change would have a clear competitive advantage. In a genuinely chaotic environment, an organization built to *thrive* on chaos will certainly do better than one built merely to *survive* the chaos (Peters, 1987). The goal is to create an organization for which the continuous "white-water rapids" are a source of competitive advantage and not a source of continuous insecurity and dread. Peters has suggested a set of principles that typify what he calls the *innovative* organization, a blueprint for designing organizations to actually thrive on chaos. A number of Peters's principles—or "prescriptions," as he calls them—for creating such an organization are shown in Figure 12-5. According to Peters, the goal of the innovative organization is to create an organization *designed* for white-water rapids, an organization whose ability to "thrive on chaos" represents a competitive advantage over organizations for whom change somehow represents a continuing problem.

The Learning Organization

MIT professor Peter Senge has suggested a different prescription for prospering in this era of turbulence and change: convert our traditional command-and-control organizations into what he calls "learning organizations" (Senge, 1990). The only organizations that will successfully adapt to the conditions of continuous change are those that are constantly engaged in learning from their own and others' experiences. Only organizations deeply committed to continuous learning will be capable of the continuous adjustments necessary for success in the constantly changing environment. Significantly, although learning may be a management responsibility, according to Senge, it is not exclusively—or even primarily—the task of managers. Organizations in general at all levels must become more "learningful." A culture of change readiness must pervade the entire organization.

Jon Spoelstra, president of the Teams Division of Mandalay Entertainment and former president of the NBA New Jersey Nets, suggests that sports organizations must change and innovate to survive in today's sports industry (Spoelstra, 1997). For Spoelstra, the key is creating an organization that not only rewards and values innovation and change, but encourages it. By creating think-tank sessions away from the office for employees, rewarding even innovative failures, and recognizing budding superstars of innovation, Spoelstra was able to create an organizational culture within the Nets organization that thrived on "little experiments," which often gave birth to "breakthrough ideas" that greatly increased ticket revenues (Spoelstra, 1997).

Sports organizations must be willing to embrace change, harness it, and realize its promise of improving and enhancing the organization. Successful organizations are those that create change, embrace change, and lead change rather than those that seek to be sensitive to change, react to change, or adapt to change (Kriegel, 1996). Sports organizations that integrate change readiness into their culture are those organizations that question existing beliefs, assumptions, and standards while seeking out opportunities to innovate, to lead, to take risks, and to challenge existing ways of doing things.

Summary

Collegiate athletics is a segment of the sports industry that has changed dramatically and continues to pose a challenge for the sports manager. The sources of change include the changing environment, advancing technologies, new structures and systems, products and services, and people concerns. Athletic directors face continuous pressures from outside and inside the organization to grow, improve, and innovate.

Managing the change involves developing a vision and translating the vision into clearly defined goals. Through force field analysis, the manager undertakes the task of understanding the factors supporting the change and the sources of resistance.

Implementing the change process includes three stages. The first stage, unfreezing or awakening, must prepare people and awaken them to the need for change. The second stage is the change or envisioning stage. In this stage the goals of the change are defined, clarified, and communicated. The third stage, refreezing or rearchitecting, requires reward structures to reinforce the change as it begins to happen to ensure that it endures over time. Without the successful completion of all three stages, the process of change becomes more dubious.

But making even the most successful change is probably not enough. One of the most significant changes for management is that in today's environment change never ends. Continuous change is the new requirement. This means that management must develop organizations built for change. Tom Peters talks about the innovative organization designed to thrive on chaos. Peter Senge speaks in terms of the learning organization, in which everyone learns from their experience and makes the adjustments required by whatever change lies ahead. Jon Spoelstra argues that successful sports organizations must be willing to challenge the status quo, question common conventions, and encourage risk taking. Clearly, good sports managers are those that can quickly shape their organizations and adapt to change in an ever increasingly dynamic environment. Excellent sports managers are those that will initiate change and create organizations where change is the norm and innovation is the standard.

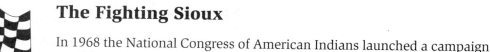

The Fighting Sioux

In 1968 the National Congress of American Indians launched a campaign to address stereotypes in print and in media. As part of the campaign, a spotlight was shone on the use of Native American images, particularly logos and mascots utilized by college athletic teams. Debates over the use of such names as "savages," "warriors," and "redmen" ensued on college campuses across the country. It was argued that the use of these names and symbols was disparaging to Native American culture, and their use represented racist treatment of Native American people. Colleges and universities as our nation's leading educational institutions should not sponsor or promote the use of these symbols that are offensive to Native American cultures. Many colleges and universities across the country supported the movement to eradicate these symbols, but some organizations including alumni groups and booster clubs suggested such names were intended to honor the bravery, determination, and spirit of Native Americans and therefore were appropriate names and mascots for athletic teams.

In 1969 Dartmouth College changed its nickname from "Indians" to "Big Green." Other schools followed including Marquette University, which abandoned its "Willie Wampum" mascot, and Stanford University, which changed its nickname from "Indians" to "Cardinals." In 1988 the states of Michigan, Minnesota, and Wisconsin issued governmental reports criticizing the use of Native American logos and mascots at educational institutions, and in 1989 a University of Illinois graduate student began to protest the use of the school's mascot Chief Illiniwek. Her protest received national media attention and was featured in a documentary, *In Whose Honor?*, which was shown on public television stations throughout the country. In 1998 the NCAA Committee on Racial Diversity issued a report stating that the use of Indian-type mascots indicates a lack of respect for Native American peoples and suggesting the practice be abandoned.

Although dozens of schools abandoned nicknames and mascots deemed to be offensive, other institutions refused to change and argued that such a change would violate school tradition, damage school spirit, and tarnish school history. Suggesting their name would perpetuate respect for Native American people, some school officials claimed they would not bow to the pressures of political correctness or to the demands of "outsiders" who did not understand the school's traditions or intent.

At the University of North Dakota, the "Fighting Sioux" nickname and mascot were challenged, and the campus quickly became divided over the issue. In 1976 the school decided to keep the nickname but adopted a generic more abstract Indian head design that was considered less offensive. The men's hockey team retained the original logo, which resembled that of the NHL Chicago Blackhawks. As national debate over the use of Native American nicknames and symbols escalated and public attention became focused on the hockey team's use of the original logo, University of North Dakota president Kendall Baker announced in 1992 that the team's logo would be replaced with the abstract logo used by other teams. North Dakota hockey alumni, including multimillionaire Ralph Engelstad, approached Baker and encouraged him to retain the original mascot. Engelstad, considered the school's wealthiest alumni benefactor was already angry with the school for forcing the resignation of his friend, hockey coach John Gasparini, after three straight losing seasons in 1994. At the time, Engelstad told Baker he would withhold millions of dollars in donations as long as current athletic director Terry

Wanless remained employed by the school (Dohrman, 2001). When his pleas for retaining the hockey mascot were rebuffed, Engelstad allegedly made it known that he wanted both Wanless and Baker ousted. By September 1998 both Wanless and Baker resigned. In December Engelstad announced a $100 million gift to the school with $50 million earmarked for a new hockey arena (Dohrman, 2001).

In 1999 the University of North Dakota alumni association presented new university president Charles Kupchella with a new logo design for the new arena. The logo, designed by a Native American artist, was remarkably similar to the old design. When the president accepted the gift, there was a public outcry on campus from faculty and students. Native American leaders of the nine tribes from North and South Dakota that had been encouraging the school to drop the "Fighting Sioux" name and logo rallied the media behind their cause. Protests on campus followed, and the president formed a committee to study the issue. In late December 1999 Kupchella wrote to the chairman of the state board of higher education that he saw "no choice but to respect the request of the Sioux tribes" (Dohrman, 2001, p. 49). A few days later, Englestad wrote a letter to Kupchella and sent copies to members of the state board. The letter reiterated Englestad's support of the new logo and the "Fighting Sioux" nickname and informed the president that construction of the new arena would stop if the president failed to utilize the new logo and retain the school nickname. The next day, the board of education voted to keep the name and adopt the new logo and suggested that because the president was in an untenable situation, they would act to resolve the controversy.

Construction continued on the arena that Engelstad developed into a marquis showplace for collegiate ice hockey. The arena, which opened in 2001, features all-leather seats, state-of-the-art locker rooms, and expansive training and weight room areas. No expense was spared either within the $100 million arena or in its landscaping. A large hedge in the front of the building spells out "Fighting Sioux" and massive plantings echo the team logo. The new Indian head logo is featured more than a thousand times within the arena itself. Engelstad retains ownership of the arena, but has leased it to the university for $1 a year. There are hopes that Engelstad will continue his support of his alma mater.

1. Identify the driving and restraining forces affecting the change process at the University of North Dakota.

2. Discuss the culture of collegiate athletics in the United States. How has this culture evolved from the early years of collegiate athletics to today? What role has cultural change played in shaping policy toward the use of Native American nicknames and mascots in educational institutions?

3. What do you suspect about the organizational culture of the University of North Dakota?

4. What factors shaped the changes that occurred in this case?

5. As an athletic director of a school that currently utilizes a Native American nickname or symbol, how would you go about effecting a name or logo change?

Bennis, W., & Nanus, B. (1985). *Leaders*. New York: Harper & Row.

Boost for Women's game. (1998, February 19). *New York Times*, p. 28.

Bruner, J. S. (1973). *On knowing: Essays for the left hand*. New York: Atheneum.

Burwell, B. (2000, May 22–28). Zero tolerance? You've gotta be kidding. *Street & Smith's SportsBusiness Journal*, p. 54.

College athletic programs. (2000, June 12–18) *Street & Smith's SportsBusiness Journal*, p. 32.

Deal, T. E., & Kennedy, A. A. (1982). *Corporate cultures: The rites and rituals of corporate life*. Reading, MA: Addison-Wesley.

Dealy, F. X. (1990). *Win at any cost*. New York: Carol Publishing Group.

Division I notes: Sport sponsorship. (1997, November 24). *NCAA News*, p. 6.

Dohrman, G. (2001, October 8). Face-off. *Sports Illustrated*, pp. 44–49.

Drucker, P. (1989). *The new realities*. New York: HarperCollins.

Heyman, I. M. (1987, July 20). Trapped in an "athletics arms race." *U.S. News and World Report*, p. 7.

Katz, N. (1993, August 6). Season ticket point system UM's price of success. *Springfield Union News*, p. 23.

King, B. (2000, June 12–18). Unearthing the A.D. of the future. *Street & Smith's SportsBusiness Journal*, p. 35.

Kotter, J. P., & Schlesinger, L. A. (1978, March–April). Choosing strategies for change. *Harvard Business Review*, pp. 109–112.

Kriegel, R. (1996) *Sacred cows make the best burgers*. New York: Warner.

Lawmakers reach deal on a stadium for Uconn. (1999, June 3). *New York Times*, p. 32.

Lee, J. (2000a, May 8–14). NCAA issues ultimatum over S.C. flag flap. *Street & Smith's SportsBusiness Journal*, p. 10.

Lee, J. (2000b, May 15–21). Bill with Uconn stadium survives to gain governor's signature. *Street & Smith's SportsBusiness Journal*, p. 15.

Lee, J. (2001a, Jan. 29–Feb. 4). Having listened, Knight panel will talk. *Street & Smith's SportsBusiness Journal*, p. 23

Lee, J. (2001b, Jan. 29–Feb. 4). UCLA group leads call for athletes to press NCAA for reforms. *Street & Smith's SportsBusiness Journal*, p. 23.

Lewin, K. (1947, June). Frontiers in group dynamics: Concept, method, and reality in social science. *Human Relations*, pp. 17–24.

Lewin, K. (1951). *Field theory and social science: Selected theoretical papers*. New York: Harper & Row.

Lively, K. (2000, February 2). U. of Vermont cancels hockey season. *The Chronicle of Higher Education*, p. A56.

Maloney, R. (2000, June 12–18). One of the "old boys" Crouthamel builds on decades of success. *Street & Smith's SportsBusiness Journal*, p. 26.

McMillen, T. (1992). *Out of bounds*. New York: Simon & Schuster.

Moran, M. (1997, November 3). A dreary day, a doomed program. *New York Times*, p. 16.

NCAA Manual. (1999–2000). Indianapolis, IN: National Collegiate Athletic Association.

Negative poll has Uconn trying to cut cost of stadium proposal. (1997, November 21). *New York Times*, p. 23.

Peters, T. (1987). *Thriving on chaos*. New York: Harper & Row.

Rabinovitz, J. (1997a, November 20). Legislature hears both sides of Uconn stadium issue. *New York Times*, p. 42.

Rabinovitz, J. (1997b, November 26). Stadium plan quickly dies in Hartford. *New York Times*, p. 31.

Rofe, J. (2000, June 12–18). Thanks to fund-raising skills, Hedges' stock on the rise at Uwash. *Street & Smith's SportsBusiness Journal*, p. 28.

Rudolph, F. (1990). *The American college and university: A history*. (Rev. ed.). Athens, GA: University of Georgia Press.

Schwartz, D. (2000, June 12–18). AD's biz role full time, seven days a week. *Street & Smith's SportsBusiness Journal*, p. 37.

Sears directors cup: Financial breakdowns of the top 25. (2000, June 12–18). *Street & Smith's SportsBusiness Journal*, p. 32.

Senge, P. M. (1990). *The fifth discipline: The art and practice of the learning organization*. New York: Doubleday/Currency.

Seyle, H. (1976). *The stress of life*. New York: McGraw-Hill.

Seymour, H. (1989). *Baseball: The early years*. New York: Oxford University Press.

Sheldon, H. D. (1969). *Student life and customs*. (Rev. ed.). New York: Arno Press.

Slack, T. (1997). *Understanding sport organizations*. Champaign, IL: Human Kinetics.

Smith, R. A. (1988). *Sports and freedom: The rise of big-time college athletics*. New York: Oxford University Press.

Sperber, M. J. (2000). *Beer and circus: How big-time college sports is crippling undergraduate education*. New York: Henry Holt.

Spoelstra, J. (1997). *Ice to the Eskimos*. New York: HarperCollins.

Steinbreder, J. (2000, June 12–18). UCONN produces another champion. *Street & Smith's SportsBusiness Journal*, p. 34.

Tichy, N. (1993, December 13). Revolutionize your company. *Fortune*, pp. 114–118.

Turner, P. V. (1984). *Campus: An American planning tradition*. New York: Architectural History Foundation.

Vaill, P. (1989). *Managing as a performing art: New ideas for a world of chaotic change*. San Francisco: Jossey-Bass.

Vermont attorney general backs hazing charge. (2000, February 4). *New York Times*, p. 19.

Williams, P. (1997). *The magic of team work*. London: Thomas Nashville.

Zimblast, A. (1999). *Unpaid professionals: Commercialism and conflict in big-time college sports*. Princeton, NJ: Princeton University Press.

Index